BRICKLAYER BILL

BRICKLAYER BILL

The Untold Story of the Workingman's Boston Marathon

Patrick L. Kennedy &
Lawrence W. Kennedy

Foreword by Bill Rodgers

BRIGHT LEAF
AMHERST AND BOSTON
An imprint of University of Massachusetts Press

ISBN 978-1-62534-306-2 (paper); 305-5 (hardcover)
Designed by Sally Nichols
Set in Adobe Minion Pro
Printed and bound by Maple Press, Inc.

Library of Congress Cataloging-in-Publication Data

Names: Kennedy, Patrick L., author. | Kennedy, Lawrence W., 1952– author.
Title: Bricklayer Bill : the untold story of the workingman's Boston Marathon
  / Patrick L. Kennedy and Lawrence W. Kennedy.
Description: Amherst, Massachusetts : Bright Leaf, An Imprint of University
  of Massachusetts Press, [2017] | Includes bibliographical references and
  index.
Identifiers: LCCN 2017020927| ISBN 9781625343062 (paper) | ISBN 9781625343055
  (hardcover)
Subjects: LCSH: Kennedy, William John, 1883–1968. | Runners (Sports)—United
  States—Biography. | Boston Marathon—History.
Classification: LCC GV1061.15.K46 K46 2017 | DDC 796.42092 [B] —dc23
LC record available at https://lccn.loc.gov/2017020927

British Library Cataloging-in-Publication Data
A catalogue record for this book is available from the British Library.

To Andrea Baird Kennedy
and
Judith McCarthy Kennedy

CONTENTS

Foreword   ix

Acknowledgments   xi

Abbreviations   xv

Prologue   1

1. Brickie, Boxer, Knickerbocker   8

2. On the Road (and Rails)   24

3. Strides, Setbacks & Laurels   55

4. "We Must Repel the Finns"   93

5. Over There   151

6. Paris or Bust   185

7. Good Times   212

8. Hard Times   238

9. The Road to Berlin   254

10. Go West, Old Man   273

Epilogue   287

Notes   293

Index   319

FOREWORD

Bricklayer Bill: The Untold Story of the Workingman's Boston Marathon is a powerful book. I say that for many reasons, one being that it explores in detail the raw beginnings of marathoning, particularly in the United States. It's also an exploration of a Boston Marathon champion's psyche, his personality, and his life in America a century ago. That man is William J. "Bricklayer Bill" Kennedy, whose triumph in the legendary race came six decades before mine.

As the book's title makes clear, marathoning a hundred years ago was no high-paying sport. Unlike the baseball stars and boxers of that era, who would earn big money, marathoners were true working-class athletes. That is, they competed just for the love of the game. Of course, marathoners were few in number then, and the fact is, these athletes—like all track and field athletes, swimmers, rowers, and others who aspired to compete in the Olympics—were obliged to follow the rules of amateurism. That made things tough. As Bill Kennedy said, the trophies and ribbons and accolades were nice, but he had to put food on the table for his wife and family! Thus Bill pursued his vocation as a hardworking bricklayer while he pursued his avocation and passion as a runner.

Bill's is a story of family and friendship and of the unique gentlemanly code of honor that has always been key to the sport. In this book you will meet the other kings of the road of Bill's era. Clarence DeMar ruled the marathon like no other, of any era. But while I respect Clarence greatly, I also respect Bill and his comrades. They struggled financially, yet nothing seemed to stop them. Not world war: they took part in the war effort in 1918. Not the Great Depression: Bill and his working-class peers traveled to jobs all over the country. Sometimes they rode in boxcars on their way to races, and unlike today, the elite runners then did not stay in fine hotels before a marathon.

The lure of the quest to win the Boston Marathon, and to compete in the Olympic Games, was at least as powerful to Bill Kennedy and his fellow marathoners as it is to current professional runners. Bill was a kind of dreamer; all the great folks in any endeavor are!

The myths of marathoning and of the sports world, the power of the journalists of the era before TV, the dearth of knowledge of exercise science, the lack of sponsorships or quality shoes and clothing—all are hallmarks of marathoning in Bill's world.

Yet it was and is a beautiful sport, and the way was paved in part by Bill Kennedy. He didn't use steroids or EPO to win a race and cheat others of their rightful places. Bill was what Diogenes was looking for: an honest man.

I love the comment in this book by Harvard paleoanthropologist Daniel Lieberman: "Why are people running 26.2 miles for charity? The Boston Marathon raises more than twenty million dollars a year for charities. And I think that's because we've always run to help each other. . . . Running has always been a communal event that was part of helping each other, and I don't think that today's marathon movement is any different."

Talk about chasing unicorns. That is part of why Bill ran, but Bill's own words on marathoning also ring true today. When you read this book, you'll see what I mean. Most people do not get it, but I believe Bill found that running improves your life. Truthfully, though Bill led a hard existence, he drank deep from the well of life. How many really do?

It's an honor to have followed in Bill Kennedy's footsteps!

Bill Rodgers
Boxborough, Massachusetts
Winner, Boston Marathon, 1975, 1978, 1979, 1980
Winner, New York City Marathon, 1976, 1977, 1978, 1979

ACKNOWLEDGMENTS

First of all, we are grateful to our late cousin Ann Louise McLaughlin for preserving Uncle Bill's manuscript as well as so many elements of our family's documented and oral history, and for bringing all of these to our attention in the closing years of her life. Our aunt Joan Kennedy Harvey brought her Uncle Bill alive in many conversations, and our late uncle Roger Kennedy shared recollections toward the end of his life as well. Eileen Lawlor Kennedy (mother and grandmother) and John and Brian Kennedy (brothers and uncles) helped the cause by sharing family memories. A special thanks to cousins Eric Coffin, Andrew Coffin, and Larry and Nicole Coffin for finding the missing chapter on transportation.

This book has been deeply enriched by the recollections, mementos, and encouraging words of our far-flung network of Kennedy cousins and shoestring relations, including Rita Bishop, Tracy Holton, Timothy Kennedy Bishop, Jo-Ellen Pearson and Mike Pearson, Steve O'Neill, Lisa Hochhauser, Cristin Laccabue, Laurie LaRock, John Mernah, Maureen Wheeler, Mary Nell Nicoletti, Tim Nolan, and Patricia Nolan Schmidt.

The staff of the Weinberg Memorial Library of the University of Scranton provided enthusiastic assistance, and we thank Betsey Moylan for her years of interest in this project as head of reference. Both Sheila Ferraro and Maggie Restuccia performed great service in the Interlibrary Loan office in securing newspapers on microfilm.

Kristen Yarmey, digital services librarian, aided by arranging for the photographic restoration performed by April V. Francia.

The staff of the O'Neill Library of Boston College also deserves thanks, as do the people who work in the microtext department of the Boston Public Library at Copley Square for their exemplary assistance to this project. (In a fun metaphysical quirk, we found articles about the post-race celebrations in the BAA clubhouse while sitting at microfilm machines in the same space where said clubhouse once stood.) Thanks also to Danielle Pucci and Aaron Schmidt at the BPL's photo archives, and to the staff at the Faneuil and Brighton branches of the library. Gratitude is due Bob Cullum and his family for allowing the use of a great Leslie Jones photograph.

The staff of the Port Chester–Rye Brook Public Library in Port Chester, New York, assisted with our reading of the microfilm collection of the *Port Chester Daily Item,* and further aid was provided by the Greenwich Public Library in Connecticut. We also acknowledge the help provided by the staff of the New York State Archives in Albany and the State Historical Society of Missouri. A good friend, Homa Ferdowsi, helped research parts of the St. Louis story.

Without the help of colleagues we never would have completed the book. We thank Brian Conniff, Joseph Dreisbach, and Harold Baillie of the University of Scranton for providing encouragement and institutional financial support. As deans and provosts, they showed personal interest in the book, as did members of the history department at Scranton. Thanks also to Dan Antonellis and colleagues at Suffolk Construction Co. for their moral support toward the tail end of the project, just as Jean Keith and colleagues at Boston University encouraged it at the very beginning.

We thank all those who have shared our excitement about this book and cheered us on. Paul Kennedy (son and brother) and his wife, Kate Boylan, have long been ardent supporters and we appreciate their helping us to keep going over the years.

Running writer Caleb Daniloff took time to furnish his crucial insights, advice, and moral support. Another writing runner, Tina

Cassidy, offered encouragement as well. A conversation with sports historian Richard Johnson was inspirational.

The late John J. Kelley shared a copy of his and Tom Murphy's book about Jock Semple, which proved a great resource. Amby Burfoot and Bill Rodgers took the time to read drafts and provide feedback and encouragement.

We also owe a debt of gratitude to Gary Corbitt, Walter Kehoe, Wayne Baker, Bill Mallon, and Steve Cottrell in the New York running community; Tom Tryniski, fultonhistory.com; Eric Reinert, Army Corps of Engineers; William Mays, *Police Gazette;* Jim Wilson, Missouri Athletic Club; and Margaret Sullivan, Boston Police Department archives.

Arthur Veasey held on to an old letter of Bill's that proved a boon. Christine Forshaw O'Shaughnessy shared her grandfather Joe Forshaw's essay from *Spalding's.* Craig Cogil of the National Oceanic and Atmospheric Administration and Harry Hillaker, Iowa's state climatologist, helped us to nail down details of the Des Moines incident.

Roger Fussa, Sara Goldberg, and the staff of Historic Newton helped us flesh out the scenery along the marathon course, and Jane Hanser pointed us to that organization in the first place.

Our heartfelt thanks as well to Steve Flynn of the Ashland Half Marathon Committee and Gloria Ratti, Boston Athletic Association historian.

Props to Dennis Doherty for inviting Patrick along on his slushy, inspirational training runs over the Newton hills. Dennis as well as Matt Migonis and Christoph Straub also took the time to read Bill's words on training and to lend the perspective of modern-day hardcore runners.

Kelly Marksbury pointed out that Forest Park is now part of Washington University of St. Louis. She also read early drafts and provided enormous encouragement, as did John Marksbury and Jamie Bransford. Rob Lind—a working-class autodidact, like Bill—showed genuine interest and provided suggestions and a morale boost on this book.

Several people and publications permitted us to reprint passages previously published in related articles, and we greatly appreciate their help and encouragement as Bill's story continued to unfold. Specifically, we thank Steve Heuser and Amanda Katz at the *Boston Globe*, Noah Rosenberg and Brendan Spiegel at *Narratively*, John O'Rourke at *BU Today*, and Jim Concannon and Terry Murphy at the *Harvard Gazette*.

Our gratitude to Brian Halley of the University of Massachusetts Press for patiently and enthusiastically shepherding this project along. Also at UMass Press, we appreciate the efforts of Mary Dougherty, Carol Betsch, Mary Bellino, Jack Harrison, and Sally Nichols. Finally, Amanda Heller's editing also helped strengthen the book. Thanks to all.

Patrick's supportive in-laws Allison and Barry Baird sacrificed their time to pitch in on the child care effort at critical points. And Declan and Oona Jean went fairly easy on their grandparents.

Most of all, we wish to acknowledge our wives for making this book possible:

Andrea Baird Kennedy deserves a survivor's medal for her role in seeing this book through to completion. She weeded and gardened for an ailing Ann Louise, acted as a sounding board, suggested synonyms when asked, cropped images, and pulled extra parenting duty again and again. Beautiful inside and out, Andrea wasn't kidding when she made those vows.

—Patrick L. Kennedy

Thanks to Judith McCarthy Kennedy for joining me in conducting research, typing up notes, tracking down sources, and editing multiple drafts of various chapters. All this in addition to stepping in and caring for Declan and Oona Jean in loving support of our work.

—Lawrence W. Kennedy

Excerpts from Patrick Kennedy, "In the Running: 1897 to 2014," *BU Today*, April 18, 2014; "Bricklayer Bill's Ultra-Marathon of a Life," *Narratively* (http://narrative.ly), October 1, 2014; "A Race against Fear," *Boston Globe*, March 23, 2014; and "Running as Tradition," *Harvard Gazette*, April 14, 2016, are reprinted with permission.

ABBREVIATIONS

AEF   American Expeditionary Force
AAU   Amateur Athletic Union
AOC   American Olympic Committee
AOH   Ancient Order of Hibernians
BAA   Boston Athletic Association
BAC   Bricklayers' Athletic Club
DNF   Did not finish
IAAC   Irish-American Athletic Club
IAC   Illinois Athletic Club
IMRA   International Marathon Runners' Association
IOC   International Olympic Committee
MAC   Missouri Athletic Club
SOS   Supply of Service
USOC   United States Olympic Committee

BRICKLAYER BILL

PROLOGUE

We don't know what flashed through Bill Kennedy's mind when the gust of wind blew him off the roof of the Des Moines Coliseum. One moment the bricklayer was five stories above the street, carefully applying the finishing touches to the mortar on a nearly complete sports arena; the next he was plunging sixty-five feet to almost certain death on the pavement below.

Nor do we know what Bill was thinking when he fell from a moving freight train outside Cleveland, when he was hit by an automobile in New York, or when he was stricken with typhoid fever in Chicago. It's a cliché that a brush with death brings to mind pivotal moments in a life, but neuroscientists do say that time slows down (or rather we perceive it to) during a life-threatening experience.[1] Maybe Bill simply thought a string of curse words as he sailed earthward. Or maybe he thought of his loved ones while delirious in the hospital. But perhaps he replayed one sunny Saturday in September 1896, when he was twelve years old. We do know it was a day that he wrote about six decades later. The day something happened in Port Chester, New York, that few people had ever seen before, anywhere.

It seemed the whole town had turned out to cram the sidewalks on either side of Main Street, a narrow, winding artery lined with multistory brick buildings. Officially, Port Chester was (and is) a "village" of Westchester County, but with eighty factories packed into its two square miles and thousands of Irish, Italian, and Polish immigrants settling there to work in them, Bill's adopted hometown was beginning to look more like a tiny outpost of the Bronx, twelve miles to the south. The state health department would report that Port Chester was afflicted with "tenement-house congestion" and "an excessive proportion of foreign born inhabitants."[2]

Most of the factory workers had Saturday afternoons off, and masses of men in coveralls and cloth caps swelled the crowds on Main Street. Bill probably hadn't seen such a hubbub since he was ten, when those same workers came out to welcome the New England contingent of Coxey's Army, the populist protest movement, as they marched through en route to Washington.[3] But this time the mood was purely festive. Women in brightly colored dresses found spots to stand alongside businessmen in dark suits and bowler hats, while children, like Bill and his seven brothers and sisters, flitted through the crowd, shouting and laughing. A giant Old Glory flew over Liberty Square, with forty-five white stars on its blue field along with the traditional thirteen red and white stripes. The guy wires that suspended the flag over the street were strung with Chinese lanterns that glinted in the shining sun as everybody gathered on Main Street, looked north, and waited.[4]

Taking a cue from the first modern Olympic Games in Athens earlier that year, New York's Knickerbocker Athletic Club was hosting a day-long series of amateur athletic contests at Columbia Oval in the Bronx. There was a fifty-yard run, sack hurdle race, pole vault, discus throw—a dozen events in all. The strangest of these was a twenty-five-mile race on the roads from Stamford, Connecticut, to the Bronx, finishing up with two laps around the track in the stadium. No such race had ever been held in America—nor (despite a persistent misconception) had any such race taken place in recorded human history until a few months earlier, in Greece. And about a mile of the Knickerbocker race would pass through Bill's hometown.[5]

Thirty men took the train from New York to Stamford that morning, were shown to dressing quarters, and changed into tracksuits. Shortly after noon, an official fired a revolver into the air and the runners were on their way, heading out of town on East Putnam Avenue. "The day," reported the *Brooklyn Eagle*, "was glorious for sport," albeit not exactly for the athletes. "The sun made matters rather uncomfortably hot for most of the competitors," not to mention that "there was scarcely a breath of wind" to relieve them. But at least "for the spectators the weather conditions left nothing to be wished for."[6]

Accompanied by a group of bicycle riders called the Harlem Wheelmen, the runners covered the first five miles with confidence. Once they passed through Greenwich's town center, the contestants' lack of experience started to show. "Several of the runners began to think that their early hopes were not warranted by the facts," noted the *New York Herald*. Soon, the telegraph poles disappeared and they were on a dusty, bumpy, rocky, rutted country road.[7]

After another couple of miles, the panting plodders crossed a bridge over the Byram River and entered New York. Soon they reached paved roads and civilization once more—Port Chester, the first official checkpoint. A waiting official dashed off a telegram to the Bronx: John McDermott and Louis Liebgold were running neck and neck to lead the pack. McDermott was "a little lank fellow," according to the *Eagle,* and he worked during the week as a lithographer. Liebgold "hadn't trained an hour for the race." The rest of the field was scattered behind them, about fifteen minutes separating the leaders from the last of the laggards.[8]

As the front-runners approached, young Bill Kennedy, spectating from a spot steps from his family's walk-up flat, couldn't contain his excitement. With no tape or cop to stop them, he and his pals leapt into the road and ran alongside McDermott and Liebgold. You can picture them hollering encouragement as they dodged the squeaky wheels of the Harlem cyclists. The boys kept up with the leaders all the way to the railroad bridge into neighboring Rye before turning back.

"Thus," wrote Bill years later, "I claim the honor of running in this pioneer race, though unofficially."[9] That spontaneous jaunt of less than a mile launched William J. Kennedy's lifelong passion for "the Marathon race," as the one-off Stamford-to-the-Bronx run was called. A few months later, the Boston Athletic Association began its own version of the twenty-five-mile run. (The 26.2-mile distance would be standardized later.) The Boston Marathon became an annual event, and it was in running *that* race that Kennedy got his name in the sports history books, along with a sketch of the circumstances of his brush with fame. They say "Bricklayer Bill" rode the rails to Boston and slept on a pool table the night before he bested the great Clarence DeMar.

But there is more to Bill's story than the oft-repeated shorthand legend, and it is about more than just running. The Harlem native survived the abovementioned five-story fall, train and car accidents, and typhoid fever as well as an extralegal prizefighting stint, a tour of duty in war, Depression bankruptcy, decades of backbreaking work, and his own bad habits to win four marathons and scads of shorter races (including one against a horse) while raising a family. He also co-founded a prestigious marathon in New York, trained younger runners (including African Americans), and promoted the sport when much of the nation viewed it as a freakish novelty.

Late in life, Bill gathered his thoughts and experiences on marathon running and typed them up, hoping to publish a book on the subject. (Hoping in vain; this was the mid-1960s, a decade shy of America's modern running boom.) Though his manuscript remained unfinished, Bill nevertheless peppered it with plenty of gold nuggets—colorful and heartrending anecdotes about the sport and his competitors, who were also his lifelong friends. So when we, his great-nephew and great-grandnephew, received his typewritten manuscript from an elderly cousin in 2010, it provided an outstanding primary source, inspiring us to research those early marathons and piece together Uncle Bill's life. In the process, we uncovered a story larger than Bill himself. It is about struggling to overcome immense obstacles, as well as about America and the way it was when a few bricklayers, plumbers, and printers could be star athletes, as big as Babe Ruth, at least for a day.

Probably the best way to begin this tale is to let Bill Kennedy do it in his own words. Here is the first of this book's many excerpts from his manuscript, which he titled "Keep Pickin Em Up." We don't know what went through our uncle's head during some of the more traumatic moments in his life, but we do know what he wrote and left behind.

IN BILL'S WORDS: START

"What in the name of God ever started you men running twenty-six miles?"

The speaker was a stylishly dressed woman, accompanied by a younger companion. We were a group of marathon runners in the lobby of the Long Beach Hotel, out on Long Island. For a moment we gazed sheepishly at the ladies in silence. Then Frank Zuna, one of our group, a big, husky plumber from Newark, N.J., laughingly spoke up and said, "Well, ladies, our mothers put us on a merry-go-round when we were little boys and forgot to take us off. So we have been going round and around ever since." This remark caused a hearty laugh from us all.

We were a large group of marathon runners who had competed in the Long Beach Marathon [ca. 1925], starting at the N.Y. Athletic Club at 59th Street in N.Y. and had run the twenty-six miles to Long Beach out on the island. Having bathed and dressed, we were seated at the banquet table ravenously looking forward to the dinner. A gentleman with a list of the results of the race approached, and reading off the names of the men and their finishing positions, made the announcement that only the men who had actually completed the race would be fed. As some of the men who had been forced by fatigue and blistered feet embarrassedly arose and left the table, at the writer's suggestion [we] all left the table and joined them in the lobby.

Thus the crowd of excited marathoners gesticulating and arguing in the lobby. These two ladies approached and enquired of me the trouble. On being informed, the elder of the two was astonished. Thus the question of the opening of this story. Identifying herself as Mrs. Jack Levy and daughter, whose husband was a prominent clothing manufacturer in New York City, Mrs. Levy graciously invited this hungry mob to be her guests for dinner. As we were debating the advisability of accepting her generous offer the chairman of the race committee approached and with apologies invited us all back to dinner stating the gentleman with the list acted without authority. At our insistence the ladies joined us, and to show our appreciation of her kind offer to feed such a hungry mob, we voted her and her daughter Honorary Members of the International Marathon Runners Assn. of which I was Pres. at the time. The ladies roared with laughter at being members of such a "wackey" bunch of men who run twenty-six miles for pleasure.

This incident was the inspiration for this story of marathon runners, though written many years later. You may wonder, as did Mrs. Levy, why men run so far for a medal or trophy. Besides this question of why do we run so far? other questions so often asked are "What do you think of along the road?" "Are you not afraid you will drop dead running so far?" and the commercial one so often asked, "Don't you get paid for running?"

The writer was a brick contractor at the time in Westchester County, and at social affairs so many of my acquaintances and friends would ask the same questions, and while some may have envied the good health and the ability to run so far, probably more of them thought I was a bit "wackey."

So in an endeavor to write of these men, of experiences plodding along the road both in training and racing, and in answer to the questions asked, it will be impossible to keep the personal pronoun out of this story, as most of the incidents are personal or eye-witnessed. Not only the winners but the losers are interesting characters. The late Clarence DeMar wrote a story "Marathon" (Stephen Day, publisher). [That] book deals with DeMar's many victories, and tells little of his competitors, of whom this story is of.

The title occurred to me from an incident back in Chicago in 1913. I was running for the Illinois A.C. at the time, and had just finished a five-mile workout on the Douglas Park track on the west side of the city. Feeling rather chesty after doing five miles under twenty-six minutes, I turned to Mr. Wilson, our coach. "How am I doing, Coach? Am I laying 'em down all right?"

"Never mind how you lay them down, keep picking them up," was his reply. Glancing at him and noting no trace of a smile, I realized he was in earnest and not wise-cracking. Later on that evening, thinking of his remark, it dawned on me. "Why sure, that's the secret of running: Keep picking them up." And I smiled at the thought they go down of their own accord.

Thus I feel that it is an appropriate title for this story of running. Most runners use it as a slogan when running. "Keep pickin em up." Or an old English one I've heard. "One foot up and one foot down, that's the way to London Town." So if you are on foot and want to get some place, "Keep pickin em up."[10]

1

BRICKIE, BOXER, KNICKERBOCKER

Nobody knows what time Pheidippides clocked. There were no stopwatches in his day, and he wasn't competing in a race when he ran twenty-five miles from the plains of Marathon to the city of Athens in 490 B.C. The Greek courier of legend hotfooted it alone to deliver the news that Athens's army had defeated the Persians in the Battle of Marathon. An imaginative Roman historian later embellished this tale with the herald's ironic, noble end: Pheidippides uttering, "Joy to you, we've won," before dropping dead of exhaustion.[1]

Later still, an English poet tweaked the messenger's dying words to the snappier "Rejoice, we conquer!"[2] Robert Browning's 1879 poem "Pheidippides" fired the imagination of American and western European schoolboys of Bill Kennedy's generation. In the late nineteenth century, European intellectuals, long influenced by the philosophers and democratic principles of ancient Greece, were welcoming modern Greece as it emerged from centuries of Turkish rule. Interest in the country's classical tradition ran high as archaeological digs yielded new artifacts and facts about the place and time of Socrates and Aristotle.

Meanwhile, railroad tracks, steamship lines, and telegraph wires were drawing the world closer together. The old monarchies jockeyed for new colonial territories. "European culture was simultaneously approaching its zenith, and its apocalypse," writes historian Richard Mandell. In response to the dizzying pace of technological and social change, the French aristocrat Pierre de Coubertin proposed reviving Greece's ancient panhellenic Olympic Games as a pan-global competition for amateur athletes. He hoped the tensions among imperial powers might dissipate if expressed on a playing field rather than a battlefield. The idea caught on, and the event was scheduled for April 1896.[3]

Though the Games were conceived by a Frenchman and held in Greece, the format of the first modern Olympics actually owed more to the Scottish and Irish track and field meetings of the nineteenth century, festivals of contests including the hammer throw, shot put, high jump, and foot races. The ancient Greeks had held foot races too, but all on tracks and none longer than three miles; there was no "Marathon race" in the games at Olympia. But to connect the new Olympics to its classical forebear, at least in the public mind, Coubertin added a road race from the plains of Marathon to the new stadium in Athens—a distance of roughly forty kilometers, or about 24.5 miles—and a tradition was born.[4]

The world thrilled that April as, fittingly, a Greek, Spiridon Louis, bested all visitors to win the first-ever marathon. One of the nineteen other contestants was Arthur Blake of the Boston Athletic Association. Indeed, several BAA athletes traveled to Athens for the Games, and they took note of this revolutionary new race. Coach John Graham and runner Tom Burke were especially impressed.[5]

The BAA contingent returned to Boston full of excitement and began planning a grand athletic meet styled after the one they'd seen in Athens. But a rival New York club, which had ignored the Olympic Games and regretted it, "now defended their position" by beating the BAA to the punch.[6] And so Olympic fever swept tiny Port Chester and the rest of metropolitan New York in September when the

Knickerbocker A.C. staged its own day of sporting events, including the 25-mile race from Stamford to the Bronx that passed the Kennedys' doorstep on Main Street. (See prologue.) To lend the games a real ancient Greek flavor, the club even planned a chariot race, reported the *Brooklyn Eagle,* although that "fell through because before the race began several of the chariots [collapsed]."[7]

The Knickerbocker festival drew crowds that were massive for that era. Extra trains were run to the Columbia Oval, and the university's stadium was "jammed up" early in the morning, reported the *Eagle.* "The gay dresses of hundreds of pretty women" caught the attention of observers, and a brass band played, "with all the vim in the world," such popular tunes as "Down in Poverty Row" and "Only One Girl in the World for Me."

The thirty men—simply daredevils, many of them—who signed up to run to the Oval from Stamford numbered a dozen more than the eighteen who had raced in Greece. The course was at least twice the distance any of them had ever even thought to run before, and indeed several of the competitors dropped out around halfway through. One threw himself against a fence, exhausted, as another sprawled on the roadside, and a third was carried into a "convenient drug store."

The road conditions certainly didn't aid the runners' performance. The marathon route followed the old Boston Post Road, a vital artery for horse-drawn stagecoaches in colonial times. But now, in 1896, sleek steam-powered locomotives moved people and goods more efficiently on steel railroad tracks, and the highways had been neglected for decades. There was no federal funding for maintenance. The historic Post Road was now cluttered with "rocks, ruts, and thank-you-marms" (large bumps), wrote an inventor who tested an early automobile over the route in 1898. (One "very rough and stony" section in Rye, the town bordering Port Chester to the south, caused the vehicle's engine to fall out, ending the experiment.) The wrong step could send a marathon runner—especially an inexperienced marathon runner, which in 1896 meant everyone—sprawling, maybe with a sprained ankle.[8]

Navigating that terrain, Louis Liebgold and John McDermott, whom Bill and the other Port Chester boys saw off at the railroad bridge to Rye, continued trading the lead for another three miles until Liebgold "became muscle bound and was obliged to drop into a walk."

In the Bronx, "the discus throwing had scarcely been finished when all the events slated on the track and field were interrupted by the cry of 'Here comes the Marathon race.'" McDermott, "his clothes purple with perspiration, but still running strong and well after his long journey of 25 miles over a somewhat stiff road, burst through the crowd amid tremendous cheering." As the lithe lithographer trotted around the track to break the tape, he "appeared to be particularly fresh and smiled and waved his arms to the women on the grand stand, who stood up and shook their handkerchiefs as he ambled past. His time for the twenty-five miles was 3 hours, 25 minutes, 55 ¾ seconds."

Behind McDermott, some of the runners "managed to reach the finish and to trot once around the track, spurred to the best possible conclusion of their effort by the cheers and plaudits of two thousands persons," reported the *New York Times*. "But the greater number of those who entered found mud and stones, hills and humidity, too much for them, and, after valiant struggles and combats with breath and strength, came back to New York in trains."[9]

The Knickerbocker games turned out to be a one-time affair: New York wouldn't see another marathon for more than a decade. But seven months later, on April 19, 1897, the Boston Athletic Association put on a Patriots' Day marathon, a 25-mile run starting in the country town of Ashland, Massachusetts, and ending at the Boston club's track on Irvington Street in the Back Bay. The race was a way to celebrate the midnight ride of Paul Revere—another military messenger given an outsize role in an oft-taught poem. But instead of starting the run in Lexington or Concord, the BAA took inspiration from its representatives' trip to the Olympics a year earlier. They chose the course that would best mimic the difficulty of the

Marathon-to-Athens route—a gradual ascent, with the hills getting tougher the closer runners got to the city, then a gradual descent for the last few miles.

The start of the Boston race was modest. Like a Wild West gun-slinger, the BAA's Tom Burke dragged his boot heel across a dirt road to make a starting line in Ashland. Just eighteen men crouched behind it awaiting his signal. Lacking a pistol, Burke simply shouted, "Go!"[10]

The contestants took off in a sprint until the thought of the distance ahead hit them and they settled into a jog. The runners and their corps of bicycle attendants kicked up clouds of dust. The cyclists offered water and lemons as needed. Behind them trailed spectators on horseback and in horse-drawn carriages as well as "motorcycles and in fact every conceivable form of conveyance."[11]

McDermott, winner of the Knickerbocker marathon, competed in the Boston event too. His main rival was Dick Grant, a Harvard track star who bucked his coaches to enter the long-distance grind. Grant gave McDermott a run for his money but dropped out on the Newton hills. (Harvard disciplined Grant with a suspension the following week. For the next half century, collegians would be a rare sight in a sport dominated by workingmen.) McDermott burst through a funeral procession at Governor's (later Kenmore) Square. At last, he circled the Irvington Oval to finish first, in 2:55:10, ten seconds faster than Louis's time at Athens.[12]

"It is a great deal better than the New York course," McDermott said afterwards of the route to Boston. "In fact, everything connected with the race was managed a great deal better. The bicycle service was great. Nobody interfered with the runners at any stage of the race." Nevertheless, the victor declared then and there that he'd just run his last marathon. "I hate to be called a quitter and a coward, but look at my feet," McDermott told reporters, pointing to his blistered, bleeding dogs.[13]

Yet McDermott came back for more when the BAA held the race again on April 19, 1898. Unlike the Stamford-to-the-Bronx run, which was the first "Marathon race" held in America, the Boston event would continue annually, making it today the country's oldest marathon.[14]

It would take years—decades, really—for it to sink in, at least for large numbers of Americans, but the evidence was clear that Pheidippides' stunt could be replicated safely (though not easily). "Consequently, the marathoners emulate the historical feat of a Greek soldier," Bill Kennedy would later write, "with the exception of the tragic ending."[15]

〜〜

The Kennedys were builders from way back. The lad who would grow up to be "Bricklayer Bill" was at least the third in a line of men to ply that trade or one related to it. His paternal grandfather, Joseph Lawrence Kennedy, was a stonemason from Tipperary who emigrated to Boston around the time of "An Gorta Mor" (the Great Hunger), Ireland's devastating potato famine. "Of sticks and stones we're not afraid in Tipperary," Bill would later recall his great-aunt telling him.[16]

Tipperary is not far from Wexford, whence hailed the more famous Kennedys. "I am positive [Joseph and his sister] were related to the President's ancestors," Bill would write in the early 1960s. "We all have the Kennedy hair." Indeed, many of Joseph's male descendants sported thick, wavy ginger manes, though if any connection to the more well-known Joe Kennedy exists, it is surely long distant. But the clan's leadership pedigree extended even farther back, according to tradition. One of Bill's earliest memories was of his great-aunt telling him, "Willie, you are a direct descendant of Brian Boru, King of Ireland." (The legendary Brian's father is said to have been Cinneide, whose descendants would carry the surname O Cinneide, or O'Kennedy, with many eventually dropping the O.)[17]

It so happens that Tipperary is also home to a strong athletic tradition. Parts of Tip, Cork, and Limerick form "a very small pocket of rich countryside, often known as the Golden Vale," which "may well have produced more world records, more international and Olympic

FIGURE 1. Lawrence J. Kennedy, father of William J.
"Bricklayer Bill" Kennedy.

champions than any other rural area in modern times," writes historian Kevin J. McCarthy. Many of them would medal in the Olympics in 1904 and 1908, including an American-born son of Tipperary natives, Johnny Hayes, winner of the Olympic marathon at London in '08.[18]

In 1855, Joseph Kennedy, then thirty-six, married another Irish immigrant, named Margaret, in Attleboro, Massachusetts. The following year they had a son, Lawrence Joseph (see fig.1). "L.J.," or "Larry," was followed by four siblings, of whom two, James and Margaret, survived childhood. As L.J. approached adolescence, the family moved to Staten Island in New York City. James and Larry grew up in the construction industry, learning the bricklaying trade while working for their father, the senior partner in the contracting firm of Kennedy & Murphy.[19]

By 1880, Joseph had moved his family to Stamford, Connecticut, while Lawrence, at age twenty-five, was out on his own, working as a stonecutter and living in a boardinghouse in nearby Port Chester, New York. There was a bar at street level, and the Irish family running the place was known on occasion to allow horses inside well into the twentieth century. Some of L.J.'s fellow boarders worked in the town's large bolt factory.

Living in close quarters with him, changing his linens, helping to cook and serve his meals, the landlady's daughter caught L.J.'s eye. A seamstress about his age, Louisa O'Brien had been born in Ireland but raised there in Port Chester since she was a little girl. After a brief courtship, Lawrence and Louisa married and moved to East Harlem in New York City. They had a daughter, Ellen Louisa ("Nellie"), in February 1882, and the following year, in December 1883, they had their first son, William John Kennedy. Raised in a second-generation Irish family in heavily Irish enclaves in the nineteenth century, "Willie," as he was initially nicknamed, reportedly spoke with a bit of a brogue his whole life.[20]

Bill and Nellie would be the oldest of nine children. Joe, Rose, and Marie came next, as the young family moved to progressively bigger apartments in Harlem. Then largely Irish and Jewish with a growing African American population, the neighborhood retained something of a frontier character when Bill was growing up: wooden shacks and outhouses shared space with the newer brick tenements; stockyards alternated with gasworks; and chickens, pigs, and goats ran about the muddy, garbage-strewn streets. Teeming with children, the district suffered from high rates of tuberculosis and other infectious diseases, and social workers battled juvenile delinquency. But wee Willie didn't have much time to idle or get into trouble; he went to work selling newspapers on the sidewalks at age seven, less than a year after his grandfather Joseph died.[21]

By 1892, L.J. and Louisa had had one more child, Paul, and had moved their family out of the city to Main Street in Port Chester. During this time three more children arrived: Owen, Regina (aka Queenie), and Vera. Poor Owen died as a child, though we don't know how or when—only that it was sometime after he turned six.

Long known as "Saw Pits" (for its sawmill and boatbuilding shop) even after the name officially changed, Port Chester was a bustling pocket of urban life surrounded by largely rural Westchester County. Nine-year-old Bill found a positively bucolic work environment caddying at a nine-hole golf course in Rye. But at age thirteen, just a few months after he'd jumped into America's first marathon, Bill joined the union, took up the trowel, and went to work for his father as an apprentice bricklayer.[22]

Bill grew up on his father's building sites, learning how to mix mortar from lime, sand, and water; how to cut bricks to a desired size with the trowel or a hammer and chisel; how to use a level, plumb rule, and straightedge; and the other secrets of a trade dating back thousands of years. Bill pushed heavy wheelbarrows full of bricks, and he carefully measured and staked cord lines where the walls would begin. Wearing a cloth cap on his head and a button-down shirt and tie under his work overalls, he would stoop over to pick up a brick from its pile, place it on the mortar bed, and tap it into place, then stoop to pick up a new brick, over and over, hundreds of times a day.[23]

The young Kennedy learned how to build walls, staircases, chimneys, and walkways. And like his old man, he learned to cuss, chew tobacco, and appreciate his union, the Bricklayers and Masons International—the oldest continuously operated union in America. He also learned to drink beer with the older "brickies" after work—which was emphatically *unlike* his old man, a near-teetotaler. The ebullient Bill and the hot-tempered L.J. would butt heads over this issue often.[24]

Not long after, Bill began his other career, in competitive athletics, when he fought in his first boxing match, at age fourteen, in

September 1898. And indeed it began as a "career," in the sense that it paid, a little: "$3.00 to the winner, $2.00 to [the] loser," Bill wrote later. "I was the loser far more often than the winner."[25]

Boxing was a wildly popular sport then, but also one struggling to appear respectable. It was less than a decade after John L. Sullivan reigned as the last bareknuckle champion, capping an era when the sport was just "as cruel as the gouging match of the frontier," according to one sport historian. Most Irish American boys Bill's age grew up idolizing Sullivan, whose portrait still adorned barrooms everywhere. What's more, for many urban youths, the sport offered freedom from tedium. "In a more and more regimented era," writes Sullivan biographer Michael Isenberg, "when people increasingly lived to the metronomic beat of the clock rather than the languid movement of the seasons, sports such as boxing encouraged defiance of convention, the urge to violate the established order of things." True enough in Bill's case. For better or worse, his career path was already prescribed, and his daily work schedule set, by his father. So the chance to defy a little convention at times must have been welcome.[26]

When Bill donned the gloves, prizefighting was technically illegal in New York. But the 1896 Horton Law had added a loophole for "exhibitions" put on by "athletic associations," giving rise to wink-wink de facto prizefights with admission fees, gambling, and pay for the combatants. Organizations that sprang up to take advantage of the law, such as the Coney Island Athletic Club, hosted the events.[27] Bill fought on the warm-up undercards, but a *Police Gazette* account of a headline bout between Joe Goddard and Peter Maher paints a picture of a typical night at Coney Island:

> The big club house reverberated with a storm of applause that fairly shook the building. . . . The big fellows were at it again viciously. On they fought not in a scientific manner but in true slugging form, and the way they thumped each other made the sports howl with delight. . . . Maher beat his opponent's bruised eye into a jelly-like pulp.[28]

A few fighters died during the Horton Law era. Moreover, those howling "sports"—the cigar-chomping, derby-clad gamblers who attended these fights—could be rough characters, and brawls and even riots broke out following some bouts. It was a brutal milieu, but for Bill and his cohorts, prizefighting meant opportunities for both glory and much-needed cash. "Irish-Americans embraced sport as a passion but also as a financial enterprise," which in the nineteenth century was "wholly anathema to British [and Anglo-American] ideals of amateurism," writes Kevin McCarthy.[29]

Teenage Bill was not yet acquainted with the amateur ideal, which—as espoused by organizations such as the BAA—stressed the physical and even moral benefits of engaging in sport for its own sake rather than for pay. After prizefighting for a few years, though, Bill would eventually come to believe that he and his fellow boxers were being exploited. Much later, he wrote of boxing:

> This is a sport which by its very nature is bound to leave an undesirable after effect on many of its contestants. These unhappy results have been pointed out to us by various sports writers and you may have come in personal contact with some of these past heroes of the prize ring, who in the vernacular of the sport world are said to be walking on their heels.
>
> It is the writer's humble opinion that this sport is comprised of some of the most selfish and disloyal men in the sport world, in that little if anything is done to help these unfortunates, these pioneers so to speak who have made possible the fight game and the big money of today.[30]

It was in training for boxing, however, that Bill started running seriously. "Road work" was common for boxers a century before Sylvester Stallone immortalized it in *Rocky*. "The best exercise for a man training for a boxing match is boxing. The next best is running," wrote John Boyle O'Reilly in his popular 1888 handbook *The Ethics of Boxing and Other Manly Sports*. Unlike his fellow Boston Irishman John L. Sullivan, O'Reilly—once a Fenian revolutionary and then co-founder of the BAA—was a proponent of amateurism and

FIGURE 2. Louisa O'Brien Kennedy, Bill's mother.

an articulate defender of boxing purely for its body- and character-building qualities. It's possible that Bill read *Ethics*. Certainly he learned that "running excels all exercises for developing 'the wind,'" as O'Reilly put it. And in running to train, Bill found that he enjoyed it, simply legging it up and down the paved streets of Port Chester and the dusty country roads nearby.[31]

A few months into his athletic career, weeks after his fifteenth birthday, and five days after Christmas, Bill lost his mother. Louisa (see fig. 2) died at age forty-three, after birthing nine children in fifteen years. The cause of death, a physician recorded, was "exhaustion from Anemia and other organic complications liver kidney etc."[32]

Bill had adored his mother. Now, he was starting 1899 as a motherless adolescent, growing up fast, making regular trips into the city to punch and be punched for a few bucks, picking up bad habits there and from the rough men he worked with on construction sites in Port Chester, and coming into his own as a gregarious, wisecracking youth. He was on a collision course with the clean-living, serious, and now grieving and overburdened man who was both his boss and his father. And in both roles, L.J. was not an easy man to put up with.[33]

〜

By the turn of the century, the Kennedys had moved to yet another, larger home. L.J. built a brick house, and an office next door, on South Street. In the neighboring wood-frame houses lived a roofer, a clerk, a gardener, a butcher, a teamster, and a machinist.[34]

Bill's father, a husky man with black hair and a red beard, was now well on his way to becoming the biggest contractor in town. Over a forty-year career he would build not only several schools, office and apartment buildings, and a large factory addition in Port Chester, but also the Connecticut State Armory, the Carnegie Library in New Rochelle, a hospital addition in White Plains, and Mount Hope Academy in Yonkers.[35]

Mount Hope Academy was essentially an orphanage run by Roman Catholic Ursuline sisters. L.J. didn't just build it; he sent his three youngest children (Paul, Regina, and Vera) to live there. After the loss of his wife, L.J. apparently found running his growing business and raising the youngest offspring beyond him. At least Paul (the authors' direct forebear) later recalled the home affectionately, visiting it annually for decades, and attending the funeral of the mother superior.[36]

L.J.'s income in 1893, the last year listed in a surviving daybook, was $985.35, about $23,600 in 2010 terms. And he still had nine mouths to feed besides his own. "I don't know how L.J. raised all those kids on the money he made," said his granddaughter Ann Louise McLaughlin. "And sometimes it wasn't even money. Someone once paid him with a barrel of sauerkraut." At least that saved him the step of buying food.[37]

"L.J. was difficult to live with for a teenage boy," said McLaughlin. Her "Grandpa" loved his children and grandchildren, she remembered, but she understood that in their youth, Bill and his younger brother Joe chafed under their father's strict regime. Chief among the boys' faults, as L.J. saw it, was their indulgence in alcohol. The old man wasn't a drinker. Not that L.J. was without weaknesses: he chewed tobacco, cursed a purple streak, and was "a little vain," recalled McLaughlin. "He liked to have his picture taken," and he concocted a skin cream he believed would remove his freckles. (He also fudged his age to census takers.)[38] But he largely abstained from booze, and he may have encouraged his employees and acquaintances to do the same, even administering the temperance oath. One daybook entry reads, "Ed Barrett took the pledge against liquors of all kinds. Also gave up playing Pool & Billiards until Fourth of July."[39]

L. J. Kennedy was described as "vitally interested in the affairs of the community." He never held public office, but he was active in the Knights of Columbus and the Grand Jury Association of Westchester County, and he was a devout parishioner at the Church of Our Lady of Mercy.[40]

The builder's godliness had its limits; at times it ran smack into his temper. The story is told that one day when L.J. was on-site, loudly overseeing the crew erecting St. Mary's parochial school, the pastor finally, cautiously approached. Mr. Kennedy, we are grateful for all your efforts, and so forth, he began. "But the neighbors have been complaining about some of your language."

"What the hell is wrong with my language?" L.J. responded, in part. (His granddaughter, while remaining ladylike, made it clear that there was much more, and much worse, in the same vein.)[41]

Still, the pastor might have approved of the prudish impulse L.J. exhibited in another surviving anecdote, one that *contrasts* with a modern stereotype about construction workers. Two young ladies in flashy hats and tight dresses were walking down the street past a worksite. L.J.'s reaction was to shake his head, *tsk,* and say, "Look at that. Those girls ought to be ashamed of themselves."

Then as the supposed hussies drew closer, a worker said, "Hey, Larry, aren't those your girls?" The shamefully dressed women were his daughters Rose and Marie Kennedy.

In any event, more than his attendance at Mass, L.J. was known for his devotion to the Democratic Party. "L.J. was a diehard union man, even though he was the one doing the hiring," McLaughlin related. "He was very pro-union, and an outspoken Democrat. So much so that when [William L. Ward, Republican national committeeman and president of Russell, Burdsall & Ward Bolt & Nut Company of Port Chester] wanted his son Evans Ward to learn about the Democrats, he sent him to meet L. J. Kennedy."

When the Nineteenth Amendment passed, L.J. seems to have urged his daughters to take advantage, confident he had raised them to do the right thing in the voting booth. When Queenie came home the evening after her first election, L.J. asked her, "Well, did you vote?"

"Yes, but I didn't really know any of the names, so I just voted for all the Irish ones."

Queenie would later recall that that was one of the few times her father ever bawled her out. Even if most of the Democrats on the ballot were indeed their fellow Irish Americans, that wasn't *why* the Kennedys voted for them, and L.J. was upset that his daughter didn't see the distinction.

Young Bill did absorb some of his father's lessons, becoming a proud lifelong Democrat and union member with a relatively non-parochial outlook. He also picked up L.J.'s tobacco-chewing habit. But there were major points of departure, too. Bill and younger brother Joe found themselves repeatedly running afoul of the man of the house. They would frequently stay out late carousing, sparking the wrath that L.J. usually spared his girls. This happened so often that even on one night when the boys happened to be long home and in bed, when L.J. was awakened by the singing of a passing drunk, he immediately shouted to his sons, "Oh, go on and go to bed!"

L.J. didn't appreciate disturbances generally. Once, a dog was barking outside, and he marched out to the sidewalk and grabbed a passer-by. "Take this God-damned dog away from here!"

The young man protested, "But it isn't my dog!"

"I don't give a damn whose dog it is! Take it away!" The conscript obediently collared the hound and hustled it away down the street.

Part of L.J.'s dismay at his sons' behavior was that he was a rising leader in the community as well as in business and was concerned about his family's reputation. He was "embarrassed," McLaughlin said, by the boys' devil-may-care attitude and antics. "Of course, they were all the same in some ways, which is probably why they argued."

In the fall of 1901, Bill fought his last bout and hung up his gloves. Trips to Coney Island weren't enough to assuage the seventeen-year-old's restlessness. He had learned his father's trade, but he couldn't live under his roof any longer. One day, Bill and fifteen-year-old Joe walked to the local rail yard and hopped a freight train bound for the West.[42]

Bill wouldn't return for years, though in many ways he never left Port Chester or his father, or they never left him. It wasn't only L.J.'s profession, party affiliation, and ever-present plug of chaw that Bill inherited. At stressful moments, there were flashes of the elder Kennedy's gruffness, too. But the essence of L.J. that lived on in Bill was that intangible quality that would make him a leader, in one realm or another, time and again.

Yet in other ways, once that freight train pulled out of Port Chester, Bill would be on the road for the rest of his life.

2

ON THE ROAD (AND RAILS)

I magine hanging on to a narrow beam underneath a boxcar pulled by a wailing, smoke-spewing fifty-ton iron horse. You're hurtling across the country at fifty miles per hour, faster than any other mode of transportation on the planet, and it certainly feels that way from where you're sitting—or rather lying, facedown. The wooden ties flash past below, and flecks of gravel and cinder sting your face as the steel wheels on either side of you squeal and clatter along the tracks.

That's how Bill and Joe Kennedy made their way west at the turn of the century. It's easy to see why the steam locomotive looms so large in the American imagination, starring in myriad blues songs and western films. Trains made a terrific noise and spectacle, and they powered the nation's expansion across a continent. The Kennedy boys were part of a great westward movement at that time, one that followed the trails already blazed and the rails already laid. In contemporary parlance, they were "hoboing," sneaking a ride by train to a new town, there to seek work. (Even perennial hoboes looked down on "tramps," who had no intention of working.)

To avoid detection, these "land stowaways" often spent a whole trip "riding the rods"—hanging on to the brake rods or beams underneath freight or passenger cars, just inches above the speeding ground. If this seems like courting disaster, it was: in the two decades around the turn of the century, at least 32,000 hoboes and tramps were killed on American railroads, whether by falls, encounters with railroad "bulls" (private security officers), or other misfortunes. Besides the brake rods, hoboes also rode on top of passenger cars (with the baggage) or, if they were lucky, inside freight cars. Bill employed all three methods at different times, and he had his own mishaps and close calls, which we'll get to in due course.[1]

Though the brothers returned to their native New York City at some point, Bill soon beat his way west again, and he spent years crisscrossing the country, a free spirit, traveling to wherever the jobs were and enjoying the journey. Apart from one stint as a deckhand on the Great Lakes, Bill worked at his trade, laying bricks. And there was nearly always work for a good bricklayer at a time of industrialization, population growth, and urbanization. The union provided job leads as well as a social network, so Bill seldom lacked for food or friends, whether he found himself on the West Coast, in the upper South, or (more typically) in the Midwest.

During a layoff one day in the spring or summer of 1904, Bill was back in New York, taking in a baseball game, probably drinking a bottle of beer while sitting on a wooden bleacher seat. In between innings, a brass band struck up the popular song "Meet Me in St. Louis, Louis." What a swell idea, Bill decided: the twenty-year-old's next destination would be St. Louis, which was just then hosting a World's Fair.[2]

That warm-weather whim would have long-term repercussions. Not least because it set Bill on a course to reunite with the pioneering extreme sport he'd dabbled in once as a lad.

⌣

Set on the banks of the Mississippi, St. Louis straddled the crossroads
of the genteel, rural South; the bustling, industrial North and East;
and the wild, dusty frontier West. And it was Bill Kennedy's kind
of town: the "Gateway City" was built almost entirely of brick. This
was due in part to a city ordinance passed after a devastating 1849
fire, and in part to the region's rich clay mines. The city had about a
hundred brick factories at the time Bill moved there, and the building boom was ongoing. Moreover, thanks to its large German colony,
St. Louis also had twenty breweries and hundreds of beer gardens to
slake the thirst of its 575,000 residents.[3]

The summer of the 1904 fair was an exciting time to arrive in St.
Louis. Officially called the Louisiana Purchase Exposition, the fair
was the city's largest event, before or since, drawing 20 million visitors to Forest Park. Amid lagoons and landscaping, white palaces and
small huts housed exhibits devoted to nations and states, metallurgy
and manufacturing, wild birds and dairy cows. Perhaps Bill heard
ragtime music composed by Scott Joplin, or took in one of the Anglo-
Boer War battle reenactments. He was likely drawn to the Irish Village for a glimpse at how his grandparents supposedly lived, and he
might have stopped by the Massachusetts and New York exhibits,
just across from each other on Commonwealth Avenue. (In time Bill
would become quite familiar with another road by that name.)[4]

But there is little question that Bill witnessed, and devoured,
the Olympic Games. Strange as it may seem now, the third revived
Olympiad—the first held in the United States—took place in the
midst of the 1904 World's Fair. The athletic program was crammed
into a corner of Forest Park, just one of many attractions. Over the
course of that summer, seven hundred athletes competed in events
ranging from tug-of-war to the plunge (akin to the high dive) to hop,
step, and jump. The field was not diverse: five hundred of the athletes
were Americans, representing their colleges or local athletic clubs
rather than their common nation. Many events drew sparse crowds.

The exception, on both counts, was the marathon—"without doubt, the most interesting and the hardest event to win in the Olympic series," declared the *New York Times*.[5] The entrants hailed from many lands, including Greece, Austria, Cuba, and South Africa. And about ten thousand spectators filled the stadium at Forest Park on August 31 to see the start and finish of the race, while more gathered at various points along the country roads, or took to their horses or autos to follow the runners. Thirty-two runners of varying degrees of experience set off at 3 p.m., running in the dry ninety-plus-degree heat of a St. Louis summer afternoon. The loop of a course was measured at forty kilometers (about 24.85 miles), same as the 1896 Olympic route from Marathon to Athens. Seven hills, from one hundred to three hundred feet high, lay along the way. Like the Boston Post Road and the roads from Ashland to Boston, these rural routes outside St. Louis were rocky and rutted and at times inches deep in dust. Runners dodged horses, autos, trolleys, and dog walkers. Just two water stations provided succor, one at six miles, the next (and last) at twelve. No wonder only fourteen of the thirty-two starters finished.[6]

"Here at St. Louis 'Tragedy and Comedy' played their part," Bill recalled. The tragedy was very nearly literal: Bill Garcia of San Francisco collapsed and was hospitalized with hemorrhaging, but recovered. And though it likely did not seem comical to him at the time, Len Tau was chased about a mile off the course by a large dog. A South African Tswana tribesman who competed barefoot, Tau still managed to finish in ninth place.[7]

It was probably with some embarrassment that Bill related the trick played by a brother brickie: "Fred Lorz, a New York bricklayer, had quit the race owing to the heat, and returned to the stadium in a horse and buggy. As he enters the gate on foot, he is greeted with a roar of applause. Lorz broke into a trot and circled the track, receiving the plaudits due the winner." Lorz said later he was joking, and indeed he bore a reputation as a prankster, but he let this gag go pretty far: "Alice Roosevelt (later Mrs. Nicholas Longworth) placed the traditional laurel wreath around him." At that moment, Lorz came clean, though it remains unclear whether he volunteered the truth or was forced to admit it when the *real* leader arrived.[8]

In any case, the real leader did arrive shortly but not too well. Thomas J. Hicks, of Cambridge, Massachusetts, had placed second at Boston back in April of that year. Missouri in August, however, did not agree with him. Five miles from the finish, Hicks was out in front but flagging. His attendant, riding along in an auto, was a kind of quack doctor, Charles Lucas. When Hicks slowed to a walk, Lucas gave him raw eggs mixed with one milligram of strychnine—the active ingredient in rat poison. In small amounts, strychnine was often taken as a stimulant at the time. To use today's terms, it was a performance-enhancing drug. Curiously (at least from our modern perspective), an athlete seeking to gain an edge with a chemical pick-me-up was not considered a cheater in Hicks's day. Even so, intentionally ingesting rat poison seems to "put the 'dope' in doping," as *Mental Floss* magazine quipped in 2010. And as if one dose weren't enough, when Hicks failed to respond to the first treatment, Lucas administered a second one a mile down the road, then washed it down with a glass of brandy for good measure.[9]

Ashen-faced and hallucinating, Hicks barely jogged into the stadium to cries of "An American! An American!" Held up by two trainers, he shuffled across the finish line in 3:28:53, which stands forever as the worst finishing time in Olympic history. Behind him (eventually) came Albert Corey and Arthur Newton. "A grand slam for America," wrote Bill.

> But the real hero of the race was Felix Carvajal, a Cuban from Havana. He had worked his way from Havana to New Orleans on a tramp steamer, beating his way to St. Louis by freight. Here he was adopted by the whales [members of the Irish-American Athletic Club] from N.Y., Pat McDonald and Co., who cut his pants off at the knees for a track suit. He was the joke of the race at the start as he ran around the track, with his heavy shoes, his shortened pants, and his shirt with the sleeves flapping over his hands. But what an ovation he received as he entered

the Stadium in fourth place, bowing and smiling at the
cheering crowd which four hours earlier had been laughing
and jeering at him.[10]

One man who did not cheer the event itself was the influential
James E. Sullivan, secretary-treasurer of the Amateur Athletic Union
and a prime organizer of the 1904 Olympics. "The marathon race was
a decided success from an athletic point of view, but I think they
should be dropped from the list of events," Sullivan argued in the
next day's *St. Louis Republic*. "I saw the finishes of the Paris [Olympic
marathon in 1900] and yesterday's races, and I think they are man-
killing in effect. Although there were plenty of machines on the road
to render assistance to the runners, they are so fixed on winning that
they do not stop until they drop from sheer exhaustion."[11]

Yet that persistence is exactly what sport followers admired—
what they called the "guts," "grit," and "gamesmanship" that these
uncommon athletes showed as they drove themselves over a distance
thought deadly to achieve their goal. So the long grind would continue to crown the Olympic program every cycle thereafter. But Sullivan held sway in the Amateur Athletic Union's (AAU) base of New
York City, and no marathon would take place there during these early
years of the century. The Boston Athletic Association, by contrast, felt
no obligation to defer to Sullivan and kept running its local marathon
annually. (A lowbrow headline writer might summarize this sentiment as "BAA to AAU: FU.")

Indeed, in the 1905 Boston race, Fred Lorz—whom Sullivan had
initially banned "for life" for his Olympic shenanigans—entered and
won. (For real, by all accounts.) From its modest beginnings in 1897,
the Boston Marathon had become a flourishing fixture of the athletic
season and the premier distance event in America. Nearly a hundred
runners entered the race in 1904, when Hicks came in second; and
seventy-eight ran in 1905, when Lorz won in 2:38:25. Thousands of
spectators turned out along the route. In fact, the crowds were so
large in places, police struggled to keep a path clear for the runners.[12]

Largely forgotten now is that outside Boston, one city far from the East became for a time a second hotbed of the marathon—thanks in part to the gritty Olympic performance of Hicks of Cambridge.

⁓

Inspired by the drama and spectacle they'd witnessed at Forest Park, members of the Missouri Athletic Club in downtown St. Louis started the Missouri A.C. All-Western Marathon the following spring. It was the same impulse that had taken hold among the men of the BAA starting in 1896. Athletic clubs proliferated in cities in those years. They ranged from the highly exclusive New York A.C. to the more working-class Irish-American A.C., and included all in between—like the BAA and the MAC, which sat toward the high end but allowed middle- and working-class athletes to join (perhaps even encouraged them as "ringers"). With lounges, gymnasiums, and competition calendars in a variety of sports, these organizations provided social cohesion and promoted the benefits of exercise. And they would soon prove critical to the success of city marathons.[13]

Despite the "Missouri" in the event's name, nearly the entire course of the MAC's marathon lay in Illinois. The route began at the railroad station at Freeburg, a bit shy of twenty-five miles to the southeast of St. Louis, and wended its way through Belleville and East St. Louis (Illinois) before crossing the Mississippi River and ending at the MAC clubhouse. Still grappling with perceptions about the distance, club officials assured the public as to the event's safety: "That the race is harmless has been thoroughly proven, and all fear of serious results has been eliminated. Statistics show that the only ill effect of the run has been the leaving of blisters on the feet, which in a few days are healed." Nevertheless, only fourteen men felt brave enough to attempt it.[14]

The Missouri club scheduled its marathon for May 6, 1905, two and a half weeks after the Boston Marathon. They hoped that would give eastern runners enough time for recovery and travel. Only one was up for it, but in his way he made a big splash, whose ripples would soon touch Bill Kennedy and thereby travel back east and even down the generations.

Representing the Cambridgeport Gymnasium, Bob Fowler traveled by train from Boston to St. Louis, arriving the day before the marathon. That evening he dined with his fellow competitors in the MAC clubhouse. Next to him sat a young athlete named Joe Forshaw. The lanky 24-year-old was already known in St. Louis for winning the Western AAU cross-country championship, but that 6.5-mile race was the longest he had ever run. Fowler and Forshaw struck up a conversation at the dinner table. Then as now, when runners gathered, they liked to talk running. The old hand was glad to share advice with the newbie, even though they'd be competing against each other the next day. Fowler "gave to me all the hints that he knew about the game," Forshaw would say later. "He told me to grease my stockings and shoes with beef grease. This I did and it prevented any blisters or sores on my feet. He also told me to eat the solid food that was prepared for us at the table, but to merely break the eggs to look as though I had eaten them. His suggestion to drink nothing but beef tea helped me, and I thank him for that."[15]

To cut to the chase, Forshaw won the marathon. "I owe my success to Robert Fowler, the Boston runner," the victorious St. Louis lad told the press.[16] Within a few years, Forshaw would in turn share those winning tips with Bill Kennedy.

The race itself was a seat-of-the-pants affair, not unlike the inaugural Boston Marathon back in '97. The start of the event was delayed because an automobile carrying one runner and the referee from St. Louis broke down en route to Freeburg. Another runner lost a shoe in the mud, kicked off the other, and labored over the last two miles barefoot. Forshaw's time of 3:16:57 was good enough to win by more than twenty minutes over the next runner in.

Observers were struck by how comparatively fresh and healthy Forshaw appeared, after the walking-dead act of Hicks the previous summer. Nevertheless, Forshaw *felt* exhausted. "Yesterday's event was [Forshaw's] first Marathon race," the *St. Louis Post-Dispatch* reported.

"And, he says, his last."[17]

A year later, Forshaw was running in an Olympic marathon in Athens.

Like McDermott in the 1890s, Forshaw had been bitten by the marathon bug. The Missouri A.C., too, was not deterred from running the event again, though the concept was still a hard sell for some locals: "Twenty-two young men whose sanity will thereby be placed more or less in question will attempt to run 24 miles," chortled a writer for the *Post-Dispatch* in May 1906.[18] (The marathon distance was not yet standardized, and the methods of course measurement were not scientific anyway.) Just as in the Ashland-to-Boston race in its early years, for long stretches the runners passed through quiet, pastoral landscapes, as the *Post-Dispatch* article painted:

> The soft rain drops hung as jewels on the fresh grass. The air was filled with an invigorating zone which came from plow and leaf, from tree and water, from heaven itself. The road just softened and dust laid with a light rain was sweet as velvet to the feet. The birds sang in the trees and the cow bells tingled in the woods. The sod tore softly before the plowshare. The smoke curled lazily up from the chimneys of the farm houses.[19]

But in the final, urban leg in East St. Louis, and surrounding the Missouri A.C. clubhouse in St. Louis, the streets were crowded with cheering spectators—an intensely interested Bill Kennedy among them. At first, Bill simply followed the marathon as a fan, not only rooting runners on from the sidewalks, but also clipping and saving race coverage from the newspapers, absorbing all the information about the sport that he could. Even then he was documenting the marathon, a practice he'd continue all his life. More important, he soon began thinking about entering the contest himself. It likely encouraged him that the runners were largely his fellow workingmen. The victor three years in a row (1906 to 1908) was a newspaper carrier from Chicago, Sid Hatch. (You'll hear his name again.) Roughly Kennedy's age, Hatch trained by running along his paper route each day in River Forest, Illinois. An increasingly sympathetic *Post-Dispatch* praised these hardy athletes in 1907:

> As usual after such an endurance test there are some that ominously shake their heads and croakingly announce the horrible effect such a performance has upon the contestants, but the facts do not bear out such statements. All of the men this morning reported themselves as feeling none the worse for their effort and as most of them are working men of some description or other they are all down to the daily grind today as if there never had been such a thing as a Marathon run.[20]

By some accounts, 1907 was the year Bill Kennedy started running seriously, at least on his own.[21] He had stopped running along with boxing as he entered adulthood, essentially the moment he left Port Chester. In those days, grown men simply didn't run around with no apparent aim. But now, to hell with what people on the street thought. Bill took up the pursuit again, this time with a passion. The previous year's Olympics—won by underdog Billy Sherring, a railroad brakeman wearing the shamrock of the St. Patrick's A.C. in Toronto—kept the event on the radar for Bill and many other sporting types. The record-breaking performance of Onondaga Indian Tom Longboat at Boston (2:24:24) in April 1907 captured fans' attention as well. A 25-miler was finally held in James E. Sullivan's territory in November 1907, when a Yonkers club hosted "the first big Marathon race ever held in the vicinity of New York," declared the *Times* (apparently having forgotten all about the Knickerbocker run of 1896).[22] That same fall a marathon took place in Chicago, and fans and experts debated the wisdom of one losing runner, who had downed a slug of whiskey every mile. "If John Lindquist's trainer had been acquainted with the real properties of the drug which he so freely and foolishly administered to his man," opined the *Times,* "he would have given Lindquist a good dose of whisky at the last mile or so of the race."[23]

But it was the following year when marathon fever truly took hold, thanks to an athlete with roots in Bill's own ancestral county of Tipperary.

Johnny Hayes was a sandhog, an underwater digger for a contractor building New York's subway system, when he won the first Yonkers Marathon in 1907. The son of immigrants from Nenagh, Tipperary, Hayes soon joined the Irish-American A.C. and secured a cushier job in the dry goods section of Bloomingdale's. Finishing second at Boston in April 1908, Hayes qualified for that summer's Olympic team.

At London, for the first time, the Olympic marathon course was measured at 26 miles, 385 yards, in order to start the race at scenic Windsor Castle and finish at White City Stadium. Legend has it that the royal family itself requested the extension, but marathon historian David Davis casts doubt on this story. What is certain is that the 1908 Games were plagued by American-British tensions (which meant, to a great extent, Irish American–British tensions). Sullivan and the AOC complained that no American flag flew alongside the other nations' flags inside the Olympic stadium. Their English hosts were scandalized during the opening ceremony when U.S. flag bearer Ralph Rose of the Irish-American A.C. apparently failed to dip *his* flag before the king. Sullivan complained again when the English tug-of-war team wore illegal shoes.

The signal controversy occurred at the Olympic marathon. Italian runner Dorando Pietri reached the stadium first, but in rough shape. Like Hicks in '04, the Italian had taken a dose of strychnine. Setting foot on the track, he took a wrong turn, then collapsed. Doctors helped Pietri to his feet, and he shuffled in the right direction, but collapsed four more times before he was finally helped—practically carried—across the finish line by British Olympic officials and announced the winner. In the meantime, Hayes had entered the stadium, and he crossed the finish line second, but unassisted. A livid Sullivan protested the decision, and after hours of deliberation, the British Olympic committee grudgingly awarded Hayes the gold medal instead. Once so ambivalent about the marathon, Sullivan soon became a big proponent. (Incidentally, Forshaw finished third and Hatch fourteenth.)[24]

These dramatic elements—A collapse at the end, like Pheidip-pides! Official collusion and chicanery! An American wins!—fired up the folks back home. "Marathon became a craze in this country," Bill Kennedy recalled. "Both Hayes and Dorando turned professional and raced in Madison Square Garden several times. Professional races were held in ball parks." As writer Benjamin Cheever points out, a 1909 marathon at New York's Polo Grounds drew ten thousand spectators. The same day, in the same city, just four thousand people attended a Yankees–Red Sox game. (The Sox won.)[25]

Not only did ordinary men and women attend marathons, but also many took to the streets themselves. It was America's first, forgotten fitness fad. Scores of rookie runners discovered the level path around New York's Central Park Reservoir, a mile-and-a-half loop. Among these runners were well-to-do ladies, according to one press account:

> Many of them wear divided skirts and running shoes. It often happens that a motor car or carriage will stop nearby and the women go to the reservoir path, accompanied by a maid. Upon reaching the path the woman will shed her cloak and display a costume suited for running. Once around the reservoir appears to be enough for most of the women, but a few go over the course twice.[26]

To be sure, vast swaths of the country remained unaware of the sport. Outside of urban centers, it was harder, even dangerous, to run in public wearing what appeared to most rural folks to be undergar-ments. Bill kept to the streets and parks of St. Louis after hearing that one of his fellow plodders had been threatened by shotgun-toting farmers in Columbia, Missouri.[27]

Nevertheless, the exhilaration that Bill got out of running, coupled with the new excitement surrounding organized races, inspired the bricklayer to start running competitively. The first step was to join the Amateur Athletic Union.

"I found out I had to be a member," he recalled, "so I got a card without informing them of my boxing for money."[28] That was Bill's introduction to the stringent rules of the AAU, which he would learn took the amateur ideal to an extreme.

⤳

Bill started training in January, most likely. At some point he seems to have read and absorbed Forshaw's how-to article on marathon running in *Spalding's Athletic Library*—that era's *ESPN Magazine* and *Men's Health* wrapped up in one. Much of what Forshaw recommended (in part passing on the tips of Fowler of Cambridge) still holds up in the twenty-first century. Beginning a regimen on New Year's Day for a springtime marathon is still standard, although Forshaw started a bit more slowly than many modern runners: "For the first month or so, I only take the weekly run." From three miles, he gradually increased the distance each week. Then in February,

> I begin taking short runs twice or three times a week, [varying] from four to ten miles; . . . the Sunday runs vary from ten to fifteen miles. I continue on this schedule until about April, when I may take one or two long runs, say about twenty miles, and about two weeks before the race may go over the full course once, walking, say, the first five or six miles, and then running the balance, the object being to measure the distance well and the speed I can stand without making too much of a hard race of it, and taking all the run out of myself before the actual race.[29]

Matt Migonis, a 2014 world champion triathlete, reviewed the *Spalding* article and told us Forshaw's schedule would be reasonable today.[30] Migonis also agreed with Forshaw's suggestion to incorporate long walks and periods of rest and recovery. Some of his other tips not so much. Forshaw would "flush the system" with a bottle of citrate of magnesia about a week before the race.

"Never heard of this," Migonis said. "Sounds kind of crazy to me."

Nor had Migonis, or marathon runner and pediatric nurse Dennis Doherty, heard of cooling off by sponging the head with bay rum, as Forshaw recommended. "I would think it'd be awful if it got in your eyes," said Doherty.

Bill Kennedy would always swear by citrate of magnesia. Most important, though, was the running. And by April, Bill was doing the long runs, and he felt good enough to attempt his first marathon. He sent in his entry for the 1909 Missouri A.C. All-Western Marathon. On Friday, April 30, Bill passed the physical exam at the clubhouse, ate dinner with his competitors, then went home and tried to get some sleep.[31]

At dawn on May Day, it snowed in St. Louis. Though the fat, feathery flakes failed to stick to the ground, temperatures remained in the thirties all morning, and frost threatened to kill fruits on the vine. Unlike on other first Saturdays in May, no birds sang in the trees along the route of the All-Western Marathon in 1909. A strong wind blew east, toward the little village of Freeburg. Despite the chill, most of the town's twelve hundred residents—largely coal miners and their families—thronged the courthouse square, which was lined with a few shops doing their annual brisk business on what had become a holiday for the denizens of the race route. This year, the buzz was doubled and tripled by post–1908 Olympics marathon fever and by the absence of three-time winner Sid Hatch, at home in Chicago with rheumatism. With Hatch out, it was anyone's race. Along with the crowds of locals, dozens of automobiles and horse-drawn buggies packed with scores of sports from St. Louis were parked along the streets of the village, waiting for the start.

To spare the competitors any unnecessary exposure to the cold, MAC athletic director C. W. Bassett waited until the last minute, but finally, just before noon, he called the thirty-nine runners to doff their coats and line up. William J. Kennedy was one of many first-timers running "unattached," not as members of any athletic club. He and the other rookies probably rubbed their hands together and hopped up and down to stay warm while casting quick glances at Forshaw and the other veterans. When the church bells chimed noon, Bassett fired his pistol into the air, and the race was on. The new guys "sprang away like frightened rabbits," said the *Post-Dispatch*.[32]

Things began with a hiccup. To make the distance conform to the new London precedent, the MAC had decreed that runners begin by completing seven and a half laps around the courthouse square. As if that half lap weren't confusing enough, Bassett lost count altogether, and the leaders (even Forshaw, who realized the error but held his tongue for fear of embarrassing Bassett) ended up running an extra lap. The unattached contingent dutifully followed before other club officials intervened.

Once the runners finally headed out of Freeburg on the toll road, the race settled into a pattern. A Missouri A.C. man by the typo-tempting Teutonic name of Joe Erxleben held the lead, with Forshaw and Chicagoan Alexander Thibeau close behind. A jam of spectators in automobiles and horse-drawn buggies and riding bicycles followed the front-runners. The rest of the competitors strung along after, choking on clouds of exhaust and coal-black dust, which a headwind blew directly into their squinting faces. Some of the men took to the boardwalk on the right half of the road, but the dust wasn't much better there, where the wooden planks jolted their bones to boot. The wind never abated and "at times half strangled them and made them bend over more like bicycle riders than long distance runners." Forshaw fell behind, while an unattached runner named Frank Johnson surged ahead to nip the leaders' heels.[33]

The scenery along the toll road was still rural—fields or woods—but now it was lined with spectators, largely curious farmers and their families. The farmers "did not take any too kindly to the autos," said the *Post-Dispatch,* nor did some of the horses, which were spooked at the sight and sound of so many "machines." Indeed, some of the motorists did not take too kindly to one another, as the heavy traffic in the narrow lane led to some scrapes. Meanwhile, the attendant bicyclists "had a worse time of it than the men they were supposed to be helping," some catching ruts and tumbling.[34]

After nine miles, the runners reached Belleville, a town about twenty times as large as tiny Freeburg. The brick-paved streets "jarred them mercilessly," but at least the athletes were cheered on by the largest crowds yet. Many fans clutched lists of the runners and their bib numbers, clipped from the St. Louis papers, and checked them off as they passed.[35]

Erxleben reached the Belleville toll gate first, at 1:01 p.m., followed so closely by Thibeau and Johnson that "a blanket could have covered all three." They were joined by no fewer than one hundred bicycle riders, who accompanied them through town. Thirty seconds and a hundred yards behind the leading trio came Forshaw. Two more runners followed before Bill Kennedy arrived, at 1:03 p.m., in seventh place, with Karl Warma on his heels. Warma was "handicapped by his name," reported the *Post-Dispatch*. "Everybody along the route seemed to think it funny to tell him that he was running a hot race."[36]

Past Belleville, the road returned to dirt, but clattering alongside now were electric trolleys, "packed to suffocation" with race watchers.[37] Meanwhile, the persistent cold wind and the choking dust proved too much for about half the runners, who one by one dropped out over the six-mile stretch to Edgemont.

After Edgemont, the leaders passed through the small city of East St. Louis, Illinois. Only here, in the final portion of the race, were policemen present to keep back the crowds. Erxleben maintained his lead as he plodded over the downtown's cobblestoned streets, up a tilted road atop a steep viaduct, and over the Eads Bridge to St. Louis. An auto raced ahead to deliver the news that an athlete wearing the cherry-red diamond of the Missouri A.C. was in the lead. The club's members "rushed out into the street shouting wildly" and joined a crowd swelling to upwards of a thousand in front of the clubhouse. All cheered and waved their hats as Erxleben broke the tape. For the first time in four years—since the first running of the race—a local athlete had won the St. Louis marathon. Erxleben's time was 2:49:10, which the *Post-Dispatch* pointed out beat Hayes's London record by six minutes, though it was still far short of Longboat's Boston record of '07.[38]

Where did Bill Kennedy end up? The *Post-Dispatch* reported that twenty men reached the clubhouse on foot. Unfortunately, the paper recorded the names of only the first fourteen. The last of those fourteen came in at 3:46:13. Likely the referees gave up waiting after that, and the newspapermen took their cue from the club, considering the six who straggled in afterwards not to have officially "finished."

Having been ahead of the majority of the field at Belleville, Bill may well have hung on and been one of those six, but it's impossible to confirm now. Bill always maintained that he finished every marathon except one, in Boston decades later. Still, just the fact that he finished so poorly if at all his first time out is a clue as to why, several years later, he counseled rookie runners not to beat themselves up for a DNF:

> It is not all young fellows who are temperamentally fitted for Marathon racing. I do not mean that it is harmful for a lad, if he is in the proper condition, but too many start out with the idea that a Marathon race is a jaunt. Maybe it is for some, but I am not ashamed to confess that upon several occasions I found it necessary to summon all my willpower to stay in the race. A man does not have to be "yellow" to quit in a Marathon, notwithstanding what anyone may say. I have always found that it was great fun during the first miles of a long race, but when one begins to tire and the legs grow heavy, when the arms begin to ache and maybe you get a "crick" in the neck, or your head rolls from side to side—then it is that a runner must call upon all his reserve force and mental powers to stay in the race. Personally, I have never felt any ill effects from marathon running, for I generally recuperate quickly, but just the same I would never condemn a fellow who stops in the long race. He alone is the best judge as to whether it is best for him to continue.[39]

It is also possible that after the race, Bill felt like the runners in a *Post-Dispatch* cartoon the next day. Captioned "How some of the tail enders feel about marathons," it showed two sweating, exhausted runners each raising a hand in solemn oath: "Never again."

Yet Bill would run the race again. And again and again.

～✑

Later that spring, Bill was working on a bank building in Little Rock, Arkansas, when he had the opportunity to emulate the English runner (and former bricklayer) Alfie Shrubb, a professional marathoner who was known on occasion to run a race against a horse. At least, Shrubb was known to running fanatics like Bill Kennedy. In Arkansas in 1909, such exploits were not well known at all, as Bill discovered, to his benefit:

> The tavern next to the [bank site] was run by a heavy man who owned a trotting horse. The bricklayers who stopped in thereafter were speaking about me running long distance races, so he asked me how far I ran. Knowing he had never heard of a man running a marathon race, I told him ten miles. He was surprised to know a man could run so far, and he asked me how long it took me so I said about 53 mins. "Why," he says, "a horse can't run it that fast." The result, we arranged a ten mile race for the following Sunday out on a country road, he to drive his horse in harness while I ran in a track suit. While I had never raced a horse, I knew from reading of Shrubb's races that a man could beat a horse in a distance race. I also had read of the pony express horses doing only thirty miles a day when they were relayed by another horse. He and some friend of his covered the bricklayers' bets. He was the most surprised man the following Sunday when I ran away from his horse. He told us he would have bet his tavern that a man couldn't beat a horse. Needless to say the local sports heard of it and he took a good deal of friendly kidding about the man beating his trotting horse.[40]

The tale is not as tall as it sounds, and not only because the poor horse was handicapped by hauling its heavyset human owner. Paleontologists postulate that man is uniquely adapted to long-distance running precisely because that trait allowed our ancestors to eventually run down prey that could sprint faster over short distances. Heck, this is probably how we caught and tamed horses in the first place. In more recent times, 1920s marathoner Johnny Miles trained in Nova Scotia by running for miles with a pony as a pacemaker.[41]

❧

Though Bill Kennedy continued to follow his trade wherever it was in demand, St. Louis remained his base. Now that he was an active participant in athletics, Bill had some cachet in the city's sport-centered saloon scene, where he enjoyed mingling with the even better-known pro ballplayers—both those who played for St. Louis's two baseball teams, the Cardinals and the Browns, and their visiting opponents, especially the New York Giants, who to Bill were like emissaries from home. Much later, he jotted down recollections from these bibulous bastions of bachelorhood:

> Every reader of sports is familiar with the present day ball player and his colorful or wacky acts. I know none of these men of today [circa 1963] as the present day ball player has no time for the rabble. But back in the old days in St. Louis it was different. The public came in contact with its sport celebrities. Back in the days when the ball teams rode to the ball park in horse drawn carry-alls, and the laughs and pleasure I had from the ball players of those days are indelibly impressed on my memory. Believe it or not, with apologies to Ripley, I have seen [Browns pitcher] Rube Waddell dash out of the back gate of Sportsman's Park to a bar room at Sullivan and Grand, still in his uniform, and serve beer to the thirsty customers. And mister, you can be thirsty in that burg in the good old summer time. Rube loved to serve and the customers loved the Rube.
>
> On one occasion [Cardinals pitcher] "Slim" Salee disappeared, and scouts were hunting all over town for him. He was finally located down in Kerry Patch on a huckster's wagon peddling vegetables. Bugs Raymond another problem child was taken off the Cards' hands by [Giants manager John] McGraw. . . . [Cardinals manager] Roger [Bresnahan] stayed out at the King's Arms Hotel, where [second baseman] Rabbit Maranville dived into the fountain, caught a gold fish, and ate it.
>
> [German-born St. Louis Browns owner] Chris Von der Ahe kept a saloon in my neighborhood, Jefferson and Olive. Chris spoke broken English and what a circus it was when Arlie Latham and other members of the Giants hit town. Latham sure could get Chris aroused. Latham used to tell a story that always got a laugh. You old timers have heard it before. Latham while playing for the old Browns. A hot liner was hit down to Arlie. He got his hands on it but couldn't hold it and it went for a hit. When the side was out and Latham came to the bench, Chris was raving.
>
> "Why, Chris, what's the matter with you? That was a hot one."
>
> "Vell," shouted Chris, "Vat am I subbosed to do, run along mit ice vater und cool it off?"

A lot of people who never knew the real McGraw didn't like the Giants manager, but he was not pugnacious off the field. I recollect back when the ball players stayed downtown in St. Louis, the life was downtown and McGraw was the attraction when the Giants hit town. He was a soft touch for any down-and-outer, and they all knew it. Give me those wackey, colorful old time athletes, who always had the time and inclination to meet their public.[42]

‿

But Bill's bachelor days were numbered.

An institution that enabled the itinerant laborer's lifestyle in that era was the boardinghouse. In his travels, Bill might sleep in a livery stable for one night, but that was no place to stay for the duration of a construction job. Yet the length of that job wasn't sufficient to justify renting and furnishing a house or apartment either. Enter the family-run boardinghouse. The place where Bill ended up in 1909 at age twenty-five was typical: Lizzie Herbert was a single mother with three daughters and six extra beds. She rented out her spare rooms to boarders who paid by the week, and she cooked for them and washed their linens into the bargain. When Bill moved in, he shared his meals (and the bathroom or outhouse) with another mason, three telephone linemen, and a Swedish shoemaker. (Knowing Bill's sense of humor from his writings, we can easily imagine him attempting to mimic the Swede's accent.)[43]

Lizzie's daughters helped with the chores, and the eldest girl caught Bill's eye. She was a pretty redhead named Nellie, the same name as Bill's older sister, but this Nellie was younger—about eighteen. She was good-humored as well as good-looking. And she took a liking to the deep-voiced, gregarious bricklayer, who stood no taller than five eight but was described by contemporaries as "picturesque."

A courtship blossomed, and the couple were soon engaged. It seemed Bill was destined to follow in his father's footsteps. Recall that L.J. met his own bride in the boardinghouse where *he* lived at age twenty-five; Louisa was a live-in niece of the proprietress. Surely that augured well for Bill and Nellie's romance.

That summer, Bill signed on with the St. Louis–based C. L. Gray Construction Company, which paid union wages, to work on some kind of convention hall in a neighboring state. The young man's prospects were good as he traveled to Iowa that spring to help build the Des Moines Coliseum.

⌣

The planned Coliseum would take up an entire city block, rise four stories high, and hold up to ten thousand people. Overlooking the Des Moines River, the venue would in ensuing decades host tractor shows, corn growers' conventions, Drake University basketball, and speeches by four U.S. presidents. Bill Kennedy was one of twenty bricklayers to work on the building, along with thirty carpenters plus other tradesmen and laborers.

On the breezy morning of Thursday, October 21, 1909, the Coliseum was nearing completion. Under a clear blue sky, the bricklayers were standing on a narrow platform on the lower level of what was becoming a two-tiered roof. Bill was pointing up (scraping excess mortar from) a portion of the new south wall that rose above him and jutted out farther south than the part of the roof holding his platform. This meant Bill had to grasp the wall with his left hand, lean over and stretch himself a bit out over the street, while reaching upward to scrape the mortar with the trowel in his right hand. It was the kind of dangerous work a bricklayer had to do sometimes; just the other day a fellow "brickie" had fallen to his death from another Des Moines building under construction two miles away. But lightning couldn't strike twice, could it?

Lightning didn't strike Bill, but wind did. Between 11 a.m. and noon, the breeze turned blustery, and as Bill pulled himself back to a standing position, a thirty-mile-an-hour gust caught him and threw him off balance. Bill lost his footing and fell from the platform. It was a descent of sixty-five feet to the sidewalk. He probably passed out before hitting the ground.[44]

In an incredible stroke of both good and bad luck, a city official the previous month had asked the site's foreman to remove some sidewalk barriers, what with the work appearing nearly done and a state fair about to increase foot traffic. So there was no reason for an unfortunate tailor named John Holmquist to suspect, as he walked down the sidewalk past the new Coliseum, that a 130-pound bricklayer was about to drop from the sky.

The falling body landed on Holmquist's head and shoulders, driving the tailor into the ground and snapping his neck. "Kennedy rebounded from Holmquist's body and landed with considerable force upon the sidewalk," reported the *Des Moines News*. "Holmquist's body lay prostrate on the walk, eyes staring into the sun." He was dead.[45]

But in that fatal collision, the forty-year-old had broken Bill's fall. As the bricklayers lifted their fallen comrade and carried him into the Gray Company office, they realized Bill was breathing, though unconscious. He was "seriously injured," reported the papers. But apparently he stayed in the hospital for only one week. "Slightly hurt internally, with no broken bones," Bill reported later.[46]

John Holmquist left a wife and five children. His widow, Emelia, sued the city and the contractor for negligence, and the case went all the way to the state supreme court. Only the contractor was found guilty, and Mrs. Holmquist received six thousand dollars.[47]

Why didn't the Gray Company take better precautions in the first place? Workplace safety was a concept still in its infancy. Not until four years later (1913) was the U.S. Department of Labor formed with the express purpose of improving working conditions, especially safety. A much stronger initiative, the Occupational Safety and Health Act, was many decades away (1970). In truth, however, construction is still a dangerous field in the twenty-first century, with falls the leading cause of fatalities. There were 806 deaths in the private construction sector in 2012, down from almost a thousand in 2005. These figures are not terribly different from those in 1909. Bill was just lucky that day, or as he put it, "My number wasn't up yet."[48]

How did Bill feel about the incident? Though it was caused by a random act of nature, another man died while he lived. Bill left little evidence as to whether he experienced any survivor's guilt, while his prevailing preoccupation was clear: "Being held for observation in the Mercy Hospital in that city for a week, before being discharged, here was plenty of time to ponder over the effect of the fall upon my running career, and decided to continue with my walking and running."[49] Perhaps it was the era. The average life span was shorter then. Bill had lost a brother and his mother by the time he was fifteen. He may have lost colleagues to other workplace accidents, or fellow hoboes to misfortune on the rails. A man couldn't dwell on such things.

And yet, there is one hint that Holmquist's death weighed on him. For a man who never received any schooling beyond high school, Bill read widely and wrote well. His spelling was better than that of many college graduates today, and his eighty-page manuscript, tapped out on a mechanical typewriter, is relatively free of typos. But Bill made a Freudian slip when he described the immediate effect of the fall:

"I was rendered unconscience."[50]

His bones intact, Bill returned to the Herberts' boardinghouse in St. Louis only to have his heart broken. Nellie had moved out and married another man. Whether it was the accident itself that frightened her, or simply the months on end that the bricklayer had to spend away from her, she had decided to break off the engagement.

This created an opening for Nellie's younger sister Jessie. The middle child, perhaps Jessie had always been jealous of Nellie; perhaps she now took pity on the jilted bridegroom. In any event, back in close living quarters, their relationship took an intimate turn. In October 1910 Jessie realized she was pregnant. The couple married on Halloween. He was twenty-six years old; she was sixteen. They continued to live in her mother's house.

Things started off on the wrong foot when Jessie complained that the engagement ring Bill hastily bought her wasn't as big or fancy as the one he'd given her sister. Jessie wasn't to lighten up with age. Though the couple stayed together for the rest of his life, raising two daughters, all indications are that the marriage was rocky at times. Younger relatives and in-laws would remember Jessie as "emotional," "an odd duck," and, in one colorfully dated term, "a Tartar." They recalled a woman obsessed with order and cleanliness who brought "drama" to family gatherings, often drinking heavily and, on at least one occasion, throwing heavy objects in a rage. For his part, Bill stayed on the road as much as ever, if not more. Perhaps it was a vicious cycle, in which Jessie's behavior motivated Bill's long absences, which exacerbated her behavior.[51]

To be fair, there is also some evidence of happy times in the couple's many decades together. Jessie dutifully showed up at some races, hugged her sweaty man at the finish of at least one, and even grudgingly attended a training session, as Bill recalled:

> Billy Rozette and I were training at Macombs Track in N.Y. City. Our wives were sitting in Bill's car watching us circle the track. My wife turned to Mrs. Rozette and says, "Do you know, I think all runners are dizzy." Startled, Mrs. Rozette turned her attention back to the track. "Yes, perhaps, but not these two." So that should make Billy and me exceptions to the rule.[52]

In any event, Jessie did not stop Bill Kennedy from competing. He ran the All-Western Marathon again in 1910. This time, the *Post-Dispatch* recorded the names of the first twenty-two competitors to finish. Bill was twentieth. The paper did not record the times for anyone after the fourteenth runner. But at least Bill definitively finished.

The winner that year was a milk wagon driver from Chicago, L. J. Pillivant. In the final yards, both he and Erxleben stumbled into blockades of overzealous spectators, on foot and in automobiles, casting doubt on the results by today's standards. The autos were becoming a persistent problem for the early marathoners. In one of these St. Louis races, Bill recalls, "I was struck by a car and knocked down, but I arose unhurt except a few minor bruises, and relieving myself of a few oaths continued on my way."[53] But other times, the consequences were more serious, either for the runners' safety or for the outcome of the race.

Regardless, Bill must have read with interest the next day Pillivant's account of how he strategized for victory:

> I trained to go 15 miles in an hour and 35 minutes. I set my pace to keep this time to the finish and my consistent plugging won. I did not stop or slow up during the race, nor did I lose my stride until I was jostled by the crowd in East St. Louis and at the west end of the Eads bridge. A fellow got in my way in East St. Louis and I hit him in the jaw and knocked him down. I lost about two steps there. . . .
>
> A steady pace is the thing that wins long races. The sprinter or the fellow who relies on spurts has got to come back to the men with the digging pace every time.[54]

Despite that advice, in the following year's race, when the temperature reached the nineties, Bill found that he really liked running in hot weather, and he threw caution to the wind. Wearing the logo of the bricklayers' union in 1911, Bill ran hard on the heels of the great Sid Hatch and Joe Forshaw as that duo battled for the lead. Frank Johnson kept pace with him, and as they approached Belleville, both Kennedy and Johnson actually passed Hatch and Forshaw.

It must have been exhilarating to be out in front, especially as so many of the other runners were dropping by the wayside, wiped out by the oppressive dry heat. "The dirt was three inches thick," Bill recalled, "and lucky was he who did not have to stop and empty his shoes of sand and pebbles, causing bruises and blisters." Frank Kern, son of the mayor of Belleville, had hoped to run a strong race at least through his hometown. Instead, that's where he stopped, ducked through the swinging doors of a corner barroom, drank a tall glass of soda, and announced, "I've quit."[55]

Even Hatch later admitted he'd thought of quitting at Belleville. But the paper deliveryman kept his steady pace, while Bill's spurt proved to be just that. The heat eventually overcame Kennedy, who dropped back while Hatch went on to win, in 3:04:56. "I didn't set out to race any individual," Hatch said. "I have my own pace, and I know how fast I can go and hold out."[56]

About a month after the race, Bill and Jessie's first daughter, Louise, was born. Bill may have suggested her name because it reminded him of his mother, Louisa.[57]

During these years, Bill soaked up more knowledge of the running game as he got himself acquainted with Hatch, Forshaw, and the other distance runners. He soon joined the Missouri Athletic Club himself. And as those veteran plodders planned trips to the running mecca of Boston and to the nation's media capital of New York, which was rapidly catching up as a marathon haven, so too did Bill turn his attention back east. Suddenly his old neck of the woods was hip.

For the marathon craze still reigned in 1911. In February, the ever-popular New York Irishman Johnny Hayes traveled to the nation's capital to meet with William Howard Taft, our most overweight president. Taft "Tells Marathon Runner Too Much Exercise Is Not Advisable," the *New York Times* trumpeted with barely concealed glee. "The President said he was a strong believer in physical exercises, although he thought great care should be used so as not to overdo it and destroy the good effects." Hayes surely nodded sagely at the tubby man's words.[58]

In May, the AAU put on perhaps the most ambitious race yet on American soil. Though the run from the Bronx to New York City Hall was only a "modified marathon," all twelve miles of road were blocked off to automobile traffic. Apparently this was the first time such an action was attempted. (It would also be the last for many, many years.) And the number of competitors? Fifteen hundred. That was a previously unheard-of figure, and a sign of road running's enormous popularity.

In winning the race, Hopi Indian Louis Tewanima "demonstrated the superiority of the red man as a foot runner," the *Times* declared. But the real story was the race's aftermath, when the halls of government hosted a scene out of *Animal House:*

The peace and dignity of the City Hall has not been disturbed in many years as it was yesterday at the wind-up of the Marathon race. . . .

Half nude men swarmed through the building, using the corridors and chambers as dressing rooms. . . . Nearly 1,500 men took possession of the building and used it as they would a public bath. . . .

A horde swarmed down upon the Board of Estimate room. This room is one of the best furnished in the City Hall. There are expensive carpets on the floor, and at one end is a large solid mahogany table said to have cost $15,000.

Many of the athletes used this as a rubbing table. The strong liniment used in rubbing them down soon ate through the polish, and left the table a wreck. The liniment was also smeared over the desks, carpets, and walls . . . with equally disastrous results. . . .

The noise broke up two meetings. The school teachers, alarmed at the noise, rushed out only to be confronted with several hundred men in various stages of nudity, for even in the corridors they were going through the grooming process preparatory to getting into their street clothes. The women screamed and beat a hasty retreat into their committee room. Lieut. Kennel of the Mayor's office summoned police aides, and they acted as escorts for the teachers until the women were clear of the building, hiding their faces as they went. . . .

When the last of the runners had departed it took a force of cleaners two hours to put the building partly to rights. Several tubs of orange and lemon rinds, empty bottles, and towels were carted away.[59]

In his own writings, Bill sheds some light on the chaos that often was dressing for a race in those days, touches on people's perceptions of the early distance devotees, and pens a somewhat idealized ode to his fellow "Men of Iron."

IN BILL'S WORDS: MARATHONS AND MARATHONERS

In the more important races, the men are furnished with a hall or gymnasium, to get into their track suits, and have their street clothes hauled to the finish by truck. Some races have no place to dress or undress. They use a barn, back room of a tavern, or behind a stone wall or bush. On two different occasions the writer has changed clothes in a taxi on the way to the start. . . .

As a sport, distance running is rather strenuous, perhaps even grueling, and to many people we are a bit on the "wacky side." Well, it takes all kinds of people to make a world, and so marathon runners. . . .

Who and what are these men who follow this grueling test of running this distance for pleasure? These "Men of Iron" who spend their spare time running or walking hundreds of miles on the highways, emulating a Greek tradition? They range in age from the youth of 18 to the veteran of fifty. They are real true amateurs, and number among their fraternity artisans, laborers, policemen, doctors, lawyers, school teachers and even a few clergymen. Their average weight is from 125 to 150 lbs. They lose an average of eight pounds in running a race. . . .

The greatest of philosophers, there is no ego in him. He knows today may be his, tomorrow will be another man's day. Note them during the race, passing a piece of orange or a sponge of water to one another, or an encouraging word. I have never known of a marathoner being sent to jail. No man who tempers his body as does he can be crooked. Mix with these men some time, attend a dinner given them after a race. You will hear no obscenity or blasphemous talk, no alibi, no bragging. . . .

While it is true that not many college boys follow our sport, as most of us are hard working men who can take it with a smile about being "dizzy," we can recall some fine gentlemanly competitors. "Pop" Weeks of Yonkers, Craig Richards, a Harvard man, Johnny Gallagher of Yale, Lon Gregory Supt. of Schools and Johnny Kelley, school teacher of Groton, Ct.

Mike Lynch ran a restaurant in Washington, D.C. Monteverde was in the book binding business in Atlantic City. Tom Morrissey chief of police. Harvey Lichenstine and Zuna were plumbers. Dr. Herman and Dr. Robbins. . . . Joe Forshaw a prominent businessman of St. Louis was on four Olympic teams, finishing 3rd at London. . . . And hundreds of other friends of mine too numerous to name. . . .

Sid Hatch "The Iron Man," running three 26-mile races in five days, traveling to N.Y. back to Chicago then on to N.Y. for his third race. At River View Park in Chicago he won a 100-mile race, also won the St. Louis race seven times and a 100-miler from Milwaukee to Chicago in fourteen hours. . . .

Right here is a good spot to tell this story Hatch's father told
me. Attending a social affair in Oak Park a local doctor, learning Mr.
Hatch was the father of the runner, says "Mr. Hatch, do you realize
that every time your son runs a marathon, he takes five years off his
life? And furthermore, his heart becomes so overdeveloped from
running that were he to stop athletics his heart would collapse."

"Well, doctor," replied he, "I would rather see Sidney running
down the street with whiskers than hobbling down with a cane. And
as to the five years off his life, the good Lord must have intended
him to be as old as Methusalem [sic], for he has already ran nearly
fifty marathons." . . .

I have great admiration for any man who ran and finished,
whether he was first or last, as Theodore Roosevelt said. To those
whose names are not mentioned, it is not for lack of appreciation of
their efforts. With apologies to you, who endured physical punishment and kept going. When in the words of Kipling "You can force
your heart and nerves and sinews to serve you, long after they are
gone, and so hold on. When there is nothing in you except the will,
which says to them, 'Hold ON,' you are a man, my son, a man."[60]

In the fall of 1911, Bill traveled back to New York for his first race in
his home region. Since its inaugural running in 1907, the Mercury
A.C.'s Yonkers Marathon had become a well established annual race
of an "estimated twenty-five miles." Interest spiked when Sullivan
and the AAU announced that the first three men to finish would be
given "serious consideration" as candidates to represent the United
States in the next summer's Olympics, at Stockholm. Held this year
on Thanksgiving, the Yonkers race also provided Bill an opportunity
to see his brother Joe in the Bronx, and perhaps other family. He
likely hoboed his way home. The train fare to New York, via Chicago,
was $32.05, a third again more than the bricklayer's typical wages for
the week, if he was working. And that was just one way.[61]

However he managed it, Bill considered the race important
enough to make the journey. He and Hatch were the only "westerners" in the field of forty-seven athletes who lined up that Turkey Day

outside the Hollywood Inn. Most of the rest were New Yorkers—such as the above-mentioned Billy Rozette—with a sprinkling of Bostonians. The mayor of Yonkers fired the starter's pistol, and they were off. The weather was cooler—officially in the thirties—than in the last couple of marathons Bill had run, but with the sun shining, it felt warmer, even "delightful," the *Times* reported. One big difference Bill surely noticed straightaway: the roads in Yonkers were largely macadam. Except for a few sections, such as where the loop of a course veered into the nearby village of Hastings, there was very little mud to slog through. That, along with the warmth and the pretty scenery—wooded parks, pastoral country estates, green cemeteries, a reservoir, and a golf course—might have made the run pleasant, but for the other big difference: hills. The Yonkers terrain proved sharply steeper than that from Freeburg to St. Louis.[62]

For most of the sixteen-mile loop, Rozette led the way, with Hatch back in fortieth place at one point early on. The last nine miles of the race, though, were run around the Empire City Raceway, on turf meant for trotting horses. "The slippery soil and grass" slowed down most of the human competitors. Hatch was the exception. The steady plugger from Chicago worked his way up to second place by the twenty-first mile, then passed William Galvin to take the lead. Hatch won in 2:34:40, beating Galvin by almost four minutes. As Bill recalled it, Hatch was so far ahead that race organizers lost track (no pun intended) of how many laps he had left. Having actually finished, Hatch "was informed he had another lap to go, and was on his way when the late Jim Sullivan discovered the error, and called him off the track," Bill wrote.[63]

And where was Bill himself? In obscurity once again.

"After thirty men had passed through the gate [of the raceway] no more were permitted to continue the race," reported the *Times*. Then the paper recorded the names of only the first ten to cross the finish line. So Bill was either one of the next twenty runners to finish or one of the seventeen barred from the track altogether. Either way, the experience had to be frustrating.[64]

And yet Bill wasn't discouraged. It was a thrill to compete in a well-run race on paved roads just outside the Big Apple, cheered on by 75,000 fans along the route, plus perhaps five thousand in the stands around the track.

No, the trip to New York only whetted Bill's appetite to return east again. And the next time, nothing less than Mecca would do.

Bill was determined to run Boston in 1912.

3

STRIDES, SETBACKS & LAURELS

Bill Kennedy was an unknown in Boston in April 1912, when he rode into town as a stowaway on a freight train. He arrived several days before the marathon, went straight to the bricklayers' union hall, and secured a job so that he could feed and shelter himself while acclimating to the Hub ahead of race day. It was surely a better reception that greeted Bill than the one his famine refugee grandparents received when their "coffin ships" docked at the same city six decades earlier.[1]

Now a member of the Missouri A.C., Bill had hoped to travel with Joe Forshaw on the club's dime, but as it turned out, even Forshaw had to pay his own way, arriving a few days after Bill. The St. Louis club was focusing its fund-raising efforts on Stockholm, where they hoped to send Forshaw as well as Erxleben for the Olympic Games that summer. As the MAC saw it, Forshaw's selection to the Olympic team was all but assured already, so his trip to Boston was extraneous. From Forshaw's own perspective, a strong showing at Boston would seal the deal. Fortunately for him, as an executive in his family's department store, Forshaw had the means to travel at least stateside "on the plush" (Bill's wistful term for buying a train ticket).[2]

It was a propitious time for Bill to make his debut in Boston. The prospect of Stockholm raised to a fever pitch the annual excitement over the Boston race, which this year would also serve as an official Olympic tryout. The large silver cups that the BAA offered to the first eight finishers would be icing on the cake. (The first-prize trophy stood more than three feet high, and a gold unicorn, symbol of the BAA, decorated each cup.) No fewer than 130 athletes signed up for the chance to impress Sullivan, the AAU, and the American Olympic Committee. The field featured several former Olympians, Forshaw and Hatch included, and other past marathon winners, such as Sammy Mellor. Contestants came from the Midwest, Pennsylvania, and in large numbers from New York, where this year's Boston race sparked "unprecedented interest." French Canadian Édouard Fabre was back after a strong third-place finish in 1911, and Louis Tewanima and Andrew Sockalexis were just two of several Native American runners entered.[3]

The city prepared for record crowds. Even former president Teddy Roosevelt wrote to friends that he hoped to come to Boston to watch the race from start to finish. For the first time, Boston's police department and parks commission made plans to rope off the streets for the last mile and a half of the race and close the eastbound side of Commonwealth Avenue to motor traffic. (In those days, the course took runners down Comm. Ave. until turning right at Exeter Street, only briefly crossing Boylston.) The Boston & Albany Railroad sold tickets for a special train out to Ashland to watch the marathon's start. After rain delayed the opening of brand-new Fenway Park until Patriots' Day, which was celebrated annually at the time on April 19, the Red Sox started a tradition when they moved the first game of their doubleheader with the New York Highlanders—later renamed the Yankees—to 10:30 a.m. so that fans could take in both the game and the marathon.[4] (Again, historic timing for Bill's arrival in town.)

Bad news and bad weather battered Boston in the final few days leading up to the marathon. On April 15, the RMS *Titanic* struck an iceberg in the North Atlantic. At least 1,500 of her roughly 2,200 passengers drowned. The disaster cast a pall over the seaport city, as most Bostonians read with horror the accounts of the sinking. Many had personal reasons for scouring the lists of survivors arriving in New York on April 19. Meanwhile, a nor'easter swept the region, turning most of the marathon course into mud.

Though the race must go on rain or shine, a measure of fortune favored the athletes as the rain tapered down to a drizzle that morning. Perhaps eager to recapture some of the spirit of the holiday, more than 100,000 fans bundled up against the chill and rain to take their places along the route. The town of Ashland was soggy but bustling as Bill Kennedy and the other runners pulled in to the local depot on the "Marathon train." Bill followed the herd of competitors and BAA officials as they traipsed through the village square, where umbrella-toting locals gathered to watch their arrival and swap gossip. Enterprising high school girls set up booths and hawked doughnuts and steaming hot coffee.[5]

The runners crowded into the Columbia Hotel to strip and undergo examination by stethoscope-wielding physicians. Hearts pronounced sound, the men changed into running togs and pinned cloth numbers to their jerseys. Next, they waded through a crowd of teenagers and other thrill-seekers clamoring to serve as bicycle attendants, each hoping to accompany a prizewinner to Boston and earn a souvenir bronze medal for himself. Bill and the rest made their selections, handing corresponding numbers to the young men, who rushed out, hopped on their bikes, and made for Framingham, where they would wait to join the race. Finally, the runners filed out and piled onto electric streetcars that took them a mile west to the starting line.

At the shot from the starter's pistol, the runners took off down the slimy country road, passed again through Ashland's town square, where the crowds cheered them on, and continued east over the slippery hills. The muck sucked at their ankles. But rather than finding their spirits dampened by the rain and mud, the runners rode an adrenaline rush caused by the high "class" of the field. There were so many strong runners competing; none of them wanted to cede an edge to any of his peers; and the amped-up performance of the elites drove the second-tier athletes to stretch themselves. If anything, the shared adversity imposed by the cruddy weather only boosted the runners' excitement level.

At Framingham, Bill recalled seeing the bike attendants waiting "until their man hove in sight." When Bill so hove, he saw his rider "proudly mount [his] bike, with a triumphant glance at those whose runner[s] had not yet appeared, and pedal along" at the bricklayer's side, "pleading, driving and coaxing" the whole way. Out of a sack slung over his shoulder, the youngster offered oranges, water, a sponge, or liniment, as needed. "My rider that day sure earned his medal. He fought for the right of way, cursing my competitors and their riders, all the time directing me to short cuts at turns in the road."[6] Indeed, at one time or another, most of the runners sought a kind of shortcut along the comparatively less treacherous sidewalks, though on the long rural stretches between town centers, there was no relief from the "veritable seas of mud and mire," as the *Herald* put it.[7]

John J. Gallagher led the pack up the long hill into Wellesley (eleven miles), beating (at 1:00:20) the course record at this point. A rare collegian in the field, Gallagher attracted much attention as "the first Yale man to ever attempt the Marathon distance," and the women of Wellesley College, wrapped in rubber coats and hats, cheered him wildly.[8] He was soon followed by a pack that included Kennedy and Hatch. The latter would later say he had never encountered such bad roads, and he'd run plenty.

In Newton, after sixteen miles, Bill encountered the course's notorious trio of hills for the first time. He wouldn't quit, but he started to fall behind. Meanwhile, the crowds grew as the runners drew closer to their goal. By Brookline, Sockalexis, the Penobscot Indian, had claimed the lead.

"Every time an Indian has competed in the BAA race, the great crowds of spectators have invariably awarded generous applause as they passed on their way," the *Globe* noted, and Sockalexis proved no exception. He ran as hard and tirelessly down Beacon Street as his father once had through the Maine woods, hunting deer to feed his tribe.[9]

But starting at Coolidge Corner, redheaded Mike Ryan—a toothpick jutting out from between his gritted teeth, his bright emerald and white Irish-American A.C. jersey spattered with brown mud—started to gain steam. He caught Sockalexis unawares at Audubon Circle, on the Brookline–Boston border, near the Fenway, barely edging him out for the lead. At Governor's Square (later renamed Kenmore Square), the crowds were swelled by many of the 24,000 fans who had earlier turned out for the inaugural game at Fenway Park, where Mayor John F. "Honey Fitz" Fitzgerald hurled the ceremonial first pitch (Fitzgerald, of course, being the grandfather of future president John F. Kennedy).

Down Comm. Ave., Ryan, now untouchable, took the right on Exeter Street. The sodden crowd filling the temporary grandstand roared as Ryan breasted the tape in front of the BAA clubhouse, "covered from head to foot with mud and glory." He had won in 2:21:18, beating even Clarence DeMar's record-breaking time of the year before. Sockalexis followed thirty-four seconds later. Hatch finished fourteenth.[10]

Bill Kennedy came in twenty-third, "back of the ruck," as he put it, but good enough to earn a souvenir bronze medal. More important, his time of 2:34:31 was a personal best, "fast enough to have won many of [my] previous races." Indeed, the great Hatch had won marathons with longer times. Bill even beat his senior clubmate Joe Forshaw, who finished thirtieth or thirty-first. The bricklayer had earned his shower, rubdown, beer, and post-race dinner in the opulent BAA clubhouse. And he was determined to come back.[11]

⌣

Fired up by his Boston run, Bill entered St. Louis's marathon just two weeks later. The 1912 All-Western turned out to be the moment when Bill joined the elites, getting his first true taste of all the excitement and even verbal jockeying that went with that status. And something else happened that Bill would never forget.

In a makeshift dressing room in Freeburg before the start of the marathon, Bill met Henry "Levi" Levinson, a young Jewish runner from St. Louis. Levinson had undergone surgery on his left foot two weeks earlier, and he asked if Bill could spare some tape for his feet. "Handing him the tape with a glance at his feet," Bill noticed that "the big toe on his left foot had become festered from a blister and was swollen to twice its size. 'You can't run on that foot, kid, you won't last a mile.'"

"Oh, I have to run, I have been training for over two months and my friends would be disappointed" was his reply.[12]

May 3 was a hot day in St. Louis. This was good. For whatever reason, Bill liked best to run in the heat. He took the lead about nine miles in—running ahead of past winners Forshaw, Hatch, and Erxleben—and reached Belleville (ten miles) at fifty-five minutes after the noon start. Two hundred yards behind him, Forshaw checked his wristwatch and pointed out to reporters in the *Post-Dispatch* automobile that Bill was a minute ahead of the record. Farther back, the bulk of the thirty-three runners sweated under the strong sun and grimaced amidst the dark gray clouds of dust.

Bill still led at Priester's Park (fourteen miles). "He was running strong, and did not show the slightest fatigue," noted the *Post-Dispatch*. Meanwhile, his rivals picked their way over the road to East St. Louis, which was "newly graded and very uneven. In some sections the racers would sink into dust, while in others they had to stumble over hard lumps and through mud puddles."[13]

At the end of twenty-two miles, Bill was still out in front by half a mile. Heading into East St. Louis, "Kennedy maintained his lead admirably." Perhaps he was about to show the Midwest what he'd learned at the big show in Boston.

But then the trio of previous champions began to close the gap. Meanwhile, "the misguided kindness of spectators" hampered the front-runner, according to the *Post-Dispatch*. "All along the line men and boys threw water upon him, until his canvas pants were soaked and heavy. In the outskirts of East St. Louis several gallons of water were thrown upon him with such violence as to almost knock him down." Eventually Bill was overtaken and lost too much ground to recover.

Erxleben won the race, in 2:36:30. He was followed by Forshaw, Hatch, Jacob Kaysing, and finally Kennedy in fifth, at 3:04:41.

But the hero, Bill and others thought, was the Jewish lad with the swollen foot. Levinson ran "with the greatest pain" that day, reported the *Post-Dispatch*, making "one of the bravest struggles in the race." He finished sixth, right behind Bill. As the latter lay on a cot in the MAC clubhouse, Levinson was carried in and placed on the cot next to his. That image flashed to mind, Bill wrote, whenever he heard bigoted talk.

> I watched in silence as they cut his shoe off his left foot, and called for the doctor. Reaching over and grasping his hand, I said, "You are a better man than I am, kid." He smiled at me faintly, thanked me, and fainted away. . . . Don't tell me that any one race has a monopoly on grit.[14]

As for the winner, Erxleben indulged in a bit of self-serving bloviation. "I won," he said, "by profiting by my experiences in the races of 1910 and 1911, which I lost through mere accidents, after virtually having won." (In reality, it was only in 1910 that Erxleben had been cut off by an auto in the final yards. In 1911 he finished third, almost five minutes behind Forshaw in second.) Moreover, Erxleben griped, "my time in this race would have been better if my attendants had permitted me to start my sprint when I wanted to." Incidentally, "Kennedy's lead did not swerve me from my intention, as I felt certain he could not maintain it," Erxleben added.[15]

Bill couldn't argue with that. Nevertheless, at fifth, the bricklayer had made a strong showing. Erxleben, Forshaw, and Hatch would all be picked for the 1912 U.S. Olympic marathon team, and Kennedy had placed but two slots away. Forshaw took notice. In the coming year, Forshaw's guidance would prove a boon to this newest member of the Missouri A.C.

⌒

Running his two best and most exciting marathons yet in just two weeks, along with witnessing the inspirational performance of Levinson, seemed to launch Bill onto a higher plane of competitive drive that spring and summer of 1912. In June he won his first race, a ten-mile run at the grand opening of Hibernian Park in Ferguson, Missouri. In so doing, he beat Kaysing, who had edged him out for fourth place in the St. Louis marathon. Then in July, Bill won the Missouri A.C.'s "modified marathon," a race of 11.6 miles on a July day that saw several contenders drop out because of the heat. Even Bill struggled under the hot sun, but with a mile and a half to go, he spotted his wife, Jessie, with their daughter Louise, waving at him from the corner of Locust and Twenty-third streets, in the Kennedys' and Herberts' neighborhood. "He seemed to take a new lease on life at this point" and held on for the win, in 1:15:20.[16]

The modified marathon victory was particularly sweet for Bill because he came from behind after trailing Chris Christensen for eight miles. A strong and cocky all-around athlete from Chicago, Christensen was something of a villain to Bill and his buddies, though one they respected.

> Chris Christensen, a Danish high diver in Europe, was also a running amateur. He was a big, handsome chap, much given to brag of his feats in Europe, and how we loved to beat him. Many a hard race I had with him and more than held my own with him. Chris afterward went into vaudeville with a running act on a thread wheel. He came to New York to get booking but had tough sledding. He offered to emulate Steve Brody and jump off Brooklyn Bridge for a three-month contract. No dice. Later Chris played the Pantage[s] circuit. He was a great athlete, and at Grant Park in Chicago he ran, walked, rowed, cycled and swam all within an hour. . . .
>
> Joie [Ray]'s advent into the running game is too good a story not to be told here, especially as Ray was the hero, and Christensen the loser. Chris at the time was Pres. of the Danish American Club of Chicago, who were putting on the five mile Western Championship

at Douglas Park. As we were lining up for the start, this fresh kid comes running up to get in the race. He was from Kankakee and had never heard of the A.A.U. Harry Keator was chairman of the Reg. Board and sings out "Say, Chris, do you want to let this boy start?" Glancing at the boy Chris says, "Sure, get his entry fee and let him get in line." Well, this boy paid his entry fee, got an A.A.U. card and we were off. Christensen was fifty yards ahead of the field in less than a mile, but "oh that fresh kid." Gradually he drew up to Chris, passed him and drew further and further away from him. Then Chris began to yell every time he passed the officials. "Who is this man? I protest." Finally this boy lapped the field to win by over a quarter mile, setting a new five mile record in his first race. What a kick Chris put up to no avail, as this kid received the special prize of a gold watch and the championship gold medal.[17]

～⌒

Some time in the next year, Bill moved to Chicago for work. Jessie, pregnant again, stayed behind with her mother and Louise in St. Louis. Bill soon found the larger, louder Windy City to his liking. He joined the Illinois Athletic Club (IAC) and made plans for Jessie and their children to join him when possible.

Determined to win St. Louis's All-Western Marathon in 1913, Bill tried something drastic. Starting in December 1912, he swore off liquor and tobacco for the next five months. His father must have been proud—maybe even awed, regarding the tobacco restriction. And just for good measure, when spring arrived, Bill adopted a vegetarian diet. None of this could have been easy for the sociable, fun-loving Irishman, especially at the end of a hard shift. But his co-workers seemed to understand or at least overlook the athlete's eccentricities, and he became a popular figure in Chicago's Local 21 of the bricklayers' union.

The Missouri A.C. made two big changes to their premier event for 1913. First, they moved the date of the marathon from the first Saturday in May to the third Saturday in April. That would be April 19, Patriots' Day in Massachusetts then. Whether by accident or design, the MAC was competing directly with the Boston Marathon. Bill and most of the top plodders of the Midwest elected to stay local this year.

The other change was to the route. For the first time, the race would be held entirely on the Missouri side of the Mississippi River. The starting line moved west to Gumbo, in St. Louis County. Traversing roughly twenty-six miles, the runners would face a few more hills in the early rural portion, but the final ten miles were over paved city streets. The finish line remained the Missouri A.C. clubhouse.

"CHICAGO STARS HERE," blared a local headline when "W. J. Kennedy" arrived with Hatch and the rest of "the Chicago delegation of marathon runners" the day before the race. By dint of his 1912 modified marathon win and his association with Hatch, Bill had made a name for himself. But could he prove himself a winner in a full-distance marathon?[18]

Thirty-two men lined up in Gumbo on the nineteenth. The usual suspects were there—defending champion Erxleben, four-time champ Hatch, and perennial front-runner Johnson—along with an anonymous pack of hopefuls. Forshaw was on hand, but as a spectator, in an automobile, one of many Missouri A.C. members and officials to ride along. As the runners readied themselves for the start, Bill Kennedy—whom the *Post-Dispatch* described as "a slight, wiry built fellow" of 130 pounds—likely cast a wary glance at Erxleben, "a bigger and stronger man" than himself. Yet Bill felt confident. At noon, Bassett fired his pistol in the air, and the athletes jumped off their marks.[19]

The day was warm, though not unseasonably hot. What slowed the pace were the unfamiliar hills on the new course, and especially the strong wind blowing from the east, right into the runners' faces.

"Hundreds of farmers lined the course that wound through St. Louis County," the *Post-Dispatch* reported. "Fruit orchards in bloom fringed the highways."

Going up the first hill, in Chesterfield, Johnson took the lead, running one hundred yards ahead of John Probst, who in turn stayed fifty yards ahead of the trio of Hatch, Kennedy, and Erxleben. The rest of the field snaked along behind, "away to the rear, all but lost in the caravan of automobiles."

Probst caught up to Johnson at the crest of the Creve Coeur hill, and Erxleben and Kennedy joined them on the way down, the whole quartet passing the first checkpoint abreast. On the next hill, Bill made his move, opening up a gap on Erxleben and the rest.

"The MAC men who were handling Erxleben smiled knowingly as Kennedy pulled away and recalled how he had led the field for 18 miles last year only to falter and lose in the last heart-rending stretch," noted the *Post-Dispatch*. "'Joe will catch him outside Clayton,' they confidently predicted, 'and then it will merely be a procession through the city.'"

But when Bill reached Clayton, where hundreds of cheering Claytonians crowded around the courthouse, the bricklayer didn't falter. Indeed, he was "appreciably widening his lead" while Erxleben "was laboring along in a bad condition" as the sun beat down without mercy. Remarkably, Joe Forshaw reached across club lines here: Rather than offering succor to his *current* fellow Missouri A.C. member Erxleben, Forshaw had his car pull up alongside his erstwhile teammate Kennedy, still his friend and protégé. He saw that the Irishman was eager to run harder and harder, perhaps thinking about a record time, and he coached Bill instead to conserve his strength, to focus on securing the win.

At the corner of Twenty-third and Locust streets, Bill again drew a third or fourth wind at the sight of Jessie and their "baby daughter Louise waving happily to him." At last, to the roar of the crowd in front of the Missouri A.C. headquarters, Bill broke the tape in 3:02:11. A gang of his friends lifted him onto their shoulders and carried him triumphantly into the clubhouse. Inside, Bill stepped onto a scale for the second time that day. This time, he weighed 118. He had left twelve pounds behind on the road from Gumbo. If his recollections are any guide, Bill quickly made that weight back in beer, possibly drinking it out of the silver loving cup he earned for first place.[20]

The *Post-Dispatch* thought "Kennedy finished in splendid shape, and could have cut off at least 10 minutes from his time if he had been forced to exert himself." But under what turned out to be grueling conditions, it's hard to fault Forshaw's counseled strategy of playing it safe. It had been the slowest MAC marathon to date, yet paradoxically Bill set the course record, this being the race's first running over the new, longer course. More to the point, "the victory was the most decisive ever registered in the history of the event." Sid Hatch—who had been knocked down by an auto but gamely came from behind to pass Erxleben—finished second in 3:14:30, more than twelve minutes behind Bill. Led to a cot next to "his townsman," Hatch looked "patently exhausted." Back out on the street, when the third runner was spotted in the distance, the knowledgeable in the crowd shouted, "Here comes Erxleben!" But as the runner drew closer, he turned out to be a younger, unfamiliar figure. "Officials hurriedly consulted programs" as Charles Lobert crossed the finish line in 3:20:40. Erxleben "staggered home in the hands of his attendants seven minutes later." Only thirteen other men finished after that.

In any event—well, not in just any event; in *the* event that Bill cared about, the marathon—he had at last joined the elite ranks. Precious few men worldwide in 1913 could say they had won one of these long grinds, whether measured at 24.5 or 26.2 miles. But Bill decided this was only the beginning.

〜〜

Indeed, Bill was just warming up. Sticking to his vegetarian diet that summer, he enjoyed a career year. In May he won his second straight MAC modified marathon, in 1:08:12, Jessie and little Louise cheering him from their usual corner. Kennedy led the field nearly the entire way—though this time Erxleben finished just thirteen seconds behind him. Also, it seems clear that Erxleben was cut off by an automobile in the home stretch, muddling the results, as happened too often in those days.

The 1913 modified marathon was also notable for featuring a partially blind runner. Kale Hopkins, representing the Missouri School for the Blind, had no vision in one eye and indistinct vision in the other. Guided by a boy on a bicycle, Hopkins came in thirty-first. Of final note on this race, the *Post-Dispatch* wondered whether Hatch, who finished sixth, was "slowing up" on account of his age. "Youth must be served, you know."[21]

Kennedy was three and a half months younger than Hatch.

Later that month, back in Chicago, Bill won a nine-mile road race that he snatched from Joie Ray in the final two hundred yards. The *Tribune* called Kennedy "one of the leading long distance runners in the west."[22]

The good news continued as Bill and Jessie's second daughter, Juanita, was born on June 7. Two weeks later, Bill nearly won the Central AAU championship at the fifteen-mile distance, but this time victory was snatched from *him* at the end, by Fritz Carlson, winner of that year's Boston Marathon.[23]

⌖

Just a week after *that,* on June 28, Bill and the rest of the Midwest pluggers toed the line at Grant Park in Chicago. It was opening day for a weeklong athletic carnival variously called the "international games," the "Olympian Games," and even "Olympic Games." All but forgotten now, this festival of sports and other attractions took place at a time when the word "Olympic" could be thrown around without concern over copyright infringement or branding confusion. Indeed, any confusion could only work to a hosting city's advantage. Essentially, if you were putting on a bunch of athletic events—some conventional track and field, some not (such as, in this case, nighttime auto polo, with a ball covered in phosphorus)—then you could call it an "Olympic Games." It didn't matter if all the entrants were from the United States and, maybe, Canada. With luck, Coubertin over in France would never even hear about it.

Chicago was still smarting somewhat after St. Louis maneuvered to wrest away the 1904 Olympics, and city boosters hoped to recapture some of the glory of their 1893 World's Fair, twenty years earlier. "Olympic games were held at St. Louis in 1904 in connection with the Louisiana Purchase exposition," acknowledged the *Tribune,* "but those events hardly equal in scope the Chicago contests."[24]

Despite the squishy nature of the event's marketing, the Chicago games drew serious attention. President Woodrow Wilson put his imprimatur on the festival by sending a message of approval and well-wishes via a Boy Scout relay run, four days and 778 miles, from Washington to Chicago. (This was more than two decades before the tradition of the Olympic torch began.) And there was nothing laughable about the competitiveness of the twenty-six-mile, 385-yard race that would inaugurate the week, "following the long established custom of opening the world's games with a marathon race." In the middle of a crippling heat wave, on a day when the *Tribune* reported five heat-related deaths so far, the field turned out to be small—eighteen entrants—but select. Kennedy faced Carlson, Erxleben, Hatch, Christensen, Ray, and 1912 Olympic bronze medalist Gaston Strobino for the honors.[25]

The race began with two laps around the track inside a stadium in Grant Park. Then the runners had to plod over sizzling South Side boulevards to the South Shore Country Club, there to turn around and head back. With the mercury hitting ninety-eight degrees, "the runners wore hats and wet handkerchiefs on their heads and water was thrown on them continually to keep them in the race. The hot pavements caused many of the runners' feet to blister and some of them even discarded their shoes." Nevertheless, thousands of Chicagoans lined the route, encouraging the athletes with rounds of applause. Policemen held up traffic at major intersections to keep the way clear for the marathon.

"Running over the hot pavements with a strong but steady stride," Bill Kennedy took the lead at Twenty-sixth Street and Michigan Avenue, about two and a half miles from the start. Hatch fell a mile behind, and in back of him other runners—especially the inexperienced collegiate athletes—fared even worse. Baking under the hot sun, eight runners dropped out. Some collapsed unconscious. Three required minor medical attention where they lay, while two or three others were rushed to the hospital. Carlson stopped on the way back from the country club but managed to resume. Then it was back to Grant Park stadium for twelve final laps.

Bill entered the stadium still a mile in the lead. What happened next is the stuff of legend.

Because of the extreme heat, the officials decided to cut the race short. Bill was so far ahead, they reasoned, there was no sense in forcing him or his rivals to continue. As the bricklayer approached twenty-two miles, they signaled for him to stop. Surely sweating through their dark formal attire, the officials waved their arms more vigorously when they realized the front-runner wasn't slowing down.

That's because Bill refused to stop. Not content with the win, he wanted to earn the credit for running a full-distance marathon. As the crowd roared, Bill blew past the officials and circled the cinder track again. And again. And again and again. Sometimes he slowed almost to a walk, but each time he kicked back into a run, always propelling himself forward.

Eventually, Hatch appeared. No slouch himself, the paper delivery-man gladly followed his friend and respected rival's lead. Now with the win back on the line, Bill put on "a burst of speed that astounded even his trainers," reported the *New York Sun*. The bricklayer completed the twelfth and final lap and breasted the tape three laps ahead of Hatch, winning in 3:05:20.[26]

A gaggle of Illinois A.C. officers greeted their champion, but Bill zeroed in on his wife, Jessie, in the crowd beyond the finish line. Sweating profusely but otherwise looking well, Bill made straight for her. They fell into each other's arms.

After Hatch, Manuel Cooper of the Chicago Hebrew Institute finished third, and Carlson finished fourth. Just six men followed. (It is not recorded whether they stopped at the twenty-second mile.) "GRIND OPENING" a *Tribune* headline nicknamed the event. "Kennedy, the crack I.A.C. long distance runner, achieved a great victory, which stamps him as one of the best long distance runners in the country." As Bill remembered it, when he stepped onto the scale, he had once again dropped a dozen pounds, falling to 118.[27]

Though some sportswriters and fans were impressed, the whole thing struck others as loony. "All the nuts are not confined in the strong wards" of asylums, quipped one wag.[28] And quoth another:

> After that marathon race of the Olympic Games Saturday you can't blame the boxing enthusiasts for claiming their sport is not the most brutal in the athletic calendar. A marathon race under weather conditions such as prevailed Saturday is not sport. Several of the contestants dropped, overcome by the broiling heat, and at least one had to be taken to the hospital. A similar toll in a boxing carnival and a flock of reformers would have been climbing the pulpits within 24 hours.[29]

Bill Kennedy was aware of such sentiments. Indeed, he battled that perception most of his life. Here he collected some of his thoughts on the matter.

IN BILL'S WORDS: DIZZY RUNNERS

Have you not often heard the expression "He is dizzy?" Some say punch drunk, or walking on his heels, wackey, or just plain crazy. Why? Because he is different from the ordinary person. The dictionary tells us Custom is the frequent or habitual repetition of the same act. Who established custom? Blamed if I know, but woe betide the man or woman who fails to follow it. They are looked upon as being queer. Recollect when you first saw a man going about hatless. Or go back to the days of the first golfers. A grown man batting a little ball around a field. The saying was, "He is a little nuts." I recollect a short poem written by an English woman, Sarah Cleghorn.

"The golf links lie so near the mill

"That almost every day, the laboring children can look out, and see the men at play."

In order to be a success at anything, one must disregard criticism and eat, work, and sleep the particular calling or sport at which one hopes to excel. Successful people, contrary to public opinion, don't just happen. They have drilled and toiled while others slept. They had visions, day dreams, and because they had the grit, the determination to keep plugging they made their dreams come true. But in arriving at this goal they had to shun the usual way of their fellow men, and thus are looked upon as queer or dizzy. Maybe we runners are "dizzy." As Zuna told Mrs. Levy at Long Beach, we have been going around and around since our mothers forgot to take us off the merry-go-round. . . .

I used to train over the roads in Westchester County, and through the back country of Greenwich, Ct. On many a winter morning I have jogged along Rye Lake clad in shorts and a sweat shirt, and exchanged a wave of the hand with men sitting wrapped Indian fashion with a heavy blanket fishing through a hole in the ice. They sit there for hours yet speaking with them they will ask "What pleasure do you get out running in the cold this way?"

One Sunday morning in January I was out for a training run when after ten miles a cold, steady rain set in. I was soaking wet. A couple pulled up along side of me and I climbed in the car, arriving in Port Chester. I thanked them and was about to get out, when the lady asked me blushingly if I knew where they could get married. "Clergyman or justice of the peace?" I asked. The lady said she preferred an Episcopal clergyman. Well, it was my home town, I knew them all, so asking them to wait ducked into a speakeasy, borrowed a coat and pair of pants, and up the avenue to the Reverend Kilbourne, who made them man and wife. They were from Worcester, Mass.

It was old stuff to me. Five years previous I had taken a couple to Judge Bailey who married them. They were from Providence R.I. Marathoners. Like Boy Scouts, do a good deed every day.

Maybe you have heard of Sam Johnson, he hails from Brooklyn and calls himself the Human Locomotive. At one time he worked for Bernard MacFadden and ran from New York to Portland, Me., on a vegetarian diet. In his own words: "[I] ran along the road with a head of lettuce in me hand. When I finished in Portland, I dashed into a restaurant shouting to the waiter. 'Bring me a Porter house steak, or I will dash your brains out with this head of lettuce.'"

Cigar Connors used to run the Boston Race with a cigar in his mouth. Geo Kirkwood finished the Yonkers Race smoking a cigar.

A. L. Monteverde [walked] from New York to San Francisco, 3,415 miles at sixty years of age in 79 days 10 min and 10 sec. It cost

Monte over five thousand dollars of his own money back in 1929. Monte lives out in Los Angeles and still walks ten miles at ninety years of age. . . .

One more on a runner and I will sign off on this subject. Frank Lalla was an A.D.T. boy for the Western Union. While on his way to deliver a telegram, he stopped to watch the start of the Port Chester Marathon. He forgot his telegram and followed the race on his bicycle, delivering his telegram some three hours later.

The message was a tip on a horse running that day at Belmont, the race was over and unfortunately for Lalla the horse had won. Result, he no longer was an A.D.T. boy, and the marathon fraternity had a new member. Five years later Frank Lalla won the Port Chester Marathon. If you ever get off a train at Rye, N.Y., and take a taxi, it will be one of his cabs you will ride in. He has a nice home, a fine wife, a boy of whom I am godfather to, and I don't think he ever regrets losing that Western Union job. Incidentally, he lives in the Italian quarter of Rye, formerly the home of [Gene] Sarazen, the famous golfer. Ironically, this section of Rye is called DUBLIN.[30]

Just six days after the Grant Park marathon, Bill breezed to a win in a fifteen-mile race at Chicago's Portage Park. Hatch finished third. Cooper dropped out after ten miles—understandable as he, too, had just run the heatstroke marathon.

To recap, in the space of ten weeks, Bill Kennedy won two marathons and three shorter road races of between nine and fifteen miles (plus his second-place finish in another fifteen-miler). Going meatless for a while seemed to agree with him.

It was probably around this time that Bill, now a top athlete in the Midwest, met August Anheuser Busch Sr., president of Budweiser, the brewery founded by his grandfather Eberhard Anheuser. As Bill recalled:

St. Louis held numerous modified marathons from five to fifteen milers. The writer won a number of these, though I can recollect taking the dust of Joe Bantle Jake Kaysing, John Probst and Irwin Biel. I won the Eberhardt [sic] Anheuser trophy two years in succession.

After my second win he gave a dinner at the Bricklayers Hall in my honor. It was no full dress affair, but a good time was had by all.

Following the dinner the officers of the union and myself toured the city in the company of Mr. Anheuser [Busch]. We made every Budweiser stop downtown, where the drinks were on [Anheuser Busch]. The old timers out in Missouri were probably not as sedate as their contemporaries in the East, but they sure knew how to enjoy themselves. Those were glorious days in sports. . . . As Shakespeare said, "Oh call back yesterday, bid time return."[31]

As the weather cooled in the fall of 1913, Bill got a hankering for "meat and foods with more oil than minerals," he recalled. "So I ate accordingly."[32] But he had established himself for the time being as the hottest runner in St. Louis and Chicago. Naturally, that meant a stiff handicap in a handicap marathon:

The Columbia Athletic Club, now disbanded, promoted a handicap marathon on the South side of [St. Louis] for two years and then dropped it. The writer took part in the first of these, in 1913. The race was held on a dark, drizzly, rainy day in the fall of that year. I was placed on scratch, and gave up to 45 min. handicap. The closest man to me had 15 mins. and it seemed an eternity sitting wrapped up in a blanket waiting for my time to start. Finally the starter sent me on my way, and with a wave of their hands, the officials and newspaper men were off down the road and I was all alone out in the wilds of Missouri. Now and then I would pass a farm house, to be greeted with "Haw, haw, you are a way behind." Even the cows in the field mooed at me.

The miles drifted by and gradually I caught and passed many of my competitors, finally reaching Gravois Road, with its sprinkling of German beer gardens. Slowly but surely darkness was setting in, when to my great joy I was met by a carload of loyal bricklayers, and from here on in I not only had company but refreshments as well. As I passed the 20-mile mark, flashlights were used to check my number. I ran the last five miles in darkness, finishing at Lemps Beer Garden.[33]

The Columbia race made for a somewhat comical ending to an otherwise outstanding race season for Bill. Now, the bricklayer looked forward to training for his return visit to Boston next April. It wasn't meant to be.

꩜

Bill woke up with a fever one morning that fall. Running a temperature of 103 to 104, he felt weak. His stomach hurt, his head hurt, and he'd lost his appetite. He may also have noticed red spots on his skin.

Typhoid fever—thought to be the disease that decimated the Jamestown colony—was still a widely feared killer in Chicago as well as other big cities throughout the nineteenth and early twentieth centuries. Up to fifteen Chicagoans per ten thousand died of it some years. The city took great pains to sanitize its water supply between 1913 and 1917, and nearly eradicated the bacterially spread disease by 1925. But that came too late for Bill Kennedy, who was stricken with typhoid in the fall of 1913, toward the end of a year that saw 276 of his fellow city residents die of it.[34]

For more than three months, Bill lay in Chicago's Post-Graduate Hospital, suffering from fever, delirium, headaches, and diarrhea. With no antibiotics then, all doctors could do was try to treat the symptoms. The weeks ground on. In December, the once hardy Kennedy "still is in serious condition," the *Tribune* told sports fans. "The athlete has rallied several times, but on each occasion when it appeared he was on the road to recovery he has suffered a slight relapse." As far as the Illinois A.C. was concerned, their star of 1913 was lost to them for 1914—and maybe forever.[35]

Still, Bill kept up his hopes as he turned a corner. "Lying there convalescing, common sense told me my running days were over, yet something kept reminding me that I had led a clean life, had put in years of exercising and road work building up endurance. This should overbalance thirteen weeks of illness." But most of the medical professionals at Post-Graduate disagreed. "The staff of doctors advised me to give up any idea of racing any more, as typhoid leaves an after effect which may harm me."[36]

The doctors had a point. Bill still wasn't out of the woods even after he recovered from the typhoid itself. According to one study of mortality in Chicago in that period, "most people survived the bout(s) with typhoid, but only by the skin of their teeth. . . . The typical typhoid survivor was so weakened and compromised by the disease that he or she would later succumb to some other infectious disease like tuberculosis, or die of kidney or heart failure." Competitive running seemed out of the question. "His battle for life has reduced Kennedy to a shell," pronounced the *Tribune* on the eve of his release from the hospital. "It is doubtful if the marathon star ever will be able to condition himself for another grind."[37]

Yet before being discharged, Bill held "a confab with Dr. McNealy, who had treated my case," he recalled.

> We discussed the advisability of running again. I spoke of my years of training and the fact that as soon as I was able I would have to go back to laying brick, which was hard manual work for eight hours, while the marathon took less than three hours. On the job you had a boss breathing down the back of your neck, and racing you had a cheery word and the applause of the crowd. So Doc says "You got something there. If you want to run, don't let anyone discourage you. Take it easy at first, but you know how to condition yourself. Go to it. And good luck."[38]

At last Bill walked out of the hospital, prematurely gray at age thirty. He was broke and owed the hospital about five hundred dollars. He had no health insurance, and he was in no condition for construction work.

But he did have friends. The bricklayers and the amateur athletes of Chicago organized a fund-raiser for Kennedy. When the proceeds were tallied, he had enough to pay his medical bills. Not only that, but also one of the locals got him a job selling sporting goods in a department store, so that for the time being he could earn a living while taking it relatively easy. The name of the store, on Chicago's State Street, had to be a good omen: The Boston Store.[39]

Jessie and the girls moved up to Chicago to be with Bill. Gingerly, gradually, he resumed running. He started with modest distances. Cooper from the Hebrew Institute got Bill a free membership there "so I could use their gym, swimming pool and track to get back in shape," Bill recalled.

> Here I made the acquaintance of a fine old gentleman, Mr. [Jacob] Loeb. . . . He was one of the founders of the Institute and would sit on a bench sunning himself and watching me running mile after mile around the track. Calling to me to join him one day after finishing my run. We chatted for a while, and never have I forgot the title he applied to me, showing [his] sense of humor. Tapping his cane on the ground he says, "Kennedy, you are a Jew's Harp. It does me good to see an Irishman like you at our Institute. It's a good omen for the future. You remind me of when I was a boy, there was a musical instrument which took no skill to play and was popular with the young. It was called a 'Jew's Harp.' " We both got a laugh out of his joke.[40]

Loeb, a prominent businessman and philanthropist, was then president of the Hebrew Institute, and later head of the Chicago Board of Education. (A decade after Bill Kennedy met Jacob Loeb, the latter's nephew Richard Loeb committed a sensational murder that was the basis for the Alfred Hitchcock film *Rope*.)[41]

As Bill's health improved, he returned to bricklaying form. And he even donned gloves and engaged in a little sparring:

> Walter Terrell, a west side plumber, was an amateur runner by day, and a good one, fought professionally nights as "Young Fitzsimmons," also a good fighter. Young Fitz used to work out in Joe Welland's gym on W. Madison St. Knowing I had done some boxing, he asked me to work out with him on rainy days when I was not working at bricklaying.
>
> In one of our workouts Welland and a couple of other boxers were needling him that the "old guy is outboxing you." Whereupon

Fitz got that left of his working on the bridge of my nose. When I got home both of my eyes were discolored. My wife took one look at [me] and let out a roar.

"Now what have you been doing?"

"I was helping 'Young Fitz' train for a fight," I replied.

"Helping him? Did he get mad at you?"

"Oh, no, it was just friendly," says I.

"Well, by the looks of you, I'd hate to see you if he was sore."[42]

It seems Bill's recovery was complete. If it was acceptable for a prizefighter to give him two black eyes, then he was probably okay. By September, he felt strong enough to enter a twelve-mile race sponsored by the Hebrew Institute. He went into the lead at the third mile, though he fell back to third by the end, losing to Hatch and Curtis Booth.[43]

By early 1915, Bill had worked his way back up to running twenty miles in training. Now, he felt, he was ready to return to Boston. In April he applied to the Illinois A.C. for travel expenses to take part in the marathon on Patriots' Day. But club officials wouldn't spend a dime on a runner whose best days were clearly behind him. They knew the toll typhoid took on a body, saw Bill's gray hair and wizened face, and dismissed him as over the hill, not a serious contender.

That wouldn't stop him. Lack of funds was a common problem for amateur athletes, and solutions were myriad. In a disquisition on the topic, Bill recounted his journey to Boston in 1915, among other travels on the cheap.

IN BILL'S WORDS: TRANSPORTATION

Now in order to take part in one of these marathons, it is first necessary to reach the city in which the race is being held. But only a small percentage of these athletes belong to clubs financially able to pay their expenses to take part in these out-of-town runs. How then do they get there? In a field of over a hundred probably not more than a dozen have had their expenses paid by a big club, some company they work for, and in some cases by their friends taking up a

collection to send them to the race, as I have had at times from the
bricklayers on the building on which I was working. . . .

Of the American competitors in my day, the Canadians would
come in a car riding six or more who shared the cost, many hitch
hiked their way, and others arrived via freight trains or blind baggage [a passenger train's baggage car]. Being able to tell of my own
means of reaching the start, I will relate a few incidents when I was
not financially able to travel de-luxe. . . .

In one of my early races I was loafing around St. Louis and
decided to go to Chicago to run in an indoor race. The weather
was mild in St. Louis, so I crossed the bridge to E. St. Louis and
climbed into a box car. After sundown the wind shifted north and
it was down to zero by the time we reached Decatur Ill[.], where
I unloaded and slept in the lobby of the R.R.Y. The next evening
with the thermometer at 10 below I rode a box car to Chicago,
jogging back and forth to keep from freezing. At every stop the
end brakeman walked up to my Pullman banging on the door
he would shout "Are you awake Brickey?" "Yes Sir." "Don't go to
sleep or you will never wake up." Arriving in Chicago at 5 A.M. in a
blizzard, I rode a Halstead St. car to the Bricklayers Hall, and slept
alongside the furnace all day, down in the basement. Three days
later I ran that indoor marathon at Riverside Rink finishing an hour
behind the winner "Sid" Hatch. . . .

Many years later Frank Lalla and I hitched it to Boston by auto.
We made it to Worcester but had to walk the last 40 miles to Boston. In the Bunker Hill Marathon the next day, Lalla finished fifth
and I walked up Bunker Hill showing the whites of my eyes in 10th
place. . . .

1933 for a marathon held at Wilmington Del., six of us from the
Cygnet club of E. Port Chester traveled by car, going down the Jersey
side. Learning at the ferry that the charge was by passenger, we put
four of our boys under the rumble seat, paying for two passengers.
For lodging at Wilmington, after trying the Y, the police station and
fire dept., we finally slept in the park. We all took a beating in the
race the next day, which was nearer 28 than 26 miles.

Hardship meant nothing to us old time marathoners, like good
steel our bodies were highly tempered to take punishment, and until
a distance runner has the stamina and will power to do so, he will
never become a successful winner. . . .

Back in 1915, being out of work in Chicago, and having been running on the roads all winter with the idea of again trying the Boston
Race. Being out of funds, I decided to beat my way by freight—hitch
hiking not then in vogue. With thirty cents in my pocket, I climbed
aboard a cattle car out of South Chicago one night. It was a cold
night, so I climbed up and slid in to the feed box, closing the lid
down on myself. It was warm enough in there as the cattle engender
heat but you can't sleep very well with them eating your bed from
under you.

I held that train down for two nights and a day, pulling into
Buffalo the second morning. The only food I had in that time was at
Toledo, where we stopped to take water. Raising the lid of my berth,
I saw the picture of a 16 oz. schooner of beer and under it "5 cents."
I was out of that box in a jiffy, across the tracks, and downed two
of those beers, grabbed two handfuls of pretzels, and back into my
Pullman. It gave the high ball.

I lay over for a day and slept in a 10-cent flop house at Buffalo,
making Albany the afternoon of the fourth day. Before prohibition
it was the custom with most breweries that an out-of-town visi-
tor could sample their product. So, paying my respects, I was the
recipient of four schooners of brew, my vitamins for the day. Leaving
Albany I arrived by freight in Springfield, Mass., at 2 A.M. I met up
with a policeman who, on questioning me, took me over to a livery
stable, where the night man put me up in the loft to sleep. On being
roused at 6 A.M. I learned that I was not the only guest that night.
I was allowed to depart with a handshake, while my fellow guests,
who were members of the local fraternity [hoboes], were forced to
manicure the horses and stalls.

Now within sight of my goal, and knowing the Boston section
of the Twentieth Century was due shortly, I decked it into Boston,
arriving on the fifth day after four days and nights on the road.[44]

As if that journey weren't epic enough, there's one part Bill left out.
What he forgot, or chose not to share in his book manuscript, but
what he told his Port Chester friend Lank Leonard, was that on the
approach to Cleveland that April week in 1915, Bill dozed off while
riding underneath a train car. He slipped and his right arm brushed
one of the wheels, opening a severe cut. A surgeon stitched him

up, and an hour later Bill was on another freight train out of Cleveland.[45]

⌣

"Fear the man with the paper bag," Jimmy Henigan once told Jock Semple. "Fear the man who comes to the race with his clothes in a paper bag. That's your real runner."[46]

When Bill arrived at the Huntington Avenue station of the Boston & Albany Railroad on Friday, April 16, 1915, he didn't even have a real paper bag. His tracksuit and running shoes (the only items he brought) were wrapped in newspaper. Ironically for a traveler toting no luggage, Bill rode into town on the roof of a baggage car.

When the train screeched to a halt that afternoon, Bill slipped off the roof, climbed down to the ground, and stretched. Asking around, he was "directed to a public bath where for two cents, I was given a towel and soap," he would recall. Refreshed, he walked down to "Newspaper Row," the block of Washington Street where most of Boston's nine daily newspapers were headquartered. "I went up to the Boston Globe, where I met Larry Sweeney, a sports writer."[47]

Sweeney was perhaps the first Boston newspaperman to play the role of consistent, inveterate enthusiast of the local marathon. He had witnessed every single edition of the big run, going back to 1897, when as a teenager he'd ridden along on a bicycle. "There is no one," wrote a colleague, "who is in as close touch with the history of the Marathon as Sweeney." Bill had come to the right sportswriter.[48]

"Larry was astonished when I told him how I got to Boston," Bill recalled. The reporter pumped the willing subject for more details about his life. With obvious pride, Bill talked of his daughters, showing Sweeney a picture of Louise wearing an I.A.C. shirt and posing amid a display of trophies won by her "Papa."[49]

"Handing me a five-dollar bill, [Sweeney] called Mr. Barnes, his boss, to whom I had to repeat my story," the bricklayer later wrote. The AAU would have balked at this, but Bill considered it a loan, and it enabled him to find accommodations in Boston that weekend.

FIGURE 3. A *Boston Globe* cartoonist illustrated Larry Sweeney's article about Bill Kennedy in 1915.

After the interview, he made his way out to Dorchester for a workout over the roads with Jimmy Henigan and the other Dorchester Athletic Club runners engaging in some last-minute training for the big race.

The next day, Bill opened the *Globe* to see this headline: "BILL KENNEDY HERE FOR THE MARATHON" (see fig. 3). Sweeney's story began: "Bill Kennedy is here! Bill, who will represent the Illinois A.C. of Chicago in the B.A.A. Marathon run Monday despite the refusal of the athletic committee of the big Chicago club to defray his expenses."

Bill had traveled to Boston the same way in 1912 in perfect obscurity. But this time, thanks to Sweeney, sports fans learned all about his long trip: "Cattle trains and freight trains do not make as much speed as trains de luxe, although Kennedy patronized all three on his pilgrimage East. Incidentally, he abhors the idea of enriching the coffers of the railway magnates." Furthermore, "he expressed genuine pleasure in being 'home' once more. If he was not by adoption a Westerner, he would be a New Englander." Readers learned about Bill's family, his occupation, his upbringing on the Connecticut–New York border, and his growing prominence in marathoning: "In the West he is mentioned in the same breath with such exponents of long distance running as Joe Forshaw, Joe Erxleben and Sidney Hatch . . . a stellar group of runners."

For years Bill had run himself sore out West—relatively speaking, the minors of the running game—where the marathon was still largely a curiosity. Now he was getting recognition back "home."

"The write-up [the *Globe*] gave me on their sports page sure made a lot of friends for me," Bill would recall, "people whom I still have the highest regard for almost fifty years later."

The 1915 Boston Marathon was the first since 1897 in which no previous winner was competing. Perhaps that meant some dark horse could take it all. Of course, there were plenty of good runners in the race. Bill's old rival Sid Hatch was there. And from Quebec came Ed Fabre, a remarkable athlete who'd finished second the year before. Raised by Iroquois, Fabre was a brawny construction worker known in Canada not only for his prowess in conventional foot races but also as a champion endurance snowshoe racer.[50]

Other entrants included Mike Lynch, a teetotaling bartender who four years earlier had weighed 205 pounds (at five foot seven) and through running had slimmed down to 145. To be sure, wrote Sweeney in the *Globe,* "Lynch will be 33 years old next July and he fully appreciates that he is too old to ever hope to become a sensation in the Marathon world."[51] (Remember these words later.)

Patriots' Day was warm and sunny—nothing like the nor'easter that had turned the course to slop during Bill's last visit. This time,

Ashland had the bright look of a circus as the runners arrived, checked in, and headed to the starting line. After much mugging for the cameras, wrote James Sullivan of the *Globe* (not the AAU official), "There were a few moments' silence."[52] Then George V. Brown of the BAA spoke.

"Everybody ready, now."

The starter fired his pistol. "Like a flock of birds liberated from a cage the runners swept forward," wrote Sullivan. "The steady pounding of many feet on the dirt road sounded like the echoes of a distant rumble of a dying thunder clap." A growing parade stretched behind the runners—automobiles, motorcycles, bicycles, and the still prevalent horse-drawn buggies.

Bill managed to stay among the front-runners for most of the race, and as high as fifth through Natick and Wellesley. "I held on for fifteen miles with the roar of the crowd cheering me on but tired toward the end," he recalled.[53] Again, Bill lost ground on those bedeviling hills in Newton.

Meanwhile, Fabre, who struggled with a sore leg for much of the race, mounted a comeback, from fifteenth place in Natick to third at Coolidge Corner. Down the home stretch he caught the leader, Cliff Horne, and finished first in 2:31:41. Hatch came in third. During the victor's press conference in the BAA clubhouse, Fabre called for and downed beer after beer until a half-dozen empties teetered on his bench.

Bill wound up in fifteenth place, in 3:01:24. This earned him a silver medal. But the important thing, after his long illness and recovery and training and train-hopping journey, was that he'd made it to the finish line. He was back.[54]

~~~

That year's race was noteworthy for another reason. For the first time, women attempted to run the Boston Marathon. "Want to know if young ladies will be allowed to run in the Marathon race," read a postcard Brown received at the BAA. "If not, why not? For women now have the same rights as men. If ladies are permitted to run, please set aside a dressing room for them. We are going to run, anyway." The postcard was mailed from Hyde Park in March and signed ""I.H.K." and "M.T.Y." Around the same time, two young women "clad in bloomers, blouses and leather gymnasium shoes" were spotted running along Blue Hill Avenue.[55] After the *Globe* reported on these unprecedented happenings, six more women sent in entry forms.

"Properly enough the B.A.A. officials paid no attention to the entries or requests," the *Globe* reassured readers after the marathon. With that kind of response, it's no wonder none of the women showed up on race day. The prohibition on women in the marathon would persist for decades.[56]

〜〜

As for Bill, he had already secured a bricklaying job in town to pay his way back to Chicago. Moreover, "I tried to pay Sweeney the five bucks [back] but he wouldn't take it," Bill recalled. "As watch fobs were the style in those days I took my [souvenir] medal to a jeweler, had him engrave it to Larry and put it on a fob. He was as proud of that present as if it cost 100 dollars."[57]

Bill didn't have to work in Boston very long. Sid Hatch "came to his rescue," Sweeney reported. "Sid is a fine sport and would not hear of his clubmate 'riding the rods' again and insisted that Kennedy travel back first class . . . as his guest."[58]

〜〜

A shock wave rippled through the marathon community later that week. The news concerned Jimmy Duffy, 1912 Olympian and winner of the 1914 Boston Marathon. Born in Sligo, raised in Edinburgh, settled in Ontario, Duffy was a tinsmith, then a stonecutter, who ran road races when he wasn't working—or carousing. "Duffy is an athletic marvel—all the more so because he does not take such care of himself as successful athletes generally do, does very little training and is by no means abstemious in his habits," declared the *Hamil-*

ton Herald. Duffy admitted beer was a staple of his training diet, and as soon as he finished the '14 BAA run in 2:25:01—one of his seven straight marathon victories—he asked for and received a cigarette, his first since . . . just before noon. As a guest of honor at a show at the Colonial Theatre that night, he asked his hosts a lot of questions about the various female cast members.

When the First World War broke out in Europe in August 1914, Duffy enlisted in the Canadian army. The 24-year-old sailed for Belgium with the same spirit of adventure that had drawn him to distance running. On April 22, 1915, his Sixteenth Battalion was entrenched outside Ypres, supporting French positions in a small wood. A gas attack pushed back the French, who had to abandon four machine guns. The Canadians were ordered to retake the wood from the Germans. They snuck in through the trees that night. Hearing the scrape of a bayonet, a German fired a flare aloft, exposing Duffy and 304 other soldiers and officers. In the ensuing firefight, all but twenty-seven were cut down.

Carried bleeding to a farmhouse, Duffy died on April 23. It was one week before his twenty-fifth birthday, and a year and four days after he'd won the Boston Marathon. "[Duffy] did not live long to enjoy his well-earned laurels," wrote Bill. "Requiescat in pace."[59]

To the marathoners he left behind, Duffy's death was a reminder of the European conflict; a tendril of war reaching across the Atlantic into the lives of still neutral Americans. Scarier still, it was a harbinger of their own involvement in the war in the years to come.

〰

After Hatch and Kennedy returned to Chicago, the latter found himself without an A.C. Perhaps the board of the Illinois Athletic Club was annoyed by the bad press they'd received in Boston thanks to Bill's hobo heroics and his gift of gab shared with Sweeney. Whatever the reason, they "gave me my walking ticket," Bill said later. "The Chicago club thanked me for what I had done for them, and all that, but added that it wished to weed out some of its runners, so I went. . . .

Sometimes the rocking-chair athletes around a club know more about a fellow's condition than he does himself."[60]

Undaunted, Bill co-founded the Bricklayers' Athletic Club, based out of his union local, No. 21, that summer. He found no fewer than two hundred colleagues who boxed, swam, ran, or played soccer or baseball, or were interested in doing so more regularly. It seems he got Chicago White Sox owner Charles Comiskey—a former employee of Chris von der Ahe, Bill's favorite St. Louis saloonkeeper—to donate land near Comiskey Park for the BAC to site its facilities. The plot measured 350 by 700 feet, big enough for a track, baseball diamond, soccer field, and handball courts. In gratitude, the local made Comiskey an honorary member. (This was a designation not to be taken lightly. President Taft's honorary membership was revoked in 1912 after he ceremonially laid the cornerstone of the Boston YMCA, which was built with non-union labor.) By the end of the year, Bill and a crew of his brother brickies, volunteering on weekends and holidays, built a one-story clubhouse, forty by twenty feet, featuring four showers, a rubdown table, and even a ladies' restroom "for the comfort and convenience of the fair sex." As chairman of the track committee, Bill oversaw the grading and construction of the track, which circled the field, and a judges' stand. The front of the clubhouse sported the union's insignia—a trowel, square, and level. Bill wore this emblem with pride while running.[61]

No hobo in 1916, Bill rode to Boston "on the plush," in a passenger car, a week ahead of the marathon—the first of the out-of-town runners to arrive. He secured a job working on an apartment house being built on Peterborough Street, not far from Fenway Park. All week he worked there nine hours a day. In the evenings, he again linked up with the Dorchester Club for final practices, running the roads with Arthur V. Roth, a tracer in an architect's office. (Roth was "frail to look upon," the *Globe* would note. Frail like a fox.)[62]

"Kennedy, through his persistence in coming here when the [IAC] failed to provide," said the *Boston American,* "made hundreds of friends [last year]. This week he'll have just as many rooting for him to come back in front."[63]

Sure enough, come April 19, Bill "was greeted with continuous salvos" along the course. And he had only come in fifteenth the previous year. The Chicagoan's popularity was based almost solely on his backstory and personality. (His being Irish didn't hurt.)[64]

Maybe it was the cheers, maybe it was his hard training all winter, and maybe it was the hot pace set by his new training pal Roth in the lead, but Bill stayed well up in front most of the way. He ran in third through Wellesley and past the Woodland Park Hotel.

Then those Newton hills again. On the second long hump, Bill lost ground, dropping back to seventh place. He sought help from his attendant,

John Dailly, a bricklayer who worked with me on a job in the Back Bay. He borrowed a bike to ride with me . . . but, as he hadn't ridden for some years, had a hard time keeping up with me on the hills. It was a cold raw day, so I [had given] him a pint of brandy, diluted with hot water and sugar, to feed to me as I called for it. Well, I called for it many times over the last ten miles, but got no response from my brother bricklayer. He just kept pedaling along with eyes front.[65]

Roth, despite his awkward-looking gait, finished first, in 2:27:16. Hatch was third, and to great cheers, Bill finished sixth, in 2:35:17. It was his first time among the prizewinners at Boston.

Inside the clubhouse, Bill took a bath and got a rubdown. And Dailly—a once and future president of the Boston bricklayers' union Local 3—finally came clean about the brandy.

In the dressing room, I questioned him as to why he didn't let me have a drink when I asked for it. He sheepishly replied, "Well, Bill, I was pretty well fagged out going up those hills, and you seemed all right, so I kind of figgered it might do you some harm, and, as I

wasn't feeling any too well myself, I drank it." You can well imagine
the laugh from the sports writers gathered around.[66]

After a celebratory dinner and a moving picture, Bill retired at
midnight. The next morning he was up at 5:30, and by eight o'clock he
was on Peterborough Street, "swinging his trowel and laying bricks as
fast as any man on the job," reported the *Globe*. "He repeatedly called
'more brick' and his helpers wondered at his capacity for work."[67]

"I feel fine except for my blistered feet," Bill told the reporter. "By
the way, I was not the only bricklayer among the runners, for James
A. McCurnin follows the same trade and is a member of the Bay-
onne, New Jersey, union."

"Kennedy was the idol of his brother bricklayers on the Fenway
job yesterday," the article continued.

> Many had seen him run on Wednesday and all had read of his great
> race. When he got on the bricklaying job yesterday morning, however,
> he had to tell them all his story of the race and again at noon and at
> knocking-off time at 5 o'clock he was forced to repeat the tale.
>
> When one suggested he ought to come to Boston a few weeks be-
> fore a Marathon and train and rest instead of working at his trade and
> training he exclaimed: "How can I? Don't I have to send the rent money
> home?" The expression won him still greater popularity among his fel-
> low workers, for aside from his running ability he had already gained
> their friendship and esteem by his companionable qualities and ever
> ready smile and word of encouragement.

Bill stayed on that job for another week. Every other evening, still
wearing his "ordinary trousers, a sweater and a cap," he ran over part
of the marathon course again, this time to train for the All-Western
Marathon in St. Louis on May 6.[68]

Sid Hatch won the All-Western in 1916, about 150 yards ahead of Bill
Kennedy in second. Within three months, both Chicagoans were
back east again, in a "26.8 mile marathon" in Johnstown, New York,
on July 29. Once again Hatch won, and Bill was runner-up.[69]

At that point Bill took a job with his father, working on a new high school building in Port Chester. He spent the rest of the year there or in the city. It seems clear that Bill was now ready to move back to "Old Saw Pits" permanently, as soon as he could save the money to send for Jessie and their daughters. It was the ideal spot, convenient enough to Boston, where he was suddenly quite popular, and to other big races in New York and the vicinity—for example, a national track and field meet that September.

> The writer sent his entry in for the steeplechase championship at Travers Island without enclosing the entry fee of two dollars. As I toed the line for the start the clerk asked for my two dollars. Having no money in my track suit, I was ordered off the line. As I started to leave a white-bearded gentleman enquired what was wrong. Upon being informed, he pulled out his wallet, and paying my fee says, "Well, Bill, if they can't trust you, why, I can." Judge Bartow S. Weeks. There were men in those days. Charlie Elbert and Hugh Brady also came to my rescue but the Judge beat them to it. Brady always sent me a four-leaf clover before a race.[70]

Judge Weeks was a veteran Tammany Hall politician, a former assistant district attorney, and president of the New York Athletic Club. Bill scored third prize in the two-mile steeplechase, the finish of which took place during a driving hailstorm that sent spectators scurrying for cover.[71]

Bill met another well-known politician a couple of weeks later when he finished third in the Brockton Fair Marathon in Massachusetts, this time behind Hatch in second and Finnish runner Willie Kyronen in first. Governor Samuel McCall presented this trio with their prizes. At least, that's what the *Globe* reported. Bill would always remember it differently.

> Sitting at a table with the late John Rodemeyer, Pres. of the Bald Headed Mens Assn. of America, at the Pickwick Arms in Greenwich, Conn. He remarked that the only man to make Pres. Coolidge smile was Will Rodgers. Asking his pardon, I told of the time I ran third in the Brockton Fair Marathon. As governor, he presented the first and second men their prizes. As he handed me the third prize, I said,

"Governor, I would like to shake hands with you." I have always cherished the smile that lit up his face, as grasping my hand he replied, "Bill, the pleasure is all mine." The crowd enjoyed it as much as did he and I.[72]

Calvin Coolidge was actually McCall's lieutenant governor at the time, and the *Globe* did report that Coolidge attended the festivities as well. With all the happenings around the fair, could it be that McCall sent Coolidge over to the marathon finish line at the last minute to cover for him, and the *Globe* engaged in some sloppy reporting? (The extent of the prize ceremony coverage is the sentence "The prizes were presented by Gov McCall.") Or did Bill get the two elected officials mixed up? Probably we'll never know.[73]

On Halloween 1916, Bill Kennedy was set "to be added to the Irish-American A.C. roster as soon as he becomes eligible to compete for the local club," the *New York Times* reported. This was a big deal. Since Bill's teenage years, the IAAC had been the athletic power of the region. Up to fifteen thousand people attended some IAAC track and field events at Celtic Park in Queens. Fans collected cigarette trading cards with images of its stars, many of them Olympians, including marathoner Johnny Hayes and nineteen others who'd medaled in 1908 at London, all while holding down day jobs as policemen or laborers. And now Bill was about to join their ranks, though under AAU rules he had to wait. "Kennedy yesterday asked for his transfer from the Central Association to the Metropolitan Association of the A.A.U.," noted the *Times*, "and it will be four months before he will be allowed to compete under the colors of the Winged Fist organization."[74] (The club's logo was a raised fist with wings.)

Unfortunately, Bill was stymied by bad timing. In a raid, federal agents had already found that a member of the club's board of directors had indirect ties to German spies, by way of his connection to the Irish independence movement. (Irish rebels hoped to obtain weapons from Germany for their own purposes.) By the end of Bill's four-month waiting period, American sentiment would start to turn against Germans, and indeed all things foreign and "hyphenated." On the ropes, the storied Irish-American A.C. would suspend operations in April, another casualty of the world war.[75]

〜✑

Two days before Christmas, Bill exchanged unwanted gifts on the race track in Yonkers. Jessie had been complaining about all the hardware he was bringing home—the trophies and other prizes taking up shelf space. As their nieces and nephews heard the story later, she told Bill, "If you bring home another silver cup, I'm going to hit you with it!"[76]

The day of the Yonkers Marathon was bitterly cold. After running out on the roads, Kyronen entered the Empire City Raceway a mile ahead of Hatch. As the Finn trudged across the finish line, his feet were "torn and bleeding and his shoes gashed and cut by jagged ice," reported the *Chicago Tribune*. "His face was numb and blue from the cold." Hatch finished second.[77]

When Bill reached the track, he was in fifth place. As he remembered it later, "a friend in the crowd yelled out and told me to slow down. The [fifth] place prize, he told me, was a camera, and the [sixth] prize was a set of silverware."

Bill thought about this. "I didn't want the camera. You'd have to buy film for it."[78] And Jessie would be pleased with the silverware.

The *Tribune* related the "farce" that followed:

Kennedy . . . jogged along until half a mile from the tape, when he suddenly stopped and threw himself to the ground.

To all urging and pleading he refused to go on, and waited for [Joseph] Carr, who was half a mile behind, to overtake him. It was a long, cold wait out there in the backstretch, and to pass away the time Kennedy finally got up and began to run—backwards. This even was too fast, and he slowed down to a walk, with a stop every minute or less to mark Carr's slow advance.

Carr was coming on all too slowly, so Kennedy halted again until the

Yonkers boy could come up. Carr seemed none too eager to overtake Kennedy, but he was too cold to follow the Chicago man's tactics, and a quarter of a mile from the finish line passed him.

Kennedy fell into a dog trot and plodded along five feet behind Carr while stopping every few minutes to fix a troublesome shoe lace. In 40 yards that lace came untied eight times, and Kennedy lost two yards every time he stopped.

The handful of spectators was in an uproar over this strange performance.[79]

The *Tribune* predicted that Bill would face charges before the Metropolitan AAU. As it happened, Bill said decades later, "the officials got on me for it, and there was an investigation.

"But they never got anything on me."[80]

4

"WE MUST REPEL THE FINNS"

Under the leaden skies of a New York City winter, Bill Kennedy slogged through piles of slush and snow as he logged his miles in training runs after work. Icy water soaked his shoes and chilled his feet and ankles. In January and February 1917, the weather in the Big Apple was what you'd expect of January and February most years in most places in the Northeast. Either the air was bitterly cold, dropping to zero at some points, or if it warmed up to the thirties, that simply meant the conditions were right for snow. One storm in early February sent fifty-mile-per-hour gusts through the streets, piling up large snowdrifts that quickly froze when the mercury dipped again.[1]

Running home in the slippery, shivery darkness, Bill had his eye on early spring. The newly repatriated New Yorker was more determined than ever to win the BAA Marathon. He'd show his erstwhile club the IAC once and for all how wrong they'd been.

The Patriots' Day run would be Bill's thirteenth marathon, "showing he has no superstitions," noted the *Boston Herald*.[2] That supposedly unlucky number would no more deter Bill than would the wintry weather. The BAA's was by far the most venerated marathon in the country. Indeed, it was the oldest annual marathon in the world, a fixture for a generation of distance runners. "We all have run in races for which we have not trained enough," Bill wrote. "But for a race such as the Boston Marathon—which has been held on the same date for [decades], and is the 'Derby' of marathon races—most men are in top form. This is the explanation of the large entry, fast time and close competition at Boston."

> Experienced runners will start three or four months before the race to train. Running three or four times a week, if unemployed even every day.
> Now for my methods. Starting with five mile runs every other day and a long walk of a Sunday. Increase the distance each week, until you are able to run twenty miles and walk thirty or even forty, which I have sometimes done. Then I cut out the walks and concentrate on running, tapering my long runs down to ten miles.[3]

On the day that winter when Bill ran twenty miles, "I felt so strong after the distance," he said, "that I knew it would take a good man to beat me."[4]

Meanwhile, in Germany, the Kaiser's military brass decided to break a previous pledge and resume unrestricted submarine warfare. That meant torpedoing, without warning, merchant ships from the still neutral United States. They would risk pushing America off the fence and into the war on the side of Britain and France, but the desperate officers gambled that stopping the flow of arms to the Allies would turn the land war Germany's way before the Yanks would have time to mobilize their army. The civilian leaders agreed, and on January 31, 1917, the German ambassador to the United States announced the new policy. President Wilson severed diplomatic relations with Germany and authorized the arming of merchant ships.[5]

In and around New York Harbor, the announcement delayed or canceled departures, held up the mail, and forced ship owners to shop for deck guns. Warehouses filled up with cargo going nowhere.[6]

Still, the country wasn't at war yet. Bill kept up his training, and on February 11 he was in good enough shape to win, during a cold snap, an eighteen-mile race, the Pennant A.C.'s invitational in the Bronx. His time was 1:51:10, the *New York Tribune* reported, "and after the first half mile, Kennedy was always in the van."[7]

By this time Bill had become captain of the Morningside A.C., based in his childhood stomping grounds of Harlem. His new club, in the opinion of the *Boston Evening Record,* was "composed of one of the best balanced long distance squads in the East."[8]

In late February, Bill and some teammates, along with his pal Sid Hatch from Chicago, entered the Bronx County Marathon. "Plunging rather than running through streets that were covered alternately with ice, mud, and melting snow," thirty competitors climbed the hilly New Rochelle roads and Bronx streets, the *New York Times* reported. "The roughest part of the going was encountered on the Fort Schuyler Road, through which the field had to splash for about one mile on the return journey. This stretch is torn up, and it was necessary for the runners to wade ankle-deep in mud, where even the automobiles following the runners would not venture to follow."[9]

Observed the *New York Sun:* "To many of the thousands who saw the runners wade, swim, trudge and otherwise struggle through the warmed-over leftovers of the early morning snowstorm it seemed as if there were many more rational things than Marathoning to do on an off day. Twelve more starters had been expected, but conditions appealed only to superenthusiasts."[10]

An unattached Swedish runner named Hans Christian Schuster won the race in 2:40:25, with the Morningside's Harry Lucas finishing twenty-five seconds behind him for the number-two spot. Kennedy finished seventh in 2:55:02, and a third club member, Harry Spies, was tenth. The Morningside men were impressed with Schuster's performance and invited him to join their club. The Swede accepted.

But Bill would have to do better than his Bronx showing if he wanted to win at Boston. Granted, he didn't expect snow in mid-April, but the snow hadn't stopped the six guys ahead of him—and some of them would be running in Boston, too.

⌒

March debuted with fair weather in the Northeast, and in Boston, Mayor James Michael Curley pronounced March 1 "Spring Hat Day for Men," according to the *Boston American.* "True to his word, the Mayor blossomed forth [that morning] in a new headdress. It is green and it is felt and it is jaunty. The hat attracts due attention."[11]

But storm clouds were gathering quickly. Attention shifted that evening from Curley's chapeau to the revelation of a German plot to help Mexico invade Texas. British intelligence agents had intercepted and deciphered a coded telegram from German foreign secretary Arthur Zimmermann to Germany's ambassador in Mexico. The telegram outlined an alliance to be proposed to Mexico if and when the United States entered the war in Europe, as now seemed likely with the resumption of submarine warfare. Under Zimmermann's plan, Germany would support Mexican efforts to reconquer its former territory in the southwestern United States.[12]

The scheme's intent was to distract Washington's attention—and siphon away American weapons and manpower—from Europe. Instead, when the telegram was made public on March 1, it inflamed Allied-leaning public opinion in the States and stunned the many Americans who had favored neutrality. Not only pacifists but also isolationists and many German Americans and Irish Americans had long hoped to stay out of the war. The Zimmermann telegram ultimately would push most of these conflicted or "hyphenated" Americans either off the fence or out of the public discourse. It triggered defensive reflexes as it stirred patriotic sentiment in the hearts of men like Bill Kennedy, as would become obvious some weeks later.

But Bill's true passion was running, and at present his focus remained squarely on victory in the Boston Marathon. And on the street corners and in the saloons and barbershops of Boston, sports fans began buzzing that month as the BAA officially announced plans

for the marathon and entries began trickling in, including those of
Kennedy, Schuster, and Spies. The coming of the annual Patriots' Day
run served as "a sign of spring," noted the *Herald*.[13]

"The Marathon fever is with us," wrote Arthur Duffey, a former
track runner, in his *Boston Post* sports column in late March. "If
you doubt it, just take a peek at some of the country roads over the
Ashland-to-Boston course any of these evenings and see the runners
preparing for the B.A.A. race April 19."[14]

But though locals had the advantage of proximity to the course,
runners from far and wide sent their entry forms to the BAA. "The
Flying Finns" were the heavy favorites. Villar "Willie" Kyronen, of
New York's Millrose A.A., was the reigning national champion at the
ten-mile distance, had placed a close second in the 1916 BAA Marathon, and had won the Brockton Fair Marathon in October and the
Yonkers Marathon in December. Hannes Kolehmainen was a star of
the 1912 Olympics, having won three gold medals and one silver in
track and cross-country events. By 1920, he would earn a gold in the
Olympic marathon. In other words, he was a great runner at his peak.
"The greatest of them all," sportswriters were saying. "The greatest of
all those runners who have crossed the sea."[15]

Like Kennedy, Kolehmainen was a bricklayer by trade; unlike
Kennedy, he was also a vegetarian—year-round. Bearing more than
a passing resemblance to modern-day Russian president Vladimir
Putin, Kolehmainen stared into a camera with the hard eyes of a
competitor. And he was being coached by a veteran marathoner, his
older brother Willie (not to be confused with Willie Kyronen). "What
[Willie Kolehmainen] does not know about the long distance running game isn't worth knowing," wrote Duffey in the *Post*. Willie also
enjoyed using the press to psych out the competition. In late March,
he dropped into Duffey's office to announce "that Hannes is training
daily for the stunt down in Philadelphia and [is] perfectly confident
that he would run away with the honors in the race."[16]

For a country on the brink of entering a global war, the strong
foreign competition in such a high-profile athletic contest meant

national pride was at stake, even though Finland was a duchy of Russia, one of the Allies. "It will be up to Arthur Roth of the St. Alphonsus A.A. or some other American runner to defend the laurels in the Ashland-to-Boston race," wrote Duffey. "Kyronen and Kolehmainen are as fast as they make 'em and it will indeed take a record performance to beat this pair of champions."[17]

April opened to the drumbeat of war. On the first, the Boston branch of the Irish American organization Clan-na-Gael met to condemn the "British propagandists" campaigning for American entry, even as Mayor Curley and a Boston College Jesuit urged a gathering of three thousand Catholic young men to support President Wilson. The next day, just over a month after the interception of the Zimmermann telegram, the president "declare[d] Germany is now at war with America," and 100,000 crowded the Boston Common to watch a flag-raising and sing "The Star-Spangled Banner."[18]

Also, Senator Henry Cabot Lodge got into a fistfight with a pacifist. Each man later blamed the other for the altercation, which began with an exchange of name-calling.[19]

In the sports world, the Morningside A.C. showed its own fighting spirit. The *Boston Evening Record* reported on April 4 that the New York runners "want a crack at our Dorchester boys" when Kennedy's club challenged the well-regarded Dorchester club to a head-to-head race of fifteen miles. Race fans knew this was largely smack talk in advance of the BAA marathon—that was the real contest. The focus on war preparedness at this moment only heightened the significance of a race that drew "the cream" of amateur athletes into "a mighty struggle for American supremacy," as the *Boston American* put it.[20]

"With the boxing championships out of the way and [preseason] baseball the only other sport to attract any great amount of attention, interest in the annual B.A.A. marathon is becoming greater each day," declared the *Evening Record* on April 5. "That the race will be as fast as ever and symbolical of the American long distance championship is assured by the class of entries received by Manager George V. Brown of the B.A.A."[21]

At the same time, Brown had to correct rumors that war would cause the cancelation of the event. BAA officials acknowledged they planned to meet with the governor of the state and would call off the run if he asked them to. This seemed an opening for one race favorite's manager—perhaps nervous about having talked too big earlier—to start lowering expectations a tad.

"Willie Kolehmainen, brother of Hannes, thinks a 15-mile marathon is plenty long enough for any of the long-distance pluggers to show them real class in an endurance run," Duffey related, saying that the Finn had pointed to "the well-known Powderhall Marathon" in Edinburgh, Scotland, which had recently been reduced from twenty-six miles, 385 yards, to fifteen miles.[22]

Congress officially declared war with Germany on April 6, two weeks before the Patriots' Day classic. The very next day, a German submarine sunk the *Canadian,* a ship that had steamed out of Boston in late March and was underwritten by Boston investors, as it carried wheat, corn, oats, horses, and artillery shells to the Allies. The Germans torpedoed the ship without warning eight miles from the Skellig Islands, off the Irish coast.[23]

The day after that, a slate-colored ten-thousand-ton raider was sighted off Nantucket, and unconfirmed reports surfaced of two Boston fishing trawlers being sunk off nearby Georges Bank. The U.S. Navy immediately warned Boston and other Atlantic ports to suspend shipping until the raider could be caught. Furthermore, the navy set mines and nets around Boston Harbor to thwart German subs, taking care to keep open two routes through which approved boats could be escorted safely.[24]

Boston was justifiably jittery. The city was two hundred miles closer to Europe than any other large port in the United States, and its ships had carried hundreds of millions of dollars' worth of meat, milk, grain, leather, cotton, iron, steel, and eventually weapons to the French and British since 1914, despite official American neutrality.

It was precisely such export activity that had prompted Germany to resume attacking merchant ships from noncombatant countries—a fatal miscalculation on the Kaiser's part. Outrage over the 1915 sinking of the *Lusitania* resurged. Soon enough U.S. troops would board those boats out of Boston: the city ranked third in the nation as a port of embarkation, sending tens of thousands of doughboys "Over There."[25]

So while today it is hard to imagine a western European power threatening our eastern seaboard, the fact is that in 1917 the German navy had Boston and other North Atlantic seaports in its sights. That raider spotted off Nantucket was not the last tub of Teutons to terrorize Massachusetts Bay. (Perhaps not even the last one that month, as we shall see shortly.) Skirmishes continued throughout the war, with the scariest incident occurring in July 1918, when a U-boat three miles off Cape Cod fired on several barges, sinking three, and even fired four shells at the shore, scattering beachgoers (thankfully, none were hurt). It was the first time the Commonwealth's coast had been bombarded since the War of 1812.[26]

Clearly, Bay Staters had reason to fear the seaborne wrath of imperial Germany. In the early days of U.S. entry into the war, those two weeks leading up to the 1917 Boston Marathon, many wondered how the region—and the country—would adapt to this new reality. The *Boston American* editorialized that war "spell[ed] doom" for hard liquor: "Now we are embarking upon a great war, the nation will probably find itself abstaining from strong drinks."[27] (On the face of it, such a conclusion might strike some as illogical, but in fact the prediction would prove somewhat prescient.)

For their part, Harvard and other colleges decided to cancel athletics at least for the season, but press commentators and military officers objected. Duffey pointed out that "neither West Point nor Annapolis, the two great government [military] schools, will eliminate their athletic training." Better, these critics argued, for the nation's young men to follow the wartime English and Canadian example and stay fit for duty through organized sports.[28]

"Shades of Pheidippides!" thundered the *Globe's* Lawrence J. Sweeney a week before the race.[29] "They're thinking of calling off the B.A.A. Marathon run of Patriots' Day on account of the war! Thinking of dropping the run that was intended to perpetuate the valor of the Greek soldier of 20 odd centuries ago . . . whose nimble feet and stalwart frame saved the Greek Army from annihilation." Why, the event's "very name suggest[ed] a martial spirit," Sweeney added.

"Already there are 25 entries," the columnist pointed out. How could the club cancel at this stage?

(This is remarkable by today's standards. A week before the race there were "already" twenty-five entries, a number that would swell to sixty-five by the nineteenth. It wasn't even until March that the race was officially announced and preparations commenced. Compare that with the 2017 Boston Marathon, which hosted 27,000 runners, most of whom were granted entry through an online rolling registration system in September 2016, fully seven months before the race.)[30]

But not to worry. The next day the BAA announced that the race would go on, for all the reasons Sweeney mentioned. "The event would be in keeping with the martial spirit of the times," the club agreed.[31]

Duffey approved: "It is pleasing to see that the Unicorn committee is composed of men with some real live blood in their arteries."[32]

If anything, these twentieth-century athletes were tougher than old Pheidippides, wrote Bob Dunbar in the *Journal*. "The Greek youth who ran to Athens from the [Marathon] plain was not compelled to do his running on macadamized roads and granolithic sidewalks, nor had gasoline fumes and cabbage-leaf cigars been invented at the time of the Persian invasion. We claim that the real heroes are the 50-odd starters in the B.A.A.'s 'holiday classic' Thursday next."[33]

❧

Meanwhile, it came to light that "diplomatic relations" had been "severed" between the two best-known foreign competitors: The *Evening Record's* Stuart Rogers revealed that "Hannes Kolehmainen and

Villar [*sic*] Kyronen, the two greatest long distance runners in the game today, and probably as great as any the world has ever known, are not on speaking terms."[34] Rogers got this scoop (and but one side of the story) from Hannes Kolehmainen's brother and manager, Willie.

Apparently the two former friends fell out after a 1915 marathon sponsored by the *Evening Mail* in New York. The Finns "had always run together. Kyronen frequently asked Hannes to help him win second prize, never once thinking himself the master of Hannes." According to Willie, "the same plans were in order" in the New York race.

> The pair alternated in setting the pace and Hannes held himself back a bit trying to bring Kyronen out of the ruck. Near the end he said he would just lope in a little bit ahead just as soon as he saw Kyronen was sure of second place. Kyronen double crossed Hannes and near the finish, after saving himself, let out a terrific sprint, catching Hannes unawares and just beating him to the tape.

The brothers took this betrayal personally. "To begin with the two Kolehmainens were the ones to bring Kyronen to this country and over here they developed him. Hannes claims he could have won the Mail race if he had run for himself instead of helping Kyronen. This is probably true."

After the incident, Kolehmainen refused to run in any race that included Kyronen. Because that meant most major races, rumors began circulating that "Koly" had given up competing. "Kyronen has boasted that he was Hannes' master at any distance and that Hannes quit because he was aware of this fact and didn't care to lose his world wide prestige."

To quash such talk "and to sting Kyronen with an overwhelming defeat, Kolehmainen is coming back to his own game and is going to run as he never ran before," wrote Rogers. "When the two meet on that day in the great annual B.A.A. Marathon of 25 miles, Han[n]es Kolehmainen is likely to set the world aghast with his running."

"The Finns, who are strong for early speed, will make the pace hot from the outset," agreed the *Traveler*. "The others will have to hustle if they hope to be in the race. Kyronen and Kolehmainen will bear close watching. . . . However, they will not [necessarily] have things their own way. The race in past years has been an endurance test and a dark horse may win."[35]

Bill Kennedy certainly respected the grit and skill of these competitors. Indeed, he had lost to Kyronen in the Brockton Marathon six months earlier. "The Finns, the greatest of distance runners, have the racial traits of patience, perseverance, and determination," he wrote. "Each one works out in his own way and most of them alone and not in groups. They are mostly fish eaters, though they object to be told so. One thing they have in common is the vapor or steam bath, topped off with a cold shower."[36]

As we shall see, however, Kennedy would differ with Kolehmainen in the matter of warm-up competitions. Boston's Cathedral YMCA (sometimes called the Cathedral Athletic Association) planned a ten-mile race over the streets of the South End, Roxbury, and Dorchester on April fourteenth, five days before the marathon. Several plodders who were already signed up for the BAA 25-miler decided to enter the Cathedral run as a last big workout before Patriots' Day. But not Kolehmainen, as Duffey pointed out: "Although the Cathedral A.A. has done everything in its power to have Hannes Kolehmainen among the entrants, the little Finn has decided not to compete in the coming run, claiming that the roads are apt to make him leg sore and hence he will save all his energy for the Boston Marathon race."[37]

Kennedy hadn't entered the Cathedral race himself—yet. At this point, he didn't even know about it. Bill (along with his brother Joe) was forty miles to the south, in Pawtucket, Rhode Island, "throwing in 2,000 bricks a day," he wrote in a letter to Sweeney. But he was almost certainly making preparations for the marathon.[38]

"Final tips before the race," Bill would later write. "Take a bottle of Magnesia one week before. Massage your feet with mutton tallow or lanolin. Tape any abrasions on toes or any place where shoe rubs."[39]

❦

Entries poured in to Brown now. The BAA manager "received 18 entries in the last 24 hours," the *Evening Record* reported on April 11, "which at the same rate would mean about a thousand entries by the day before the race." In reality, the total wound up at sixty-five, a typical figure in the marathon's early decades. (And not all of those entrants would show up on race day.) But that was a healthy number of runners in an era when so few people ran long distances for sport. Moreover, the international composition of the field heightened the sense of size.

"Looks to be a most cosmopolitan list of athletes in the big Marathon this year and America is going to have a tougher time than ever in winning the big laurels," Duffey wrote in the *Post* on April 13. The *Evening Record* listed some of the representatives of various nationalities: "There is Villar [*sic*] Kyronen, the wonderful little Finn; Hans Schuyster [*sic*], recent winner of the Bronx Marathon, who is a Dutchman; George Luosalo, Italian; Carl Linder, Scandinavian; Bill Kennedy, the stalwart Irish plugger; and several others." In addition, "Greeks just arrived from Greece are figuring largely in the run this year," noted the *Globe,* naming George Costarakis, Otto Alenius, and Spiros Catapodis.[40]

"One Greek," the *American* reported, was "a forty-third cousin to Miltiades," the Athenian general who defeated the Persians at the Battle of Marathon in 490 B.C. That may seem a thin qualification, but with his entry form, Leimtros Antonopoulos "sent word to Manager Brown that he felt confident of covering the route and furthermore, of finishing right up there in the front ranks."[41]

Nor were the dreaded Canadians totally absent from the competition, though most were now fighting with the British in Europe; 1915 winner Édouard Fabre was said to be coaching a fellow Montreal *habitant,* Edmund Martineau, to follow in his footsteps across the finish line at Exeter Street. "The latest Montreal crack," the *Boston Journal* related, "is a strong plugger, carrying his 185 pounds with ease. For training he has been running a 15-mile course over the mountains," presumably the peaks of Mont-Royal (highest point: 763 feet above sea level, dwarfing Heartbreak Hill's 236). "Recently he was clocked for this distance in 1 hour 27 minutes. As the Canadian entries for the grind in the past have made very creditable showings, it is expected that Martineau will be among the favorites." (This despite his scofflaw past: the *Herald* revealed that Martineau had until recently been banned from amateur competition for racing in an "unsanctioned snowshoe contest.")[42]

The earlier-mentioned Italian in the race, incidentally, was an opera singer, menacing the field with his formidable lung power. As one tickled reporter put it: "Grand Opera and the Marathon. No one would ever think of connecting the two. However, George Luosalo of Maynard, Mass., has done the trick."[43]

(The profusion of runners with exotic surnames even caused some newspapermen to issue a tongue-in-cheek note of protest. The *Boston Traveler*'s typesetters and proofreaders announced in a short item on April 13, "We have struggled along with names like Kolehmainen and Giannakopulous because those boys became famous in the track game, but we're hoping that Michael Demitrius Ematracupolos, who won the 880-yard run at the Samaclair A.A. games in New York the other evening, either changes his name or never gets famous.")[44]

While not a foreigner per se, there was even a fellow arriving from the "Pacific Coast," a fact that literally made headlines in Boston at a time when even the fastest possible cross-country trip would take several days, on multiple trains. The entry of Tacoma, Washington's, P. B. (or possibly P. D.) Allen meant that "nine States will be represented," reported the *Transcript*.[45]

Others entrants needed no introduction to Boston race fans. In winning the previous year, Dorchester native Arthur Roth had become the first bona fide Bostonian to win his city's marathon. Roth had beaten Kyronen once and thought he could do it again as he sought to become the first champ to repeat since J. J. Caffery in 1900–1901.

Another past local winner, Clarence DeMar, was mounting a comeback after a long break from running. DeMar was entered for the first time since he'd won the race in 1911, setting a record with his time of 2:21:39.5 and earning a slot in the 1912 Olympics. Perhaps DeMar couldn't know that he would win the race again, and again and again, eventually earning the nickname "Mr. De Marathon." But he was ready to win again *this* time, Sweeney suggested in the *Globe:* "The Melrose boy is serious in his determination to regain the crown."[46]

Finally, the hosting club had its own favorite standard-bearer. Albert Frederick Merchant, perennially a strong finisher in the marathon and fresh off a victory in a Washington's Birthday ten-miler, had recently joined the BAA and felt sure that this was *his* year, that he would at last "carry the Unicorn to victory." Just for practice, Merchant ran the entire Ashland-to-Boston route himself one day a couple of weeks before the race, with George V. Brown accompanying him in an auto.[47]

The 1917 field looked *so* strong, in fact, that more and finer monitoring was called for. "In anticipation of a great race several extra watches are going to be on hand to take the times at intermediate distances along the route," the *Evening Record* reported on the eleventh. "It is thought that records will go by the boards this year, and [in order] that the runners may get full credit for their efforts, plenty of timers are to be on hand."[48]

This would prove problematic for Merchant.

〜◯✓

Before taking leave of his brother and their worksite of the moment in Pawtucket, Bill sent a letter to his pal Sweeney at the *Globe.* Kennedy, the scribe told readers, "has never won a B.A.A. Marathon run, but he has experienced the sensation of winning other big Marathons. He will never be satisfied until he does lead a field of runners over the Ashland-to-Boston route, and despite the fact that his hairs are gray, he avows that this is the year he is going to 'cop.'"[49]

Bill also told Sweeney that after the race, he and his Chicago friend and rival Sid Hatch planned to "volunteer their services for Uncle Sam."

"'But first, we must repel the Finns,' writes the picturesque Kennedy, and the expression indicates clearly that Sir William's mind is very much inclined to Marathonitis, and that he, as do other qualified judges, regards Villir Kyronen and Hannes Kolehmainen as the most dangerous men in the holiday run."

In the next passage, we get a glimpse into how the old-time amateur runners traveled, communicated, and even fed themselves as they made their way to, and prepared for, a big race:

> [Kennedy] has followed his trade for years, and if he can land a job in Boston Monday morning he will work right up to race day. Just how he plans to come to Boston, whether by the brake-rod or parlor car route, he does not state, but it is reasonable to suppose that this year he will make his contribution to the New Haven railroad, for he writes:
>
> "Keep on the lookout for a pal of mine from Chi, Charles Mellor. He is a good, game kid. I sent him information 'which can't be bought' as to how to reach Boston. Tell him I will arrive Saturday and have enough dough for him and me to eat on for the next month or so. Let him look me up at the Bricklayers' Hall."
>
> Kennedy is also authority for the statement that Sidney Hatch will arrive in town early next week.

"Yep," Sweeney summed up, "Bill Kennedy will be with us today and the arrangements for the B.A.A. Marathon run next Thursday may now go on."

As it happened, Mellor had followed in Bill's footsteps that year, taking the "brake-rod route" to Boston, and even injuring himself in the process. It happened when he jumped a freight train on a bridge near Albany, the *Herald* would report: "Swinging on to a car, his body swung around and struck against a girder on the bridge, leaving a big bruise on his thigh."[50]

Luckily for Bill, his own trip to the Hub this year was less harrowing. On Saturday, April 14, the same morning that Sweeney's readers learned of Kennedy's imminent return, the bricklayer himself was riding from Rhode Island "on the plush," Bill later recalled, "the Morningside A.C. of N.Y. paying my expenses." As he watched the scenery pass his window, Bill thought he would work out that afternoon by running the last ten miles of the BAA marathon course.[51]

Upon his arrival in Boston at noon, however, he learned he was just in time for that day's ten-mile race sponsored by the Cathedral YMCA—the run that Hannes Kolehmainen had spurned to "save all his energy" for the marathon, now five days hence. Kennedy welcomed the chance to meet up with his fellow plodders and run that ten-mile workout in competition, on crowd-lined streets, rather than alone. He made haste for the South End.

⌣

Registration had closed two days earlier, but Bill Kennedy was a veteran marathoner who had, after all, been written up in that very morning's *Globe*. The club made an exception and accepted his thirteenth-hour entry. In the Cathedral clubhouse, he donned a faded tracksuit and wrapped his head in a white handkerchief. An uncommon sight yet, the look was becoming his trademark. (Some New Yorkers even nicknamed him "Handkerchief Bill.") Then, with a bit of time to spare before the start, he chewed the fat with club members and other runners. Here Bill's written recollection contradicts part of his own legend as told by others. This is what Bill wrote in the 1960s:

> Sitting in the [Cathedral] club house chatting with [illegible]. He mentioned a runner who had been sleeping on the pool table at the club. Upon investigating, who was it but my old protege from Chicago Chuck Mellor. Needless to say we had a pleasant reunion and to my amusement he whispered that he had been getting meal money by playing pool with the members. When first we had met on the N.W. side of Chicago, Chuck was racking balls for Johnny Coulon in his pool room, and it took a darn good player to beat him.[52]

So it was *Chuck Mellor* who slept on the pool table. Indeed, Bill shared this same story with the *Globe* just a few years after the fact, in 1923. How did the nugget then come to be associated with Bill himself? Simply put, Mellor's injurious journey by brake rod from Chicago was so reminiscent of Kennedy's own 1915 trip that reporters started getting the two mixed up. (An *American* article the day before the Cathedral race even called Chuck Mellor "Bill Mellor.")

Then, over the ensuing decades, as sportswriters swapped tales of the marathon, they conflated the original teller of the pool table story (Kennedy) with his subject (Mellor). Eventually the legend entered print. Seeing as Bricklayer Bill did in fact sleep in stables, cattle cars, and other makeshift quarters over the years, it is not surprising that over time he came to symbolize the hard life of the early marathoner—a life that was clearly also lived by Mellor and others.[53]

The Cathedral run started in the South End, by Holy Cross Cathedral, seat of the Roman Catholic Archdiocese of Boston. (Despite sharing initials with the better-known Young Men's Christian Association—then a more overtly Protestant group—the Cathedral athletic club was a chapter of the rival Young Men's Catholic Association.)[54] Veering into Dorchester and back, the five-mile route took in portions of Massachusetts Avenue, Columbia Road, and Blue Hill Avenue, covering territory that is now predominantly black and Latino but was then largely Irish and Jewish. As in a pickup stickball game in which trees and hydrants stand in for bases, the club deputized the Elevated Railway post on the corner of Blue Hill Avenue and Morton Street to serve as the halfway point marker. Upon rounding it, runners headed back to the Cathedral clubhouse over the same route, completing a ten-mile course.

It was a handicap race. Club official Frank McGrath assigned higher time penalties to the faster runners, forcing them to wait antsily behind the starting line for a period, while they watched their slower rivals disappear (gradually) into the distance.

"Limit man" George Carney of the St. Alphonsus Association was the first runner to set off, fully six minutes and forty-five seconds before Jimmy Henigan, the "scratch man"—the last runner allowed to start. McGrath assigned Kennedy a penalty of 3:30, meaning Carney got a three-and-a-half-minute head start on the Morningside captain, who in turn had a three-and-a-quarter-minute lead on speedy Henigan of the Dorchester club. Henigan was the reigning ten-mile champion of New England and the national junior cross-country champion. Most of the roughly thirty competitors received spots in the space between Carney and Kennedy.[55]

Six inches of snow had fallen on Boston just five days earlier, covering Braves Field and postponing the baseball team's home opener, but on this Saturday afternoon, the streets were dry and the sun was out. The temperature (about fifty-three degrees) was cool enough to be ideal for runners but warm enough to hint at spring, and thousands of spectators gathered along the route, the event's biggest crowd yet. "There were at least 2,000 persons jammed into the space between Union Park street and Harrison avenue at the start and finish of the race," the *American* reported. "Captain Driscoll of the East Dedham street station had forty policemen present to keep a clear path for the runners." And in a sign both of foot-race fever season and of Yankee establishment respect for this Irish-run event, the BAA's George Brown was on hand as an official timer.

For the first five miles, dodging autos along the cobblestoned streets, Carney and his St. Alphonsus teammate J. Madden "led a merry chase to the rest of the field," as the *Post* put it. "It did not take the other competitors long to gradually fill in the gap," but Carney and Madden still led "by a comfortable margin" at the first checkpoint, the corner of Columbia Road and Blue Hill Avenue. "At this point of the race neither Bill Kennedy nor Jimmy Henigan was given much consideration, Kennedy running in 12th place, while Henigan appeared almost hopelessly in the rear in 20th place."

On Blue Hill Avenue, the course started to slope downhill toward the halfway-point turnaround, and Kennedy, "the husky bricklayer," began to pick up steam. "Racing along with Tom Henigan, Kennedy ran almost stride for stride with the brother of Jimmy, and passed many of the runners until at Morton street he turned the corner in eighth place." Jimmy Henigan was still some distance behind, in seventeenth place.

Now the runners were struggling up the same hill they had just breezed down. "One by one they gradually began to fall back, which enabled both Kennedy and Henigan to get within striking distance of the leaders." Chuck Mellor was making steady progress too, despite the bruise on his thigh suffered during his freight-hopping journey.

"As the runners turned the corner at Blue Hill avenue and Columbia road, the final leg of the race, the pace was telling on Carney and Madden, the former appearing in such condition that it seemed only a question of time before he would have to quit the grind," noted the *Post*. "In the meantime Kennedy and Henigan were running like mad to catch the rapidly tiring field, and as they rounded this point Kennedy was in third place while Jimmy had caught some of his field and had come from 16th to 12th place."

Henigan pressed on up Columbia Road, passing one runner after another until he was in fourth place. Madden tired at last and fell behind. Mellor streaked by him and "dogged Henigan for a couple of miles and then dropped back, leaving Henigan to go after Carney and Kennedy," according to the *Herald*.

"Rounding the corner of Massachusetts avenue and Columbia road the race had finally sifted down to a battle between Kennedy, Carney and Henigan for the leading honors," noted the *Post*. Carney was still in first but flagging, and his many supporters in the crowd called out to him, trying to buck him up.

"Kennedy with a handkerchief wound round his head . . . showed surprising speed," the *Herald* reported. The seasoned plodder held back, reluctant to take the lead until Everett Square, about a mile and a half from the cathedral. Then he let loose with a burst of speed and leaped into first place—"passing Carney as if he were anchored," in the *Post*'s turn of phrase, as the new leader "set full sail for the finish."

But Henigan "did not allow any grass to grow under his feet. Realizing that he would have to get a hustle on if he hoped to overtake the two leaders, he set out full tilt. . . . Stride by stride he began to overcome the distance."

But there wasn't enough road left. "Kennedy was still running strong as a bull and had secured more than a 75-yard lead over Carney while the St. Alphonsus boy seemed to suddenly come to life and proved to be a factor in the race," impressing fans with his "wonderful grit" as he battled the two better runners.

The three turned, one by one, onto Harrison Avenue, the crowds thickening on either side, Driscoll's patrolmen keeping the sea parted. Kennedy had a clear view of the finish line. "Urged on by the crowd who were cheering him to the echo he let out another burst and crossed the finish line," according to the *Post,* "romp[ing] in an easy winner" and looking as if he could go another ten miles.

Following seventy-five or a hundred yards behind, Carney also received an ovation, as did Henigan, about the same distance in back of him. The crowd cheered again for Mellor in fourth and for the rest of the finishers. In a post-race ceremony, the Reverend William Finigan of the cathedral parish presented the first six runners with trophy cups. "I'm afraid I tipped off my real form," Bill told Sweeney. He needn't have worried, however. Most of the attention was focused on the local boy Henigan.

"The winner was the dark horse," declared the *Globe,* "but the real sensation . . . was Jimmy Henigan." Kennedy had covered the course in 53:58, but Henigan had done it in 51:07, breaking his own 1915 record, and winning the time prize for the third year in a row.

Nevertheless, said the *Post,* "the race gave a line on the possibilities of what the two outside runners—Kennedy of New York and Mellor of Chicago—may do in the big B.A.A. Marathon, next Thursday afternoon." The *Globe* posited that Kennedy "showed enough of his true form to demonstrate that he is in the best form of his career, though he hid his gray hairs with a knotted handkerchief."

Then again, what if running ten miles that hard just five days before the marathon was a bad idea? What if Kolehmainen had been wise to skip the Cathedral race?

That evening, Bostonians learned that police had raided a native German's home in suburban Melrose and confiscated a stash of rifles, pistols, ammunition, and dynamite fuses. The man was not arrested, and, strangely, there would be no follow-up in the news at any point afterwards, nor does there seem to be any surviving record that would illuminate this case, but on the day it was reported, the incident served as yet another reminder of the impending conflagration.[56]

Bill rented a room for the week at the Cathedral YMCA. Of course, he couldn't let his old Chicago pal go back to sleeping on the hard pool table downstairs. Just as Sid Hatch had spotted Bill his return fare in '15, so Bill now split his bed with the penniless Mellor—not an especially problematic arrangement for itinerant laborers raised in large families and accustomed to overcrowded flophouses. "I had a square room," Bill wrote later. "We doubled up in a single bed and our meals cost us 15 cents apiece. We had a loaf of stale bread we used to eat between times. . . . Porterhouse steaks and feather beds do not always make winners."[57]

On Monday, Bill started work on a building on Washington and Pleasant streets in the South End, not far from the Y. He would keep working right up until the eve of the marathon.

George Brown of the BAA kept busy over the last few days before the marathon, driving over the course, inspecting the roads, and making arrangements with civic and police officials in each town along the route. He made sure to relay the runners' concerns about the automobile traffic and exhaust that had been thickening every year. In the rural early portions of the course, plans were made to spray water over the dirt roads shortly before the race, in order to tamp down the dust clouds that the runners, cars, and bicycles would kick up otherwise. In the final urban mile, the Boston police agreed again to rope off the sidewalks along the last leg of the course, through the Back Bay.[58]

Most of the runners took practice spins on part of the route at some point that week. Kennedy and Mellor ran more than ten miles of it early Tuesday morning before work, two days before the big event. On Wednesday, Bill walked over part of the course with his new Morningside A.C. teammate Hans Schuster.[59]

It was also a week when war pressed closer. On Tuesday, naval officials reported sightings of mysterious aircraft near the Portsmouth Navy Yard, less than sixty miles away in southern New Hampshire.

The yard's commandant speculated that the Germans had established an airbase deep in the woods of the White Mountains, and the sheriff of neighboring Rochester responded by gathering an armed posse to comb the area for it. What might sound zany today was nothing to scoff at in April 1917, when no spy satellites circled overhead and such an installation theoretically could have remained hidden for some time. The good sheriff's efforts notwithstanding, if it appeared the Germans were casing the navy yard in Portsmouth for bombardment, then Bostonians had to worry that the next target would be their own Charlestown Navy Yard, where even then 4,500 welders, riveters, drillers, and other workers were outfitting six vessels for battle. Remember that the Kaiser's submarines may already have been prowling the waters outside Boston and other Atlantic ports. Indeed, that very evening brought news of a U-boat lurking off New York Harbor firing upon an American destroyer (one captained by a Rhode Island native), the torpedo missing by thirty yards.[60]

The encroaching swirl of threats reminded longtime marathon watcher Larry Sweeney of 1898, when, a few days before the race, "the country was plunged into a ferment over the impending war with Spain, which was declared April 21 of that year. In other years the race divided interest with the Chelsea fire, the San Francisco earthquake and the Titanic disaster, but notwithstanding the B.A.A. run attracted hundreds of thousands of spectators."[61]

"Inasmuch as April 19, Patriots' Day, was originally chosen as the day for running the fixture," Sweeney continued, "and as American history is full of important events that occurred in April, the Marathon race has ever attained its place, despite the important happenings that had to do with American destiny and American lives."[62]

But the most alarming news hit town the next day, Wednesday, April 18, the day before the marathon. That morning three Coast Guard stations on Cape Cod reported hearing the heavy firing of artillery guns in foggy Massachusetts Bay. The firing went on for about ten minutes and was estimated at just thirty miles from the entrance to Boston Harbor. (There were unconfirmed rumors of additional gunfire that night.) Strangely enough, the navy released a statement confirming the noise but admitting (or protesting) ignorance: "The department is without information as to the nature of the firing or whether warships were engaged." Nor was the incident ever fully explained. By the following day, navy officers were refusing to comment further. But their initial confirmation of the gunfire was enough for the *American* to scream atop its front page, "NAVAL BATTLE IN MASSACHUSETTS BAY." That was the most widely read headline in Boston that evening, and surely on many people's minds as they tried to get to sleep that rainy night, maybe fourteen hours before George Brown was scheduled to fire the starter's pistol in Ashland.[63]

At the stroke of midnight, a terrific rumble split the air in Boston's North Square. German attack? No, a group of motorcycle hobbyists embarking on a ride along Paul Revere's route to Lexington and Concord. It was an early start to the holiday festivities. As Sweeney predicted, the saboteur and submarine scares did nothing to limit turnout or enthusiasm on Patriots' Day 1917. If anything, the opposite. "This year, the interest in the race is fully as great as ever, despite the fact it divides attention with gigantic battles and U-boat raids almost at our own door yard," wrote John Moran in the *American*. "The indications are that close to half a million people will see the race at one spot or another along the twenty-five mile route."[64]

The rain stopped, the clouds parted, and as the sun rose on eastern Massachusetts, tricorne-hatted Minutemen fired a volley over the Battle Green in Lexington, where a "preparedness parade" was held. In Boston, the Sons of the American Revolution met at the Old South Meeting House. A costumed "Paul Revere" mounted a horse in North Square and set off for Lexington, accompanied by a National Guard cavalry unit, with Mayor Curley and former president Taft following in automobiles. Bands played "The Star-Spangled Banner" at the start of a ten-mile road race in Jamaica Plain that morning and

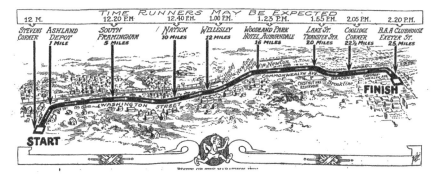

FIGURE 4. A *Boston Globe* cartoon map of the marathon course as it was in 1917.

later at Hibernian Hall in Roxbury, where a celebration marked the
first anniversary of the proclamation of the Irish Republic.[65]

Running gear in hand, Bill Kennedy and his fellow athletes trick-
led in to Boston's South Station soon after 8 a.m. George Brown of
the BAA spotted Bill in the crowd and delivered a message from his
brother: Joe hoped Bill could return to Pawtucket on the morrow,
Friday.

"I should love to go," replied Bill, "but I am going to win this race
today and I shall have other engagements."[66]

The runners boarded a special train that chugged out of the station
at about 9 a.m. and arrived at the Ashland Depot at 9:50. In Ashland's
town hall, doctors examined the entrants to make sure they were fit
to run twenty-five miles. A *Post* cartoonist imagined this process
to include whacking an impervious, smiling man in his washboard
belly with a mallet and proclaiming, "You are in fine condition." But
Kyronen wasn't laughing when doctors told him his condition was
just borderline. He would be allowed to enter the race only if he
promised to quit at any point if so advised. The docs felt he suffered
from an "athletic," or enlarged, heart. Hatch got the same diagnosis.[67]

Finally, at 11:55 a.m. that Thursday, April 19, a winnowed-down
total of forty-eight runners gathered behind the starting line at
Stevens Corner, about a mile west of the town center. Picture them,
Kennedy would write later: dozens of men "clad in shorts, augmented

by officials, friends and well-wishers, lined across a road, awaiting the report of a gun to send them on their way. With the Red Cross nurses, ambulance and doctors, it may remind you of a battlefield, were it not for the holiday spirit of the spectators and the colorful dress of the women." An idling motorcade stretched behind the runners, with hundreds of fans piled into open-air Tin Lizzies, Hupmobiles, Locomobiles, and other horseless carriages, ready to tag along with the official vehicles filled with BAA men, medical staff, state troopers, supporters from the various athletic clubs, and sportswriters for the city's nine daily newspapers. (Sweeney of the *Globe* sat in a White touring car, a step up from the bicycle his teenage self rode when following the first Boston Marathon in 1897.) The sun shone from high in the sky, and the roads, dampened in the previous night's rain, were rapidly drying.[68]

Bill again wore the white handkerchief, but today his head covering sported a patriotic twist: a small silken American flag, sewn on by the wife of a bricklayer buddy, the improbably named Johnny Brick. The flag itself was apparently a souvenir given to Bill by Governor Samuel McCall at some event that week, or sent to him. Perhaps the governor had remembered Bill from the Brockton Fair in October, or he'd read and appreciated Bill's sentiments ("We must repel the Finns") in the *Globe* the preceding Saturday. The ornament attracted the crowd's notice, and a youngster ran up to Bill and asked him where he got the flag. Spectators hushed up to hear Kennedy's response, delivered in his deep voice: "Governor McCall gave it to me, young fellow, and told me to bring it to Boston first."

"You bet you will," the boy shouted. "That flag is always first."[69]

The crowd erupted with approval, and the cheering continued as the town's church bells clanged to mark noon. Brown fired his starter's pistol. The runners were off.

✄

Prescott Dean jumped out into an early lead. The roar of the crowd was joined by the roar of the auto engines. Bugles sounded, blown by military recruiters working the roadsides. American flags strung from telegraph poles billowed in a strong east wind, which also blew in the marathoners' faces. The wind slowed their pace, but they pressed on, up and down the rural rolling hills, headed back east toward Ashland's town square and then Boston beyond. The surrounding motorcars churned up dust and stones and spewed clouds of exhaust, forcing runners and their bicycle attendants into a shifting slalom course.

Belying thermometer readings in the fifties, the now blazing sun made the afternoon feel fairly hot to the runners. Bill welcomed the warmth. Moreover, the cheering masses on either side of the Boston route were his favorite spectators of all. "The most appreciative and enthusiastic sportsmen and women that man has ever competed before," he called them. (Even though some rooters could be *overly* enthusiastic, reaching out to clap runners on the back in "Atta-boy!" fashion—not always a welcome gesture after miles of exertion.)[70]

But despite the conditions and Kennedy's confidence, it was the smart money pick, Kolehmainen, who overtook Dean for the lead within the first mile. The Finn led the pack as they curved past the Ashland Depot on their left, and he stayed out front as they crossed the Sudbury River. Heading into South Framingham, the leader saw the road was barred by a railroad crossing, but the passing train cleared the way before he reached the tracks. Three and a half miles and all his rivals behind him, Kolehmainen reached the first checkpoint at about 12:23 p.m. (almost three minutes behind the course record, owing to that easterly wind). Close on his heels, the BAA's Merchant was in second, with Schuster of Morningside third, followed by Hatch, Kennedy, then Mellor. "The automobiles became thicker" in Framingham, reported the *Herald,* "and the going was extremely difficult." Other fans cheered on the runners from a special spectator trolley, which clanged and clattered along the tracks that ran parallel to much of the course.[71]

By Natick—seven miles in after forty-four minutes—Kolehmainen was still in first, and "he moved like a piece of well-oiled machinery," scribbled Sweeney from his seat in the *Globe* car. The runners passed pretty Fisk Pond on their right. Kennedy had managed to move past Hatch into fourth place. But the three leaders were still fifty yards ahead. And Hatch as well as Kyronen were not far behind. Hatch worried Bill more than Kyronen did. Chicago's seasoned "old-timer" was surely playing a waiting game back there, conserving his energy, ready to pounce the moment Kolehmainen appeared to weaken. But Bill bet on beating Hatch at his own game. He kept his eye on the leaders.

Sure enough, on an easy ribbon of road between Natick and Wellesley, Bill detected a slight slackening on the part of the Finn in first. Merchant and Schuster failed to take advantage but instead slowed their own pace accordingly. This could be the moment. But not two-fifths of the race had been run. Was it too early? Or was Hatch even now making his move behind him? Kennedy had to decide in an instant: it was time. He began to pour on the speed.

Bill caught the leaders napping, as the *Post* put it. Before they knew what was happening, he passed the trio and opened up a 25-yard lead on them. The Irishman had decided to "set such a killing gait that either they or I would have to come to grief before we would reach the B.A.A. clubhouse," he would say later.[72] On another day, in another race, this might have seemed crazy. But today Bill was feeling good. Less than ten miles in, he was going for broke. Time would tell whether he'd chosen wisely.

No sooner had Bill taken the lead than the men heard a high-pitched wail. It was the siren song of hundreds of cheering young women lining the road ahead of them: Wellesley College, an eye-catching, if ear-splitting, landmark of the Boston route. The "college girls," as the era's newsmen called them, waved and screamed and sang their school anthem. They were overdressed by our modern standards, in long skirts and ruffled shirts or their white college sweaters, but many of them chose the brightest colors and flashiest patterns they could find. And with the energy of youth, the "throng of beauties" egged on the athletes as if at a Harvard pigskin tilt.[73]

But Bill had other things on his mind as he crested the hill of Central Street. His own clubmate Schuster, winner of the Bronx Marathon in February, had bolted ahead of Kolehmainen and Merchant, and now he was gaining on the bricklayer, making the latter's lead seem tenuous. So at first, when a young woman dashed into the street to sprint alongside Bill and place something in his hands, the front-runner was flustered. Then he registered that she was handing him a full-size American flag. He took the banner with a smile and a slight bow, and held it aloft for the next mile.

The sight of the Stars and Stripes caused a sensation along Bill's path: contrary to the forecast, a Yank was leading the pack! A thunder roll of wild applause carried Kennedy toward Wellesley Square. By now it was clear that something special was happening this Patriots' Day. "The crowds approached in number those which lined the course in the halcyon days of marathoning a decade ago," reported the *Boston Evening Transcript*—the days "when Longboat and Hayes and Fowler were heroes of the hour." And many onlookers recognized "Bricklayer Bill" Kennedy from previous races or from the press he'd earned since he first rode the rails to Boston in 1915. As Bill ran through the square, a clergyman from one of the nearby Protestant churches stepped into the street and said, almost in a whisper, "Good luck, Bill." The marathoner sensed those words came from the bottom of the minister's heart.[74]

Finally, Bill handed off the flag to his bicycle attendant, who in turn passed it to George Brown, riding along in his auto. With Schuster still nipping at his heels, Kennedy needed his full concentration. It was 1:02 p.m. Eleven miles down, fourteen to go.

As the men raced up Washington Street, the motorcars continued to dog them. "Never before have as many automobiles clogged the roads and endangered the runners," proclaimed the *Evening Transcript*. "At times the clouds of dust were so thick that the runners were enveloped in it." Even more of a nuisance were the young boys on bicycles—not the attendants but just joy-riding kids. Pedaling furiously, the knickers-clad youths zipped among the runners and automobiles, "reckless of their own personal safety [and disregarding] the rights of competitors, officials or newspapermen all along the route," the *Transcript* complained. Bill had to smile, though. Perhaps he recalled his own antics at age twelve, when the Knickerbocker marathon came through Port Chester. True, the kids on bikes could be "wild at times," he said later, but their cheers were so earnest, "you can't help loving them."[75]

Over the next quarter hour, Schuster stayed Kennedy's shadow. Would he sneak past, going on to beat Kennedy for the second time in two months? They were teammates now, and Schuster surely appreciated Kennedy's help thus far, but like any marathoner, the Swede was in it to win it. He had to be hoping Bill would lose steam the way Kolehmainen had earlier. Meanwhile, Kolehmainen himself was making a comeback. The Finn and the BAA's Merchant steadily eroded the Morningside men's lead until just five yards separated the pairs as they crossed the bridge over the Charles River into Newton Lower Falls. What's more, Kyronen, the forgotten Finn, was suddenly showing signs of life. He had passed Hatch to take the fifth position.

Just after the falls, the runners passed an eighteenth-century paper mill on their right. Then they took on a hill of underrated toughness, ascending more than fifty feet over a distance of more than half a mile. At the top, they approached a fork in the road, where giant signboards pointed right toward Beacon Street and left to stay on Washington and the course. Bill looked for the big Irish cop usually posted here. Every year, their eyes met, and if Bill wasn't doing well, the patrolman would look genuinely pained. Well, Bill wouldn't disappoint him this year. Once he spotted the officer, Bill straightened up somewhat, doing his best to appear fresh. The cop smiled, pleased to see his fellow Gael not only running strong but in the lead, and he let out a "Go on, Bill me bye" as Kennedy ran past, fourteen miles under his belt.[76]

The order remained Kennedy, Schuster, Kolehmainen, Merchant, and Kyronen at 1:27, as the leaders passed, on their left, the gables and wide front porches of the Woodland Park Hotel. Nestled between two golf courses, the resort hotel marked the sixteen-mile point. At that moment, the open-air motorcar carrying race manager George V.

Brown happened up alongside Bill, who couldn't help but overhear one of the other passengers asking Brown, "Can he make it?"

It was a fair question. Kennedy had taken the lead so early, and Schuster and the others had forced him to run so hard, that it was natural to wonder whether the gray-haired workman could sustain the pace. Brown paused, seeming to weigh his response, and Bill held his breath waiting to hear it.

Finally, Brown spoke: "He'll win."[77]

Bill's heart leaped, and he sped onward, staying in first at the next intersection. There the course makes a ninety-degree right turn onto Commonwealth Avenue. Schuster followed his club captain, "holding on," Sweeney wrote, "like grim death."

"Then," noted the *Post*, "came the difficult part of the course."

The nickname "Heartbreak Hill" wouldn't start to catch on until the 1930s, when then cub reporter Jerry Nason is widely credited with coining it. As early as 1916, however, an unbylined *Globe* article (probably penned by Sweeney) referred to the swath of Newton between Washington Street and Boston College as "the heartbreaking hills of Commonwealth av."[78] Since the course nadir at Newton Lower Falls, the men had traveled mostly uphill from a height of sixty feet above sea level to about one hundred. Now, over the next four miles, Kennedy and the rest needed to crest three peaks, the last being the highest, at 236 feet above sea level. That's not an insane climb, but it is about the last thing anyone wants to tackle after having run more than sixteen miles already. The final hill would be about twenty miles from the Ashland start. Twenty miles is what Amby Burfoot and others call "the Wall." It's the point at which the untrained marathoner runs out of carbohydrates, and even a trained athlete has exhausted his normal reserves.[79]

These hills pose a tough hurdle in the twenty-first century, when runners have the benefit of protein gel packs, frequent water stations along the route, their pick of highly engineered running shoes, and reams of research and training guidance at their fingertips. In Kennedy's day, a century ago, the pioneering plodders were more or less making it up as they went along. They wore hard, black (and therefore heat-absorbing), low-traction, unventilated leather shoes meant for bicycling, or possibly, in a few cases, flimsy canvas jobs intended for basketball. Even in the 1920s, recalled Jock Semple, "the chiropodist's station at the finish line in front of the Lenox Hotel looked like a butcher shop." The men were fortunate to have bicycle-riding attendants who could tote a limited supply of refreshments, but there were no official water stations on the route. And while the course was at least a mile shorter, it was dirt in the earlier portions and macadam later, both materials that generated voluminous dust clouds when subjected to the stampede of man and machine that was a contemporary marathon. Moreover, these athletes grew up hearing, and still often heard, that running too hard for too long would kill you, just like it did poor Pheidippides.[80]

Little wonder, then, that the era's experienced runners normally slowed to a *walk* when they hit the hills. Just the day before, under the heading "Where So Many Fail," the *Globe* expounded:

> The long Commonwealth-av hill in the Newtons is the one spot in the course that some of the newcomers fail to figure properly. When it is reached about 16 or 17 of the 25 miles have been covered and, when they strike the hill, most of the veterans shift from a jog to a fast walk. The long rise has killed off many an aspirant for a leading place in the B.A.A. classic, and walking up the hill well exemplifies the theory of a few seconds lost, much wind and all-round stamina saved.

But that was yesterday. This was race day, Patriots' Day 1917. There was too much at stake. Schuster and the Finns and Hatch and the rest were too close behind. Push came to shove at the hills, and Bill kept running. So did his rivals.

"The leading dozen men all appeared strong as they struck up the first incline," reported the *Post*. They passed Georgian revival mansions with big front yards, and stands of young copper beech trees, their branches yet bare. The trolley rumbled along to their left. Up the first hill they ran, climbing more than fifty feet along a curving 1,200-yard span of road, the Brae Burn Country Club on their right.

Merchant was the first to show pain. A cramp struck his leg, and he started swinging his fist downward, punching his thigh with every step. "He had made the fatal mistake of accepting the pace of such fleet men as Kolehmainen, Schuster and Kennedy," wrote Sweeney. After struggling over the first hill, the BAA's champion began to fall back. There followed a dip, then a quick speed bump of a hill, and next a gradually downward-sloping mile.

Meanwhile, Schuster was looking less and less "fleet" himself. He had stayed on Kennedy like an attack dog since Wellesley College, but the pace was taking its toll, and now he'd hit the Wall. Drooping, he fell out of his lockstep with the leader and began to lose ground.

The runners passed a cemetery on their right, followed by Bullough's Pond on their left. (Newton's present city hall would be built just to the right in 1932.) Then they tackled the second major hill, an eight-hundred-yard rise along about half a mile of road, plus another speed bump.

At this point, Hannes Kolehmainen had gained a new lease on life. If anything, he seemed to enjoy the hills, and it appeared he had been husbanding unguessed-at energy reserves all along. Certainly, breaking away from Merchant and gaining on Schuster boosted his confidence. He passed the fading Swede to take the number-two spot. On the sidewalks, knowledgeable fans likely nudged one another and pointed. Reporters in the autos raised their eyebrows and jotted notes. Gamblers on the trolley reached into their pockets or readied their palms for cash transfers. The much-vaunted Finn was on track to surmount Newton in second place. It was not for nothing, after all, that Kolehmainen had been one of the top two picks to win. This could be when the Olympic gold medalist retook the lead.

Still, Bill wasn't worried. At least not about Kolehmainen. What he did fear were cramps. His natural tendency was to lean forward while running uphill, which he'd found could make him cramp up at the wrong moment. So today, Bill ran the hills deliberately keeping his head well up and his chest out, while landing on his heel with a slightly higher stride. It might sound effortful, but his goal was to "run relaxed, take hills with a rolling stride as does a pacing horse."[81] So far this afternoon, this method had paid off. Now, after crossing the intersection with Centre Street and passing a few shops, Bill faced the final, "heartbreaking" hill. Officially Waban Hill, it was a ninety-foot climb up half a mile of road.

Here, Kyronen could have used some of the front-runner's advice. Cramps were precisely his problem at present. The Finn's coach was Pete Hegelman, veteran of the six-day walking races of the nineteenth century. "Stick to Kennedy," Hegelman shouted at Kyronen from his car. "Don't let him get away!"[82] Kyronen grimaced and clutched his stomach. He "struggled manfully," wrote Sweeney, and just managed to crest the hill, but then he ground to a halt. A car carrying one of the BAA's official physicians pulled over. The doctor ordered Kyronen to quit the race, as he had agreed to do before the start if his condition worsened. To Hegelman's consternation, Kyronen assented and hopped in for a ride to the clubhouse. Merchant, meanwhile, looked to be going to pieces, though the BAA man managed to stagger on.

As for Bill Kennedy, all his training in the hard Manhattan winter, his past Boston experiences, his strategizing—it was all bearing fruit. "Kennedy," wrote John Hallahan, the sportswriter from the *Herald,* "was not to be denied." The bricklayer seemed to breeze up the big hill as easily as he might cover level ground. "He had the speed and stamina and, instead of weakening, just romped away to a nice lead." By the time Bill crested the hill at Hammond Street, he had opened up a two-hundred-yard gap between himself and Kolehmainen in second.

There was yet another dip-and-speed-bump combo. Kennedy passed the Waban Hill Reservoir on his left. Then it was a steep, calf-hammering descent of half a mile. Over the bare branches on his right, he spotted the Gothic bell tower that heralded Boston College's arrival, a few years earlier, on the site of Amos Adams Lawrence's old farm. This year, Bill saw that the heavens-reaching tower had been joined by a Jesuit residence hall, squatter and less imposing but done in the same High Medieval style. Bill probably couldn't help but admire the stonework and compare it to that of the churches his father had built.

There might have been some wistfulness in his gaze, too, as he took in the growing Catholic university, the kind of school he might have attended had circumstances allowed. "One of my regrets in life was that I never had the opportunity to get an education," Kennedy wrote later. Then again, he added, "I have lived life and have never lost any sleep over it."[83]

The bellowing, suit-clad students lining the road—all men, nearly all Irish American, and many now bound for battle overseas—gave their elder an ovation as he ran by. Bill waved back while chatting easily with his bicycle attendant. The pair passed the Lawrence Basin (since filled in) of the Chestnut Hill Reservoir as they approached the bottom of the hill and crossed the border into Brighton.

"On reaching Lake street, Kennedy was running strong," reported the *Herald* of the race's official twenty-mile mark. "There was no apparent shortening of his stride." It was 1:54 p.m. On the mercifully flat segment of Comm. Ave. that followed, Kennedy ran calmly past the rolling green hills of the St. John Seminary grounds on his left, briefly on the outskirts of Boston proper.

Little did he know what was happening behind him. Not that Kolehmainen seemed to pose such a terrible threat. The Finn did make it to Lake Street still in second place, but fully a minute behind the leader. While to one reporter Kolehmainen seemed just as confident and full of wind as Kennedy, another thought he looked leg-sore and tired.

No, it was the new third-place runner who looked like trouble.

～～

Bill had never run against Clarence DeMar before. Calling to mind *The Natural,* DeMar had mysteriously taken a years-long break from marathoning after winning the Boston race in 1911 at age twenty-three and competing in the Olympics the following year. Why the early retirement? A doctor had told him he had a "weak heart," for one thing. For another, the devout Baptist was leery of the spotlight, ever conscious of the sin of pride. Moreover, he had intensely disliked his Olympic experience in Stockholm, where he bristled under the coaching he saw as unnecessary for someone who had won the Boston Marathon on his own. Not to mention that DeMar felt he was busy enough working at his printer's trade to support his mother and five younger siblings, while taking courses part-time at Harvard, and in his spare time serving as a Sunday school teacher and a Boy Scout leader.

Nevertheless, he couldn't give up running altogether. Somewhat under the radar, each year he entered two or three lower-profile races of five to twelve miles, and he usually felt good afterwards. Eventually, DeMar's prickly, defiant nature won out, and he decided to show that doctor how wrong he'd been.[84]

"DeMar has trained for this year's race even more conscientiously than he trained for any previous race," claimed the *Globe* the day before the 1917 Boston Marathon. "For a whole year he has devoted about every thought to again winning the race and breaking the record once more." Every night for several months, after his shift in a Dickensian printing shop—a hot, dark cellar, where pots of molten lead spewed poisonous fumes—DeMar ran seven and a half miles, northward from Boston to his family's house in Melrose. As race day came closer, he likely ran the distance both to and from work. And unlike Kennedy and many of the others, DeMar eschewed tobacco and alcohol all year round, not just for a few months before the big race. He was fit, he was still young, and he was on a mission. "DeMar is bent upon proving to the skeptics that he never was a 'has been!'"[85]

Earlier in the afternoon, DeMar had labored back in the ruck. He was checked in twenty-second place at South Framingham. But he had made steady progress, coolly picking off stragglers with every mile his feet put behind him. He'd clambered up to sixteenth place by Natick (seven miles from the start) and to eighth place by Wellesley (ten miles). At last among the elite, DeMar moved up only one place over the next six miles, but by that point he was "running faster and stronger than any other man in the race," wrote Sweeney. That was at

Woodland. Once he turned the corner onto Commonwealth Avenue, "DeMar apparently reveled in the hill-running." He passed the fading Kyronen, Schuster, and Merchant, and even slipped by the sturdy-plodding Hatch. DeMar was coming from behind just as inexorably as he had in 1911, when he advanced from fifteenth place in Natick to third at Woodland before going on to win.

Now, in 1917, DeMar was in third place once again. At Lake Street, he was two minutes behind Bill Kennedy but showed no signs of slowing down. And what Bill almost certainly did not know, as he embarked on the marathon's final leg, was this trivia tidbit: DeMar still held the speed record for that portion of the race. The last time he ran the race, the Melrose man went into overdrive *after* the hills. He pasted the competition over the final five miles, especially the two and a half from Coolidge Corner to the finish, which he covered in 14:13. With that feat, he demolished even the great Tom Longboat's record of 17:58. "Never before has, and it is doubtful if ever again will, a runner cover the last five miles of the B.A.A. marathon as fast as did DeMar," wrote Sweeney in 1911.[86] And indeed, DeMar's performance had not been matched in the intervening years.

In short, this final, critical length of road belonged to the surly scoutmaster.

⤳

Bill turned right onto Chestnut Hill Avenue, ran downslope to Cleveland Circle, and took a left onto Beacon Street, entering the town of Brookline, a thickly settled, largely upscale streetcar suburb jutting into Boston proper. From here on in, the roads were tar, and the way was lined with multi-story brick and stone residential and commercial buildings. "The crowd grew more dense," observed the *Post.* All the louder now, "the applause of the spectators seemed to fire the runners to greater effort." Bill started to increase his lead on Kolehmainen, but the latter responded with a speed burst, keeping Bill to his two-hundred-yard advantage. In turn, Kolehmainen tried to cut into the gap, but Bill picked up his own pace, just managing to stay the same distance out front, as if the two were positively charged magnets. DeMar, Schuster, and Hatch, in that order, trailed across the 150 yards behind Kolehmainen.

Bill was a few blocks from Washington Square when a joyous cacophony erupted up ahead on his right. He looked, listened, and smiled. It was a crew of bricklayers and plasterers working on an apartment building on the corner of Beacon and Tappan streets. The men had paused in their labors to give their brother "brickie" an unforgettable cheer: They were pounding bricks together, battering the air with a clatter of flinty claps that echoed off the other buildings and drowned out even the most enthusiastic palm-clapping of the crowd below. On top of that din, the workers lifted their voices in a full-throated chorus of encouragement as Bill ran by with a giant grin and a heart swollen with gratitude.

The relentless swirl of unofficial traffic reached new heights of chaos on Beacon Street. Kids on bikes zigged and zagged across the runners' path. The Brookline cops kept shooing them off the road, but the lads would simply dart down a side street, then reappear a block later.

Not every youngster was making trouble, though. Clarence Edwin Knibb was an eighteen-year-old Boy Scout from Belmont. He had volunteered as a bicycle attendant for one of the athletes who was now struggling well out of contention. Riding dutifully along with his charge nevertheless, Knibb suddenly noticed a runner sporting the BAA's unicorn emblem. It was Fred Merchant. He had fallen so far behind that he was out of sight of the referee monitoring the leaders. Not long before Coolidge Corner, Knibb saw Merchant slow to a halt and climb into an automobile, which sped off. Poor Merchant. Like Kyronen earlier, he was clearly quitting the race, too exhausted to continue. Young Knibb returned his focus to the task at hand. He had to be ready in case his own man should suffer a spell and require medical assistance, just like Kyronen or, apparently, Merchant, or any number of other runners who dropped out in pain. As a Scout, Knibb was prepared for such emergencies, being on track to earn his merit badges in first aid and lifesaving by the summer.[87]

No, this young man wouldn't be causing trouble for anyone.

Except Merchant.

Meanwhile, Bill Kennedy ran into a Coolidge Corner that was jammed with thousands of cheering spectators. Up on his left were the yellow Tudor gables and clock tower of the S. S. Pierce building. To his right, Bill spotted a familiar heavyset figure waving from the sidewalk. It was another bricklayer friend, Jack Nason. (Yes, a mason named Nason.) Jack, his wife, and their three children had left their triple-decker house across from St. Mary of the Assumption church and joined the holiday pilgrimage out of the Marsh, Brookline's working-class Irish enclave. The Nasons and their neighbors had strolled up Harvard Street to the Corner to mingle with a crowd that included many of their employers, everybody enjoying the festive atmosphere of the marathon. As Bill approached, Jack reached out and handed him a thermos of hot tea with sugar. "It sure hit the spot," Bill later wrote, "pepping me up for the last two miles."[88]

Bill passed the Coolidge Corner checkpoint at 2:11:14. Kolehmainen made it through next, with DeMar breathing down his neck. Almost instantly after the checkpoint, DeMar passed the Finn to take second place. Behind Kolehmainen followed Hatch, Schuster, and Mellor in succession. Merchant, having left the course, was not checked.

About two and a half miles of macadam separated Bill from the winner's laurels, if he could just hold off DeMar, the champion of 1911—not to mention the inexorable Hatch, who was now making a move on Kolehmainen. The men had been running down a rather steep drop, almost thirty yards, for the past mile. One final calf-punishing dip remained before they would reach level ground.

And it was on that decline that the journey's exertion caught up with Bill at last. When he hit the bottom of the hill, his legs and feet turned to stone. He felt tired, faint. His stride shortened. Meanwhile, DeMar and Hatch (now in third) were running like sprinters, on pace to overtake the flag bearer. Just like that, after all the miles Bill had led, the holy grail of his kind was about to slip from his grasp. Yet in his weakened state, all Bill could think about was quitting. As he put it later:

A Marathon isn't so much a test of a runner's muscular or lung endurance as it is a test of heart endurance—his grit, willingness to fight on when that something inside that no one has ever defined tells you that you ought to quit.

There is always a time in a distance race when you've run yourself out and your mind begins to say: "You're a darned fool for going on." Then is when the test comes. [You need to] get a hold on your mental strings, shut out those thoughts and forget that your better sense is telling you to do what hundreds of others have [done] and have not been disgraced [for it].[89]

So how would Bill get a hold on his mental strings this time? As he was squaring off in his head with the voice of his more sensible self, other voices started to penetrate the bricklayer's haze. Louder, external voices. Trying to tell him something urgent. Then he noticed Hallahan of the *Herald* shouting and waving his arms at Bill from the Grant motorcar he was riding in. Bill stared at the reporter's wildly waving arms. Then he looked down to find his own arms were "all tied up," the runner remembered later, wrapped across his chest. "I got them down and to working in no time."[90]

Once Bill resumed pumping his arms properly, he must have started the blood flowing back to his ears, because he began to listen to what Hallahan, the other reporters, the boys on bikes, and the fans had been yelling at him. It was something about Hatch. Hatch! Bill snapped to attention. The competitor whom Bill knew best and feared most was challenging DeMar for second place, clearly angling to take Bill down next. *That's* what they'd been telling him. Bill needed to get moving again. As if on cue, he reached Audubon Circle and crossed the border into Boston. For the first time all day, the road opened up before him as the Boston cops blocked all unofficial vehicles from the course. No more motoring gamblers or cycling preteens spinning dust into his face. Perhaps, too, this is when the sugar in Nason's tea kicked in.

Whatever the formula, it all acted as a tonic on the weary plodder. With a jolt, Bill recovered his senses, "regained some of his form and picked up," said Hallahan. Crossing the railroad bridge, Bill lengthened his lead on the neck-and-neck duo of Hatch and DeMar. From behind ropes, the Boston fans rooted for the man wearing Old Glory as he bore right, traversed the expanse of Governor (now Kenmore) Square, and ran down broad Commonwealth Avenue. Classy brownstones flashed by on the right, while a tree-lined mall ranged along the left—a narrow link in Frederick Law Olmsted's "Emerald Necklace." A cool breeze blew along Comm. Ave. "The wind was sweet to me," Bill would recall. Probably the hot tea was causing him to sweat more, making the breeze all the sweeter. (Modern scientists have confirmed this paradoxical cooling effect of hot beverages, long a folk wisdom staple.) Now Bill ran "harder than ever," wrote Sweeney.[91]

At the intersection with Massachusetts Avenue, Bill kept going straight. Recall that in those days, the course continued down Comm. Ave. for another four blocks before it turned right onto Exeter Street, crossed Boylston, and finished in front of the BAA clubhouse (site today of the Boston Public Library's 1972 Philip Johnson building). The crowds were so large, the BPD had detailed more than four hundred officers to hold them back behind the ropes strung alongside the mile and a half of the route that lay within city limits. These thousands of Bostonians waved flags and emptied their lungs for the grateful bricklayer. No runner "was ever accorded a greater reception" along the race's home stretch, wrote Hallahan.[92]

Spurred on, Kennedy widened the gap between himself and the hard-charging DeMar and Hatch to more than a minute. When the latter two reached Mass. Ave., Hatch finally passed DeMar. Behind them, Kolehmainen languished in fourth, the feared Finn firmly out of the running. And behind *him* was Chuck Mellor. In spite of his bruised leg, the Chicagoan had run a solid race, consistently in sixth or seventh place at nearly every checkpoint, and he'd earned his position of fifth going into the final mile.

So it must have been particularly galling to Mellor when he saw Fred Merchant sneak under a rope and rejoin the race ahead of him.

FIGURE 5. Crossing the finish line first in 1917. "Bill Kennedy used to object to having his picture taken when he finished," Clarence DeMar later wrote, "saying that his wife always remarked on how old he looked!"

Mellor distinctly remembered passing Merchant before Coolidge Corner, and he knew this was the first time he'd seen him since. Yet nobody else seemed to notice. Mellor ran like mad to catch up, but Merchant was running on a fresh set of legs after his lift in an auto.

All for naught, though. Merchant wouldn't deny Kennedy victory that day. Nor would Hatch, nor DeMar. Bill was too far ahead now, and he picked up new speed as he turned the corner onto Exeter Street and headed down the final few short blocks bisecting the Back Bay. "Cheered on," wrote Sweeney, "by the largest crowd that ever witnessed the finish of a Marathon run," Bill crossed Boylston Street and headed for the length of red yarn that was stretched across Exeter Street, the BAA clubhouse on his left and the Lenox Hotel on his right (see fig. 5).

Bill broke the thread with a wide grin plastered across his face. A thick layer of grime coated his body from head to foot. Since leaving Ashland two hours, twenty-eight minutes, and thirty-seven seconds before, he had lost eight pounds. But he had won the Boston Marathon. On the sidewalks, men roared and waved their hats in the air while women waved handkerchiefs. Rushing forward to greet him, one BAA official placed the traditional Greek laurel wreath on Bill's head while another covered his shoulders with a towel. Silver-haired BAA elders applauded from their perches in the windows of the elegant clubhouse. After acknowledging the cheers of the crowd, Bill was ushered into the building, where he immediately called for telegram blanks. He dashed off two identical messages—one for his father, the other for his wife. Ever mindful of his limited budget, the victor kept it short: "I won."[93]

The news flashed over the wires from coast to coast. Kennedy's triumph "was as popularly received as it was generally unexpected," said the *Post.* The story of an American's victory in "the American Marathon" made the front pages across the country, alongside reports of Allied victories in Europe. That had to be an encouraging combo. If a homegrown athlete could best the foreigners in a contest of physical prowess, and if "Over There" the German lines were already "crumbling," as some papers said, then perhaps this war would be won handily and our boys would be home by Christmas. Especially since, as Sweeney reported, the marathon winner was a "future United States soldier—for 'W.J.' intends shortly to enlist in the service."[94]

But before all that could happen, what about the rest of the marathon field? And what of Bill's recuperation and celebration in the BAA clubhouse? A couple of minutes after Bill broke the tape, Sid Hatch finished in 2:30:19. DeMar followed at 2:31:05. Kolehmainen was fourth. Merchant was fifth with Mellor right behind him, and the latter lodged a protest almost immediately, alleging that Merchant had hitched a ride. This sordid business would have to be sorted out later. Behind that pair came Schuster and then future (1919) BAA Marathon winner Carl Linder. The 1916 winner, Arthur Roth, finished twelfth. Moran of the *American* would joke about putting the family jewels in hock as a result of Roth's poor showing. (At least, we think it was a joke.)

Prescott Dean, the man who had jumped into the lead right off the starting line back in Ashland, now crossed the finish line in a dead faint, collapsing into the arms of a waiting policeman. Unfortunately, the cop miscalculated Dean's weight and/or momentum, and both men tumbled to the ground. The coincidence in Dean's starting *and* ending the race in dramatic fashion makes us wonder if he was one of the era's "collapsing acts" that Bill wrote of, reasonably skilled runners who were nonetheless guilty of the misdemeanor of embellishment for maximum crowd sympathy or admiration.[95]

Inside the clubhouse, Bill was relaxing after a shower and a rubdown. On the table next to his was Willie Kyronen. That's where Kyronen's trainer Pete Hegelman found his charge after the latter had dropped out on the final Newton hill. As Bill recounted the reunion: "Pete came over to Willie, bawling him out with 'I told you to stick to Kennedy. Why did you quit?' Looking up at him, Willie says, 'Yah, you say stick to Kennedy but my belly he say quit, and when my belly say quit, I quit.'"[96]

As he replayed the race in his mind, Bill remembered the lad in Ashland who had encouraged him with the shout "That flag is always first!" just before the crack of the starter's pistol. "I would give anything to see that kid," Bill told A.J. Rooney, a sportswriter from the *Traveler.* "All the way I thought of what that youngster said and will never forget his words as long as I live."[97]

"Many persons appealed to Kennedy for the flag he wore on his head," wrote Rooney, "but he would not part with it. He will wear it again next year, if he runs." The *Globe*'s Sweeney, however, wrote that Bill was holding on to the "perspiration-laden handkerchief" for a different reason: "William J. allowed that he would always keep the shirt, pants and shoes he wore in the race, but the oddly patriotic head covering would be presented to the donor," Mrs. Brick.

Meanwhile, Hatch wasn't broken up about being second best for the day. "I would rather have Kennedy win than anyone else," he told the *Journal.* "Naturally, I expected to win, but there is some satisfaction in having a friend finish first. I just couldn't go any faster and that's about all there is to it."

The time came for the awards ceremony. Runners, trainers, BAA members, and reporters crammed into the cherry-finished banquet hall on the second floor of the opulent Gilded Age clubhouse. Clouds of cigar smoke wafted up to the bronze-finished heavy beamed ceiling, the tobacco staining the cream and green wallpaper as it rose. Bill appeared to be "in grand trim" as he addressed the crowd, according to the *Herald*. "Besides winning the race, Kennedy made another Marathon record yesterday," the *Globe* reported. "He made the most glittering speech of acceptance ever heard during the presentation of prizes." Though none of the papers published Bill's remarks in their entirety, several did run excerpts.[98]

"I am the happiest man in Boston," Bill began.

> I had a hunch all along that I would win the big B.A.A. Marathon, and now that I have won, everybody can realize just how I feel. To begin with let me thank the people of Boston and the officials of the B.A.A. for the treatment that I have received in the race. I have run in Marathons all over the country . . . but never was I treated better or raced in a better conducted race than the Boston race.

Bill added that he had "never found a warmer, more cordial citizenship" than he encountered in Boston, that the handling of the event was "magnificent," and finally, that he "would rather win the Boston event than any five [other] Marathons."

Vice President Edward E. Babb presented Bill with the handsome first-place trophy—a large silver cup with two handles. According to Sweeney, Babb quipped:

> "We hear, Bill, that you are going to celebrate your victory. Now you have a chance," indicating the use for which the prize is intended, other than for ornamental purposes.
>
> "I sure would like to," rejoined the victor, "but I notice that the decorations that hang from the top are clusters of grapes and not blossoms of hops. You know beer is my speed." And everybody joined in the laughter.

Sweeney summed up the feeling in the room: "He has claimed St Louis, Chicago and New York as his 'last hailing port,' but 'Bill' can hang up his hat right here and call it home, if he wants to. The brick-laying fraternity of Boston and its vicinity would be quite happy to refer to 'Bill' as 'Mr Kennedy of Boston,' and so would all livers [*sic*] of clean living, manly, patriotic athletes."

That patriotism was key to the impression Bricklayer Bill Kennedy made on the Boston sporting crowd of his day, and consequently to his persistent popularity in the coming decades. When he donned that flag bandana, he tapped into the zeitgeist not only of that moment in time but also of that place—a proud but nerve-wracked city that needed a win on a grand stage. Sweeney reminded readers that Bill

> stated long before yesterday's race that this was the year for American runners to show their mettle. He was enthusiastically patriotic when he allowed himself to be quoted as saying that Americans should endeavor this year, above all others, to prove to the world that America is supreme in all branches of endeavor.... He warned other American runners that despite kindly feelings for all alien athletes, they must needs be repelled in the greatest of all Marathon races, if only for the moral effect.

Sure enough, Bill "carried Old Glory to one of the most popular victories achieved in this or any other country." And he punctuated his win by re-vealing his plans to enlist in the military, despite being over the draft age.

But Bill Kennedy was not the only prizewinner that day, nor even the only American in the top ranks. Both Sid Hatch and Clarence DeMar had joined him in besting Kolehmainen and the rest of the multinational competition, and both would also enlist. "Aside from the pride that must surely have swelled the heaving breasts of the trio of panting Americans as they concluded the great race from Ashland to Boston," Sweeney wrote, "theirs was a striking exemplification of the ruggedness of our American long-distance leaders."[99]

Besides being Americans and future soldiers, the trio shared some-thing else in common: "Not one of the first three finishers was thought of so well before the race as some of the others in the field," said the

Herald's Hallahan. That underdog story dovetailed with the hopes of a nation about to start punching above its weight. For despite its industrial output, America was, to an extent hard to remember today, a rural nation with a strong isolationist tradition. These were the early stages of its emergence as a world power. The massive mobilization for war hadn't truly begun, and the fear was real that in jumping into the fray among the mighty empires of Europe, the Yanks would find themselves in over their heads. So it must have heartened the home crowd to learn that a handful of underrated upstarts could beat the odds in the big race.

Kennedy and Hatch were remarked upon for another reason: they were "old." That is to say, thirty-three. "Both Kennedy and Hatch are two of the oldest marathoners competing today," wrote Jack Kelleher in the *Journal,* "which bears out the claim that it doesn't matter how long a distance runner has pegged away at the game." Hatch "demonstrated that he is the most consistent marathoner of all time," wrote Kelleher, who earlier that week had added a year to Hatch's age and reported he might retire soon.[100]

Some of the papers inadvertently exaggerated Bill's age as well. Blame the typhoid that prematurely grayed his hair and lined his face, not to mention a life on the road. The *Globe* and *Post* reported that Bill was thirty-five (the age that entered the unofficial public record ever after). The *Boston Daily Advertiser* upped him to thirty-eight, and the *American* claimed he was "just ducking the forty-mile stone." The *Globe* was correct, nevertheless, when it stated that "Bill Kennedy is the oldest runner that ever led a field" in the BAA grind. He was in fact the first Boston Marathon winner over thirty, a half decade older than the previous oldest winner (Édouard Fabre, twenty-eight in 1915), and at least a decade older than the rest, most of whom had been in their early twenties or even teens.[101]

"The lesson here stuck with [Clarence] DeMar," writes marathon historian Tom Derderian. "High mileage works and age is not a handicap." In his comeback at age twenty-nine, the returning 1911 champion had surprised fans with a "sterling effort," wrote Hallahan, and his third-place finish wouldn't deter him from competing again.

"If these two old fellows improve with age," DeMar said to Sweeney, nodding at Kennedy and Hatch, "why isn't there a chance of a young fellow like myself emulating their example?'" (And so it was borne out that DeMar would enter the race pretty much annually throughout the next quarter century, winning it another six times, to become the event's all-time most prolific champion. As to the doctor who'd warned him in 1911 that his heart was weak, DeMar later said, "I read in the papers a few years later where he dropped dead of heart trouble. I always felt he was listening to his own heart instead of mine.")[102]

Then there was the hoariest of the day's runners by far. The *Post* devoted this paragraph to the Boston Marathon's first well-known *unofficial* participant:

> Long after the 35 scorers in the B.A.A. event had passed the mark—4 hours, 11 minutes, to be exact—aged Peter Foley, carrying his 61 years with the freshness and elasticity of youth, trotted up Exeter street, gazing defiantly at the B.A.A. clubhouse, which was then housing the officials who had turned down his entry blank, and on to a private dressing room to don his street clothes and go to his home supremely happy.[103]

After the awards banquet, the reporters hopped into their White touring cars and other automobiles and rushed to Newspaper Row to type up and file their stories. That evening, the race was talked about at Patriots' Day parties all over town, from a fireworks show at Braves Field to a "war rally" at the Boston Arena.

And after several months of self-denial, Bill almost certainly celebrated, as Babb had hinted, indulging in beer (in whatever vessel), a victory cigar, and his first late night in some time. Eventually, he must have gone to bed. After all, he had to get up early for another day on the job, laying brick.

✎

The next morning, presumably leaving his "fine big silver trophy" sitting in his shabby YMCA room, Bill walked through the drizzle to his building site in the South End (see fig. 6).[104] But he did not return to anonymity when he arrived at work at seven or eight a.m. He was greeted by the applause of his colleagues and the flashbulbs and queries of a contingent of newspapermen. The *Traveler* reported:

> Before he raised his trowel from the mortar bucket he was given a great reception by his fellow workmen. All shook hands with him and each said: "I knew you would finish first." Kennedy, who is a modest fellow, did not say any more than he did yesterday after the race. He thanked his fellow workmen for their kind words and the encouragement they gave him prior to the race. He told them he might try again next year.[105]

Moran of the *American* marveled that "bashful Bill" was "back on the job this morning, just as if he wasn't the most famous athlete in the country." But after all, the reporter stressed, Bill's primary duty was to see that his family "grab their three squares per diem."[106]

"It's great to win the Marathon," Bill told Moran, "but it doesn't buy any steaks, or potatoes or onions these days. And there's Mrs. Kennedy and the two little Kennedys out there in Chicago."[107]

That wasn't to downplay his accomplishment, Bill added. "This race was the crowning achievement of my life," he said. "Four times I have tried to land first honors and on three occasions I failed. Yesterday I came through. Words would fail to adequately express the sensation I experienced when I felt sure that none other than I had passed between the standards that marked the finish line."[108]

Atypically, a reporter came from the *Boston Evening Transcript*, a staid broadsheet geared to the city's old money Yankees. The *Transcript* carried hardly any sports coverage to speak of, but something about Bill's story seemed to fire the imagination of at least one of its writers. The front-page piece began by quoting the late John Boyle O'Reilly, the nineteenth-century Irish revolutionary who had escaped from an Australian penal colony to settle in Boston, where he became a respected poet, editor, and, appropriately, co-founder of the BAA.[109]

> The Boston poet of an earlier generation who wrote "The dreamer lives forever, but the toiler dies in a day," never heard of William Kennedy, sturdy descendant of that poet's own race . . .

BILL KENNEDY, MARATHON VIC-TOR, RIGHT BACK ON HIS JOB AS BRICKLAYER.

Here, and Kennedy, yesterday hero of 150,000 Marathon spectators, as he appears today. Bill is a bricklayer and was at work on a Pleasant street building this morning, just as though he wasn't the most famous man in the land.

FIGURE 6. From the *Boston American,* April 20, 1917.

In the early afternoon of yesterday, beneath the rays of a warm April sun, "Bill" Kennedy toiled twenty-five miles over the heart-breaking hills between Ashland and Boston, amid the gas exhausts and blinding dust of an endless stream of motor cars, and through a maze of small boys on bicycles, and broke the tape a winner in the twenty-first annual American Marathon of the Boston Athletic Association. A "toiler for a day," to be sure. But [by morning Bill] was practicing his other profession, going about his business with that same calmness of spirit which marked the two hours and twenty-eight odd minutes he spent on the Ashland-Boston road yesterday. And bricklayers will admit that their day's labor can properly be classed as "toil."

Thus "Bill" Kennedy belies the poet's words. For, if we take into consideration the winner's own words this morning, as he chatted with his fellow workers on the job, he looks forward to a long and rosy future. . . .

"Will I try it again? Of course, I will. Caffrey won it twice, didn't he? So why shouldn't I go in next year and win again? And I'm going to hide these gray hairs again with that little flag that did the trick yesterday. And he'll be a wonder who beats that flag to the tape."

Kennedy is a remarkable specimen of manhood. The gray hairs to which he referred were very noticeable beneath the little flag, and his years are written in the lines of his face. But his physical condition, both before and after the long grind, amazed the physicians. He lost eight pounds in this race, a very normal decrease when the heat of the day is considered. He has no mock modesty; he was quite willing to talk about the big event of his life. He was sincerely and outwardly elated over the outcome; most of all for the happiness it will bring to his wife and two children at home, and his father in Portchester, N.Y.[110]

The bricklayers toiled for a time, but before long the drizzle turned to rain, and the men stopped work for the day. That had to be a relief to Bill, no matter how remarkable a specimen he might have been. He took the opportunity to wander up Washington Street to Newspaper Row to finish his conversation with "Spargo" of the *Traveler*. (Sports columnists in those days often used pen names; Spargo's true identity has been lost.) Bill hadn't a chance to speak long with the *Traveler* writer back at the building site. Now, perhaps because he was well past the initial adrenaline rush of victory, and away from the audience of his brother brickies to boot, Bill spoke more quietly and philosophically than he had earlier.

"Kennedy seems to have bumped around the earth in a way that has given him a keen appreciation of human nature in its various phases, and is keen enough mentally to absorb a lot of knowledge that doesn't come in books" was Spargo's assessment.[111] When the columnist asked how he felt after the race, Bill responded: "Well, I was pretty tired. I've heard a lot of the boys say they weren't when they have won or finished in other years, but any time you hear anyone make that statement you can bet he's pulling off a little bravado stuff. There isn't a man living can run 25 miles as fast as he can and not be tired."

It was here that Bill revealed his inner battle on Beacon Street, when he had hit his own Wall, his legs felt heavy, and he had begun thinking seriously of quitting the race. This is when he spoke of shutting out those negative thoughts and getting a hold on one's mental strings, of how a marathon is less a test of a man's lung endurance than it is "a test of heart endurance—his grit, willingness to fight on." But, he added, marathons don't only take place on the road:

> The greatest example of the truth of what I've just said . . . is the
> case of a married man with a family and making $12 or $14 a week.
> Many a time that man realizes he is on the toughest Marathon
> in this life, but the right fellow never quits. He goes on trying his
> best when his better judgment tells him he's up against it. I know,
> believe me, for I've been over those jumps myself.

Meanwhile, the prize for fifth place was in limbo. That same rainy Friday, the race's referee, Colonel George Billings—a week shy of retirement as head of the BAA's athletic committee—had the sad task of investigating the charges against Merchant, leveled by both Mellor and Schuster. Clarence Knibb, the Boy Scout, showed Billings the spot where he had seen Merchant get into the automobile. Merchant and his trainer—one Harry Potter—ridiculed the youngster's assertion and stuck to their story that Merchant had run the whole way. But at an inquiry that Friday afternoon, more and more evidence came to light. Two other runners' bicycle attendants were certain they had passed Merchant and not seen him again. Newspapermen stationed between Coolidge Corner and the finish never saw him either. Finally, a Boston motorcycle cop had seen Merchant walk through the crowd on the Comm. Ave. Mall and slip under the rope and back onto the course near the Patrick A. Collins memorial. Indeed, nobody supported Fred Merchant and Harry Potter's version of events but Fred Merchant and Harry Potter.

In the end, Billings had to disqualify Merchant from the race and award fifth prize to Mellor (as well as sixth to Schuster and so on). Furthermore, reported the *Globe,* Merchant would probably be asked to return his unicorn emblem. On top of that, he would have to meet with a committee of the New England chapter of the Amateur Athletic Union, who would quite likely bar him from further amateur competition.[112]

And as for Potter, he faced expulsion from Hogwarts.

All kidding aside, the incident generated some possibly unfair remarks aimed at Potter, who was, of course, not an adolescent English wizard but in fact an aging American Indian marathoner. The commentary came, alas, from Bill's pal Arthur Duffey. The *Post* columnist seemed to be giving voice to Merchant's quondam supporters who were struggling to understand how the local boy, who had been looked upon so favorably before the race, had gone so far astray.

> Just whatever possessed Merchant to undertake such a plan is problematic with both athletic followers and B.A.A. officials. His many friends have been trying to find a reason for the local plugger resorting to such tactics but they are unable to do so. But whatever may be said there is no question that Merchant was ill advised in the race. It is also reasonable to presume that had Merchant been in his right senses he would never have tried to get away with such tactics. After a runner has something like 20 miles over the dusty roads his mental balance is not what

it should be and no doubt he foolishly listened to the remarks of his
would-be advisers.[113]

Sure, it is possible that Potter suggested Merchant cheat, but it is
unclear why Duffey would leap to this conclusion, and given the era's
regressive racial attitudes, it's unfortunate that Duffey would make
such an assumption about the relative virtue of the white runner and
his Indian trainer.

In any event, Duffey shared an additional speculation that seems
a great deal more solid: "The officials will be on the alert more than
ever in any future contest."

Would that it were so, for Bill's sake. The Merchant scandal—the
first such in two decades of the marathon—didn't really affect Bill,
who finished in first, well ahead of the cheater. Notwithstanding Duffey's sensible call for improved checking afterward, the next time one
of Bill's rivals was suspected of cheating, Bill would be in a position
closer to Mellor's, only he wouldn't be as fortunate as Mellor in the
outcome, and there would be a lot more at stake.

But right now, Bill deserved to enjoy his victory in the nation's
premier marathon. It was a win twenty years in the making, and he
had earned it against a stellar field. Tallying his rivals' career honors,
Bill had bested seven Olympians, including a four-time gold medalist
(Kolehmainen), a silver medalist (Hatch), a bronze medalist (DeMar),
and four who were also Boston Marathon winners (DeMar, Roth,
Linder, and Mellor). (If you're keeping score, the one non-medaling,
non-Boston-winning Olympian was Schuster, who had topped Bill in
the Bronx County Marathon in February.) Plus, Bill had given the city
of Boston something to cheer about after its month of war jitters.[114]

Bill celebrated with Chuck Mellor that Saturday, the last night of
their stay in Boston. They started in the afternoon at a saloon in Pie
(or Pi) Alley, one of the city's oldest streets. Technically a private way,
Pie Alley was a shortcut northward from the Newspaper Row end of

Washington Street over to Boston's old City Hall, and it was lined with bars and eateries. At peak times, these almost literal holes in the wall were jammed with off-duty or lunch-breaking printers, teamsters, lawyers, cops, students, bankers—in short, Bostonians (at least male ones) from all walks of life. The mutton pie and mugs of ale served by the Bell in Hand (founded in 1795) and other establishments drew a range of sorts to the alley, said one contemporary *Globe* writer, from a "bibulous riff-raff of no particular identity" to "young men of wealth and fashion."[115]

On another day, Bill might have been lumped in with the unidentified "riff-raff." But this was the Saturday after he'd won the Boston Marathon. Bill's picture had been in just about every paper in town for the past forty-eight hours. Almost as soon as he and Mellor walked into the joint, heads turned and elbows nudged. The athletes made their way to the bar and each put down a nickel—about the last they could spare—to order the round of beer that would give them free rein at the lunch buffet. This was "the cheapest way to eat," Bill wrote later, adding that while he and Mellor had won first and fifth prize in the marathon, "we couldn't eat those cups, nor cash them in and remain amateurs."[116] As they waited for their brew, one big man in a business suit finally took it upon himself to approach the runners. The man put directly to Bill the question that the other patrons had been whispering to one another.

"Are you Kennedy, the winner of the marathon?" asked the gentleman, who introduced himself as Edward Geary. Bill responded in the affirmative. "Come up and join my party," Geary urged.

"As Chuck and I were rather short on cash," Bill recalled, "we gladly complied."[117]

Geary turned out to be one of five junior partners in the stockbrokerage firm Hornblower & Weeks. "Mr. Geary has charge of the banking department and is one of the alert and energetic young men of State street," the *Herald* wrote of him in 1906. In Geary's tale, we see barriers tumbling at the turn of the twentieth century. Born in Ireland, Geary had lived in South Boston most of his life and had started his career as a lowly clerk. Ultimately, he and another Irish-man, James Phelan, impressed their boss, John W. Weeks—a former Republican congressman—so much that he elevated them to partner status in spite of their "race" and party. (Phelan was active in Demo-cratic politics.)[118]

At the Pie Alley saloon that night, Geary was apparently the alpha male of his group, which probably consisted of State Street colleagues and/or fellow members of the Elks, of which he was a division chief. It seems clear that Geary bought at least one round for the runners and encouraged his pals to do the same. In the course of the conviv-iality, Geary asked Kennedy, "I read where you have two daughters out in [Chicago], is that correct?" Bill confirmed the fact, and Geary opened his wallet. "Here is a small present from me."[119]

At that, Geary "gave me two 10-dollar bills, one for each [daugh-ter]," Bill recalled. In one stroke, the stockbroker had about doubled Bill's bricklaying wages for that week. "Boy, I could have kissed him. A lucky thing, though, he didn't give a third for myself, or I would have automatically become a professional for accepting money."[120] That's what Bill wrote in a letter to Hallahan fifteen years later. After an addi-tional thirty-plus years passed, however, Bill thought that "possibly I *should* have been declared a professional as he revealed more of the evening: "Later on we all adjourned to the Elks Club, where the winner was introduced to the crowd in a speech by this gentleman [Geary]."[121] On Somerset Street, just a couple of blocks away from the Alley, the Boston Lodge (no. 10) of the Benevolent and Protective Order of Elks seemed to be the upwardly mobile ethnics' answer to the city's more traditional fraternal organizations, such as the Freemasons, where at the time Catholics were neither welcomed by the resident old-stock Yankees nor even allowed to tread by their own pope. By contrast, the Boston Elks' membership rolls were packed with mostly Irish sur-names, plus a scattering of Jewish and Italian names.[122]

The toasting continued. And what happened next was no sur-prise for a gathering of a tribe that had made their way in a new land by pooling their resources and helping one another out. Like the

Celtic chieftains of legend who gave generous gifts of gold to their
champions, the men of Lodge 10 sought to show this Kennedy their
thanks for a victory in which they could all share as both Irishmen
and Americans. As Bill recalled, "Geary passed the hat around, and
dumped the contents on my table, considerably more than expenses
had been."[123]

The incident, and Bill's retelling of it, illustrates the tension inherent in amateur athletics in that period. Back then, nearly every athlete
not wearing baseball or boxing gloves was an "amateur," expected to
abide by a code that brooked no form of remuneration. The Amateur
Athletic Union, which ruled this world with an iron fist, was rooted
in upper-class notions of the purpose of sport, but its hard stance
on money was ill-suited to the blue-collar competitor. Notice that
from beginning to end of this anecdote, Bill recalled his impromptu
pub crawl with the Elks in terms of its financial implications. It was
because he was "short on cash" that he readily agreed to drink with
Geary and company in the first place. Now he was leaving the lodge
with more in his pockets than he had walked in with. Should Bill,
then, be considered a "professional" going forward? If so, what about
Clarence DeMar? As marathon chronicler Tom Derderian points
out, DeMar picked up sponsorships in the 1920s, appearing in print
ads as a pitchman for running shoes. He was almost certainly com-
pensated for that. As why shouldn't he have been? DeMar had a large
family to support.[124]

The matter of "expenses" is important here. Uncommonly, the
Morningside A.C. had paid for Bill's train fare to Boston, which was
permitted, but did the club cover his lost wages on travel and race
days? Unlikely. And then Bill seemed to be on his own for accommodations, as he secured one of the cheapest rooms imaginable, in
the dormitory-style housing of the Cathedral YMCA. Moreover, he
split what meager living quarters he did have with Mellor, doing a
good turn for another, less fortunate runner—someone in the position Bill himself had been in just two years earlier. Working on the
South End building for three full days and likely two half days—he

took Thursday off to run the marathon; Friday's rain forced an early whistle; and four-hour Saturdays were standard—Bill made no more than $22.40. Out of that, he had to pay for his room (probably fifty cents a night) and board (fifteen cents per meal) at the Y—so roughly six bucks. The train back to New York would set him back another fin. Not to mention that his eventual trip home to Chicago would cost $18.75. And speaking of Chicago, remember Bill had to set aside the lion's share of his earnings to send back to his wife and two kids in the Midwest.

And that was just one of the many, many races Bill traveled to over the course of four decades. Thanks to Geary and the Elks, Bill broke even on this one trip. But did that make him a "professional?" Did Bill and his fellow plodders make a living from such rare, sporadic gifts? Not remotely. Did they even come out ahead over the course of their athletic "careers"? Did competitive running pay for itself? Of course not. Bill likely spoke for Mellor, DeMar, Hatch, and the rest of the marathoning fraternity when he wrote:

> Many women have spoken enviously to my wife of the money her husband must make by running. Yet in many cases not even expenses are paid, and that in every case, the writer lost from two to five days' pay as a bricklayer to take part in an out-of-town race. . . . Knowing my way around [I] can truthfully say, that any amateur athlete is a lucky man to have folding money in his pocket after he returns home from an out-of-town athletic event.[125]

All of which was beside the point. For these men, running the marathon was its own reward. They were driven to compete, but they also loved the experience—the exhilaration of the finish, the camaraderie of the road, and, as Bill wrote, the runner's true prize: "the memories of the wonderful people I have had the honor and good fortune to meet." The Elks were counted among these people. Bill would remember Geary's gesture for the rest of his life, writing, "His name and face are impressed in my heart." (Albeit his name was impressed in corrupted form: Bill repeatedly recalled Edward Geary's first name as "Edwin.")[126]

The sportswriters too were counted among the friends Bill had made. And indeed, that Saturday night Bill stopped in to say his good-byes to Sweeney and the *Globe* staff. He had lost Mellor somewhere along the way, and after the many toasts to his health, Bill appeared "joyful and fit as a fiddler," Sweeney wrote. "Bill is a character, original and attractive, and a fine, modest winner to boot. Good luck to him."[127]

The next morning, Bill climbed onto the train to New York and settled into a "plush" seat. As the marshes, beaches, and small towns of coastal Rhode Island and Connecticut flashed past his window, Bill possibly thought about plans for a hundred-mile race, an idea that he and Sid Hatch had, well, hatched and discussed that week. (The pair dropped this ambitious plan as the post-Boston glow wore off and other tasks occupied them.) He may have thought, too, about how and when he would enlist in the military, now that he had conquered Finland. But first, Bill looked forward to a return visit to Port Chester to see his father and show off his trophy to old friends, as well as to a hero's welcome in Harlem, where the Morningside club planned a dinner for their captain. Much like aged Peter Foley, Bricklayer Bill Kennedy was heading home supremely happy.

5
OVER THERE

Bill quickly found out that volunteering for Uncle Sam was not going to be as simple as waltzing into a recruiting office and being handed a rifle, particularly not for a skilled laborer in his thirties. Along with many Americans in that spring of 1917—not having thus far paid enormously close attention to the deepening catastrophe that was the trench war in Europe—Bill was all of a sudden swept up in romantic visions of battle. The U.S. government's war planners, however, were mindful of what had happened in Britain during its own honeymoon phase of the conflict. With no draft early on, 2.6 million men rushed to enlist in combat, and the military accepted them without any regard to their unique talents and experience. That left gaping holes in the nation's manufacturing workforce and leadership network at a time when both were critical.

To forestall such a fate here, the Wilson administration reluctantly adopted the Selective Service System. The embrace of compulsory conscription did not come naturally to a people bred from liberty-loving pioneer stock, long isolated by two expansive oceans, and raised on George Washington's warnings against foreign entanglements. But

Germany's submarine attacks and plotting in Mexico had engendered a new sense of crisis, and rather than succumb to fear, Americans preferred to respond with positive action. (Not all of this action was exactly positive: a widespread campaign of repression against German Americans would culminate the following year in the lynching of Robert Prager outside St. Louis. The mob who killed him didn't know that Prager had attempted to enlist in the U.S. Navy but been rejected for medical reasons, nor did they realize that many German immigrants had fled their homeland because they despised the Kaiser and Prussian militarism.)

The purpose of the Selective Service, then, was to allocate America's manpower in a rational way. The war effort would be massive, requiring not only fighters but also the engineers, purchasers, radio technicians, typists, horsemen, cooks, medics, and ambulance drivers, among others, who would support them. Moreover, farmers, ranchers, butchers, and the like were needed on the home front to produce food for these fighting men; gun makers, sewing machine operators, and other factory workers were needed to arm, clothe, and otherwise supply them; and railroad workers and merchant sailors were needed to transport all of those goods. And almost before anything else, carpenters, plumbers, electricians, and bricklayers like Bill Kennedy were needed to build the bases where hundreds of thousands of soldiers would be trained before heading overseas. Under the new Selective Service System, such essential workers, however brave or well intentioned, wouldn't be allowed to go storming to the front.[1]

On June 5, 1917, the system was launched with bunting-lined parades and speeches in every town. Ten million American men aged twenty-one to thirty came forward to register with local draft boards. (More than 4.7 million eventually served in the armed forces.)[2]

Bill Kennedy, though over the draft age, tried to sign up with the army engineering outfits in New York and Missouri. Both rejected him. The army's vetters likely took a pass for the same reason the Illinois A.C. had refused to support Bill's Boston bid in 1915. His gray hair and lined face made it hard to ignore his advanced age, at least relative to that of most prospective doughboys.

But what about everything he'd told the press in April about how he planned to enlist? Would that turn out to sound like so much smoke-blowing? No, Bill couldn't give up on the military just yet. But for the moment, he'd have to take a supporting role in the war. On the Fourth of July, the bricklayer rode the train back to Boston. Navy installations on the South Shore just outside the city offered plenty of jobs in the war effort. And Bill picked an appropriately patriotic day for his return. He celebrated the holiday with a run—a ten-mile road race sponsored by the Ancient Order of Hibernians (AOH) in North Cambridge. (Living in that neighborhood then, and quite possibly enjoying the day's festivities, was four-year-old Thomas P. "Tip" O'Neill Jr., who would grow up to be speaker of the U.S. House of Representatives.) Bill claimed third prize, behind winner Jimmy Henigan and an up-and-coming middle-distance runner named Fred Faller. Carl Linder finished fourth.[3]

That evening, the bricklayer found lodgings in Quincy. The next day he started a job helping to build a new training camp annex at the Hingham Naval Ammunition Depot. Bill and fellow workers put up seventeen barracks as well as a hospital, guardhouse, storehouse, and office. The men were among the 200,000 construction workers hustling that summer to construct thirty-two cantonments nationwide. It was all part of America's scramble to mobilize its underprepared military, which at that time wasn't remotely the world's biggest, nor even in the top ten, nor even by some measures in the top twenty.[4]

The Hingham annex opened in mid-August. "Blue jackets are in camp from nearly every State, more arriving each day," reported the *Globe*. As many as five hundred naval recruits at a time filled the camp. If all went according to plan, those men would soon be under sail on the North Atlantic, with orders to hunt down and destroy the feared German U-boats.[5]

After completing the annex, Bill stayed on in Quincy for the rest of the summer and fall. There he continued "working for the

Government," reported his union newsletter with censorship-enforced vagueness. First, it seems he took a job "in Hingham," at the ammunition depot itself, perhaps loading matériel or guarding it. (Many extra watchmen were hired that year to prevent German sabotage; the armory held "enough TNT to blow Boston off the map," a local photographer wrote.)[6]

Then in early October, Bill was surely one of the 2,800 union bricklayers, carpenters, plumbers, electricians, ironworkers, steam shovel operators, and "dredgemen" hired to transform a Quincy swamp into a Brobdingnagian shipyard. The planned Squantum Victory Plant would assemble a fleet of the great destroyers with which the navy aimed to sweep the piratical German U-boat menace from the seas, as the contemporary press put it. Working ten-hour shifts, seven days a week, Bill and other craftsmen and laborers erected a veritable small city with astonishing speed. Within a few weeks, the compound sprouted not only the warehouses and workshops essential to shipbuilding but also the shipbuilders' bunkhouses, a restaurant, a police and fire station, a hospital, utility plants, a movie house, and an "Italian general store," among other buildings. Construction began, too, on the enormous steelwork structure in which the destroyers would be built, and on the giant launch slips that would see the big boats off.

"The work now going on at Quincy is the most important that the country is undertaking today," a Shipping Board official told the *Globe*. "The destroyer is absolutely essential to the safe conduct of our troops and supplies across the seas and is practically the only guarantee against the U-boats." Hence the rush; the contractor planned to finish by February.[7]

A patriotic spirit ran through all the workmen at the huge plant, claimed a *Globe* report, in part prompted by posted "propaganda" proclaiming: "This work is more than a construction job. IT IS OUR CHANCE TO HELP WIN THE WAR. Our work must be done in the same spirit as the work of our friends, brothers, sons who will fight our battles. This plant is being built to guard their lives. A delay on our part may mean death to them."[8]

That would strike a chord with Bill Kennedy. His brothers were wearing khaki already. Joe shipped out on Bastille Day with an army engineering regiment bound for France. Paul had joined the Connecticut National Guard in 1915 and his unit was activated upon U.S. entry into the war; he too would land in France before long. So of course Bill wanted to help the cause. But the reminders of their service also reminded him that his younger brothers were showing him up. The lads represented the first generation of their family with the opportunity to fight for America. Their grandfather Joseph had landed in Boston during the famine and was too old to serve by the time the Civil War broke out, while his son L.J. was too young. The Spanish-American War came and went when Bill, Joe, and Paul were still boys. Now that the Kennedys' moment had arrived, Joe and Paul were "Over There" or en route, while Bill was working in the back of the house. He knew the shipyard project was important to the war effort, but it didn't truly scratch his itch to serve.[9]

A long line of horse-drawn carriages, about thirty in all, delivered a procession of dignitaries to the soggy Brockton Fairgrounds on October 5. Despite torrents of rain, 25,000 fairgoers greeted Governor Samuel McCall and his guests—officers of all ranks from the armies of Britain, France, Canada, and the United States. Underneath their smart dress uniforms, some bore battle scars; one British subaltern wore his arm in a sling and carried three bullets in his body. A cannon boomed as the governor made his entrance, escorted by marching detachments from the Charlestown Navy Yard and the State Guard. A sixty-piece brass band at the front of the parade and a hundred-piece band at the back played the "Marseillaise" and "Rule, Britannia!" Gertrude Van Deinse, nationally known soprano, sang "The Star-Spangled Banner" while the men doffed their hats. President Wilson telegraphed his regrets.

The 1917 Brockton Fair was the most patriotic that anyone could recall. Largely a horse show, the fair also featured a hot air balloon ascent and a water-pumping contest between antique fire engines. And almost as soon as the governor arrived, along came the marathon.

The course started back in Boston, in front of the BAA clubhouse, and wound its way south, down the cobblestoned streets of Mattapan and over the hilly dirt roads of Milton, finishing up with one lap around the fairgrounds' track. Just twenty-one hardy souls braved the rain and mud that day. The race pitted Bill Kennedy, Clarence DeMar, Arthur Roth, Willie Kyronen, and Hans Schuster against one another in a bit of a rematch of their April run *to* Boston. The men battled a headwind most of the way. Leaving the city, Kyronen ran out front. The defending Brockton champ kept glancing back at Kennedy as the latter steadily gained ground. As they crested the Blue Hills, Kyronen suffered yet another stomach cramp, and Kennedy took the lead. Only this time the bricklayer had miscalculated. The climb wore him out, and he fell behind Linder on the way down. Then DeMar made his move, "running like a deer." From back in eighth place, the printer overtook one rival after another until he'd put Linder in his rearview. Kyronen, reviving, rode hard on his heels, but to no avail. At the fairgrounds, "a mighty cheer went up." DeMar finished first.[10]

A loudspeaker crackled with an announcement: The winner's time of 2:24:04 broke the course record, which DeMar himself had set in 1911, the last time he'd run the Brockton Fair Marathon. The crowd "rent the air with cheers" again. Coming after his respectable return to the long-distance game in April, DeMar seemed to be regaining his status as a leading "marathonist," as the *Globe* called him.[11]

Kennedy finished fifth, behind Linder and Roth. At the awards ceremony, Bill took in the spectacle on and around the fairgrounds— the soldiers and sailors in formation, the bands, the Allied officers, the flags and bunting. Uniformed Joe and Paul must have leaped to mind. And as the runners chewed the fat while washing up after the race, they could hardly have avoided talk of the war and volunteering. A couple of the guys could sympathize with Bill. The army had rejected Linder—one of the day's prizewinners, in a 25-mile race—for flat feet. "Comment is hardly necessary" on that decision, remarked the *Globe.* DeMar, too, was rebuffed when examined by the navy. Years spent in the dark print shop, squinting at beds of type, had diminished his distance vision.[12]

But by next spring DeMar would be drafted into the army (albeit after an extra examination because of "runner's heart"). And some of the other regulars were already absent from Brockton's marathon. Single, unemployed 23-year-old Chuck Mellor had registered for the draft in June and would soon be "Over There." Sid Hatch was in basic training and would see action by the spring as an army foot messenger. Meanwhile, from the ten-miler ranks, Jimmy Henigan— Kennedy's competitor in the Cathedral race in April and the AOH run on Independence Day—prepared to run his last fixture that fall before enlisting. "Smiling Jimmy," too, would soon travel to Europe with the army.[13]

Bill Kennedy took the train back to Quincy that evening no closer to his goal of enlisting, but no less determined.

⤜⤛

Fate intervened with a stroke of luck—or better, a lucky strike. In early November, the Building Trades Council of Greater Boston and Quincy called a general strike to protest conditions at Squantum as well as at the Watertown Arsenal. Bill and virtually every other union tradesman employed on a military site in the Boston area walked off the job.

Despite their patriotism, the workers remained adamant that their employers—Aberthaw Construction Company, in the case of Squantum—should not use the war as an excuse to steamroll their concerns or roll back the gains they had fought for in recent decades. It was a gutsy move given the timing: the Bolsheviks had just taken power in Russia, exacerbating the American establishment's already zealous opposition to any form of worker organization. In Quincy, that opposition ran the gamut from histrionic to threatening. One company official moaned: "If we can't arouse our workmen to their sense of duty and encourage them to go back to work we might as

well stop trying to fight this war now. It would be better for this country to stop building destroyers and other ships and save the money
to buy off the German Emperor." Meanwhile, at the gates of the yard,
army troops stood with bayonets fixed to their rifles.[14]

Gutsy, but not anomalous that year. Work stoppages hit shipyards
in California, too—and everywhere in between. The Boston strike
was one of 4,450 in 1917, the most ever in the United States. The
strife swept Montana copper mines, midwestern munitions factories,
and logging grounds in the South and the Pacific Northwest. Hard-
pressed by rapid mechanization, increasingly ruthless efficiency standards, and other destabilizing workplace changes in their lifetimes,
the nation's workingmen leaped at the jobs offered by wartime con-
tracts but also recoiled at the breakneck pace of work and the hard
anti-union stance of many employers.[15]

For Bill Kennedy, the resulting week of downtime was an opportunity to regroup and relaunch his effort to join the army. (This
might seem an awkward or dichotomous position for the striking
bricklayer—delaying a military project while seeking to enlist in the
military—but remember that Bill's and his colleagues' beef was with
the contractor, not the government.) Going over the heads of the New
York and Missouri regiments that had denied him, Bill sent a letter
of appeal directly to the War Department in Washington, perhaps
mentioning his loyal work completing the Hingham cantonment,
and probably adding a line about his recent victory in the "American
marathon" in Boston (a victory over younger men, and Olympians
to boot).

It worked. By late November the army accepted him and assigned
Private Kennedy to the 23rd Engineers, a road-building regiment.
" 'Bricklayer William' is well beyond the draft age, but he will not be
known as a 'slacker,' " declared his union newsletter. With "the well
wishes of a host of Bostonians" ringing in his ears, Bill took the train
to Missouri to report at Jefferson Barracks, just south of St. Louis.
It was a brief chance to hug and kiss Jessie, six-year-old Louise, and
four-year-old Juanita good-bye before heading back east for training.

The family likely shared a Thanksgiving dinner, carefully planned to adapt to wartime rations on meat and wheat. They had to wonder if it might be their last holiday together. But "[Kennnedy's] wife backed him up in his resolve to enter the service," noted Sweeney at the *Globe*.[16]

Turning to his next goals, "Kennedy writes that he is going to get into good shape and try for the position of cross-country coach when he gets to the 23d's camp at Annapolis Junction, Md.," Sweeney added. More important, the gray-haired, well-traveled brickie wouldn't be content to stay a buck private. "One resolve in the letter is characteristic of the veteran Marathoner. It is: 'I am going to try just as hard to be a good soldier and win the stripes of a sergeant as I did to win the B.A.A. Marathon, and I feel I will be successful.'"[17]

～∞⁓

Enlisting when he did, at the end of November 1917, Bill had to break his commitment to run the Yonkers Marathon. He didn't miss much. Most of the familiar names were absent from what the *New York Times* called a "mediocre field." The winner, Joseph Georgio, had never run a marathon before and finished in 2:59:51. The real hero was Chicago's Frank Gillespie, who showed up twenty-five minutes late and still managed to come in sixth. "It is doubtful if such a poor field has competed" in the event before, the *Times* complained.[18]

That was the last running of the Yonkers Marathon's first iteration. The Yonkers Marathon familiar to readers in the twenty-first century began in 1934. The race Georgio won in 1917 was the last of a string, sponsored by the Mercury A.C., that began with the nation's first, forgotten marathon boom, following Johnny Hayes's Olympic triumph in 1908.

It was the same story in Brockton, where Bill had run what turned out to be his last race before enlisting. The Brockton Fair Marathon was suspended during the war and never came back. The All-Western Marathon in St. Louis—the first marathon Bill ran or won—was also discontinued during the war, never to return. Hatch, Kennedy,

DeMar, and so many other of the day's leading marathoners were headed "Over There," and with them went the star power that had drawn crowds to the big foot races. Not to mention that those crowds were about to lose much of their young male sporting element. Count the first batch of annual city marathons, indeed the Hayes marathon boom itself, among the lesser-mourned casualties of the Great War. Some races, like Yonkers's, wouldn't return for decades, while others, like Brockton's, disappeared for good.[19]

Only Boston would soldier on.

A few days shy of his thirty-fourth birthday, Kennedy arrived at Annapolis Junction, which soon changed its name to Camp Meade. Bill's and other recruits' first task: build Camp Meade. Or at least triple it in size, to accommodate the thousands of servicemen still arriving. Kennedy's regiment, five thousand strong, was made up of civil engineers and technical college graduates as well as tradesmen, laborers, and contractors. All were put to work on the expansion. The hasty erection of tented platforms barely kept pace with the influx of recruits, and a hard winter blew cold winds and waves of disease through the overcrowded camp: flu, scarlet fever, measles, mumps, meningitis, and other nasty ailments. Those engineers not in quarantine were kept busy building roads and bridges to support the heavy traffic of new troops and goods from the closest railroad stations and major towns. Bill and his Company I built a plank road to Belvoir, Maryland.

When not engaged in construction work, the men drilled like soldiers, including rifle practice, albeit with rifles left over from the Spanish-American War—and an insufficient number of rifles at that; the firearms had to be rotated among the companies.

Despite these hardships, morale was high at Camp Meade. Officers organized trips to Laurel for dances and movies, and sightseeing excursions to Washington, DC. The musicians in the regiment formed a band, playing dented secondhand trumpets and tubas. And most of all, the men played sports. Each company had its baseball nine. A ring was built to hold frequent boxing and wrestling matches. Organized athletics provided a "legitimate form of entertainment," as one officer of the 23rd wrote, during the men's precious free time.[20]

Indeed, sports were a key part of the routine at all cantonments. The young men who flooded into camp were pumped up for the "Great Adventure," as Teddy Roosevelt billed the war. The typical camp had "an atmosphere like that of a college campus on the eve of a big game," said one observer. Secretary of War Newton Baker, along with groups such as the Young Men's Christian Association, wanted that rambunctious energy channeled in the right direction. Football games, swim meets, relay races, often with cash prizes to the winning company or battalion—such contests tapped the natural aggression and competitive spirit of these youthful warriors-to-be. And it kept them out of trouble, away from what Baker called "unwholesome diversions and recreations." You know: brothels.[21]

So the YMCA and like-minded "welfare organizations" held equipment drives, collecting used balls, gloves, and bats to donate to the troops. Newspapers covered the results of inter-company games, and crowds from neighboring towns came to root the boys on. For some recruits fresh off the farm, the military provided their first experience with organized sports, period—never mind niche sports like distance running. (Clarence DeMar wrote that "a soldier from Georgia, hearing I was a runner, asked me how far I could run. When I told him 25 miles he had me branded as a colossal liar for several days.")[22] At Camp Meade, Bill Kennedy, by dint of his age and experience, most likely pitched in with this effort by coaching runners, as he had intended.

Moreover, Bill received some good news on New Year's Eve: the AAU named him to its All-America track and field team for the year just ending, 1917. As the "Marathon leader," the name of William J. Kennedy would be published in *Spalding's Official Athletic Almanac*, the bible of the sporting world in that era.[23]

Then tragedy struck. On February 5, 1918, the *Tuscania*, the ship carrying the 23rd Engineers to the front, was torpedoed and sunk by a German submarine off the Irish coast. So Kennedy's friends and family learned the next day.

Except that the 23rd Engineers weren't on that ship. "Kennedy, Marathon Man, Not Aboard Tuscania," clarified the *New York Tribune* on February 10. The scare was somehow fitting for a man who seemed to have nine lives. It was in fact the 20th Engineers who sailed on the *Tuscania*. Most of those 2,400 troops were rescued. Still, two hundred died. They were the first mass casualties of America's involvement in the war.

A week later, still at Camp Meade, Bill was promoted to the rank of sergeant. In late March, he and the bulk of the regiment boarded trains for Jersey City. On March 29, the men streamed up gangways to the twin-stacked USS *George Washington* as it docked at Hoboken. The following afternoon, the ship steamed out of the harbor to join a convoy about to cross the Atlantic. The untested soldiers were bound for the muddy, mortar-pocked fields of France.

In the meantime, the elders of the BAA determined "that the entire energy and resources of this organization should be concentrated upon the task of winning the war." To that end, the club took the unprecedented step of turning the 1918 edition of the marathon into a servicemen's relay race. The athletes were enlistees in training at Camp Devens, Naval Cadet School, and other army and navy units. The fact was, not enough "full-fledged Marathon runners" were around to field a typical race, Sweeney pointed out. The other reason for the change was "the omnipresent horror that a 'slacker' might emerge as the victor of the historic classic."[24]

And so a novelty marathon. Fourteen teams of ten men each covered the course, passing along a baton containing an appeal to buy Liberty bonds: "We will fight to the limit; we expect you to buy to the limit." With a 10:30 a.m. start time on a cold day, there were far fewer spectators than usual. "The crowds along the course, smaller than heretofore, maybe, seemingly, could not comprehend it all," wrote Sweeney. "The significance of the thing was beyond instant absorption."[25]

Camp Devens won in 2:24:53, the first man across the finish line being a cross-country runner originally from Cork, Ireland, named James Sullivan—no relation to the AAU official.

⌇

The *George Washington* landed at Brest, France, at noon on April 13, 1918. For all his travels, this was Bill Kennedy's first time abroad. His unit, I Company (alternately known as Company I, or India Company), was dispatched to the ancient river port of Saint-Nazaire, where Caesar supposedly built a fleet of ships, and Druids once performed rituals at the prehistoric dolmen still standing in the center of town. With the imminent arrival of more American troops, horses, trucks, and equipment, this small town was about to get a whole lot bigger, and the men of Company I got to work on a new dam and pipeline that would boost the Saint-Nazaire water supply. That project suffered a series of setbacks, and a sergeant matching Bill's description was heard by a superior to gripe "that the dam would never be finished, and if it was finished it would never have any water in it, and if it had any water in it, it would get out."[26]

The 23rd Engineers were just a few thousand of the more than 1.8 million American soldiers who would land in France that year. And not a moment too soon. With newly Bolshevik Russia dropping out of the war, 750,000 German troops were freed up to reinforce the Kaiser's redoubts on the Western Front. The Germans hurriedly launched a series of vicious attacks intended to bring the war to a close before the Yanks had time to gather their forces. In May and June 1918, several U.S. Army and Marine units provided key support to the French in repelling "the Hun's" advance at the Marne River. In particular, nearly two thousand Americans died defending the region of Château-Thierry, sixty miles from Paris. At the cost of their lives they bought time for the lion's share of their fellow doughboys to cross the Atlantic and disembark in ports like Saint-Nazaire, where

Bill and the other engineers prepared to accommodate these vast American Expeditionary Forces (AEF), as the U.S. troops in Europe were called.

Even in the midst of supervising the dam-building project, Bill had running on the brain. The *Boston Globe* reported that Bill "applied for the position of athletic director at one of the Army camps overseas," where the YMCA as well as the Knights of Columbus and the Jewish Welfare Board kept up their campaign to protect the boys' moral fiber.[27]

At least Bill's outfit didn't lack for female company: an English fox terrier bitch attached herself to Company I in Brest, and she became the unit's mascot, tagging along with them to Saint-Nazaire. The little dog was a familiar and welcome sight around camp, forever at the cook's heels before meals. When "Taps" was bugled, she would leap into a bunk and nestle against the neck of one or another of the burly construction workers. And on visits to town, she grew jealous when any Frenchwomen approached her engineers—the terrier studiously ignored the *mesdemoiselles* or refused to let them pet her. One Bob Fife primarily took care of her, but we can detect the hand of Bill Kennedy in the mascot's moniker, whether he had in mind his sister or his first true love among the Herbert girls: the dog's name was Nellie.[28]

Finally, in late August and early September, I Company (with Nellie in tow) headed northeast, as nearly the entire spread-out regiment converged on the Toul sector. There the men would do the work they'd left their families in the States to do: build, repair, and maintain roads and bridges. The highways built by the 23rd were crucial to the movement of troops, artillery, supplies, and intelligence as the AEF prepared for its first independent offensive, the Saint-Mihiel drive. Led by General John "Black Jack" Pershing, half a million American soldiers, accompanied by 100,000 French, sought to oust the Germans from the strategic town of Saint-Mihiel that September. Kennedy's company, plus a supporting wagon unit, camped at Belleville-sur-Meuse, just seven miles from the front line. In the middle of a

week-long rainstorm, the men opened up two quarries and worked
night and day on a road through Griscourt, despite a constant stream
of troops and trucks, and on a road to Pont-à-Mousson, which was
under fire from the Germans' outer forts at Metz. Poor Nellie hated
the sound of artillery explosions. "When she heard the crack of the
big guns anywhere close she would hunt the nearest hole and almost
bury herself there," wrote one of Bill's fellow road builders in Company I.

"Traffic conditions made road work exceptionally difficult," according to an official history of the 23rd. "A cut-off and bridge were con-
structed by continuous work for three days, relieving traffic from the
line of direct artillery fire." Frustrating for the engineers and skilled
tradesmen like Kennedy, there was little time for perfectionism. The
conditions "precluded any refinements in road building at this time,"
wrote the regiment's chronicler. "The principal work done consisted in
ditching, the scraping off of mud—a considerable item—the building
up of the shoulders, the patching of holes and ruts, and widening."[29]

Writing for *Stars and Stripes,* the military's newspaper, Sergeant
Alexander Woollcott (on hiatus from his job as drama critic of the
New York Times) described both the challenges the engineers faced
and the importance of their labors:

> Parts of those roads, never perfect in their prime, had not known the
> turn of a wheel in four long years. All through those years they had
> been scraped and torn and upheaved by exploding shells. From the ear-
> ly months of the war they had been broken and sliced by the network of
> French and German trenches. . . .
>
> Add to all this the fact that for many days and nights these roads had
> been steadily pelted with summer rain.
>
> The men assigned to the repair of the roads moved at the heels of the
> infantry. The work was under way at dawn on September 12. . . .
>
> As for material, what better could you ask than the crumbling stone
> [of] poor ruined villages . . .
>
> With such tools and such stuff, the holes were filled, the detours
> were made, the [booby traps] nullified. Then, in a twinkling, new roads,
> wonderful roads, came into being. Caught in a traffic jam and looking

wistfully over the rolling countryside, you might say to yourself, "If only there were a short cut 'cross country through all that wire and trench tangle," and jogging that way again next morning, you would find a road cut through, a well-trod road already black with patient, slow-moving traffic. . . .

It was all the difference between confidence and wild hope, between perfected plans and impromptu action. Here was none of the fearful strain and tension which marked those critical July hours. . . . Here, instead, was an enormous good humor, and it was worth getting tied up for a few hours just for the overwhelming evidence that the Yankee is that most terribly offensive weapon, the soldier who fights with a grin.[30]

Despite what often seemed like chaos on the ground, the planning of Pershing and his inner circle paid off: the Germans abandoned Saint-Mihiel and retreated. The 23rd Engineers got to work rebuilding roads in the devastated no-man's-land. Kennedy was struck by the sight of gaunt, bearded soldiers recently freed from German prison camps. "I was going into Metz," he recalled, "and they were straggling along the road looking for an allied camp to get something to eat."[31]

Company I was preparing for the next offensive, and some overzealous reconnaissance details even found themselves behind German lines on November 11, 1918, when they learned that the armistice had been signed. The war was over.

⌣

Bill later heard about the Pheidippidean feats of his old Chicago pal and rival Sid Hatch, whose 132nd Regiment had fought hard to dislodge the Germans from positions along the Meuse River just twelve miles upstream from I Company's camp. On October 11, Hatch was carrying a message through the dense and hilly Bois de Chaume forest. The woods hid enemy trenches, machine-gun nests, and artillery guns. Hatch ran with care but speed up and over the shady steep ridges. Then the thunder burst of a German shell blew him off his feet. He landed in a hole, stunned. When he recovered his senses, Hatch crawled out of the hole (either a foxhole or a crater) and continued on to battalion headquarters to deliver his message. Upon completing his mission, Hatch helped carry ammunition rather than seek medical attention. Eventually, a sergeant noticed he was wounded and ordered him to the aid tent.

Just one example of Hatch's bravery, this incident earned him the French Croix de Guerre with palm leaf. He and his fellow foot messengers proved as valuable in the chaos of this first modern war as were their antecedents in ancient times.

"Although telephones, visual signals, and pigeons were used in maintaining liaison, runners gave better service than all other means together," wrote one officer documenting the battle at Bois de Chaume. "The messengers of the 132nd maintained communications at the risk of their lives." Hatch was one of several who "distinguished themselves repeatedly."[32]

Once the shooting stopped, the engineers' workload only grew. Throughout November and December, the men of the 23rd rebuilt bombed-out roads, filled in trenches, blew up tank barriers, and tore down machine-gun nests. Bill and the rest of Company I charted and destroyed unexploded land mines across the battle-scarred landscape. They filled in shell craters and dismantled the Germans' road camouflage (clever messes of burlap tarpaulin and tree branches that had stymied spy planes). And they resurfaced and patched forty-five miles of highway that the army of occupation trod en route to Germany.[33]

Meanwhile, President Wilson landed at Brest aboard the *George Washington*, the same transport ship that had brought Kennedy and the 23rd Engineers to France. Troops cheered and bands played "The Star-Spangled Banner" when the commander in chief disembarked. Offering prayers of gratitude, French villagers knelt alongside the railway as "Wilson the Just" rode to Paris, where 2 million people greeted him with more fanfare.[34]

That same week, most of Bill's regiment came to camp at their new headquarters at Souilly. It was a pleasant reunion, as many of the engineers hadn't seen one another since they were all aboard the *George Washington* in April. With the president on the Continent gearing up for peace talks at Versailles, and progress now visible on their road repairs, the tension and urgency of wartime dissipated, and a sense of relief and even celebration permeated the camp. Someone secured a printing press and resumed publication of the 23rd's often jocular newsletter *The Highwayman.* The regiment's basketball league started a new season, and Bill's company, "The Big Eye," made it to the championship game, only to fall to Company A by the now laughably low score of 36–26. Company I also fielded a jazz band, though a few of their instruments were dinged up in a late-night fender bender.[35]

The builders had some reason to feel good when they thought back on their performance over the previous months. "Under the worst conditions of roads, torn and destroyed by four years including the hardest fighting of the war around Verdun, and with insufficient engineering equipment, in the midst of a traffic amounting to 12,000 vehicles a day by one point, supplying a rapidly advancing army," wrote an army historian, "the 23rd Engineers established the record that no blockage of traffic in the whole of the large army area was due to the failure on the part of any road to carry its proper traffic." And they made it through "the fuss" intact. "Exposed to heavy enemy fire and bombing, the escape from any death casualties directly traceable to shellfire or gas was a remarkable fact." Many of the men earned promotions or other honors. Even Nellie received two gold service chevrons and a campaign badge, which she wore on her khaki collar.[36]

But the men also paused to reflect on the losses suffered by less fortunate units. More than 53,000 American troops were killed in combat, more than 204,000 wounded. That was a far cry below the 1.35 million French troops killed over their much longer tenure at war. In general, it was easier for the Yanks to maintain their optimistic, can-do spirit after only two to three major offensives. Nevertheless, for the troops who were in those offensives, the experience could be brutal, and many came home with shell shock or lingering effects of gas attacks—including hardy athletes like Hall of Fame pitchers Grover Cleveland Alexander and Christy Mathewson.[37]

In particular, the engineers were stirred by the sacrifice of the units that supported the French at Château-Thierry in May. *The Highwayman* printed a poem eulogizing the two thousand Americans who died "on the road out of Chateau-Thierry, by the hill where we halted the Hun." One line would soon prove prophetic for Bill Kennedy:

> Some day that road will be teeming
> With pilgrims who venture to go
> To Humanity's Holy of Holies
> On the road by the Bois de Bellau.[38]

Between the reconstruction and the ongoing peace talks, not to mention the time it would take simply to mobilize the number of transport ships needed to cross the Atlantic back and forth and bring them home, hundreds of thousands of AEF troops were in for quite a wait before they could embrace their loved ones. The men grew restless. Racing to their salvation came the YMCA and its rival welfare organizations, especially the Knights of Columbus, or K of C ("the Caseys"). The groups donated baseball equipment to troops and hosted boxing matches, among like efforts. Soon the army appointed a chief athletic officer, Colonel Wait Johnson, to coordinate with the YMCA and oversee competitive sport programming as an official, even integral, element of the military schedule. (This was a coup for the forces of wholesome fun versus the proponents of no fun at all; Johnson earned his appointment when he persuaded superiors that a return to eight hours of basic-training-style drills per day would not boost the veterans' morale.)

Bill Kennedy must have sat bolt upright when he read the news in *Stars and Stripes*. With the blessing of Pershing himself, Johnson and the Y unveiled a dizzying schedule of athletic events for spring 1919.

A giant elimination tournament across France, Luxembourg, and the German Rhine Valley would determine the champions of the AEF in baseball, football, basketball, boxing, wrestling, tennis, and track and field. Conveniently for our purposes, "track athletics attracted the keenest of interest throughout the greater part of the A.E.F. athletic programme," Johnson wrote later. And principal among the track and field events was a modified marathon.[39]

The structure of the tourney followed that of the American Expeditionary Forces. Contests would pit, in succession, companies, battalions, regiments, brigades, divisions, and corps against one another until the cream rose to the top of the First, Second, and Third armies, the General Headquarters, the District of Paris, and Bill's own Supply of Service (SOS), which encompassed the Engineers. The best teams from those six organizations would meet in the AEF finals in Paris on Memorial Day weekend.

But there was more: the athletes who excelled at the AEF finals would go on to compete against their counterparts from a score of Allied nations in an enormous "athletic carnival" in Paris. Johnson scheduled this Inter-Allied Games to take place on and around the Fourth of July, just in time for the expected conclusion of the peace conference. With funds from the YMCA, the U.S. Army would build a 22,000-seat stadium to host the extravaganza.

Despite some obvious limitations, Johnson's goal was nothing less than a revival of the Olympics, which hadn't been held since 1912. "The Inter-Allied contest will be the logical successor of the Olympiads," declared *Stars and Stripes*. Indeed, "the Paris meet will in some respect overshadow the Olympic games themselves." Naturally, the defeated Central Powers were not included in the competition, but that "will not be an important loss, for the reason that Germany, Austria and Turkey have never been real devotees of sport." (Nineteenth-century Prussian Friedrich Ludwig Jahn, with a good claim to being the father of the modern fitness movement, likely turned a somersault in his grave at this point.) Johnson's plan was remarkably ambitious—audacious, even. What's more remarkable is the fact that he pulled it off.[40]

For Bill, this was his chance to run in international competition on foreign soil. As long as he didn't get stuck working construction on the stadium with his fellow engineers, he could spend his spring getting back into running shape and working his way up through the SOS and AEF meets. If the conditions were right and he ran as well as he knew he could, then Bill would finally compete on the world stage, going head-to-head against the best that the French, the British, the Italians, and the rest had to offer. Though the longest race planned for the Inter-Allied Games was just ten miles, it was nonetheless referred to as "the Marathon," and it was the "blue ribbon" event, as Johnson called it. After all, "European countries would rather win the Marathon than any other individual event," Johnson wrote. American servicemen, too, ate up news of the marathon, perhaps because of its roots in military legend. In any case, Bill had a new goal. And it was a vision far grander than the inter-company basketball championship of the 23rd Engineers.[41]

The Games Committee got to work planning the construction of the new stadium, to be built in less than six months. Fortunately, Bill was not detailed for that assignment. As the AAU's All-America marathon runner for 1917, the last year of serious competition stateside, Bill was needed in the AEF track and field tourney, as both a runner and a coach. His first race in fourteen months took place in Paris on Christmas Day 1918. The distance is not known. (*Stars and Stripes* dropped some details as it struggled to cover the massive sports program, not to mention the peace talks and other hard news, all in eight pages once a week.) But Bill placed third. He still had it. Nevertheless, when an army team that boasted several "winners of noted American distance contests," probably including Bill Kennedy and Sid Hatch, competed against French soldiers in a cross-country run that winter, most of our boys finished between eighty-third and ninety-third. So the Yanks had work to do to get back into shape.[42]

Throughout early 1919, Bill was granted leave for days at a time to travel to and compete in SOS events. He won two races, including a modified marathon at Dijon. Clearly, he was cutting the mustard. In late March, the engineer was ordered to Paris to train for six weeks for the SOS finals. The "City of Light" would be Bill Kennedy's home for the rest of his stay in France. There, he ran with an elite group that included former Olympians, college track champs, and Irish-American A.C. stars. By day, the athletes trained at Paris's Colombes Stadium. By night, they got up to the very sort of thing the YMCA wished they wouldn't. After months of fighting, marching, road building, trench digging, KP duty—all of it—few were about to pass up the opportunity to live a little.[43]

"Military discipline was practically gone so far as the athletes were concerned," wrote Clarence DeMar, who joined the group in Paris that spring. Apparently even DeMar, the devout Baptist, would at least tag along with his fellow soldiers as they sampled the Parisian nightlife. In his memoir, he drops a startling claim into the middle of this otherwise humorous anecdote:

> A group of us were practicing one day and, in trying to cross the Seine to a section where Algerian troops were stationed, we were stopped by a military police [officer]. We made believe we didn't understand English, but we couldn't fool him. He said he could tell Americans with or without clothes. So we ran up a way and crossed another bridge and came down to the forbidden area, where at night time American soldiers had been killed in drunken brawls and their bodies thrown into the river. On our way back across the forbidden bridge we again encountered the M.P. This time he was perplexed. His orders did not cover Americans returning.[44]

The laxity and debauchery even caused concern that the athletes weren't taking their task seriously enough, to the detriment of America's chances in the eventual international competition. "Athletes sent to Paris to train for the A.E.F. championships and the Inter-Allied games, whether officers or enlisted men, should be made to train and not spend all their time 'seeing Paris,'" a *Stars and Stripes* columnist finger-wagged. "Not that anyone begrudges them a good time, but their duty to their fellows, to the A.E.F., and to the United States demands that they keep themselves fit for the athletic contests in which they are to represent the A.E.F." The columnist—one Franc Terror—pointed to a possible coal mine canary in a recent exhibition race on the Seine, when "the American crew exhibited anything but good condition. At the finish most of them dropped exhausted at their oars, while the winning New Zealand crew hardly showed the pace at all. This does not speak well of American training methods."[45]

As one of the trainers and nominally an authority figure, Bill had his hands full corralling his charges. He reported directly to Captain Harry Maloney, who oversaw track athletics for the AEF, and the two seem to have shared a flexible disciplinary philosophy. "I would be disloyal did I not mention . . . Captain Maloney," Bill wrote later. The Dublin-bred Irishman "was a former captain in the Boer War and a fine soccer player." Kennedy continued:

> He put me in charge of the enlisted men, and oh the laughs and headaches he handed over to me. One word from me and they did as they pleased, my stripes didn't mean a thing to that bunch. And the officers whose dormitory was on the floor below. Of a night when they didn't make the curfew, they would barge into our dormitory, wake me up, and I would have to put them to bed. Two of my star boarders from New York were Lieuts. Joe Higgins and Andy Kelly. Also an old pal from Chicago, Lieut. Early [sic] Eby of Phila. via Chicago. Capt. Maloney was a swell guy. He would say to me the next morning, "Sergeant, did ye take care of a couple of my boys last night?" We would look at each other and smile. "Yes sir, I fixed them up." "Good bhoy."[46]

But despite winking at broken curfews, the two coaches were serious about whipping the athletes into shape. Maloney would soon gain renown among sporting types for training Gene Tunney to his breakout AEF boxing championship. As for Kennedy, it didn't matter how late "the bhoys" got in or how little sleep he got himself. Ever the workman, he was up with the rooster and on the road with his runners. Bill coached the top long-distance men, who were grouped into a squad representing the District of Paris. (It seems the army shuffled Bill between the SOS and the district depending on where he was most needed at any given time.) Two of the best distance runners were Fred Faller and Frank Zuna. Faller was a clockmaker from West Roxbury. He had run against Kennedy in the AOH race in Cambridge back on July 4, 1917. Zuna was the "husky plumber from Newark" whose wisecrack about the merry-go-round you may remember from this book's prologue. Both men had served in the SOS's Advance Section, where Faller was a corporal and Zuna a cook.

Bill got along especially well with Zuna, who had a priceless marathoner origin story. As a youngster in Newark, Zuna was shooting craps. The police came to break up the game. A cop grabbed Zuna by the coat, but the lad fled, leaving the cop holding his coat. The cop chased Zuna for four miles before giving up. At that point, Zuna realized he must be a pretty good runner.[47]

In the AEF, Faller was considered the best at the ten-mile distance, a distinction Zuna craved for himself. "Zuna was on my back that he wanted to beat Faller," Bill recalled. "So I would get up at five a.m. every day and work him ten miles for speed, massage and rub him down before breakfast."[48]

Then the day of the SOS finals arrived—May 4, at Le Mans. In the modified marathon, Faller, Kennedy, and Zuna finished first, third, and fifth. Afterwards, in the showers, Bill glowered at his early-bird mentee in half-mock exasperation.

"You big Polack lug," Bill barked. "What am I getting up at five o'clock for? You can't even beat *me*!"

Zuna just grinned and winked. (He did not inform Bill that he was of Bohemian, not Polish, descent.)

All three had performed well enough to qualify for the AEF finals at the end of the month. To be held at Colombes Stadium in Paris, this premier event would determine America's representatives in the

Inter-Allied Games. It would take place on a Memorial Day weekend freighted with significance as never before in their adult lives. Pershing himself would drape medals about the winning athletes' shoulders. The men prepared to spend the next four weeks training like mad, eyes fastened firmly on the finals.

Then the Knights of Columbus made a muddle of that.

Perhaps feeling elbowed aside as their Protestant rivals the YMCA were running the official show, the Catholic "Caseys" hit upon a brilliant stroke of thunder theft. Midway through May, the K of C announced that on the thirtieth—two days before the AEF modified marathon—it would host "the greatest relay race in the history of Europe and probably of the world," as one American reporter put it. Ten teams of twenty men each would cover a sixty-mile route, starting at the emotional flashpoint of Château-Thierry—"now recognized as the shrine of all Americans," proclaimed *Stars and Stripes*—and finishing in the Place de la Concorde, the largest and grandest public square in Paris. Each soldier would run three miles, and the first to finish the last leg would deliver a message into the hands of President Wilson. The top three teams would win gold, silver, or bronze medals, plus cash prizes.[49]

May 30 was not only Memorial Day itself (as it was every year in that era) but also the first anniversary of the day the U.S. Army's Seventh Machine Gun Battalion stood their ground at Château-Thierry, turning the tide of the war, as the Americans now saw it. And though the race was not a marathon, the invocation was hard to miss. *Stars and Stripes* perpetuated the conflated myth rooted in 1896 when it trumpeted, "This race should rank next to that ancient race on the plains of Marathon."[50]

It was a coup. Technically, the Knights' event existed "outside the regular program of sports," as one observer noted. But it was such a good idea, of course every soldier-athlete wanted to take part, and how could Johnson and his superiors say no? The obvious drawback for Bill and his elite runners was that it meant two major races a mere forty-eight hours apart. Moreover, even though no individual in the relay would run more than three miles (versus eight miles in the AEF modified marathon), the K of C race quickly sucked much of the attention away from the putatively more important AEF finals, which after all would still determine the entrants in the international "Military Olympics," as some were calling the Inter-Allied Games.[51]

No matter. Bill gamely set about picking his twenty-man team. He organized a qualifying race on May 23 at the University of Paris athletic field. The first twenty to finish made the District of Paris squad. That list does not survive, but it likely included Faller and Zuna. A full score of solid runners was maybe a lot to ask for, and Bill had to be content with some filler material—for example, "Spike" Webb of the Naval Academy. As Bill recalled: "I put him in the Chateau Thierry to Paris Relay. As a runner he was a good coach." But the single tryout was the best he could manage on such short notice. These twenty men would have to do.[52]

Dawn broke on Memorial Day 1919 with solemn services at burial grounds across the French countryside. President Wilson, General Pershing, and nearly every officer and soldier of the AEF paid their respects to the fallen that morning.

Finally, at about 9:45 a.m., ten men took positions on the bridge over the Marne River at Château-Thierry. A lieutenant colonel read aloud to them the message they were tasked with delivering:

> On the anniversary of their successful repulse of the German advance at the bridges of Chateau-Thierry, and in memory of their faithful comrades who gave their all for the cause of democracy, the officers and men of the 7th Machine Gun Battalion send to the President of the United States this message of their respect and esteem for him and of their ardent devotion to the land he represents.[53]

A Knights of Columbus official handed each soldier a bamboo tube containing a typewritten copy of the message. At ten o'clock the official waved a flag in the air, and the runners were off.

In their three-mile increments, the teams of runners traversed sixty miles of the Marne battlefield, passing through Essômes-sur-Marne, Meaux, Claye-Souilly, and Livry-Gargan en route to Paris. Back in November, this landscape was a wasteland of ruined villages, wrecked bridges, shell craters, and the occasional cross topped with a helmet inscribed "Soldat Americain Inconnu." Now, on this clear spring day, the evidence of war remained—tumbledown cottages and stone walls—but there were signs of rebuilding and rebirth. Colorful canopies of flowers hung over the roads in some villages, where French men and women cheered on the passing American soldiers. "There was a warm, smiling sun out," noted *Stars and Stripes*, "and a slight breeze was blowing over the poppy and wheat fields."

Clarence DeMar's leg of the race began at Meaux, and by the time he passed his baton to his Third Army teammate at the next checkpoint, he'd moved his team up from fourth to third. But that was all he could do. (The Third Army would in fact finish, well, third.) For a marathoner, it must have felt anticlimactic to be done running in just three miles, not to mention frustrating to have the rest of the race out of one's hands along with the baton.

Bill Kennedy, fortunately, would be running the final leg, so he would at least get to cross a finish line, and if his District of Paris teammates performed well, he had a fighting chance to win the thing. Any anxiety he harbored while waiting at the last checkpoint, a few blocks inside city limits, would have centered on what was happening back there over the first fifty-seven miles. Bill was relying on nineteen links in a chain, any one (or more) of which could easily break down and render his task impossible. But he had some good runners behind him, so there was reason to be hopeful as he stretched and jogged in place to warm up.

At about 3:42 p.m., Bill and his nine rivals sat wrapped in olive drab blankets, glancing at one another and at the murmuring Parisians and doughboys crowding the sidewalks and spilling into the street. Mostly, the athletes stared eastward up the Avenue Jean Jaurès, waiting for the first of their compatriots to appear.

In the distance, the crowd stirred. Spectators craned their necks. A bugle's peppy-officious *ppblat-ppblat* echoed down the street, followed by the chugging of a motorcar. The car itself came into view, its soldier driver proceeding slowly as MPs struggled to keep the crowds back. At last, the auto cranked to a stop in front of the runners, who rose and strained to listen for the news.

"Embarkation Center man leading," hollered the doughboy behind the wheel. "Get ready there." He nodded at Private Matthew Lynch.

Bill and the rest looked on as Lynch whipped off his blanket, pressed his elbows close to his sides, and rubbed his palms together. Soon, Lynch's sweaty teammate arrived and thrust the bamboo tube into the private's outstretched hand. Lynch took off down the avenue. An MP raced ahead of him on a bicycle, trying to clear a path. The other nine runners watched the leader recede into the distance, the crowd's roar rolling away with him. Inevitably, all nine turned about to face east again. Who would get the chance to catch Lynch?

Before too long, coming in two hundred yards behind Lynch's handoff man, the nineteenth District of Paris runner appeared: Bill's team was in second place. In a moment, Bill's right hand clutched the baton, slippery with the sweat of nineteen athletes, as he hoofed it down Avenue Jean Jaurès, determined to make it a race.

Little is known about Lynch except that he was fast. The length of two football fields behind, Bill could barely see his quarry down the narrow street packed with civilians. Upon crossing the Canal Saint-Martin, the avenue became the slightly broader Rue La Fayette, lined with pale stone apartment buildings four to six stories high, decorated with wrought-iron balconies and topped with mansard roofs. This scenery was broken up by the odd church or park, and by public squares and large intersections where cross-streets poured into the *rue* at sharp angles. The crowds grew larger. Bill drew closer. Running hard, he was gradually shortening the gap between himself and

Lynch. But could he shorten it enough in time? Rare it was that he had to expend so much energy in so short a distance. There could be no careful strategizing in this race, no holding back in the early portions. He simply had to run very fast for three miles, in hopes of passing a fleet-footed youth who'd gotten a big head start.

Lynch and then Kennedy took a left on Rue Halévy. Lynch seemed to be tiring. To their right, the steroidal, opulent Opéra Garnier towered above them for more than a block. Then Lynch entered the biggest public plaza yet, Place de l'Opéra. "He found nothing but a vast wall of faces, masculine and feminine, American, French, British, Belgian, Italian," recorded *Stars and Stripes*. "He heard a confused shouting, and at every stride there shot into his ears the good old, plain, old voices of his buddies, cheering him, praising him, urging him on." Lynch straightened up and quickened his pace as he took a right on Boulevard des Capucines.

Bill was probably less than a hundred yards behind now, and still gaining. More MPs on bicycles and motorcycles with sidecars came to escort the runners. After a few blocks, the men passed on their right the Église de la Madeleine, a nineteenth-century Catholic church that looks like a pagan Roman temple—the jarring but very French result of mid-construction pendulum swings in national power between secular and religious forces.

Lynch took a left on Rue Royale, Kennedy in hot pursuit. It was the home stretch. The two runners pounded the pavement, slinging themselves straight down the solid corridor of the *rue,* their eyes drawn to a giant gray pencil on the horizon. It was the Egyptian obelisk that marked the Place de la Concorde, their goal. The obelisk grew larger, and Bill drew ever closer to Lynch. By the time they reached the end of the *rue,* Bill had managed to pull within two yards of the front-runner.

The young private streaked into the wide open of the enormous plaza. It was filled with American servicemen in their state-trooper-style hats, as well as other Allied soldiers and thousands of French civilians in flat caps and the increasingly common straw boater. A smattering of women in the crowd wore dark long dresses even in the spring warmth. Fronting on the river Seine, the Place de la Concorde was built for a king (Louis XV), before it hosted the execution of a king and his queen (Louis XVI and Marie Antoinette). There was no guillotine today, but beyond the finish line stood a pair of modern artillery cannons, Allied soldiers climbing atop the barrels for a better view. Other spectators shinnied up lampposts. Newsreel crews aimed their hand-cranked cameras at the finish line.

Lynch ran along the narrow path that the MPs cleared through the crowd. Bill charged up behind him. After all the lost ground he had made up, he couldn't fail now. But it was going to be close.

A French press photographer waited to capture the finish. On assignment from Agence Meurisse, he would produce the dramatic picture of the winner that would be printed in newspapers the world over. Ignoring the horde of bicycles and officials advancing ahead of the runners, the Meurisse man zeroed in on the winner and closed the shutter. He had the shot. Against the spectacular backdrop of the plaza, it showed the victor as a grizzled veteran who covered his gray hair with a khaki bandana—William J. Kennedy.

Alas, the photographer was mistaken. Young Lynch had been obscured by the passing scrum of MPs, but it was he, not Kennedy, who crossed the finish line first. Realizing his error, the Meurisse man turned around and rushed to cover Lynch as K of C officials in military-style uniforms placed a laurel wreath on his head. It was too late for his action shot, though. Nobody seems to have captured on film the moment of Lynch's victory. The result in the next day's papers, including the *New York Times,* must have caused some readers to scratch their heads: the great relay race was depicted with just one photo—an excellent photo—showing Bill Kennedy coming in second (see fig. 7).

Lynch was whisked off to meet President Wilson at his hotel. But that night Kennedy, DeMar, and all two hundred relay runners and various officials were treated to a banquet at the Palais d'Orsay Hotel, and the following night (May 31) they joined Wilson in attending a

FIGURE 7. Paris, 1919. Bill Kennedy finishes second in the Château-Thierry relay race.

show at the Palace Theater. Bill wasn't going to complain about all the festivities, especially not in such esteemed company. Still, his thoughts must have turned repeatedly to the next morning's race.

~~~

The hullaballoo had hardly died down when Bill—probably still recovering from the post-relay revelry—and the rest of his team took their places on the track at Colombes Stadium on June 1. Though now it almost seemed like an afterthought, the stakes this day were higher, and the distance longer: the top performers in the AEF finals' "modified marathon" of eight miles would represent their nation in the Inter-Allied Games ten-miler on July Fourth. About ten thousand spectators filled the stadium, roughly split between American soldiers and French soldiers and civilians. General Pershing looked on from a grandstand box.[54]

Faller leaped out to an early lead as the runners circled the track twice, then left the stadium to run a course on the Colombes streets.

Behind him trailed Joe Stout, Bill Kennedy, and Clarence DeMar. Faller got so far ahead, the only drama centered on who would take second place. You can almost see the twinkle in Bill's eye as he recounted his strategy in this race, which would finish with three more laps around the track:

> After five miles Faller had a long lead on Stout, who was fifty yards ahead of me. I would put on a sprint and catch up to him only to have him open up on me again. This happened several times. [Before returning to the stadium] I again pulled abreast of him and gasped, "Take it easy, bud, you can beat me in the sprint." Joe did and I got my breathing regulated and [when] we hit the track I let go with everything I had, which took him by surprise. I gained about twenty-five yards on him which he never got back.
> Under the showers later, Joe says, "Good Lord, man, how old are you?" "Why?" I asked. "Well, when you asked me to take it easy along the road, I did, feeling sorry for your grey head, but when we hit the track I couldn't see you for the dust you kicked up."[55]

Faller sprinted to the finish, winning in 48:16, a full lap ahead of Kennedy. Stout joined them in qualifying for the Inter-Allied Games. DeMar in fourth earned the right to march with them in the Games' opening ceremonies.[56]

Two days before the Inter-Allied Games kicked off, Bill finally managed to beat Faller—in a practice run. Still, finishing ahead of his trainee by a hundred yards, Bill had some reason to hope.

The Games began on June 22, at the brand-new Pershing Stadium in Joinville-le-Pont, outside Paris. Completed just in time, the horseshoe-shaped reinforced concrete stadium was full to capacity (22,000) with spectators, military and civilian. As presidents Wilson and Poincaré and Premier Clemenceau watched from the grandstand, Kennedy, DeMar, and the rest of the 150 American athletes marched to a fanfare in the opening ceremonies. DeMar recalled, "It seemed very light stepping, indeed, to walk in a running suit, after having marched with full equipment."[57]

Over the next few days, Bill and his fellow distance runners attended the other track and field events and rooted for their sprinting brethren and other Americans as they competed against the French, Italians, and other Allied athletes. For various reasons, there was practically no English presence in the Games, with the exception of rowing. The British Commonwealth, however, was well represented, with plenty of athletes from Australia, New Zealand, and Canada. Friendly wagering flourished. Bill recalled:

> [Earl] Eby was a Philadelphia sports writer. I knew him out in Chicago where he was a good middle distance runner. During the Inter Allied Games at Paris, he was in the finals in both the 440 and 880. The man he had to beat was Mason of New Zealand. We all had a bet down on Eby in the 440, and won. We then switched to Mason and won again. We had a riotous time that night![58]

Not all the sports fell under standard track and field categories. DeMar marveled: "One of the novel features of these games was a camel race on the track. But the camels couldn't seem to get the idea and frequently turned and went in the reverse direction."[59]

Meanwhile, on June 28, 1919, defeated German diplomats signed the war-ending treaty in the Hall of Mirrors at Versailles. Despite the most idealistic efforts of Wilson, the agreement called for heavy reparations payments and the loss of coal- and iron-rich territory Germany had held before the war started. The seeds for another conflict were planted.[60]

On Independence Day, dark clouds formed, thunder rolled, and rain poured just after General Pershing took his seat at his eponymous stadium. One doughboy cracked, "As soon as 'Black Jack' arrives, the barrage starts."[61]

It was a dark day for Bill Kennedy as well. He was supposed to run in the sixteen-thousand-meter (about ten miles) modified marathon, the "blue ribbon" event that would cap the Games this July Fourth. Instead, the night before the race, his knee had become infected, requiring emergency surgery. He would spend the next sixteen days in the hospital. The precise nature of his injury is no longer known, but Bill's discharge papers called him "5 percent disabled."[62]

In Bill's absence, AEF coaches put Nick Gianakopoulos in the race. The stadium was bursting with thirty thousand spectators as Jean Vermeulen, a French private with one arm hanging limp from a battle injury, ran neck and neck with Fred Faller. The Frenchman pulled away at the end, beating Faller by more than a minute. Americans and French alike gave the plucky Vermeulen their full-throated approval and thunderous applause. An AEF brass band played "The Star Spangled Banner" then "The Marseillaise" as the Stars and Stripes came down the flagpole and the Tricolor went up, signaling the turning over of the stadium to the French as a parting gift.

Bill missed all of it. His replacement, Nick the Greek, finished seventh. After all the engineer's training and slogging through the long tournament, the Military Olympics turned out to be a letdown.

But he didn't regret the experience. The races he did run were fun, and so was the camaraderie and the "seeing Paris." Bill and every other doughboy would agree that Johnson's athletics program was a smashing success compared to plan A, drilling for eight hours a day.

But the experience also whetted Bill's appetite. The big stadiums and fancy tracks, the diversity of the crowds and languages spoken. He was eager to return to the States, yet just as eager to come back to Europe when normalcy returned. He'd already won the "American Marathon" in Boston, and fate had denied him his shot in the great Inter-Allied Games.

Nothing would do now but to run in an Olympic marathon.

6

PARIS OR BUST

Clad in blue denim overalls, Bill Kennedy steamed west across the Atlantic on the USS *Great Northern* in August 1919. The overalls were issued to all doughboys to protect their army uniforms, so that after a week at sea the men would "not look as if they had just come out of a delousing shop," as *Stars and Stripes* put it. At last the soldiers on deck caught sight of the Statue of Liberty—a most welcome sight, though it obscured the impending curtailment of one long-cherished freedom: the Volstead Act, a.k.a. Prohibition, was then coursing through Congress, to pass in October and take effect in January 1920. A glass-half-full (no pun intended) optimist, Bill might have reasoned that the timing was good if he wanted to cut out the booze while training for the Olympics, scheduled for summer 1920 in Antwerp, Belgium.[1]

The *Northern* docked in New York City, and Bill made straight for Port Chester, where he received a hero's welcome. "We're quite sure the old champ will again don the running suit which has so often flashed home in form," declared the local *Daily Item*. "Welcome home, 'Bill,' old boy." After staying with L.J. for a few days, Bill reported to Camp Merritt in New Jersey for his official discharge.[2]

For the next several months, Bill was a blur of activity, logging hundreds of miles of train travel between family, work, and races. First, he returned to St. Louis to reunite with Jessie and their daughters—Louise (see fig. 8), who was now eight, and Juanita, six. But soon he got a bricklaying job in Mississippi County, Arkansas. With the leadership credentials he brought back from the army—having served as a sergeant and an athletic coach—Bill was elected president of the bricklayers' union local in the county seat of Blytheville. Yet he managed to return east in January to run a race in Brooklyn with the Morningside A.C., which honored him with a lifetime membership. Back in Arkansas again, Bill trained in earnest for the 1920 Boston Marathon, which would once more (as in 1912) double as an Olympic tryout. His knee still bothered him, and for the first time his training included more walking than running. Bill tried to persuade Jessie to bring the girls to Boston to watch him race, "but the Mrs. wouldn't stand for it," he told his pal Hallahan, who'd jumped from the *Herald* to the *Globe*. Bill rode east in a Pullman, but alone.[3]

Come race day, Bill quickly realized an Olympic slot wasn't in the cards this cycle. He struggled along in fifteenth place for most of the race. As he recalled it, a younger runner kept pace with him, thinking the veteran was just conserving his energy for the home stretch, until Bill set him straight:

> One must stay up within hailing distance of the leaders, never allow them to get away. There was only one Boston race that I can recall in which a man, comparatively far back, half-way along the course, captured first prize. He was [Peter Trivoulidas], the Greek. He followed me into Wellesley the year he won. I was having trouble with my feet. He looked at me and asked if I was Kennedy. I told him I was, and he replied, "Well, I am going to stay with you."
>
> I felt I did not have a chance, as my feet were in bad shape. I told him "You better get going, for you never will win staying with me." He took my advice, and it will be recalled he caught Roth in 1920, four miles from the finish and won handily.[4]

FIGURE 8. Bill Kennedy with daughter Louise, circa 1920.

A Greek national and a busboy at Wanamaker's in New York, Trivoulidas won the 1920 Boston Marathon in 2:29:31. Bill finished fifteenth. He would have to shift his focus to 1924. That was his next shot at Olympic glory. And considering he would be forty years old by that time, it might also be his last.

〜〜

Bill's first step toward that end was to finally uproot Jessie and the girls and resettle in Port Chester. It had been his goal for years now, and the war hadn't changed that. If anything, the postwar New York running scene was growing by leaps and bounds. The AEF athletics program had proved a watershed in the story of sport in America. As one contemporary noted, "4,000,000 men are marching back to the ranks of citizens with a new idea of the place recreational athletics has in the life of a nation." Athletic clubs and gyms burst with new members, new clubs sprouted, and—important to Bill and his fellow plodders—road races were revived or conceived anew across the metropolitan region. And of course the nation's premier running event, in Boston, would be a significantly shorter trip from "Old Saw Pits" than it had been from St. Louis.[5]

Not that running was the only reason for Bill and Jessie to move. After a decade spent with her family, it seemed fair to return to his. Indeed, in St. Louis, Jessie may not have been thrilled about living so close—two doors down—to her sister Nellie. (It seems Bill stayed friendly with Nellie, his old flame and first fiancée, and that probably didn't sit well with Jessie.) The move would make economic sense, too. In Port Chester, Bill—no longer the brash teenager at odds with his father—could make money working on big construction jobs with L.J. and perhaps eventually establish himself as a contractor in his own right. Finally, it's possible that living in Mississippi County, Arkansas, in 1920, of all places and all times, Bill had seen the ugly side of the turbulent changes rocking the nation. The area would become notorious for a lynching the following year, and it could hardly have been hospitable to someone like Bill Kennedy in an era when the Ku Klux Klan was gaining power by stoking fears of Catholics, labor unions, and alcohol. Perhaps that sealed it. By the end of the year the Kennedys were living in Port Chester, safely within the orbit of New York City.

∽∽∽

Bill worked hard throughout the early 1920s, first with his father, then getting his own business off the ground, as he'd intended. Indeed, the work sucked up so much of his time that he found it difficult to train as hard as he needed to for the Boston Marathon. He placed fourteenth in 1921. "The leaders were half drunk from celebrating by the time I finished," Bill later quipped about his showing in years like this.[6]

But Bill was pleased to see his friend Zuna win. With a time of 2:18:57, the Newark plumber broke the record by two minutes and twenty seconds. "A fine lad," Bill told the *Globe*, "and a fine runner. Not a yip from me. I'm through. I found that I did not have the will-power to push myself, and am only sorry that my little daughter Louise came over to see her daddy licked. I guess the old man has gone by and he's all done, but before hanging up my shoes let me say 'Well done Frank Zuna.'"[7]

Bill wasn't really ready to hang up his shoes yet. But he was taking a greater interest in passing on his knowledge and developing younger runners. In 1921 he took under his wing Albert "Whitey" Michelsen, who finished fifth that year, in 2:30:35. It was Whitey's first marathon. The 27-year-old plumber and former boxer hailed from Stamford, Connecticut. Bill signed him up with the Cygnet A.C., the club he now represented. It straddled the Byram River, with members in Port Chester, New York, and East Port Chester, Connecticut. It was easy to see Whitey's potential, and the Cygnets were fortunate that by dint of Bill Kennedy's reputation and the club's geographic convenience, the Stamford lad picked them first.[8]

The 1921 Boston Marathon was also notable because it was the first witnessed by a young Johnny A. Kelley. Much later they'd call him

"Johnny Kelley the Elder" to distinguish him from John J. Kelley, who started a successful running career in the 1950s. But in 1921, Johnny A. Kelley was thirteen years old. His father took him by trolley from Medford to Kenmore Square, and they wandered behind the crowds on Commonwealth Avenue, trying to find a sight line. "A big Irish policeman saw me and held the rope up so I could get a better look," Kelley remembered later. Standing in front of the rope, the lad had a perfect view of Zuna striding to victory. "I remember my father saying, 'He doesn't even look tired, look at him.'" Fascinated, Kelley made up his mind to run the race himself one day.[9]

In 1922 Bill finished thirteenth. He'd improved just one spot per year over his 1920 showing. The bricklayer laughed off a reporter's question about how he sneaked in the time to train while running a business and raising a family. "I can lay 2,000 bricks a day," Bill responded, "and what more trainin' does a man want than that?" The press continued to report Bill's age as matching his appearance rather than his birthdate. "Kennedy is forty years of age," claimed the *New York Evening Telegram* after the '22 Boston grind, with "youth's ambitious fires long since quenched." In fact, Kennedy was thirty-eight, and in his heart he harbored a fiery desire to compete on the global stage. He had two years to claw his way back. And he had reason to hope: his time that day was a respectable 2:32:50.[10]

The winner wasn't exactly a spring chicken either. Clarence DeMar was thirty-four in 1922 when he cut forty-seven seconds off Zuna's record of the previous year. This was DeMar's first Boston Marathon win since 1911, and it would prove the beginning of a decade of dominance for the printer. To Dr. Arthur White, who'd been examining BAA marathon entrants since the turn of the century, the relatively advanced age of men such as DeMar and Kennedy was an asset, not a liability:

> It takes years to build up the mental and physical qualities, the power to punish one's self and the developing of power to be punished, required by a marathoner. A youngster is inclined to give up quicker and to quit when he finds there are men in front of him and he cannot be first. . . .
> It is wonderful what condition these veterans keep in. It is wonderful

what reserves of stamina and endurance they possess. Their poise and equilibrium are remarkable.[11]

White knew of what he spoke, but his would remain a minority opinion for some time. Bill would have to work extra hard to sway the majority, especially at the American Olympic Committee.

⌣

Bill ran local races in New York as well. In the fall of 1922, he ran a gauntlet of contests marred by intrusive automobiles. The incidents show how prevalent the "machines" were becoming on the streets of Manhattan—as almost everywhere else—thanks not only to accelerating efficiency practices in the factories but also to the boom in consumer credit that marked the Roaring Twenties. Horseless carriages were no longer just toys of the rich.

It all started after September 24, when Bill won a nine-mile road race sponsored by *Il Popolo,* a New York Italian newspaper. Beating Zuna by two blocks, Kennedy finished the run in 47:33. So far, so good. The win was a nice way to celebrate the twenty-fourth anniversary of Bill's athletic career. (He had fought his first bout on September 24, 1898.)[12]

Then on October 1, Kennedy was running against Zuna, Whitey Michelsen, and a host of other New York regulars in a 10.5-miler of the Greek-American A.C. Over the last five miles, Bill ran neck and neck with Frank Titterton, former Metropolitan cross-country champion. After a long stretch down Eighth Avenue, the course turned onto Fifty-third Street for the home stretch. The *Tribune* reported what happened next: "An automobile slowed up just as Titterton made the turn. He barely flashed by ahead of the machine. Kennedy, only inches behind, very wisely did not make the attempt to cut in ahead of the car and he lost four yards before getting clear for the run to the tape."[13]

Titterton won with a time of 1:06:03. Kennedy followed in 1:06:07. Four yards and four seconds behind, thanks to the driver of that infernal machine. But that's not how the loser played it in his comments afterward, noted the *Tribune:* "When the officials expressed their regret at the inadequate protection from the traffic, Bill dismissed the subject with this remark: 'Frank would have won anyhow. He is much younger and a far better runner than I.' Score one for clean sportsmanship."[14]

Then on October 8, in the Paulist A.C. six-mile race, Bill *benefited* from an auto incident. On West Sixtieth Street, with about a block to go, Bill was in first. A runner named Johnny Bell was just a few feet behind when he collided with an automobile. Kennedy won in 36:45; Bell followed in 37:10.[15]

Finally, on October 12, Bill was *struck* by an automobile. This time it was the Columbus Day modified marathon, sponsored by *Il Popolo.* The course was fourteen miles over the city streets, then two miles around the track at the New York Velodrome. Bill ran with the pack of front-runners for most of the race. He was in seventh place when "an automobile delivery truck crashed into Kennedy at 138th Street and Seventh Avenue, sending the runner heavily to the street," reported the *Times.* "He sustained painful bruises of the mouth." Bill took a taxi to Harlem Hospital. A doctor put three stitches in his lip— where Bill would bear a permanent scar—while the concerned taxi driver waited. The same driver gave Bill a lift to the Velodrome and refused to take any payment for the ride.[16]

Ahead of the Boston run in April 1923, Bill penned a letter to his good friend at the *Globe,* not knowing Sweeney had fallen ill. Covering for his elder colleague, Hallahan ran Bill's letter in his column the day before the race:

> *Dear Larry— Well, it's about time for another B. A. A. classic and I expect to take another crack at it. The Cygnet Club of this place will also be represented by John Rosi, a Finn, who will plug along and finish, and by "Whitey" Michelsen, who finished fifth the year Zuna copped. He is a great runner up to 10 or 12 miles and may*

go through for the distance. He trains hard and deserves to do
well.

Larry, did you ever ponder over the "why" of the Marathoners—
three months of hard training, running three or four times a week
from five to 20 miles, cutting out the smokes and chews and going
to bed at 9 or 10 o'clock? And most of us are rewarded with a survivor's medal. I always feel ashamed to [show] the gang of "brickies"
on the job what I got. They can't understand it as it is when they see
me running home from work.

Still there is the lure there. It's a pleasure to run, far more exhilaration than in walking, and every Marathoner I ever met was more
or less a dreamer. They always feel that their day is coming and they
are going to win and as for determination they are the personifica-
tion of it. I have heard them say along the last five miles when they
knew the winner was in, 'This is my last race," and five minutes after
the finish they will tell you, "Well, I will win next year," and most
winners come from that kind. Go along the list and look them over.

Another thing, they are absolutely square. I never knew one yet I
would not loan every nickel I had to, for I know they will pay back.
Some of them are tough birds, but they are honest, and during the
war, Longboat, Duffy, Hatch, de Mar, Mellor, Zuna, Faller, Dwyer,
Monteverde, Cameron, Corkery, myself and a bunch of others were
"over there," and every one of this gang is over 30 years of age.

Well, to get back to the race. Boston is sure an attractive place
for a runner to show in, for they appreciate the grind it is and give
all the boys a big hand. It's my vacation every year—the Boston
Marathon. I take a couple of days off from laying bricks and run the
race. And Larry, every mile of the course brings pleasant memories.
There are so many faces and voices I recognize along the course. I
love them all. . . . The Protestant clergyman [at] Wellesley. . . . The
numerous bricklayers are always for me, and since the war there
are some of the boys from the 23d Engineers who yell at me. [The]
big Irish cop [in Newton]. He knows and I know I am licked but we
understand each other. Then along the grade to Coolidge Corner, I

always know there is a cup of tea waiting there, if I need it. Mrs. Jack
Nason, a bricklayer's wife, and Jack and the family are pretty well
grown up now since first I got the tea from them. . . .
    So long and good luck, will see you April 19. You will be lolling
back in the cushions [in a motorcar]. I will be sweating and tired.
You will be leaning out and say—"six minutes behind, Bill, they
can't last—keep going."

                                                    Au-revoir,
                                                    Bill Kennedy[17]

In Ashland that Patriots' Day, Bill got an unwelcome diagnosis
from the BAA's examining physicians: the 39-year-old had a heart
murmur and shouldn't run. "Full of fight," Bill "declared that if he
was to die, the Boston marathon would be an appropriate setting."
Entering at his own risk, the bricklayer ran his best race in years,
battling his way from thirteenth place at South Framingham to fifth
at Coolidge Corner before finally finishing eighth, in 2:33:47. It was
Bill's highest placement and his first time among the prizewinners
since before the war. What's more, another examination in the BAA
clubhouse after the race found no more heart murmur. "I needed a
little exercise," Bill cracked.[18]

And "I am still getting [exercise] at seventy-nine," Bill wrote
decades later, looking back on the '23 race. "So to my readers who
may feel that they have a weak heart, forget it and live your own life."[19]

That was also the year Clarence DeMar solidified his status as the
marathon's superstar. Despite having been sick with erysipelas in January and February, in the midst of the training season, and despite
an automobile running over his foot and tearing his shoe half off at
Coolidge Corner, DeMar "copped first honors" in the 1923 Boston
Marathon. He was the first runner to win the race twice in a row since
J. J. Caffery in 1900 and 1901, and he was the first *ever* to win it three
times—a record he would only build on throughout the twenties.

Also noteworthy: the BAA tweaked the course around Ashland
that year to avoid railroad crossings. No more would passing freight

trains hold up the race for a minute or more, giving the front-runners extra time to get farther ahead and altogether dashing the hopes of the plebes in the rear.[20]

But bigger changes to the course were to come.

Perhaps still on a high from his doctor-befuddling Boston finish, Bill went on to even stronger placements in two prominent marathons in the next two months. First, Bill and his protégé Whitey Michelsen represented the Cygnet A.C. in a track marathon run entirely inside brand-new Yankee Stadium. The "Cathedral of Baseball" boasted a capacity of seventy thousand when it opened on April 18, 1923, with a Yankees win over the Red Sox on the strength of a Babe Ruth three-run homer. The stadium cost $2.5 million to build. "When we stop to consider the modest sums expended for baseball plants 25 years ago," the *Globe* mused, "we wonder what the fans of 25 years hence will see." The enormous size and cost of the stadium, the crushing long balls of the "Sultan of Swat"—it was all appropriate for the biggest team in the biggest sport in a nation increasingly big on, well, bigness.[21]

The stadium hosted the *Daily News* Silver Jubilee Marathon on May 20, just over a month after Opening Day. As Bill recalled it, "the News furnished the tickets for free. Result, 60,000 spectators." The *News'* competitor the *Times* printed a more conservative attendance estimate of "more than 25,000 persons." Either way, it was a big crowd for a round-the-track marathon. Argentine heavyweight Luis Firpo, the "Wild Bull of the Pampas," served as the official starter. The crowd of 25,000 to 60,000 persons gave a big ovation when Firpo took the field, "resplendent in pink haberdashery and oxford gray suit."[22]

Once Firpo fired the starter's gun, thirty-eight contestants, including most of the day's top New York distance runners, left their marks and circled the cinder track. One down, 114 to go. (The 115 laps would total twenty-six miles, 385 yards.)

"Around and around the track we went until some of us were dizzy," Bill recalled. "A race on the track becomes rather monotonous." At the eighth lap, Bill took the lead, only to give way to Frick. On the thirtieth lap, Michelsen took the lead, but Frick passed him as well. At this point, the front-runners had lapped the laggards several times. "As nature does not seem to have evenly matched the men in speed and endurance," Bill wrote, "they are soon divided into groups many yards apart." Eventually, twenty-five of the thirty-eight starters dropped out.[23]

Michelsen took the lead on the forty-fifth lap, trailed by Kennedy. On the seventy-sixth lap, "Kennedy spurted to the front, and the crowd cheered him liberally as he passed" his pupil, reported the *Times*. "His advantage was only short-lived, however, as Michelsen once more assumed the lead on the eightieth lap and gradually drew away from Kennedy."

Whitey broke the tape a lap and a half ahead of Bill in second. "The crowd stampeded and what a time the following men had to finish," Bill recalled, "being knocked hither and thither by the crowd on the track." M. J. Dwyer finished two laps behind Kennedy, followed by Frick.[24]

"Five others were still plugging along when the eighth man staggered across the line," reported the *Times*, "but the race was stopped, as there were only eight prizes to be awarded."

Both Cygnet men broke the track marathon record of 2:52:45 which had stood since 1909, when Matt Maloney established it at Madison Square Garden. Michelsen's time was 2:48:23; Kennedy's, 2:50:52.

After the race, Bill wrote, "I drank a hooker of whiskey and became ill."[25]

As if to prove the Cygnet showing wasn't a fluke, Whitey and Bill finished first and second in another full-distance marathon less than a month later, on June 16. On the road from Laurel, Maryland, to Baltimore, Zuna led the pack of thirty-nine runners for twenty-three miles before the Cygnet duo passed him.

Whether owing to the humidity or the condition of the roads, Bill felt that was the hardest marathon he had ever run in. But at least he and his teammates Michelsen and John "Iron Horse" Rosi had been promised "carfare and hotel expenses to Baltimore and return," he recalled. "After the race that night we waited in the lobby of the Southern Hotel for the committee to pay us our expenses. Finally a gentleman had me paged, informed me he was sorry but the committee had no funds left and were unable to pay us." Baltimore, by the way, is roughly 240 miles from Port Chester.[26]

Yet that was the life Bill chose. He knew the risks inherent in amateur athletics, especially when dealing with clubs or races that were new or off the beaten path. For all the hoopla that attended running a marathon at Boston or in Yankee Stadium, Bill wasn't too high and mighty to ride a late-night train to Portsmouth, New Hampshire, reach town at two o'clock in the morning, crash for a few hours at a near-stranger's house, run (into a headwind) a thirteen-mile handicap race to celebrate Portsmouth's tercentenary, finish second, go home, and then take the time to write a courteous letter to the race committee to thank them "for the fine treatment accorded me and to congratulate you for the excellent manner in which your race was handled," as he did that August. The people of Portsmouth had come together to support a road race as part of their hometown celebration, and Bill wanted to reward that impulse. Perhaps that good karma would return to Bill and his own hometown someday.[27]

Nineteen twenty-four. An Olympic year. At age forty, Bill faced long odds to make the team and the trip to Paris. But then, he wasn't just any forty-year-old. His return to the elite at Boston, his record-breaking performance at Yankee Stadium, and his second-place finish in Baltimore would remind the American Olympic Committee that this "veteran of many Marathons is far from slipping," as the *Globe* put it. Besides, he deserved a bone if the AOC could throw one, just on the basis of his career. (Think Martin Scorsese finally getting an Oscar, for *The Departed.*) After all, in some races, Bill had beaten some of the men the committee sent abroad some years: Hatch, DeMar, Forshaw, Erxleben, Mellor, among others.[28]

But that and ten cents wouldn't buy Bill a cup of coffee if he couldn't prove himself in the Olympic tryouts in the winter and spring of 1924. The Boston Marathon in April would serve as the principal trial race. The results of marathons in Baltimore and Detroit would be considered as well.[29]

Bill couldn't make it to Detroit, but he and a platoon of Cygnet A.C. runners entered the Baltimore race—run again along the route from Laurel, but much earlier in the year, on March 8. The men ran "over a hard course laid out in rolling country," reported the *Washington Evening Star,* "and for a large part of the grind a strong wind blew directly into the faces of the contestants." Michelsen led the field of fifty-nine most of the way, until about a mile and a half from the finish, when Zuna breezed past him and won by several blocks, in 2:41:39. DeMar came in third, Kennedy ninth. Bill would have to do better in April.[30]

Zuna won the Detroit Marathon, too, on March 29. Topping two of the three trials in the space of three weeks, Zuna seemed assured of a place on the Olympic team.[31]

On April Fools' Day 1924, the BAA made a very real, unfunny announcement. After years of typically Bostonian resistance to change, the Boston Marathon would conform to what had become the standard Olympic marathon distance of twenty-six miles, 385 yards, first occasioned by those damn royals (as many a marathoner struggling over the last 1.2 miles has referred to them since) at London in 1908. The starting line would move west to Hopkinton. Despite griping in the press about tradition, this change had to happen if the race purported to be an Olympic tryout.[32]

And indeed, as the date drew near, further official announcements suggested that Boston's would be *the* tryout, as if the Baltimore and Detroit races hadn't happened. The Patriots' Day run "will start the

Olympic ball rolling," as one New York sportswriter put it, reporting word that "the first six men to finish, regardless of previous performances, will be sent to France." Zuna hastily entered the race, without having trained for it.[33]

Taking a shotgun approach, Bill's Cygnet A.C. planned to "swoop down on Boston with a team of eight marathoners," while "twenty-five Cygnet A.C. rooters will make the trip to Boston and will follow their representatives over the course" in automobiles. Some of the Cygnet runners visited Boston's Newspaper Row the day before the race. "When Bill Kennedy introduced Frank Martin, the colored Marathon runner of the Cygnet A.C. in the Globe office yesterday, as the 'Smoked Irishman,' Martin with a broad smile remarked: 'I guess I'm the only 'dark horse' in the race tomorrow.'" (This good-natured Rat Pack–style joshing may seem politically incorrect today, but then again, in 1924, in much of the country, it wasn't politically correct to be seen with, much less to be friends and clubmates with, an African American.) Sticking with the color theme, the *Globe* added that "Michelsen is in the pink."[34]

Going over the chances of non-Cygnet competitors, Bill told reporters to keep an eye on Frank Wendling of Buffalo. Then the Byram River boys traveled out to Tebeau's Farm in Hopkinton to stay the night. With 170 entered in the marathon, Tebeau's and other farmhouses and inns from Hopkinton to Framingham were filled with "a collection of lighthearted fellows," said the *Herald*, "that would do your heart good, and cannot be duplicated at any other time or place in the world. The marathoner is a type in himself."[35]

The runners shared a unique camaraderie. The next morning they'd compete against one another; and yet they were friends, or even teammates. And in an era when road running was still relatively uncommon, it was only in this milieu that they were surrounded by like-minded souls.

That said, this was an Olympic qualifying year. Only six of them would make the cut. The stakes had to weigh heavily on the men's minds as they tried to sleep that night. That went double for the handful, including Bill, who were pushing the age envelope and might not get another chance.

~~~

As Patriots' Day dawned, the runners gathered in Ashland at Odd Fellows' Hall for their usual pre-race examination, then took trolleys to the new starting line on the outskirts of Hopkinton. An old-school New England town of three thousand, Hopkinton boasted famous son Daniel Shays—the Revolutionary War hero who then started his own rebellion—and a quarry that produced the granite for Boston's Custom House Tower. Hopkinton also happened to be the home of the BAA's George V. Brown and his dairy farm, with a herd of Guernsey cows and a prize bull named Rockingham Peerless.[36]

When the town's church bells bonged noontime, Brown himself fired his pistol, and the marathon got under way. The runners weren't in Hopkinton for long. They reached Stevens Corner, the old starting point, in about nine minutes. With cloud cover, cool temps, and a cross-wind, the weather was ideal as many marathoners see it, less so by Bill's lights. At least a little rain overnight had tamped down the dust. Albert Geiger Jr., chairman of the BAA athletic committee, drove on to Boston in a truck carrying the runners' street clothes. On the vehicle's side panels an appeal in paint read: "Help Olympic fund. Send money to any newspaper."[37]

Early on, DeMar battled Zuna, Michelsen, and Mellor for the lead. Still working the chill out of his bones, Kennedy ran a ways back, in twenty-third at Natick, a bit behind Linder in eighteenth. State police on motorcycles ran interference for the front-runners, keeping the path ahead clear. But without blocking off streets, as is done today, there was little the authorities could do about the growing auto caravan behind.

Meanwhile, against the fast pace set by the leaders, scores of newbies dropped out across the miles. According to the *Globe*, just 80 of the 170 entrants would finish. Drawn by visions of Paris, the young hopefuls found the going too tough in real life.

Take Ralph Williams, of the Hurja A.C. in Quincy. This was his first marathon, and well before the halfway point, he'd had enough. "Several contestants are said to have recalled seeing Williams quit at the ten-mile mark," one columnist reported later.[38]

After the Natick checkpoint, DeMar took the lead. Heading into Wellesley, William Churchill, a rare entrant from California, passed DeMar. (This was somewhat ungracious, in that DeMar had put up Churchill, a fellow American Legion member, at his home the previous night.) But on the hill, DeMar snatched the lead back from his West Coast friend, and the defending champ was cheered by the women of Wellesley College, many of whom this year were clad in full-length fur coats. Buffalo's Wendling kept pace with the pack, as Bill had predicted. So did Victor MacAuley of Nova Scotia, though as a Canadian he wouldn't factor into the race for the six U.S. Olympic slots.

Bill ran twenty-first at Wellesley, but here he began a steady climb, running "powerful all the way." He was nineteenth at Newton Lower Falls and fourteenth at Woodland Park. Going up the "heartbreaking hills" of Newton, Bill passed three more runners, while Zuna dropped out with stomach cramps. Michelsen was struggling as well from a heavy cold. Coming down the hill alongside Boston College, Bill ran in tenth place. Linder had come from behind too, to sixth.[39]

After Lake Street, rookie runner Ralph Williams suddenly appeared amidst the elites. This was strange, as officials and reporters had not seen Williams at three previous checkpoints—Natick, Wellesley, and Newton Lower Falls.

Over the last five miles, Clarence DeMar ran away from the field, a mile ahead of Mellor in second. The first-prize trophy was all but in his hands once more. Now the battle raged purely for the other five Olympic spots. At Coolidge Corner, Bill was running in eighth place. Ahead of him, in ascending order, were DeMar, Mellor, Wendling, Churchill, the Canadian MacAuley, Linder, and Michelsen. Kennedy was one slot away from making the Olympics.

On Beacon Street, Michelsen dropped out. Bill was the sixth American!

On Commonwealth Avenue, however, Williams passed Kennedy. If Williams held his position, *he* would be the sixth Yank to the finish, taking the Olympic slot Bill had toiled toward for years. Now stuck in eighth place, the gray-haired bricklayer gave it his all, but he had been running hard for almost twenty-six miles, and his legs just wouldn't cooperate.

DeMar reached the BAA clubhouse a mile ahead of Mellor. The printer scored his fourth victory with a world-record-breaking time of 2:29:40. Wendling and Churchill followed Mellor, both half-walking. "Linder with his dog trot, finished in fifth place and the long lope of MacAuley carried him to sixth place, while Williams was seventh and Kennedy, the gray-haired veteran, was given a big hand by the crowd as he broke the tape" in eighth, squeaking into the prize-winners but just shut out of Paris.[40]

Curiously, Williams's bicycle attendant did not show up at the clubhouse to partake in the banquet and receive his souvenir medal.

Contenting himself with the silver cup and the applause, Bill joked with reporters, "My legs shortened up on me towards the finish," and asked, "Supposin' they ran this Marathon business in heat?" The clubhouse scale showed that once again, the wiry workman had lost eight pounds, the most of any of the eighty finishers. At least outwardly, Bill was ready to laugh and shrug off the loss of his Olympic dream along with the spare weight.[41]

His Cygnet A.C. teammates weren't so easygoing, as you'll see shortly. Indeed, the sportswriters weren't all that certain either that the best man had claimed the number-six slot. (Remember, MacAuley was Canadian so didn't factor into the AOC's selection.) Hallahan for the *Globe* wrote: "Another newcomer in Marathon running finished seventh, Ralph A. Williams of the Hurja A.C. of Quincy. He was away back in the early stages, so far back, in fact, that he was not checked by the checkers at several of the stations. Because of this there was some doubt as to his having covered the full route."

George Trevor of the *Brooklyn Daily Eagle* spelled it out: "It was hinted that the Quincy man had received an automobile 'lift' during a crucial stage of the journey."[42]

The BAA's Geiger assured reporters that Williams was legit. And, bowled over by DeMar's unprecedented accomplishments, the Boston sports press was reluctant to sound a sour note amidst the fanfare. This was not an era when journalists were inclined to question authority. Still, Hallahan allowed a hint of skepticism to creep into his wrap-up of the Williams issue before returning to the theme of the marvelousness of DeMar—who was, after all, the man of the hour. "Williams ran a strong race," Hallahan wrote, "probably husbanding his strength too much over the final miles, *for he finished as fresh as a daisy.*"[43]

The AOC met in the BAA clubhouse that afternoon and made it official: DeMar, Mellor, Wendling, Churchill, Linder, and Williams were going to Paris.

But that wasn't the last word.

⸏

After the dejected Cygnet men returned to Port Chester, they sent a letter to the BAA protesting Williams's seventh-place prize on the grounds that "he did not run the full distance," the *Globe* reported on May 2. Geiger insisted that Williams ran a kosher race, telling the *Globe* that "unofficial checkers," whom he did not identify, "saw [Williams] pass at all except two points and at these places the runners were so bunched he could have easily been overlooked."[44]

The *Globe* put the question to William Prout, AAU president and chairman of the Olympic selection committee, who was in town to referee a Harvard track meet. "That's a matter for the referee of the race and the games committee of the Boston A.A. to decide," Prout responded, continuing:

> I talked with Referee Geiger this afternoon on the point and he told me that there was no grounds for protesting Williams. As it was Williams' first race of prominence, some claim he could not have done so well.

Other runners have declared that Williams did not pass them, while another says that he and Williams were running together at Newton Lower Falls. The fact that Williams did not wear a number on his back might have led to some confusion in the matter. The Olympic committee may have to act upon Williams' right to go to the Olympic games, but it must be more convincing than what has been brought forward, if he is to be sidetracked.

Meanwhile, a growing chorus of columnists was drawing attention to the controversy, starting with Trevor at the *Brooklyn Eagle.* "I still have telegrams [from Trevor] and Rod Thomas of the Washington Star offering to fight for my selection," Bill wrote decades later. Port Chester native Ed Sullivan, future television host but then sports columnist for the *New York Bulletin,* went so far as to call Williams "a contemptible cheat who had robbed Kennedy of his life's dream."[45]

Back in New York, Prout quickly called for an investigation. Bill Kennedy headed into the AAU office for a meeting. It turned out to be less investigative than pleading. "The committee asked me not to protest as it would hurt the drive for funds," Bill recalled. Remember Geiger's truck? ("Help Olympic fund.") In those days, the athletes' travel to Europe for the Olympics depended on the nickels and dimes of ordinary Americans. If Bill's club persisted in openly suggesting that the committee had picked a cheater for the team, they risked discouraging donors. Then, too, Bill was forty years old. "I was informed that being a younger man than I, [Williams's] chances of being a potential winner were better than mine." And finally, the carrot: Bill "was assured we would be matched to run a race at Yankee ball park for place on the team."[46]

That sounded reasonable. A large track and field Olympic trial meet was already scheduled at Yankee Stadium for June 7. It would be simple enough to add to it a distance race including Kennedy and Williams in a rematch. So there was still hope.[47]

Bill never heard any more about this race. June 7 came and went. Twenty thousand spectators took in a full slate of races at the stadium:

a ten-thousand-meter walk, a two-hundred-meter dash, and so on. No marathon.[48]

"The Cygnet A.C.," Bill recalled, "wanted to take it to court."[49]

Instead, Bill met privately with Fred Rubien, secretary-treasurer of the AOC. Perhaps Rubien had a less imperious manner than Prout. Perhaps he got through the conversation without mentioning Bill's age. Whatever it was, Bill listened to Rubien and went home to think about it.

Bill didn't record what he did while turning over the issue in his mind. We imagine he went for a run.

Plodding along the Boston Post Road and the streets of Port Chester, as he so often did, perhaps up and down Main Street and through Liberty Square, Bill might have remembered his first encounter with the marathon back in 1896. How McDermott and Liebgold seemed like superheroes. Bill's own daughters were teenagers by this time, but our family members who were children in Port Chester in the 1920s and 1930s recalled handkerchief-topped "Uncle Bill" often running past with a smile and a wave. Were he to encounter any of his nieces or nephews, or any local kids at all, playing in the street during this particular (hypothetical) run, Bill might have thought about the purpose of the international Games. However jilted by the committee, he believed in the Olympics, and he probably agreed with the message in AAU official Herman Obertubbesing's public plea for donations around this time: "Every man, woman and child in the United States should be interested in the success of our Olympic team for the value that it is going to be in an educational way—to teach our boys and girls that a clean body makes a clean mind."[50]

Bill was no saint, but he aspired to a marathoner ideal. Recall the description of "these Men of Iron" that he hoped to publish in a book (perhaps not unlike John Boyle O'Reilly's *Ethics of Boxing and Other Manly Sports*). "I have never known of a marathoner being sent to jail," Bill wrote. "No man who tempers his body as does he can be crooked." And he related with approval the words of Augustus

Johnson, another black friend and runner from Port Chester: "Colored folks ask me, why do I run so far when I don't get paid for it? My answer is, If I can instill in one colored boy the desire to emulate me and live a clean life, I am well repaid."[51]

And for all the tortuosities and hypocrisies in the rules and regulations concerning amateurism, Bill was a proud amateur. He hoped the youth of America would choose amateur athletics over the seamy underworld of prizefighting, as he remembered it. He certainly didn't want those youth to get the impression that there was something seamy about road running.

So, Bill could fight Williams and the AOC and in so doing tarnish the marathon in the eyes of the public, or he could let it go, sacrificing his own nearly lifelong ambition for the greater good of the sport he loved.

Whether he really mulled all this on a run or on the train home from the city or the next day laying brick, Bill did come to a conclusion.

"I decided to forget it."[52]

But planted in the Olympic summer that followed were the seeds of a new and larger role for Bill Kennedy in the years to come.

⚘

Meanwhile, what about Zuna? Talk about getting the shaft. The plumber had won two marathons in three weeks—two marathons that were initially announced as Olympic trials along with the Boston race. Zuna dropped out of the Boston Marathon, but did his wins at Detroit and Baltimore count for nothing? Others wondered that too, and eventually Zuna was added to the team, somewhat grudgingly, as an alternate. Of course, Bill Kennedy would never complain about his friend getting his own Olympic shot. And yet, the inclusion of Zuna, who did not finish the supposedly definitive trial at Boston, highlights the unfairness of the exclusion of Kennedy, who did.[53]

Unfortunately, the Olympic committee wasn't done mishandling its marathon team. DeMar and probably the other veteran runners felt that Zuna deserved to be a true member of the team and that Williams should be the alternate. Once the athletes had sailed to France and settled in, U.S. Olympic marathon coach Mike Ryan (winner of the 1912 Boston Marathon) observed them in practice runs and started to suspect DeMar was right. Ryan scheduled a fifteen-mile trial race to determine who really was the weakest link. The race was held on a hot day on a grass track. Williams quit after three miles.[54]

Ryan recommended promoting Zuna over Williams. The committee agreed: Zuna would start in the marathon at Paris in July. "ZUNA VINDICATED" read headlines at home.[55]

"Then," wrote DeMar, "the authorities pulled the prize boner." Instead of dropping Williams to alternate status, the committee dropped Carl Linder, the 1919 Boston Marathon winner, who had placed fifth in April and finished fourth in the fifteen-mile trial. "I have always wondered just which of the Olympic officials wanted to gamble on a youngster like Williams winning the big race as a dark horse," said DeMar. "Linder had won a place as a regular member of the team, and he was still in good condition. Williams had not shown that he was any better than seventh man and a sub. This trick destroyed any hope and morale that any of the men had left."[56]

On July 13, the day of the Olympic marathon, "as one would expect in Paris in July, it was hot," DeMar recalled. "It was certainly grueling work racing under the hot sun, and it required all one's determination and patriotism to keep from quitting or at least slowing down to a walk."[57]

A hot day. Steam must have come out of Bill Kennedy's ears when he read about the race later, at home in Port Chester.

Finland's Albin Stenroos won the race and the gold medal. Stenroos, a woodworker, was a veteran athlete at thirty-five years old, and his gaunt, grizzled appearance led reporters to think he was forty or even forty-five. Evidently, that had not bothered Finland's Olympic committee when selecting their team.[58]

DeMar got the bronze. Zuna came in eighteenth.

Williams did not finish.[59]

~~~

To play devil's advocate for a moment: a stellar rookie outing can happen. Whitey Michelsen, for example, ran a spectacular race the first time he entered a marathon—2:30:35 at Boston in 1921 (the first of many achievements for Whitey). Moreover, let's acknowledge that Bill, if indeed he was cheated in the 1924 Boston Marathon, was cheated out of seventh place, not first or second or third or so on. Had he run a little harder that day, there wouldn't have been any controversy. Lastly, there is no proof that Williams hitched a lift, and there never will be.

But did the AOC make the right selection? As far as we're concerned, the proof is in the pudding: Williams's DNF at Paris. (How far Williams ran before quitting was not officially recorded, though Bill thought it was fifteen miles.) And to fast-forward briefly, Williams started and dropped out of the next Boston Marathon, in 1925. That was his third and final grind. In other words, Williams never, in his extremely short running career, finished a marathon definitively or uncontested. He crossed the finish line at Boston in '24 under protest, without having been checked at three or at best two checkpoints. As marathon historian Tom Derderian points out, Williams dropped out of the Olympic marathon at Paris because it was too hot, then dropped out at Boston in '25 because it was too cold. Then he was never heard from again. (In an athletic context, that is; Williams may well have gone on to design suspension bridges or find a cure for erysipelas.) And yet, Williams is considered an Olympian, while Bill Kennedy spent that summer "3,000 miles from the scene of action," as Trevor wrote, "pound[ing] the Boston Post Road training for a race that he will never run."[60]

"However," Bill would write, turning the page on the subject, "to err is human, and officials come under this category as well as the rest of us."[61]

〜⌒〜

Later that summer, on another hot day, Kennedy and Zuna ran a Labor Day marathon from the New York Athletic Club to Long Beach,
Long Island. It was Long Island's hottest September 1 that century
so far, registering ninety-two degrees in the shade. Five people died
in incidents related to the heat.[62] Officials shortened the race by two
miles. Bill was leading, but this time, unlike in Chicago in 1913, he
did not insist on running the extra miles. He lost twelve pounds but
finished first by more than a mile. Bill recalled:

> The first prize was a bronze figure of Mercury mounted on an Onyx
> pedestal. It stood six feet high[,] too heavy for me to carry so I was
> told it would be shipped to me by express. I was handed a receipt.
> "One bronze statue paid in full." The receipt is in my scrap book.
> The statue, I never even had the pleasure of seeing it. I brought the
> matter before the Metropolitan Assn. of the A.A.U. They informed
> me that the chairman of the Committee absconded with the funds
> to pay for it so I was out of luck.[63]

It was an ignominious coda to an aggravating summer. Another
man in Bill's shoes might have become bitter after these events. Okay,
the loss of the statue was easy to laugh off, and Bill did. But earlier,
his Olympic dream had crumbled amidst possible shenanigans and
definite ageism. That would embitter anybody.

Bill chose to tackle the injustice in another way. He had a lot of
work to do in the next few years.

IN BILL'S WORDS: PRIZES

After all these hardships in reaching the starting line, what do
the winning runners receive for their efforts? Many people are
[under the impression] that amateur athletes get valuable prizes,
or that they are merely a subterfuge, something to be turned in
later for cash. In the case of boxing I have personally known of this
happening, but it is very rare for a runner or trackman [to sell] his
prizes. . . .

In order to give a trophy that is valued at more than fifty dollars, it is necessary to get permission from the A.A.U. This request is usually granted to a recognized club. In some races, however, a club ignorant of this rule may take it upon itself to give prizes exceeding the value.

This happened in a Marathon race in Conn, in which valuable radios were the prizes. Later on the men were notified to return same, which turned out to be rather difficult getting them back. I had a good laugh when I ran into Jimmy Roach of New Haven and asked him "Did you get your radios back yet?" With a mournful expression on his face, he says, "I wish I had never heard of that race. I have written to them all and none has replied. Now I hear Mel Porter is down in Panama. Am I supposed to go down there after that radio?"

Some races give good prizes to the first eight or ten to finish and bronze medals to the next twenty-five finishers. The balance of the men run for exercise. A club promoting its first few races as a rule will give good trophies, but the value of them decreases each year until they can no longer draw a first class entry, and it passes into oblivion. In a race in Baltimore back in twenty-eight, I received one half of a book end for fourth place, the fifth man received the other end. The entry blanks of a ten mile race at Macombs Park in New York read "Bronzed figures to the first three men to finish." Harvey Frick was first, I ran second. We got our bronzed figures—plaster of paris figures of a Roman Emperor painted bronze. The kind you used to buy off a peddler for twenty-five cents. And we had to pay fifty cents entry fee. Frick was wild. He took his and smashed the emperor against a post. . . .

Down in Salisbury Md. they held a marathon. . . . Oldag of Buffalo won with "Whitey" Michelsen in second place. At the banquet that night, a very lavish affair, where we all had an enjoyable time. In presenting the second prize to Michelsen, a gold plated medal, the toastmaster described it as a beautiful solid gold medal, asking him to say a few words. Now Whitey was not much of an orator, but he was a stickler for the truth, and what a laugh we runners had when, looking at the prize, he hefted it, looked at the toastmaster, turned to the guests and said, "This is not gold. It is plated."

Yet a race such as the Boston Marathon, with its historical background, a million spectators, the publicity, and the prestige that goes to the winner, would draw just as many entries was the first prize but a blue ribbon.

These prizes are but a part of that old commercial question "What do you get out of running?"

An additional reward is the wonderful people you come in contact with as an amateur, men and women of all stations of life. The amateur is more often welcome to their home than is the professional, due to the fact that he receives no remuneration for his performance. I have been the guest of so many wonderful people, that I wish space permitted me to name them all, and incidentally most of them were in the New England states.

All amateurs meet up with them. During my 104 marathons, twenty-eight of them in Boston, fifty years of competition and eighty thousand miles of running and walking, I have had the honor of meeting four Presidents of the U.S., several Governors and many Mayors and prominent people through my foot running . . . Honeyboy Fitz, Gov. Curley. . . .

During the depression years I stayed with a Mrs. Goslin and her three sons over in Dorchester. I often wondered if Harold came back from "Over There." At another time a bricklayer, Johnny Brick, had me at their home for a week in Somerville. After the race Mrs. Brick had a hard time keeping tabs on us two bricklayers. . . .

Meeting these wonderful people and the many others were my prizes. Medals and trophies were "junk." Many were given away, others sold during the Depression for old gold, and there is a box full of bronze medals down in the basement. The real prizes was a sense of humor and the memories of the wonderful people I have had the honor and good fortune to meet.[64]

7
GOOD TIMES

t was bedlam. Tebeau's Farm, Hopkinton, on the morning of Patriots' Day 1925, was filled with wiry men eating massive breakfasts of
steak, ham, eggs, and potatoes—or feeling too nervous to eat more
than a bite of toast; trooping up and down stairs; yelling, chatting, joking, laughing; renewing friendships (and rivalries); taking the BAA
doctors' physical exams; and preparing to run their hearts out. No
doubt Bricklayer Bill—fresh off a third-place finish in the Baltimore
Marathon in late March—was in the thick of the commotion, enjoying
every minute.[1]

But as the runners caught up, scuttlebutt surely circulated regarding the previous summer's Olympics. DeMar, especially, felt no com-
punction in airing his complaints about the marathoners' shoddy
treatment in Paris at the hands of the AOC. His teammates Zuna,
Wendling, and Linder were all there at Tebeau's that day as well, and
they could corroborate.

In a sense, those farmhouse walls contained all the contradictions
of the Jazz Age, at least as they related to marathon runners and their

struggle for respect. And Bill was in the thick of that as well. The mid- to late 1920s were good to the "prosperous contractor," as the Associated Press now called him. Not only did Bill succeed in business, but he could still run a pretty good marathon, too, with top-five finishes even in his forties. And he kept getting the loudest cheers on the course. By promoting the sport, individual runners and their collective cause, and his hometown of Port Chester, Bill exemplified the exuberant boosterism of the Roaring Twenties, when prosperity, change, opportunity, and excitement seemed to course throughout the country.[2]

Yet at a time when Americans glorified professional sports stars such as Babe Ruth and Jack Dempsey, and worshipped adventurers such as aviator Charles Lindbergh, marathon runners were generally small potatoes. Of course, Patriots' Day was still magical. On that one day each year spectators, newspaper readers, and radio audiences all turned their eyes and ears to Boston, and the workingmen marathoners had their time in the spotlight. But for the rest of the year, the runners enjoyed precious little prestige.

The great DeMar himself garnered scant recognition outside of April. More than once, while out for a practice run, he was apprehended by vigilant police officers who mistook him for a miscreant. On one occasion in 1926, DeMar, who lived in Melrose, just north of Boston, went for an early morning run through Wellesley, where "an eagle-eyed policeman" spotted "the fleeing figure of a fugitive streaking down the highway." DeMar finally convinced the officer he had nothing to do with an apparent crime wave "and that he was not running away from anything." Police on patrol were not the only ones who eyed runners suspiciously in the 1920s. Many viewed them as kooks, oddities who ran around in their underwear.[3]

Even in Boston, some sportswriters still puzzled about why marathoners did what they did. "It may be that they are just 'nuts,'" one wrote, that the "Marathon bug is a mild species of insanity." Another termed it "Marathonitis . . . a disease that first showed up in 1896."[4]

As a spokesman for his brethren, Bricklayer Bill reacted to such comments, somewhat mirroring the then nascent PR industry, though in more homespun fashion:

> Tom McCabe . . . wrote an article for his paper the day before the Boston Marathon in which he facetiously wrote that the squirrels in the trees were waiting for the marathon nuts. I got a kick out of the story, but [fellow runners] appealed to me to protest to the writer.
> Calling on Mr. McCabe I pointed out to him that we were not the only nuts around Boston, that during the previous November seventy thousand people sat through a cold rain to watch the Yale-Harvard football game, and that the National Golf Championship was held there during the summer with thousands of spectators following the finals, soaked to the skin by a torrential rain. At this point Tom burst out laughing, saying "You are right, Bill, we are all nuts."[5]

Sure enough, McCabe changed his tune, defending marathoners in 1926 by comparing them to other athletes and enthusiasts. "To our way of thinking the marathoner is no more a nut than is a golfer who pedals around a golf course in the pouring rain, and we have seen many a one do this," he wrote in the *Herald*. "The marathoner who runs 26 miles 385 yards is no more a nut than the baseball player, football player, the oarsman, or any other athletic sharp you care to mention. He is no more a nut than the football fan who sits, or stands, for an afternoon in the pouring rain, to watch two teams founder around in a quagmire. Is he?"[6]

Another contradiction played out beginning with the 1925 Boston Marathon, this one related to "the so-called evils of liquors and tobacco," as Bill put it.[7] Remember that for every flapper there was at least one dour opponent of frippery and fun. The fast pace of the twenties generated a nostalgia that, in some ways, became negative, turning people against new ideas. Some longed for an America uncomplicated by automobiles and airplanes, by world war and a League of Nations, by reform ideas and women voting, by jazz music and short skirts, by radical immigrants and black people living in northern cities. For some, Prohibition, the Klan, or a crusade against teaching evolution or for restricting immigration could provide comfort. Bostonians of this stripe found reassurance in the victories of the sober, serious, and religious DeMar.

And DeMar seemed a cinch to win in 1925, for his fifth time. McCabe went so far as to write: "Dee Mar-athon will be run tomorrow. Say what you will, the name of Clarence DeMar, the Melrose soldier, has come to be so closely wrapped up in all that is good in the American distance classic that it is more than a coincidence his name so aptly fits the name of the contest itself."[8] Bill Kennedy agreed that DeMar "will be a hard man to beat because of the conscientious way he goes in training for the event."[9]

The AAU designated the 1925 race as the "Marathon Championship of the United States." In keeping with Olympic regulations, the BAA ended the tradition of bicycle attendants for the runners, instead providing "relief stations" for "first aid" along the route.[10] Bill, for one, would miss these attendants:

I have always felt nostalgic, thinking back to the twelve years in which I had an attendant. True, they never made me run any faster, but there they were at my side with a sack hanging from their shoulder containing [refreshments]. If you finished among [the first eight], your attendant also received a medal, and they were as proud of it as though it was through their efforts alone you came through to place. . . .

I am sorry to say I can not recall the names of all my attendants much as I regret but I know I never let any of them down, though at times it was tough going to get them that medal. . . .

Al Upham, a local runner, [rode] with me one year, and brought me home in sixth place the first time I was in the major prizes. He knew every foot of the course and was a real asset, with his coaching and advice. One year I had a young Italian rider who spoke broken English. I was a pretty tired man after twenty miles, and stopped several times for a rub to get the cramps out of my legs. While rubbing me he kept pleading for me to stay in the race.

"Please, oh please, no quit," he would say with tears in his eyes. I knew he wanted to bring me in, as much as I wanted to call it a day I hated to let him down, so I ran walked and rested, and in answer to his prayers finished in time for him to get his medal.

For several years I had the same rider, an elderly Scotchman. To the best of my recollection his name was Laughlin. He was as faithful as a dog; he never left me no matter how far behind I fell. Many riders would leave their runner when they felt he had no chance to get in the medals. They would ride ahead in hopes of picking up a runner who had lost his rider, and stood a chance to be in the money. Not my rider. He suffered every mile with me when the going was tough. He must have been a machinist, for, when he peeled an orange for me, I would suck it with a wry face. His finger nails were a whole lot cleaner when we finished, than at the start.

One of the few indoor marathons I took part in was at Riverview Park, Chicago. The notice to entrants stated "bring your own handler." For my handler I chose a fellow bricklayer member of Bricklayers Union #21 of Illinois, "Scotty" Gribben, now deceased. What we didn't know about running at that time would fill a big book. We arrived at the starting line without even a sponge or towel. There were about eighty starters in the race; each one's handler had water bucket, sponge, oranges, chocolate, towel, and stimulants. I looked at Scotty. He looked at me, and, with a knowing wink, he says, "Don't worry, Kid." The track was separated from the infield by a wooden fence, or rather a railing, upon which the handlers would place their refreshments then run along the inside of the enclosure, encouraging their man. Along about the fifteenth mile I had more refreshments than any man in the race thanks to Scotty."

Tellingly, the BAA made big changes to the checking system. The *Herald* reported: "For the first time, too, at the various relief stations will be placed official checkers whose duty it will be to remain and check every runner in the race. There will be no more checking of the first group of 30 or 40 to pass a given point, then a hurried trip to the next checking point, there to renew the action." And for the runners' part, "every man in the race should be certain he has cloth numbers issued to him, pinned plainly in view on front and back of his uniform. The checking system will be more rigid than ever this year, and if a man is not checked at each station he will get short shrift at the finish line."[12] These new policies were almost certainly aimed at preventing another Ralph Williams–style debacle.

Though no bicyclists would ride along with refreshments, the runners could carry goodies themselves. At Tebeau's, they again encountered Burgess Gordon, a doctor and medical researcher from what is now known as Brigham and Women's Hospital. Gordon had examined the runners for a study the previous year, and he and Bill Kennedy had corresponded since then. ("Many thanks for your most interesting letter," the doctor wrote to the bricklayer. "The observation of the various physical changes in your running, the diets, and your methods of conditioning, are the best I have ever read from a layman.") This morning, the doctor was handing out small sacks of glucose tablets for the runners to pin to their shorts and consume during the race. Gordon theorized that the extra sweet stuff would keep the men's blood sugar levels normal as they ran. Bill happened to agree, on the basis of his own experience drinking tea (or sometimes brandy) with sugar added to pep him up during a race. Chuck Mellor, however, "refused his allotment with a disdainful wave of his hand," Bill recalled. "Stuffing a wad of tobacco into his mouth, he said, 'Here's my candy.'"[13]

Bricklayer Bill's usual hopes for a warm day were dashed when he saw snowflakes that morning. Temperatures reached "a numbing 33 degrees," marking the 1925 race as the "Frostbite Marathon." Only 95 of the 121 entries toed the line as "a bitter, bleak wind . . . whipped snow flurries" in their faces. Many runners wore gloves, and veteran plodders sported long-sleeved shirts; "some even wore long drawers." Chuck Mellor "tucked a newspaper, we think it was The Herald, in under his jersey just before the race started and it served as a great protection for his chest when the wind blew bitterly on the wide stretches between Framingham and Natick." (Yes, this was a *Herald* report.)[14]

Bill started poorly, reportedly "bothered by cramps, caused no doubt by an injudicious breakfast." By the time he had reached Newton Lower Falls, Bill had fallen to twenty-seventh position. Then nature called. As Tom Derderian relates, Bill "stopped in a garage to use the toilet (New England bushes have no leaves in mid-April)." The *Herald* reported the bricklayer "must have used up five or ten minutes in the garage before again taking up the journey. At any rate his rest did him a lot of good." Running faster than most of his rivals over the second half, Kennedy "climbed in the last 12 miles to a fighting ninth position. . . . The old man, running like a sprinter, was just nosed out of eighth position and the last of the prizes by Nestor Ericksen of the Finnish-American AC."[15]

As for Mellor, whether it was his inky windbreaker or his plug of chaw, the thirty-one-year-old Chicago mechanic had a very good day. Mellor scored his first triumph at Boston, finishing in 2:33, seven seconds ahead of DeMar in second. (Frank Zuna and Whitey Michelsen followed.) So the one guy who'd chewed tobacco instead of glucose won the race—"much to the chagrin of the doctors and the delight of the Fourth Estate," Bill wrote later. "I imagine by now Dr. Gordon can laugh this one off himself."[16]

Bill was certainly in a jovial mood himself after being "given a great reception by the crowds who always have recalled him for the grand victory he scored in 1917," wrote Hallahan. Added McCabe: "The old man deserves worlds of praise for his efforts. His happy-go-lucky way and his smile have won him many friends. If the amateur running game has nothing more to point to, it has a man worth his weight in gold in old Bill Kennedy."[17] When Bill met up with the victorious Mellor in the BAA gymnasium after the race, "they fell into each other's arms and hugged one another. It was a spirit that one seldom sees in athletics."[18]

By contrast, the pre-race favorite, DeMar, was visibly unhappy with his second-place finish. "As DeMar stood reflecting in a far corner of the big room, surrounded by a few of his intimate friends, the difference between victor and vanquished broke in on him through the haze and in his blunt manner of speech he blurted out: 'You don't get so many cheers when you lose'.... Clarence took his defeat calmly, yet it hurt him. . . . Immediately he was dressed he wanted to leave. He wanted to go home to his mother, where he knew real solace and solitude awaited him."[19]

DeMar would win more Boston Marathons, but—always the stern Sunday school teacher—he never appealed to the crowds the way Bill Kennedy did during these years. (Notwithstanding that Bill generally praised his rival as "a great runner, full of grit and determination," in just one example.)[20]

But there was more than personality involved in the popularity equation. Sports writers delighted in contrasting the lifestyles of DeMar and Mellor, echoing the cultural divide of the 1920s. One major issue was "the deadly weed." DeMar's "spectacular triumphs," such as in '24, gave "moralists abundant material for preaching abstaining from tobacco in all its nefarious forms."[21] This camp believed that because the great DeMar neither smoked nor chewed, that meant anyone else hoping to be a winner must also abstain. Then, "just as folks had begun to accept that creed as definite and unyielding, along comes Chuck Mellor, who starts his victorious race with a workingman's portion of chewing tobacco in his mouth and whose first request after finishing is for a cigar." Mellor reportedly "took no refreshment of any kind in the long run, but a cud of tobacco answered his purpose until he neared the finish." When questioned about relief stations, Mellor claimed: "I did not take a thing all the way. Never care to. It always reminds me of a drowning man grasping at a straw."[22]

The press also mentioned Mellor's penchant for liquor (a subject dealt with quite openly despite Prohibition). No stranger to either alcohol or tobacco, Bill offered his take, starting with the words of humorist George Ade:

"'Tis better to pinch hit in the World Series than to sit on the bench all your life." This often comes to mind in conversation with people,

who on learning I run marathons express surprise and say, "Then
you never drank or smoked."

With some people it was sort of an embarrassment to admit
that I was guilty of same. Then Ade's wisecrack comes to mind and
the thought I would have been rather a lonesome guy sitting on
the bench if I had led such an abstemious life. Then I think of an
old New York saying "Early to bed, early to rise, you never meet the
regular guys."

It is not for me to quote on the morality of drinking but I do
believe that tobacco is more harmful than drinking. I have never witnessed one glass of beer making a person ill, but I have seen many
an instance of the first-time use of tobacco making people very sick.
The great philosophers preached temperance in all things, which is
proper. This pertains to food as well, for what is more revolting than
an over indulgence at the dinner table.

What effect liquor may have on a person must be judged by each
one for himself. My advice to athletes would be to leave it alone,
especially the young man—an older one may possibly need it. . . .

After most marathon races beer is served to those who care for
it, and most of the men after losing eight pounds in three hours
of running are doggoned dry. Yet as I said previously DeMar, Sid
Hatch, Miles Cameron, all great runners, were tee-totalers. . . .

I have used brandy diluted with warm water and sugar, with
beneficial effect. On the other hand [in a fifteen-mile race in Bellville,
Illinois] with a safe lead at twelve miles I foolishly took a drink of
whiskey from my handler. I immediately began retching and was
forced to quit the race.[23]

Even after Mellor's victory in 1925, the press portrayed him as
undisciplined, chiding him for not allowing "his training to inter-
fere with the pleasures of life, which included smoking and chewing tobacco" as well as eating "whatever appeals to his palate." Chuck
was a workingman who enjoyed life. He had at one time been Bill's
hod carrier but was apparently "unequal to such hard work." Yet as a
married man, he had to make a living and took "whatever he [was]
able to turn his hand to," for example, laboring "a few years as a shoe-
worker." Chuck certainly felt free to pick and choose what he would
do in life at any given time: "Only two weeks ago he definitely decided

to retire from marathon racing for good, but as the date of the BAA
fixture approached, the call to his love became so compelling that
he again resumed his training, such as it is, and he outran the man
whom everyone believed was invincible."[24]

Fourth-place finisher Michelsen, by contrast, was a Kennedy asso-
ciate who was the very picture of discipline. He proved himself equal
to carrying the hod on Bill's job sites, without complaint. One day
that September, he worked up until 4 p.m., then made his way to Yankee Stadium, where he won the AAU fifteen-mile championship run.
"One would think that carrying a hod would stiffen Whitey's running
muscles," reflected the *Globe*. "Judging by what he did in that 15-mile
race, we have another guess." Proud of his protégé, Bill was quick to
point out that in addition to being a bricklayer's helper, Whitey had
worked as a carpenter and a tinsmith and "can turn his hand to anything that means hard work."[25]

Apparently Michelsen and Mellor were not the only runners Bill
ever hired:

> Now here is a tale of insurrection. I was contracting up in West-
> chester County, and had a team of runners working for me. I had
> to make a rule of no race talk on the job, as we had a habit of all
> getting together and discussing pro and con, during which all work
> ceased. Whitey Michelsen and a runner named Vickery from Texas
> were carrying the hod. John Rosi a Finn was scaffold man, Allyn
> Manning and myself were laying brick. Clarence Mead was driv-
> ing the truck and poor Frank Lalla was digging ditches. I tried to
> impress on them, that out of respect for the boss (by advice from
> Ed Sullivan) they should not finish ahead of me, but judging by the
> frequency that they beat their boss, they no capech English.[26]

On Columbus Day 1925, Bill realized the culmination of months of
work on two fronts. Most publicly, it was the day of the inaugural
Port Chester National Marathon. Bill helped launch this high-profile
race in his hometown with the help of local freelance sportswriter

Tommy McNamara. The pair presented their idea to the Port Chester Chamber of Commerce, which agreed to sponsor the race in conjunction with its Merchants'-Manufacturers' Exposition on Columbus Day weekend. (The village now boasted 140 factories, including the headquarters of the Life Savers candy company.) The Chamber and various local clubs—such as the Moose and the Sons of Italy—pitched in to purchase silver cups and other prizes, hoping to attract elite athletes and the publicity they would bring.[27]

We don't know just how long Bill had mulled over this idea, but he surely took inspiration from his boyhood experience running the Port Chester section of the first American marathon in 1896. Now, almost three decades later, the route of the new race was nearly the same as that early experiment, except that it was run in reverse, literally drawing attention from the big city to the little village. The "Port Chester National Marathon Race" started at the USS *Maine* monument at Columbus Circle, in Manhattan, and finished at Liberty Square in Port Chester.[28]

It was a coup for Bill and "Old Saw Pits." Including headliners DeMar, Mellor, Zuna, and local favorites Michelsen and Kennedy himself, fifty-six of "the foremost distance runners in this country and Canada" competed in the first running of what "promises to become as important an event in the fall as the famous Boston marathon is in the spring," claimed the *New York Times*.[29] More than 250,000 turned out along the route. In Port Chester, spectators crammed both sides of South Main Street, where American and Italian flags fluttered overhead. Fans even took to the rooftops to watch as local hero Whitey Michelsen appeared first, to the strains of "hundreds of auto horns barking." A mighty cry of "Come on, Whitey!" rolled down the street "like a peal of thunder," according to the local *Daily Item*. "The blond haired runner was greeted by a tremendous ovation as he crossed the line, smiling and showing little effects of the long grind."[30]

Michelsen broke the tape in 2:29:01.8. Whitey's performance at Port Chester that day is now considered the first sub-2:30 marathon in the world. (Despite DeMar's impressive performance at Boston in

GOOD TIMES 223

1924, the course was later re-measured and found to be short of the regulation 26.2-mile distance.) DeMar and Zuna followed. Bill finished in eighth place to a great ovation. When told of his protégé's victory, "Kennedy seemed as much pleased as though he himself had won the race." Their clubmate John "Iron Horse" Rosi came next, clinching for the Cygnet A.C. the team prize, a bronze figure donated by the Knights of Columbus and presented to them at the expo that afternoon.[31]

The day was a smashing success, and more excitement was in store that evening, as the runners and friends gathered at the Chester Tavern for a post-race banquet. The affable innkeeper "fairly out-did himself in preparing a fine chicken dinner," which the hungry runners wolfed down. Speeches followed the meal. As he spoke, "Kennedy was visibly affected by the wonderful tribute paid him when he reached Rye and Port Chester." Then a fiery DeMar "brought the athletes to their feet cheering . . . as he bitterly complained about the manner in which the last Olympic marathon team was picked." DeMar pulled no punches, charging that AOC officials with scarcely any knowledge about marathon running had played politics in choosing the team, and he decried "the disgraceful and utterly impractical manner in which the men were handled last year in France," reported the *Daily Item*.[32]

Immediately following the banquet, Kennedy, DeMar, and two dozen other top runners formally convened to found the International Marathon Runners' Association (IMRA). No surprise when Kennedy was elected president. For all his adult life and then some, Bill had been a member, and at times a president, of the bricklayers' union. Now it was time to start a runners' union. No surprise, either, that DeMar was elected secretary. Who better to articulate the athletes' grievances? Going forward, the plodders could advocate for themselves as an organized force.

The new group wasted no time in taking action. They resolved to petition the national convention of the AAU, meeting the next month in Pittsburgh, that their runners' association "be allowed to choose the team which will represent America in the 1928 Olympics; that the association be allowed to decide whether or not the team should have a coach, and if so, that it be allowed to pick the coach, and that the members of the Olympic team be chosen on the basis of their records for a year's work and not according to their showings in a single race."[33]

Such a policy would not have benefited Bill personally in '24, but it would have been fair, and that's what he and the other association officers wanted. The runners believed "that they themselves are better qualified to know who are the best long distance runners in the country and feel that by selecting the team themselves, America will be represented by the best runners and not by those who happen to belong to some more influential club." It was the opening salvo in a fight to make the 1928 Olympiad a saner one for the marathoners. They were tired of being jerked around by the whims of the AOC.[34]

Before long, Bill and his union tested out their new collective power by weighing in on the revival of the Brooklyn-Seagate Marathon, an annual fixture before the war. Organizers at first floated a full marathon course from Brooklyn to Jamaica in Queens and back. But that plan was scrapped when "Bill Kennedy, veteran distance runner and President of [the] Marathon Runners' Association, expressed on behalf of some of the country's prominent marathoners a preference for the twenty-mile route." Accordingly, a course of about twenty miles, beginning and ending at the Brooklyn Armory, was adopted for this modified marathon, held in late February. That way, the race fit into, rather than disrupted, the runners' training for the Boston Marathon in April.[35]

For after all, "no matter what they may say, the Boston race is the best Marathon in the country," Bill told the *Globe* in April. "It may not have the championship title hanging on the result [this year, 1926]. This honor has been conferred on the Baltimore Marathon, but if you asked me which race—and I guess if you asked the other men—they would rather win, I have no hesitancy in saying that they all would be unanimous in saying the Boston A.A. race."[36]

For his part, the Finnish Olympic champion Stenroos had a complaint about the Boston course, after training on it in the days leading up to the marathon: "I do not think it is full length. . . . In Finland we measure everything with a steel tape. Has the Boston course ever been measured with a tape?" Apparently the Rain Man of the race game, Stenroos was right: the course was later found to be 176 yards short of the official twenty-six miles, 385 yards.[37]

After the previous year's hype over the tobacco-chewing Mellor's victory, the press whipsawed when a young teetotaler with the marathon-perfect name of Johnny Miles won the 1926 race in record time on a bitterly cold Patriots' Day.

"The forces of reform once more are back in the saddle," gushed the *Herald*. "Last year the long-distance hike was won by a runner who lunched at intervals during his gallop over the course on plug cut, nibbled shamelessly right in the open. He smoked cigars and had no compunctions about taking a hooker of anything short of third rail vintage, if somebody else was buying." Miles, by contrast, "could qualify for honorary membership in any of the 'anti' leagues. . . . He doesn't chew tobacco and neither does he smoke. . . . He doesn't partake of the cup that cheers in any of its various forms."[38]

Abstinence alone didn't explain Miles's victory. Hailing from Cape Breton, the island at the northern tip of Nova Scotia, Miles was used to the cold. The twenty-year-old had trained that winter "running over the snow-covered roads" around the coal mining town of Sydney after his shift delivering groceries with a horse-drawn wagon. (Miles was "particularly chummy with a smart little pony that was used for the delivery team," reported the *Globe*. "He used to take it out in the evening with only bridle and reins and use it as a pacemaker as he ran along for several miles. The pony seemed to enjoy this also!") At times, Miles was "compelled to wallow through four feet of snow [and] was forced to leap out of the path of trolleys."[39]

After that, a chilly April day in Boston didn't faze him. DeMar and Stenroos battled for the lead through most of the race, but Miles passed them by at Lake Street and held on for the win, stunning the experts with a time of 2:25:40. Bill Kennedy, described by the *Globe* as "the most popular runner of all," came in eighth.[40]

Miles's unexpected win soon took on the flavor of a morality tale. "I could never have won the race on my own strength alone," Miles told the press. "There was a supreme power behind it, which aided me. Without this spiritual help I could not have been successful."[41]

It turned out that Miles shunned not only tobacco and liquor but also swearing—and running on Sundays, when he served as a Sunday school teacher. A *Globe* writer described him as "a good living, steady youth, with no bad habits, religious, but not priggish or goody-good."[42] Miles's story struck a chord with thousands of clean-living Bostonians, and their adulation turned him into an instant celebrity. At several gatherings in his honor, Miles "shook hands with at least 10,000 admirers," presumably all with good firm handshakes, for while he "underwent the handshaking ordeal with a smile," he revealed that "if the present state of affairs continues he soon will have to take such steps as Pres. Coolidge has adopted in forgoing the handshaking custom."[43] Miles even preached two sermons, one at the Tremont Temple Baptist church, the other before Canadian organizations. The burden of his text "was that clean living is the thing that makes athletic success—and other kinds of success—possible." Well-wishers filled North Station when he departed Boston.[44]

⌒

Meanwhile, in Philadelphia, John "Jock" Semple was laying floor for the Japanese exhibit at the Sesquicentennial Exposition. On the grounds of what is today the South Philadelphia Sports Complex, the exposition was due to open on May 31 and continue through the summer of America's 150th anniversary. For Semple, laying floor

was the latest in a string of jobs—shipyard joiner, concrete worker—
since the 23-year-old had landed in Philly on the boat from Scotland.

"The men I worked with talked about the Sesquicentennial Marathon," Semple recalled later. Starting in Valley Forge, this full-distance
grind would be the highlight of the fair's opening week festivities.
Semple had run cross-country races as a teenager back in Clydebank,
so he decided to try his hand, or rather feet, at the marathon. He ran
up to ninety miles a week in training. When he dislocated his shoulder at work, he ran with his arm in a sling.[45]

The morning of June 2, Semple hitched a ride to Valley Forge,
where he and threescore other hopefuls took their places behind the
finish line along with Olympians such as Stenroos and DeMar. One
gray-haired Irishman nodded at Semple and said, "Do well."

"I was surprised that anybody even talked to me," Semple
remembered.

"At the gun I trotted out, but soon I moved up with the lead pack
which included Clarence DeMar. I fell back a bit as the course wound
along the [Schuylkill] River, then moved inland."

Depending on your source, between a hundred thousand and 1
million Pennsylvanians lined the "rough hill and dale route," as the
Times called it. Under a "blistering sun," the Finnish gold medalist
Stenroos dropped out at the eleven-mile mark, one of about thirty
runners (half the field) to quit. Out front, DeMar opened up a mile-
long gap on Michelsen.[46]

"You're number ten," a spectator shouted at young Semple as the
front-runners approached the city. Taking heart, Semple "ran like
hell in the hot sun." Then, at the University of Pennsylvania and the
22-mile mark, a leg cramp hobbled the Scotsman. He dropped back
to eleventh place.

Still in first, the star DeMar ran through the main gate of the
exposition grounds, passing under an eighty-foot replica of the Liberty Bell decorated with 26,000 light bulbs. He entered the horse-
shoe Sesquicentennial Stadium (later JFK Stadium) and circled the

track, winning by a quarter mile in 2:42:50. Michelsen, Wendling, Zuna, and Kennedy followed. Rosi finished ninth, once again securing (with Whitey and Bill) the team prize for the Cygnet A.C.

Semple came in eleventh. "I had lost 15 pounds and lay gasping on the grass," he recalled. "People brought me water, while one man, the man who had said hello at the start, directed the relief efforts." That friendly veteran was Bill Kennedy.

"You did well," the bricklayer complimented Semple. "Stay with it. But don't be surprised if it takes you at least three years to run a decent marathon.'"

Bill was "dead right," Semple would admit in retrospect. The young Scot lay on the grass for another half hour, then took the subway home.

He'd be back. Like so many before him, Semple had caught the marathon bug. Later in the century, the name Jock Semple would become virtually synonymous with the management of the Boston Marathon.

The second annual Port Chester Marathon went off without a hitch in October 1926. An unfortunate *un*hitching occurred, however, when a drawbridge swung open in New Rochelle just after the top six leaders went by. Bricklayer Bill was among the half dozen who got "a four minute jump on the rest of the field." Bill then moved up a few notches, "overtaking four men during the final five miles or so of the race," and came in third to a "thunderous" ovation, behind the winner De-Mar and runner-up Michelsen.[47]

"Port Chester people, literally all of them," turned out for the marathon, said an editorial writer for the *Daily Item*. The holiday event had become more than a race for this scrappy workaday burg. "It has stirred our pride in our own community—on every face in that huge gathering yesterday was written the thought: 'My home town is doing this—people all over the country will be reading about us when the results of this race are published.'" For a little village, "Port Chester, it seems, knows how to do a big job in a big way."[48]

By now Bill was president not only of the IMRA but also of the Connecticut AAU. (He had moved just across the river to East Port Chester, later renamed Byram.) And he soon used his bully pulpit to wade into a controversial matter. About a month after the marathon, Bill came out in favor of a proposed AAU rule closing American amateur athletic competition to foreign nationals who had lived in the United States for three years or more without applying for citizenship. The proposal was deemed likely to fail, but if passed, the measure "would debar such foreign athletes as adopt America as their permanent home but fail to become naturalized citizens. The outstanding competitor in the public eye to whom this would apply is Willie Ritola, Finnish distance running star," who had lived in the States since 1913 but competed in the Olympics for Finland.[49]

Bill was "a strong advocate" of the proposal, reported the *New York Times*. The son and grandson of immigrants himself, and a friend to many Italians in Port Chester, Bill was hardly a xenophobe. But he felt the rules for competitive athletics should be similar to those of labor unions: "A bricklayer by trade, Kennedy said his own union organization compels foreigners to become naturalized citizens of this country if they expect to enjoy union labor privileges." That was the evening before the motion was scheduled to come up for a vote, one of at least 160 rule changes that Bill and other AAU delegates considered at the group's three-day annual conference in Baltimore. But J. J. Walsh, who had proposed the citizenship rule, failed to show up for the conference. At the last minute, Bill changed his mind. The proposal was defeated unanimously.[50]

⌒

Bill's experience with the AAU gave him a new perspective on the role of officials. He gained a (mostly) better appreciation for their efforts and sacrifices, and the challenges they faced:

So much criticism has been heaped upon the heads of officials of the Amateur Athletic Union in their handling of amateur sports that one hesitates to add to it. Yet this story would not be complete were it omitted, for where there is athletic competition, there are officials.

The longer we live, the more convinced we become in many of the old axioms. The great are the easiest to meet, and the more a person knows, the least conscious is he of it. This holds true in all walks of life. Therefore at many track meets some men never having achieved any distinction themselves, on being appointed an official, strut before the public issuing orders in a belligerent manner, making a nuisance of themselves to both the athletes and spectators, and usually get the "razz" from the boys in the gallery. . . .

While truth compels the writer to admit there are many officials of this sort, they are in the minority, and more than counter balanced by the quiet efficiency and conservative bearing of the majority of officials. . . .

At an indoor meet the officials dress formal and many of the boys in the gallery give them the Bronx cheer for no other reason. The writer recalls one night on his way to act as an official at Madison Sq. Garden. All dressed up in a tuxedo, Chesterfield overcoat and hard hat [bowler], of meeting a bricklayer friend, who persuaded me to forget the track meet and attend a beefsteak dinner over in Yorkville on the East Side of New York. You can picture the incongruity of the scene, with a bib apron over my duds, a beef steak sandwich dripping gravy in one hand and a stein of beer in the other. Far more enjoyable than the Garden meet.

Getting back to the boys in the tails, many of them would like to dispense with the formal wear, were they not requested to dress formally. These men receive no remuneration, except possibly the starter and clerk of course at most meets. Consider the hours they have given of their time. Many of them the finest people one could meet, [who] from back in 1888 down to the present, by their association with the Amateur Athletic Union have fostered and set a standard of amateurism, which is followed in the United States.[51]

❧

Nineteen twenty-seven, the year of Lucky Lindbergh's trans-Atlantic solo flight and the greatest Yankees team of all time, included a measure of glory for Bill Kennedy, "the best known bricklayer in the country."[52] He must have smiled at the forecast for Patriots' Day: It was going to be a hot one. The national championship was back in Boston. The course was newly re-measured and extended by an MIT professor to conform to the Olympic standard distance. Technology advanced at the finish line as well, as the BAA installed amplifiers and ordered checkers to phone in the checkpoint results so as to announce them to the throngs waiting by the clubhouse.[53]

The usual rowdy crowd of marathoners stayed overnight at Tebeau's Farm in Hopkinton. Johnny Miles, however, chose instead to sleep at the Hotel Somerset in Boston, where "there won't be any fiddles to bother him." The *Herald* aired concerns that Miles "has become rather softened, so to speak, because he has more than ordinary luxury about his training diet this year. He has been in town for a fortnight, training for the race. . . . His mother has cooked for him, bringing eggs and bread from Canada with her so that his diet would not be upset."[54]

In contrast to the wintry weather of the previous two meetings, the mercury on April 19, 1927, reached eighty-five degrees in the shade in some places. "The sun was blistering," according to the *Herald*. "It made the tar on the road ooze and boil. It shriveled the shoes and the soles of the feet. It caused the eyes to water and to blur and to burn. It created an odor of burning, baking macadam and oil that was nauseating."[55]

Even Bill felt it was a little much. He suffered over the first five miles. "I would like to have dived into that lake between South Framingham and Natick," he said later.[56]

Despite the heat, many of the runners perked up passing Wellesley College. "Naturally the boys like to make a showing going by the college girls, and they stepped up high and fast as the bevy of girls was reached," noted the *Herald*. There were few college boys to root for in these years; this was still a workingman's marathon, with "a collection of athletes that includes men of every walk of life. There is the plumber, the bricklayer, lawyer, baker, milkman, miner, electrician, painter, carpenter, letter carrier and whatnot," reported the *Globe*.[57]

DeMar, the printer, was highly motivated to beat Miles, the teamster, and regain bragging rights. "I was racing Miles that day. In all my other marathons I've raced against time, but this race it was Miles, the fastest marathoner ever. I just wouldn't let Miles keep the lead but would spurt ahead every quarter mile."[58]

In a way, DeMar needn't have worried. The Canadian's training in the extreme cold left him profoundly unprepared for a scorching hot day like this one. Moreover, Miles's father and trainer had made a fatal miscalculation. The science of running shoes, like the science of road paving, was in its infancy then. In an attempt to make his son's shoes more lightweight, the elder Miles had sliced off the bottom layers of the rubber soles. Now they were practically slippers. Johnny's fleet blistered and bled, and by mile seven, he dropped out.[59]

The lack of water surely didn't help. Since 1925, the BAA had provided the runners with refreshments and water and prohibited any other assistance. In '27 the club made its own miscalculation, reasoning that since the "athletes did not avail themselves of such things" the year before (never mind that it had been forty degrees cooler then), club members could simply carry water in official cars this time. But the supply quickly dried up, and runners dropped out by the score.[60]

As for DeMar, he revealed in his autobiography that he had been "very, very tired and thirsty" during the race, but fortuitously had "found a car with a pail of ice water on the running board" and "took a few swallows of the cold liquid. It refreshed me, and I had often drunk ice water in practice. So every time I could find that car I drank a lot. It helped save the day for me."[61]

Even without Miles to contend with, DeMar was "pushed all the way, and pushed hard," and "in the last three miles it looked for a time as though either [Karl] Koski or Kennedy might catch the wily Melrose veteran, but DeMar came through the six-mile stretch of heart-breaking hills in the Newtons with a rush that carried him out of sight."[62]

Koski finished second, and "the big surprise of the race" occurred when Bill Kennedy "came romping along in third place," his best showing at Boston since his 1917 victory. Bill received "an ovation almost equal to DeMar's," according to the *Times*. "Those who know the genial, whole-souled fellow were tickled through and through with his third-place success," declared the *Herald*.[63]

Those who stayed the course lost weight: DeMar over five pounds; Koski, nine pounds; and Kennedy, eleven. "The heat was something terrific," Bill told a reporter, "but once I was able to keep going, I felt well, only to hope that I might overtake Koski and DeMar. There was no overtaking them and I had to finish third, which is pretty good for an old man, don't you think?" Indeed, it was pretty good, particularly in relation to the field that brutal day. Only those first three managed to finish in under three hours. Out of the 186 men who started at noon, just thirty-four reached Exeter Street by 4 p.m., when the officials and reporters stopped keeping track and abandoned the finish line.[64]

Ever fickle, the press proved rough on the previous year's winner. The fact that blood was oozing through the thin soles of Miles's sneakers within the first few miles of the race mattered little to some. Marathon historian Tom Derderian characterizes reporter Bill Cunningham, heretofore Miles's "biggest fan," as "taking furious offense" that Miles did not finish. Cunningham was indeed harsh: "Miles should have finished the race if he had to crawl across the line on his hands and knees after the hour of midnight with his bleeding feet wrapped in newspapers. Good losing is as much a part of the code as good winning." (Incidentally, although Cunningham played football at Dartmouth, there is no evidence that he ever started, let alone finished, a marathon himself.)[65]

McCabe at the *Herald* weighed in: "Like Jack Dempsey, Johnnie went soft between races. The kid from the country could not withstand the glamour that went with becoming a hero overnight."[66]

Another young runner who'd suffered shoe trouble was Ray Carr of Brookline. In the clubhouse, Bill Kennedy, who could make a friend anywhere, noticed the eighteen-year-old with his knee in a cast and one shoe missing. That afternoon Bill ended up resting at the Carr home in Brookline, not far from the marathon route, before heading to the post-race banquet at the Hotel Statler. Impressed with Carr's story, Bill shared it with *Globe* reporter Joseph F. Dineen.

Young Carr was a laborer on the buildings and grounds crew at Harvard College. Two days before the marathon, he was moving boxes of books from Widener Library. A case slipped from his grasp and landed on his knee, injuring the bone. "On the day of the race his knee was tightly bandaged and stiff, but he was entered and determined to run." Carr lagged far behind the leaders at Audubon Circle, a mile and a half from the finish line, when more misfortune befell him: "A pacer on a bicycle ran into him and knocked the shoe that had been half on off altogether. Carr ran the rest of the way to the finish line minus that shoe," coming in thirtieth. Nevertheless, Dineen concluded, "his own personal victory was just as great to him as DeMar's."[67]

While Kennedy took a quiet nap at the Carrs' residence in Brookline, DeMar went home to Melrose for a celebration where thousands cheered him. In the evening, the "Marathon king" returned to Boston to rejoin "Smiling Bill" and about forty others for the annual meeting and dinner of the International Marathon Runners' Association. Eschewing the spotlight and "modest, as always," DeMar "fulfilled his duties as secretary of the association . . . while an eager, impatient world waited outside."[68]

From there, DeMar and Kennedy hurried over to Loew's Orpheum, where both were introduced to the audience. Here the printer-marathoner spoke briefly. He wasn't terribly comfortable on a stage, and in fact had recently turned down an offer to work in a local vaudeville theater. "They see enough of me in the marathon," DeMar said. He was back setting type the next morning.[69]

A few days later, doctors who had examined DeMar as part of a medical study "declared that he has a condition of 'hypertrophy of the arteries,' which would automatically bar him from future Marathons," reported the *Globe*. The condition "causes many famous athletes to die young." As it turned out, DeMar lived another thirty years, during which he ran and won more marathons.[70]

～⌒～

As 1928 dawned, the Olympics loomed large. Kennedy, DeMar, and the rest of the IMRA worked harder than ever behind the scenes, pushing for a say in the team's selection. For Bill, this became practically his sole goal, once he was definitively knocked out of contention personally. An auto struck him while he was on a training run on the roads outside Port Chester. His hip was injured in the accident, and for a time he was "hardly able to walk." Though he was determined to run even if he had to "crawl on his hands and knees to the starting post" at Hopkinton, Bill still had sciatica in his hip on Patriots' Day.[71]

And so, for the first time ever, after fifty-six marathons, Bill Kennedy—"perhaps the most popular of all marathoners," according to the *Herald*—dropped out of the race, at the tenth mile. (DeMar won, and Jimmy Henigan finished second.) "The ancient bricklayer" at least had some good luck: after he started to walk the remaining sixteen miles to the BAA, injured hip and all, he "was picked up by a spectator and driven to the finish."[72]

Not that he'd entertained serious hopes of traveling to Amsterdam for the Olympics, but his DNF drove a coffin nail into his prospects. Now, the one way that Bill could achieve a significant triumph was through his efforts with the runners' union.

Fortunately, those efforts began to pay off that spring. The AOC announced that the Boston race, while significant, would be but the first of a series of tests. This was a big deal. Previously, as the *Times* put it, "the Boston A.A. marathon has been fixed as *the* official Olympic tryout. This year the order of finish in the Boston marathon will count heavily, but performances in other marathons will also be considered." These included races in Baltimore, Detroit, Long Island, and New York City throughout May and June.[73]

It was just what Bill and the IMRA had fought for: a larger sample of results would determine the makeup of the team. Moreover, when the association held its biannual meeting in Boston, the *Globe* hinted that "something interesting will develop as regards the training plans for the men selected for the Olympic Marathon at Amsterdam in August." President Kennedy was surely happy to announce that the Olympic committee had agreed not to meddle in the runners' training that summer. At last, the marathoners had earned the trust of the committee and were getting the respect they deserved.[74]

Clarence DeMar was certainly pleased with how much better the marathoners were treated in 1928 after the problems they had faced in 1924. He wrote:

> On the 1928 Olympic marathon team besides Henigan, Ray and my-self were: Harvey Frick of New York, Bill Agee of Baltimore, and Whit-ey Michelsen of Stamford Conn. Our protest in 1924 had borne fruit and there was no coach or trainer this time, but just a manager, a man named Sullivan from New York. There was no bother of any kind this time from advice, orders or even suggestions. We marathoners ran or not in the time allotted to us on the ship and after we arrived in Amster-dam our training was entirely under our own supervision. This system was ideal.[75]

With veteran union man Bill at the helm, and no-nonsense DeMar often stirring things up, the marathoners' collective action had paid off.

꙳

Bill continued to be a mainstay and driver of the Columbus Day race, though the local paper noted he found it "more difficult each year to take time from his contracting business to whip himself into shape for a grind." The success of the Port Chester Marathon was "an indication of the strength of the New York City marathon culture, [which] now centered around the Port Chester event," writes mara-thon historian Pamela Cooper.[76]

But in early October 1929, the village's Chamber of Commerce, which sponsored the event, was already signaling that hard times were ahead. The chamber's secretary revealed a shortfall of $400 for expenses and warned that there might "be no more marathons sponsored by the organization."[77]

The *Daily Item,* editorializing for financial support for the event, asked, "What are a few dollars of any man's money" compared to "the investment of physical strength and moral courage which men like Kennedy throw into their ideal of wholesome athletics for the betterment of American youth?" Small donations poured in. The next day the paper reported that not only was the budget for 1929 met but also, "because of the generous response during the past 48 hours . . . the future of the great race is practically assured and the event which has done so much to advertise Port Chester will continue into the 1930's."[78]

Bill's friend and protégé Whitey Michelsen won the 1929 Port Chester marathon for the third time, beating DeMar by about one hundred yards with a time of 2:38:31.[79] Bill Kennedy—"the dean of all American long distance harriers"—came in thirteenth out of forty-eight starters and "received his usual big ovation."[80]

The stock market crashed a few days later. The financial devastation and widespread unemployment that followed would soon threaten both the Port Chester and Boston marathons at a time when their cities needed them the most. In "Old Saw Pits," Bill would have his hands full keeping the marathon running.

8

HARD TIMES

In the wake of the Wall Street crash, Americans endured bank runs, foreclosures, job loss, and privation throughout the early 1930s. At the Depression's nadir in 1933, a quarter of the nation's workforce was unemployed. In Boston and New York, as elsewhere, newly homeless families huddled in "Hooverville" shantytowns.

In Port Chester, the Kennedys were hit along with everyone else as the construction industry virtually collapsed. Bankruptcy left Bill, Jessie, and their teenage daughters in straitened circumstances, and Bill's athletics avocation naturally suffered:

> During the depression years I was hanging around my old home town Port Chester dead broke and living in two attic furnished rooms. Like a million other business men of the time I had lost my business, my home, and had my furniture in storage. I received an invitation from an athletic club to referee a set of games at Stamford Conn, on Labor Day of that year though no mention of expense money. Being out of work and broke, I was in a quandary as to [how to] get to Stamford, seated in a tavern where most of the local sportsmen gathered, trying to get someone with a car to drive me

up, when in walked a carpenter friend of mine looking for me. "Go
get your tools at once, I am working at Corning, N.Y., and the boss
told me to bring a bricklayer." Well, I forgot all about the track meet,
ran home, got my tools and an hour later was on my way.

Have never been in Stamford since, I have heard from friends
that I got a panning from the local paper, and while I regret disap-
pointing the club, I have been eating regularly ever since.[1]

Bill and most of his peers kept competing, though. And crowds
kept lining the roads to cheer them on, eager for some normalcy,
some reason to celebrate—and possibly some quick cash. The 1930
Boston Marathon was at the center of a gambling scandal, likely
driven by the mushrooming numbers of men lacking legal income
streams. "The annual B.A.A. marathon race has surged into a gambling proposition of such proportions as to rival even the fabulous
and world-famous Calcutta sweepstakes pool," the *Herald* reported.
No fewer than three lotteries sold tickets in a system based on runners' bib numbers. One such lottery was operated by "the Albany
syndicate," which gamblers considered "the biggest in the world." On
top of that, three *phony* lotteries fleeced would-be bettors out of an
estimated total of $200,000. A grand jury probed one of the genuine
lotteries, which had begun at the Marlboro, Massachusetts, American Legion before growing so large that it attracted the attention of
both the law and criminal elements in Boston.[2]

The BAA itself had nothing to do with any of this activity, and so
would escape with its reputation intact. But greater, more existential
challenges loomed for the old club.

As for the results of the 1930 race, Clarence DeMar won in 2:34:48.
It was his best time ever, his first time wearing rubber-soled shoes,
and his last-ever victory in the Boston Marathon. Scotsman Jock
Semple, who had hitchhiked from Philadelphia for his first Boston
Marathon, finished seventh, his feet blistering in a pair of borrowed
shoes. A while later, Johnny Miles turned onto Exeter Street in eleventh place. Then he looked back and noticed Bricklayer Bill Kennedy
struggling along some yards behind, in twelfth. They were both out

FIGURE 9. Johnny Miles and Bill Kennedy crossing the finish line together in 1930. Courtesy of the Boston Public Library, Leslie Jones Collection.

of the prizes at this point. Miles slowed down and reached out his hand. Bill clasped it, and the two ran across the finish line together in a tie. "The crowd went wild," the *Herald* reported. Though the official scorer marked Miles as eleventh, his gesture was "one of the finest bits of sportsmanship," according to the *Post*.[3]

As threatened in 1929, the Chamber of Commerce pulled its sponsorship from the Port Chester Marathon. From here on in, the race was Bill's baby. His Cygnet A.C. joined forces with the Don Bosco Catholic Club to keep the event alive in 1930. Bill led a committee in soliciting donations of dimes and dollars to cover race expenses— permits, police, prizes, postage.[4]

DeMar won the race, capping off an extraordinary year for the 42-year-old. (Since winning the Boston Marathon in April, he had also won a Pawtucket-to-Woonsocket marathon in Rhode Island in May.) Bill Kennedy, serving as toastmaster at that evening's banquet, stressed that the race "was really a community affair" and made it clear that the two sponsoring clubs would establish a permanent Marathon Fund.[5]

The Cygnet–Don Bosco partnership continued the following year. The 1931 Port Chester Marathon, starting in Manhattan at the New York A.C. at Seventh Avenue and Central Park South, was won by Dave Komonen, a Toronto shoemaker originally from Finland. "Clad in Komonen-made boots," he ran "neck and neck" with Jimmy Henigan much of the way. Henigan had beaten the odds in winning that year's Boston Marathon at age thirty-nine. Now, as he battled Komonen passing through Pelham, "an automobile . . . struck jogging Jimmy on the leg. Henigan buckled slightly, but held his balance. He slowed up to inspect the damage, but soon regained his speed in time to discover that Komonen was fifty yards ahead of him." Whitey Michelsen came in third, with DeMar in fourth.[6]

All the publicity concerning the marathon's financial straits seemed to pay off, even during the race. "As I neared Rye on the Post Road," Bill recalled, "a gentleman with a van dyke beard stepped out of the crowd, and grasping my hand pressed a twenty dollar bill in it. George Mertz a mill owner. Well I had the good sense not to throw it away. Every little helps as the old woman says."[7]

Bill, however, was disgusted with his eleventh-place finish and time of 2:57:54: "I would rather finish twenty-first. . . . Then I would not have to worry about the places where, if I had run faster, I might have pulled out with a prize."[8]

As if dips in his running times and business fortunes weren't enough, Bill soon suffered a great personal loss. His father, 75-year-old Lawrence J. Kennedy, caught pneumonia on December 19, 1931. He died on Christmas Day. Hundreds of people filed into Our Lady of Mercy in Port Chester to pay their respects to L.J., whose casket lay on the altar amidst a garden of floral arrangements.[9]

The local *Daily Item* editorialized:

The death of Lawrence J. Kennedy has removed a rugged character from our community life. Mr. Kennedy was a strong, independent spirit—some of the stuff that was in him, he must have given to his son, "Bill," one of the greatest and most beloved and one of the few truly amateur athletes in America.

It was unfair, as some newspapers did, to record Mr. Kennedy's death simply as that of the "father of Bill Kennedy"—and none would be quicker to so declare than "Bill." For "Larry" Kennedy was a man in his own right—a man of courage and of conviction. There are told about him many stories reflecting his quality of mind—he might, for example, have won place and affluence had he chosen to be a Republican, but he elected rather to be a sincere Democrat. On the other hand, he achieved little favor with hidebound Democratic chieftains because he insisted on not only voting for but frankly espousing the cause of an occasional "good Republican."

"Larry" Kennedy was a simple soul, an humble man—but he had in him much of that most precious of all character minerals, the salt of the earth.[10]

Despite these setbacks, Bill maintained his joy in running. A few months after his father's death, he wrote another letter to Hallahan at the *Globe*. Coming at the time it did, this set of reflections perhaps holds more poignancy than his missive of a decade earlier. Here is the 1932 letter:

I am well, but broke. Business is ——, but as long as I have my health that is the serious thing. I will try to write you just as I feel.

Am looking forward to the race with a great deal of interest this year, as I have been out of work so much this Winter that I have had much time on my hands. I have done over 500 miles on the road in three months for this year's run. I know many of the runners, not working, have been running every day. Yet, strange to say, the importance of an Olympic race psychologically affects so many that they make a poor showing. Look back over each tryout and it was poorly run; all since 1912.

Speaking of Marathon runners; don't you ever wonder what is
the lure of it? What does a Marathon runner think of?

Well Johnnie, I ran an average of 1000 miles a year for the past
25 years, some do more, some less, but that average is about 130
hours, along with your mind wandering here and there—building
air castles—tragedy and comedy. He thinks and pictures so many
things. Sometime I will tell you a lot of them.

The lure of the Boston race is far greater than any in the country
and, for me, the world. I can only speak of my own thoughts; but I
have been close enough to runners for 30 years that I also know their
thoughts, hopes and chances—to win the Boston Marathon, the
dream of every Marathon runner. Sometimes I hardly believe I realized that hope 15 years ago; I am still dreaming and actually believe
I am going to win again.

All Marathon runners are dreamers; we are not practical. The
hours we spend each day every year, strength and energy we waste
over miles of long, lonesome roads and the pot of gold at the end of
the rainbow is a survivor's medal, and mine, which has been left in
Boston as a remembrance to someone who has befriended me.

Boston, to see the name in print, to hear it spoken, sends my
blood racing as does the sounds of "The Star Spangled Banner."
I reached the heights in Boston and also I gazed down into the
depths. I used to beat my way in there unnoticed, cold, and half-
starved and then I met Larry Sweeney of the old Globe (Lord have
mercy on him) and after that everyone seemed to be my friend. . . .
Meeting all these people gave me an incentive to show them I appreciated their interest, so I tried hard to win. . . .

The people up there appreciate the runners more than anywhere else; no slurs, no wisecracks—just kind words, cheers and
applause. . . . Some three or four years ago, the time I finished third,
some little kid on a bicycle, about 12 years old, pulled alongside of
me at Coolidge Corner. To listen to that boy crooning to me, the
words of sympathy his little heart was pouring out to me to keep me

going you wouldn't think I was 50 years and he 12. Seemed like he
was the old warrior and I, the child. . . .

Prizes don't mean anything to me anyhow. . . . I wouldn't give a
damn if I fell dead over the line at B.A.A. Tuesday, just as I was over,
a winner.

The Olympic bait doesn't mean a thing to me. They wouldn't
take me when I wanted to go. Hell, I can beat my way to Los An-
geles anytime. But I want to beat the men they do send. There was
never a time if I had six weeks to train and not work or worry over
the wherewithal to run my home and family, I couldn't beat any
man in the race.

Do you know I have seldom come to Boston in any other race in
the last 15 years in shape. I dissipated last year before the race, and
even the night before, but I ran the course, only to punish myself for
not training.

Another attraction in Boston is the old-time runners you meet.
Who can but help love [A. L.] Monteverde, the biggest dreamer of us
all, and probably the wealthiest; little Jimmy Henigan, DeMar, with
his honest but peculiar ways and short answers. A lot of old boys are
disappearing, but I try to keep in touch with some of them.

Can't you lean back, close your eyes and picture Tom Longboat
and his funny teeth; Festus Madden, over whom I have many a
laugh; Fred Cameron, who became an amateur again in Chicago;
great old Sid Hatch, lovable "Chuck" Mellor, Joe Forshaw, a million-
aire; Fritz Carlson, Mike Ryan and his red head leading the parade
in '12; Arthur Roth, Cliff Horne, Billy Rozette, now well-to-do in New
York.

Poor Harry Jensen, dying at his home in New Jersey, wife and
two kids penniless. Good old Johnny Hayes and a few of the old boys
around New York visit Jensen and try to help. Jimmy Duffy, killed in
France; youthful Johnny Miles, Linder, poor Sockalexis, Tom Lilley,
and a host of others who have been cheered along the long, long
trail? They all know "What price glory." The handshakes, and then
oblivion, true to Boston runs and their few friends.

And that survivor's medal, well, I would rather a piece of my
overalls, I can use them if I GET A JOB. But I will be there Tues-
day, glad to see the bunch. My feet will be blistered, my legs weary,
every muscle aching, but my heart will be happy at the cheers of the
crowd. I will be giving them all that's in me and looking forward to
that little thin string in front of the B.A.A., a cot to lie down on, and
get those damn shoes off my feet. So long, old pal, I will be in the
prize winners.

"Bricklayer Bill Kennedy"[11]

The day before the race, Bill walked the course. In Wellesley, he
stopped in at Angelo Dischino's grocery store and paid the owner
the ten cents he owed him for a bottle of soda he'd had on credit
the previous year. "Mr. Dischino asked Kennedy why he didn't wait
until tomorrow and pay as he was running through," noted the *Globe*.
"Kennedy said he expected to be passing through that part of town so
fast Tuesday that he wouldn't be able to see the place."[12]

As it happened, Bill finished twenty-second in the 1932 race, in
2:49:58. The winner was Paul de Bruyn, who would go on to compete
for his native Germany in that summer's Olympics, in Los Angeles.
The '32 Boston Marathon is also notable for the first appearance of
future star John A. Kelley. A hothouse gardener from Arlington,
Massachusetts, Kelley liked running "because it's a healthy recreation, and cheap," as he told the *Herald*. Though he did not finish
the race that day, Kelley found the marathon scene welcoming, and
he quickly became a regular. "These runners are a friendly bunch,
democratic in their one common sport," he would say. "There is no
caste system in marathoning. [The] fellows don't care what club you
represent and what your background is. . . . They don't begrudge you
anything if you win and you don't envy them if you don't win."[13]

Bill Kennedy stepped down as president of the International Marathon Runners' Association in 1932 in order to focus on keeping the

Port Chester Marathon together.[14] He assumed almost total responsibility for the race that year as the Don Bosco Club pulled out and
the Cygnet A.C. folded. The committee that used to manage the event
decided to suspend operations rather than try to raise the nine hundred dollars needed for race expenses.

"Kennedy," reported the *Item*, "took the matter into his own hands,"
declaring that "as long as he can run, the Port Chester race will be
held."[15]

Bill co-founded the Inter-State Sports Club, with runners from
the New York and Connecticut communities of Port Chester, East
Port Chester, Glenville, Rye, and Mamaroneck. He moved the race
date to the Sunday after Columbus Day, just in case anyone was lucky
enough to have work on the Monday holiday. He contacted his running buddies far and wide and received much-needed support, the
Item reported:

> Bill has explained to all prospective runners that this year's race, as he
> is planning it, will not be as elaborate as it has been in the past. Prizes
> will not be as costly and no expense money will be paid the runners. Yet
> there will be numerous famous participants. When the runners com-
> pete in the race this year, they will be running mostly for Bill Kennedy.
> He is out now soliciting funds. . . . He has his heart set on having this
> fixture continued and has reduced the cost to the lowest possible figure.
> So let all who can afford it give a little something to help the good cause
> along.[16]

With a flurry of letters, Bill secured the entries of de Bruyn,
Michelsen, and other elite runners, and each agreed to bring a few
clubmates along. "None of us expect any expenses, we know how
things are," read a typical reply, from Mike Lynch in Washington,
DC. Meanwhile, Bill walked the streets of Port Chester raising funds
to meet the costs of organizing a race that started in New York City
and stretched across several discrete municipalities.[17]

Of course, he had to stop to eat now and then, right? While having a bite at Muzzy's Lunch one day that fall, Bill got to talking old

times with the proprietor, Fred Temple. They reminisced about the day, sixteen years earlier, when Temple had walked from Port Chester to White Plains, a distance of about six miles, in an hour and twelve minutes. In fact, Kennedy had trained Temple for that feat, which the latter undertook to win a bet. And, gee whiz, remember Temple had made a cool twenty-five dollars on the wager? . . . Bill walked out of Muzzy's with a donation to the Port Chester Marathon fund. Possibly he missed his true calling as a politician.[18]

In the midst of all this planning and pavement pounding, the Kennedys experienced some unwelcome drama. On a Saturday night a week ahead of the marathon, Bill's younger daughter, Juanita, then nineteen, went out on a date in Greenwich with her boyfriend, George Bishop. The 26-year-old had a few drinks, though reportedly not enough to get certifiably drunk. Driving Juanita home in the early morning hours, Bishop crashed into the rear of a parked sedan, which began leaking gasoline. The Greenwich police arrived and arrested Bishop for reckless driving. To make matters worse, a "spectator at the scene" dropped a lit cigarette into the spreading pool of gas, and Bishop's car burst into flames.[19]

A patrolman took Juanita to Greenwich Hospital, where she was treated for a cut on her chin. In court on Monday, Bishop was fined twenty-five dollars. The incident wouldn't deter Juanita from marrying him later. But that week, with Bill Kennedy's own cash flow problems and fund-raising challenges, it is unlikely that he offered to help pay the fine.

~~~

By this time, Jock Semple had moved from Philly to Lynn, Massachusetts, and was the 1931 New England marathon champion. On October 12, 1932—a few weeks after finishing second to Michelsen in a track marathon at Rockingham Park in Salem, New Hampshire— Semple defended his New England title by winning a marathon in Manchester, New Hampshire.[20]

The next day [Semple recalled] I got a letter from Bill Kennedy asking me if I'd hitch down to New York, for the Portchester [*sic*] Marathon. I looked at the date: it was two days away. My legs were still sore from Rockingham and Manchester, yet I had to go for Bill's sake. He was the founder of the Portchester Marathon and he needed top-flight runners. He was having trouble getting sponsors without big names, and though it meant running two marathons in four days, I went.

When I arrived I was shocked. Bill had come up with the idea of a "handicap" marathon to attract newspaper attention and he had put me on scratch. Not only were my blistered feet killing me, but I had to wait 45 minutes while the other runners were sent off ahead of me. I've never been so restless. Pat Dengis was allotted 15 minutes, but in a fine gesture offered on behalf of my sore dogs, he forfeited half of it.

Bill Steiner, an Olympic runner from New York, and I were the last of three groups to go off. I was so stiff I felt as if I were running on stilts. By 10 miles I began to unwind and by 20 miles I had caught the entire field, except for Dengis. Soon I pulled even with him, but then I died. Only encouragement from my friends along the course kept me moving. I took sixth and finished with the second fastest time, and I was happy for the two silver medals I received, but nothing beat the appreciative look in Bill Kennedy's eyes as he took me aside and said, "Thanks, Johnny."[21]

Frank Lalla, a rookie runner from Rye, led a field of thirty-eight to win the race. But it was the nineteenth-place finisher, "Leslie Marshall, Port Chester deaf mute," who captured fans' hearts, reported the *Item*. Perennially dead last, Marshall always impressed with his persistence. Now Main Street went berserk when he appeared running his best race yet:

> From the time he strode across the village line until he broke the tape, he was given an ovation by police motorcycle sirens, automobile horns, cheers and wildly waving hats and banners. Although the game little 52-year-old veteran could not hear the cheers, he could not fail to sense the hysterical spirit of the crowd. He responded with his unfailing grin and waved. Refusing a ride, he signaled that he felt fine and walked to the dressing quarters.[22]

Despite talk of eliminating the annual banquet, runners gathered after the race at the Port Chester Veterans of Foreign Wars hall. Dinner was cooked by VFW chefs and served by veterans. (No surprise that the commander of the VFW post was one Bricklayer Bill Kennedy.)[23]

Reviewing the enterprise, the local paper editorialized:

All Port Chester used to be proud of the annual "Port Chester National Marathon," [but this year] the whole thing seemed so formidable that the usual group of enthusiasts was lacking when the time for tackling the preliminaries had arrived. We were prepared to abandon the whole thing, and that without any feeling of chagrin. But there was one man who refused to let either himself or Port Chester be beaten—Bill Kennedy, one of the greatest and most famous of all American long distance runners.

Bill Kennedy put that race over yesterday as virtually a one-man job—of course he had the support and assistance of a loyal few, but Bill's courage, tenacity and unselfish zeal were basically responsible. He was too busy doing other things to actually participate in the race—but he was nonetheless the hero of the occasion. . . .

What a fine thing it would be if in every field of civic endeavor and in every situation requiring similar idealism, we had a Bill Kennedy ready to assume the whole burden on his shoulder if others were unwilling to share it with him.[24]

⌣

Times were hard, too, for those managing the Boston Marathon. Little noticed at the time, the thirty-year bonds that the BAA had sold to finance the construction of its classy clubhouse back in 1888 came due in 1918, during the Great War. So the club got an extension until November 1, 1932. Terrible timing. If an economy has peaks and valleys, this was the Death Valley of the Depression. Although Franklin Delano Roosevelt would be elected president later that month, he wouldn't take office until March, and his pump-priming policies wouldn't take effect until later still. (Nor were they exactly aimed at upper-crust social clubs.) More to the point, BAA officials discovered that an employee had embezzled their reserve fund. Running a deficit, the Unicorn club couldn't pay its bills.[25]

The April 1933 gathering of the International Marathon Runners' Association in Boston turned into "a protest meeting against the feared discontinuation of the Boston classic." The entire assemblage hailed a resolution proposed by A. L. Monteverde "that the Chamber of Commerce, Boston newspapers and other civic organizations support the sponsoring organization in the future, if such support is necessary to carry on the race."[26]

Moreover, voting to forgo its own dues that bleak year, the IMRA offered instead to contribute to the BAA if that was what it took to keep the Patriots' Day plod going. This was remarkable. The group's rank and file—largely "working men (or seeking, if not actually working)," as Derderian puts it, or "the poor man's club," as Kelley called it—were willing to pool their meager resources to keep the hoary rich men's club afloat. "Each [runner] would give a few dollars a year to aid in the upkeep," the *Herald* reported. "They believe this American Marathon is the greatest race of its kind. They receive the best treatment in this race that is given anywhere. Runners of their type do not ask for much. Many of them hitchhike to races so that they might have enough to pay for entry fees."[27]

Billy Garcelon, chairman of the BAA athletic committee, assured the runners that the race would go on. "Even if something happened to the Unicorn building, some of the members would band together and stage the race. That is what the club thinks of it and what it means to sport and the local public."[28]

Out in Hopkinton, innkeepers in the 1930s found that runners weren't arriving until the night before the race, or even the morning of. "The BAA marathon, never distinguished for the millionaires who competed in it, has been touched by the depression," the *Herald* reported from Tebeau's Farm the day before Patriots' Day 1935. "The inn and the surrounding houses are deserted."[29]

The town came to life the next morning, as did the roads along the race route. Johnny Kelley won his first Boston Marathon that day, despite stopping twice in the last mile to throw up. After that, it's unclear if Kelley could stomach the scaled-back repast in the clubhouse: "The traditional beef stew was omitted from the clubhouse fare, with Good Friday clam chowder and fish cakes taking its place," reported the *Herald*. "There was plenty of beer, too. The ice cream went first, with the runners working back from dessert." Someone offered runner-up Pat Dengis "a big pitcher of beer, and Pat obligingly took a few gulps, not bothering with a glass."[30] (Prohibition had been repealed sixteen months earlier.)

That was the marathoners' last meal in that building: the BAA filed for bankruptcy a few months later. "The Association's principal assets—the opulent furnishings of its clubhouse—were liquidated in a fire sale," John Hanc writes in his official history of the club. "The elegant fixtures, the paintings, no doubt even some of the ceramic tiles on its Turkish baths, were stripped and sold at a fraction of their value. The clubhouse itself was sold to Boston University, which used it as a dormitory and office building." It would eventually be torn down to make way for the expansion of the city's central library, next door.[31]

The BAA, as it had been since the Gilded Age, was no more. Already, the various sports programs it once fielded—like the rowing crew that had sculled on the Charles, or the ice hockey team that had packed spectators into the old Boston Arena for tilts against amateur counterparts from Montreal and New York in the prewar days—were things of the past. The storied Boston Marathon seemed bound for the dustbin too.

It was George V. Brown, the longtime manager of the race, who stepped up to salvage the club. He convened emergency meetings of "a small group of other determined members" at the Lenox Hotel to work out a way to keep the club in business, at least on paper. Most important, in his other role as manager of the Boston Garden, he hosted the BAA's annual indoor track and field meet, which still brought in paying customers. It was enough to subsidize, and save, the historic and beloved Boston Marathon.[32]

After all, the race couldn't go bust with another Olympic year coming up. "The Boston Athletic Association is known in track centers all
over the world," said Garcelon, one of the determined few. "The club
has given Boston more favorable publicity than any other." For the
good of the city, the marathon would go on.[33]

⌒

What Brown did for the Hub in the springtime, Kennedy did for "Old
Saw Pits" in the autumn. From its low point in 1932, the Port Chester
Marathon bounced back to a respectable sixty runners in 1934. More
volunteers pitched in, though Bill was still raising the last $175 the
day before the race. Well-known Broadway columnist Ed Sullivan
(the future TV variety show host) helped draw attention to his native
village by serving as the official starter. Decked out with flags and
bunting, Main Street was a "riot of color" as Pat Dengis led the pack
to the finish line in 2:31:30. (Bill finished fourteenth.) The great Johnny Hayes, 1908 Olympic gold medalist, acted as honorary referee and
was the special guest speaker at the post-race banquet, which turned
into a testimonial for Bricklayer Bill.

"Bill Kennedy is one of the finest men ever to put on a racing shoe,"
said Hayes. "He has been the mainspring in marathon running in the
United States for years, and the Port Chester National Marathon is an
institution you all have reasons to be proud of."[34]

"I don't want any praise at the expense of other runners," Bill
demurred in his remarks. "I want the Port Chester National Marathon race to be a race for the runners, not one for the glory of officials
as is the case with so many of our races. We want to make this race
the outstanding race of the country and will continue to make that
our goal until we succeed."[35]

Though the Columbus Day run would always more or less play
second fiddle to the one on Patriots' Day, in another sense the efforts
of Bill and his volunteers did succeed. With so many regular Port
Chester folks chipping in their hard-earned nickels even in the worst

of times, Bill pulled off his hometown marathon's revival year in, year out, throughout the Great Depression.

～

"Fascist sympathizers and anti-Fascists, numbering 400 on each side, clashed in Columbus Circle today during a Columbus Day celebration just before the Port Chester Marathon was to start," the *Item* reported from New York City in October 1935. "Fists were swung and heads were pounded with sticks bearing placards calling Premier Mussolini 'World Public Enemy Number One' and the other uncomplimentary terms. Thirty mounted policemen, with detectives and foot policemen, waded into the fighting crowd."[36]

The cops restored order, and eventually the race went on. In "the closest duel" in the history of the Port Chester contest, Rhode Island's Les Pawson edged Pat Dengis by three seconds. Pawson's time was 2:37:49—not bad, considering the course distance had been miscalculated, as it turned out. "The boys who finished," revealed the *Item*, "ran 27 and 8/10 miles," a significant error.[37]

New York's German-American Athletic Club, coached by Max Silver, won the team prize in Port Chester for the third successive year. Coach Silver, however, was not long for the German-American squad. He had agreed to coach his "long-distance runners for the important Port Chester Marathon" and a Thanksgiving Day event, but afterwards, along with other Jewish members, Silver resigned in protest of the club's increasingly pro-Nazi sympathies.[38]

The events that fall were not the last time that ugly international politics marred amateur athletics. More protests, and more fighting, were to come.

9
THE ROAD TO BERLIN

In retrospect, Adolf Hitler looms over the 1936 Olympic Games as a specter of prewar menace. But in 1931, when the International Olympic Committee selected Berlin as the '36 site, Hitler had not yet come to power, and the siting was actually intended as an act of postwar reconciliation. Originally slated to host the 1916 Games, Berlin lost its chance when World War I broke out in 1914.

Once Hitler did take over as Germany's chancellor, his henchman Joseph Goebbels convinced him the Olympics would be a useful propaganda tool. But then Americans (at least the ones paying attention) learned more and more about the Nazi regime's persecution of Jews. Even in the years before the secret construction of concentration camps, German Jews were hounded out of the professions, barred from the stock exchange and swimming pools, and disenfranchised. The new Germany was no place for a global gathering of amateur athletes, argued a growing coalition of American Jews, Catholics, labor unions, and many athletics officials, led by AAU president James Mahoney. These critics pushed for a U.S. boycott of the Olympics to protest Nazi policies. In New York, ten thousand marched for the boycott in November 1935.[1]

On the other side, AOC president Avery Brundage hated the boycott idea. The son of a deadbeat stonecutter, Brundage was born in 1887, about four years after Bill Kennedy. In fact, the two competed in some of the same amateur meets in Chicago before World War I. Brundage went on to the 1912 Olympics in the decathlon and pentathlon. Back in the United States, he became a wealthy construction company owner and maintained his lifelong involvement in amateur sports. Brundage and Kennedy intersected again in 1926, when they served together on the Track and Field Committee of the AAU.[2]

"Brundage believed strongly in the Olympic spirit, and particularly in the principle that politics should play no role in sports," writes Daniel James Brown in his chronicle of the Berlin Games. "He argued, reasonably, that it would be unfair to American athletes to let German politics deprive them of their chance to compete on a world stage." And yet, Brundage's sentiments were suspect: "He consistently lumped together Jews and Communists" and implied that the Jews, not the Germans, were the ones stirring up "Old World hatreds." Politics making strange bedfellows, the privately prejudiced Brundage was backed by a coalition that included African American athletes and commentators, who relished the chance to undermine Hitler's notions of Aryan superiority by beating his champions on the track and the field.[3]

In December 1935 the boycott proponents were defeated in a close vote at an AAU convention. For better or worse, America's Olympians were going to Berlin.

And Bill Kennedy was going with them.

The Boston Marathon in April 1936 would serve as an Olympic qualifying event, as it quadrennially did in those days. The *New York Times* observed that the Boston course "is such a tough one that the Berlin marathon should seem mild by comparison, since that will be over relatively flat countryside."[4] The BAA emphasized that "this is an Olympic tryout. All but official and press cars will be barred from the course."[5] In fact, this was the usual rule, one often ignored.

While rules might be overlooked, attitudes about race and religion were becoming difficult to brush aside. Prominent among this year's entrants was Bill Steiner of New York. He had come in third in Boston in 1934 but missed the event in 1935 to run and win the Jewish Olympic Marathon at Tel Aviv. Steiner had recently shifted his allegiance to the Millrose A.A. Like Max Silver, he no longer felt welcome in the German-American A.C.[6]

Meanwhile, Jock Semple finalized his own split—with his first wife. Four days before the Boston Marathon, a probate judge granted Semple a divorce from the former Isabel Robertson of Ontario. They had married in September 1929, and she had deserted him in December after "a lot of continual bickering," Semple testified. The missus claimed "he was spending too much time training for Marathon races."[7]

Semple's mentor Bill Kennedy didn't expect to make a big comeback this year—at age fifty-two, he just wanted to run—and he was starting to find some of the well-wishes almost painful. "As I left home nearly a dozen hoped I'd win," he related to DeMar, "and I told each of the darn fools that there were at least twenty in the race with a better chance than I."[8] (At least, that's how DeMar remembered Kennedy saying it. Either the bricklayer was getting crotchetier or DeMar was projecting somewhat.)

From the moment George V. Brown fired his starter's pistol into the Hopkinton sky on Patriots' Day 1936, it was another, unrelated Brown, who took and held the lead. Ellison "Tarzan" Brown was a Narragansett Indian from Rhode Island. He worked at various times as a farmer, woodcutter, stonemason, and stevedore, but these days he was "one of that vast regiment of unemployed," as the *Globe* put it.[9] The previous year, Brown had run wearing a shirt made from the fabric of his late mother's dress and a pair of shoes that fell apart on him with five miles to go. He ran those last five miles barefoot, and

still finished thirteenth. This year, with the sponsorship of the Prov-
idence Tercentenary Committee, Brown's feet were shod in the new
"S.T.A.R. Streamlines." Custom-made by a single local shoemaker,
Sam T. A. Ritchings, these were white buckskin shoes with elas-
tic innersoles and perforations for ventilation. Semple, Kelley, and
DeMar wore their own pairs of the Streamlines.[10]

Kelley, the defending champ, had the best chance of catching
Brown, who remained in the lead at every checkpoint. Behind him
in second place for three miles, Kelley figured the front-runner had
to be tiring himself out. Sure enough, the Narragansett began to
lose steam as he climbed the Newton hills. Kelley smelled blood. He
closed a half-mile gap down to a few yards. At the top of the last and
highest hill, Kelley passed Brown, giving him a pat on the back as
he did so. Kelley later said the gesture was intended to be friendly,
but Brown bristled. "Maybe he thought he was going to go by, but I
didn't," Brown would say.[11]

Rather than fading further, Brown regained his strength and sailed
past Kelley, the latter's hard-fought gains all in vain. His spirit broken,
Kelley fell back to fifth place. Despite slowing to a walk later, and a
moment of panic at Cleveland Circle when Brown lost his vision, the
Indian held on for the win, in 2:33:40.[12]

"It delighted the crowd thronging the sidewalks," wrote a *Globe*
editor, "to see a copper-skinned, 100 percent American [win] the
race. He triumphed in the very oldest sport, and he did it in a way to
bring credit on the original proprietors of New England."[13]

What's more, the Native American was headed straight for Berlin.
His Boston victory qualified him for the Olympic marathon team,
along with Kelley and runner-up Bill McMahon, an unemployed
plasterer from Worcester. Brown would join a handful of Jews and
eighteen African Americans in seeking to humble the white suprem-
acist German state that summer.

And at long last, perhaps as a kind of consolation prize in recognition of his career-long contributions to marathoning, Bricklayer Bill
Kennedy was invited to travel abroad with the team. Not as a runner

or even as a coach, but as a kind of royal rooter. More than a fan, but not an official, he was part of the entourage, an elder statesman of the running game, just along for the ride. It would be the trip of a lifetime.

The S.S. *Manhattan* steamed out of New York Harbor on July 15, 1936. As it crossed the Atlantic that week, the 668-foot luxury liner bustled with 330 athletes, among other passengers, trying to find space to train. Runners such as Louis Zamperini, the five-thousand-meter star, circled the decks, often staggering about on the high seas. John Kelley got to know Bill Kennedy as a "rough character" pacing the decks of the *Manhattan* with a plug of tobacco behind his lip. The burly rowers of the University of Washington's eight-oar crew took up residence in the dining salon. Indeed, some wrestlers and boxers ate so much that they could no longer compete in their weight class by the time they landed.[14]

And every night, the young Americans partied. Technically, the AOC forbade the athletes to drink while in training, but this rule was flouted throughout the voyage. Unfortunately, one swimmer, Eleanor Holm Jarrett, flouted the hardest, and perhaps paid for the sins of the team. After a night of "drinking heavily of champagne," Jarrett was fired from the squad, though Bill told a Port Chester audience later that "nothing would have been said, but for the fact that she continued drinking the next day." (Bill acknowledged spending time at the bar himself.)[15]

The team doctor reported that Jarrett was nearly in a coma from excessive drinking, but she denied that. In fact, Jarrett reportedly told another Olympian many years later that Brundage had propositioned her and she had turned him down. Kennedy told his hometown audience that Jarrett had a sharp tongue. Perhaps she used it when spurning Brundage's improper advances and, stung, Brundage abused his power as AOC president to retaliate.[16]

Bill didn't know that backstory, but he showed his old-fashioned upbringing when he suggested that the men and women might have better sailed on separate ships. "With both girls and men on the same boat, there was certain to be more partying and less attention to strict training than otherwise would have been the case," he said, before going on to scotch his chances of elective office should he live beyond 1968. "Too, I think older more matronly women should have been used as chaperones for the girls—the chaperones I saw were all very attractive, younger women who themselves liked to dance, drink cocktails and have a good time."[17]

Still, Bill disagreed with Jarrett's firing. "Seeing as how some of the officials were drinking themselves," he felt that the best course would have been to forget the whole incident.[18]

At last, land. When the ship docked in the port of Cobh, in southwest Ireland, a small vessel came alongside to take a few passengers ashore. Bill recalled one entrepreneurial Corkman who climbed aboard:

> An old newsboy, about 50, went about selling papers and as no one had seen a newspaper for [six] days he sold out. On scanning the news we discovered the papers were of different past days. Hailing him and remonstrating him. With a twinkle in his eye he says, "Sure how do you expect a poor ould mon to make a living, phwats the difference to ye boys, tis news to ye."[19]

Next, the *Manhattan* stopped in Le Havre, France; steamed up the English channel to Cuxhaven, Germany; and turned down the Elbe River, where the athletes first saw boats flying swastika flags. The team disembarked at Hamburg and took a train to Berlin. In the station, an oompah band greeted them with a Sousa march. Tens of thousands of Berliners lined the streets to cheer the American athletes as they rode past in buses to city hall, where Brundage received the keys to the city.[20]

For Bill Kennedy, this trip was all about closing old wounds. At this stage of his life, as a veteran of the Great War, returning to Europe and meeting such a wonderful reception from his old foes, Bill was inclined toward reconciliation, like the IOC officials who'd awarded Germany the Olympics in '31.

What he, along with most Americans, yet failed to realize was that Hitler's regime was many factors worse than the Kaiser's. And what Bill and the U.S. athletes didn't see behind the cheering crowds was the level of orchestration on the part of Goebbels, the Nazi propaganda chief. This whole Olympic business was for Hitler and company an enormous PR stunt aimed mainly at buying Germany time to build up its arsenal. The idea was to show the world how friendly, cosmopolitan, and *not* warlike the Germans were—even as the nation prepared in secret for war.

So when Bill and the U.S. team arrived, "all would be pleasant," Daniel James Brown writes. The Berliners had been instructed how to act. The "Juden Verboten" signs had come down temporarily. The anti-Semitic rag *Der Stürmer* was taken off the newsstands. Streets were swept, geraniums were placed in flowerboxes, Gypsies and homeless people were removed to a faraway detention camp.[21]

On opening day, August 1, Bill realized he had no way of getting into the sold-out Olympic Stadium to watch the ceremonies. Not being in the official delegation meant that he had to secure his own entry to the games.

> The writer had no ticket and none could be bought. Watching the number of important [personages] being admitted on passes. The thought of "One Eyed" Connolly and gate crashing occurred. Taking an American Legion card from my pocket, beautifully embossed with the American Shield and three gold stars, representing fifteen years of membership. Assuming a dignified manner, I nonchalantly flashed my card as I walked past the guard, who smilingly nodded his head.[22]

This ploy worked once, but Bill didn't want to chance it again. He would ask Avery Brundage for help. Seeking him out at the Avalon

Hotel in Berlin that evening, Bill was told that Brundage was in a meeting. So, the bricklayer explains,

I left a note in his box telling him of my plight of getting in to see the games. Returning the next morning, the clerk handed me an envelope in which was Avery's gold embossed pass and a note asking me to leave it at the desk each evening, and to pick it up each morning as he wanted to keep it as a souvenir.[23]

And so Bricklayer Bill got to witness the world's biggest sports extravaganza yet. The Olympics had been steadily growing as a national showpiece since the modest postwar event at Antwerp in 1920. "Each of the following Games—Paris in 1924, Amsterdam in 1928, Los Angeles in 1932," writes historian Benjamin Rader, "was more extravagant than its predecessor." Despite the Depression, the Los Angeles event set the modern standard for extravagance, but Hitler cleared even that bar. More than 110,000 roaring, saluting spectators filled the stadium for the opening ceremony, when the athletes of all the competing nations marched past Hitler's viewing box to the thumping music of a brass band. The ceremony climaxed with the arrival of the torchbearer—the first time the Olympics featured a relay carrying the flame from Olympia, Greece, to the hosting country. Trumpets blared as the runner brought the torch up to an altar and ignited a blaze in a giant cauldron.[24]

Bill was dazzled by the spectacle along with everyone else. Indeed, like most of the visiting Americans, he was impressed by the Nazis' handling of the entire Olympic program. "You can't beat the Germans for efficiency," he told Port Chester Rotarians that fall. However, Bill offered an unflattering, even chilling, portrait of life in Germany when he described the athletes' housing:

They were quartered in Olympic Village, situated in a wilderness section 12 miles from Berlin and which was really nothing more than a prison camp. It was surrounded by a high barbed-wire fence which was constantly patrolled by soldiers. No one was allowed in or out without a pass—and no one allowed in after nine o'clock at night under any circumstances. Athletes were required to be

inside the stockade by nine o'clock and to be in their quarters by
ten o'clock. That sort of thing made for discontent because it was a
discipline which Americans particularly resented.[25]

As for the competition that week: Despite all the Nazis' planning,
and in the face of their fiercest racial beliefs, it was an African American, track runner Jesse Owens, who proved the star of the Berlin Olympics. Owens won four gold medals—in the men's two hundred meter,
long jump, one hundred meter, and sprint relay—setting world records
in the two hundred meter (20.7 seconds) and long jump (8.06 meters).

Hitler must have been furious at this turn of events. When Owens's
teammate Cornelius Johnson, also black, won the high jump competition, the dictator abruptly left his stadium box. As Rader puts it,
"This action led to the potent myth that Hitler had refused to shake
the hand of Jesse Owens."[26]

But apparently Hitler composed himself and resumed his pleasant
false front. Despite criticism in the American press for the supposed
cold shoulder, Owens himself maintained that "Mr. Hitler had to
leave the stadium early, but after winning I hurried up to the radio
booth. When I passed near the Chancellor he arose, waved his hand
at me and I waved back at him. I think the writers showed bad taste
in criticizing the man of the hour in Germany."[27]

Although Kennedy didn't go as far as Owens there, he remembered matters more or less the same way. At least he did that fall, well
before the war, telling the Rotarians that Hitler had been "human like
all the rest, and really didn't snub Jesse Owens." (Bill made no such
comments in his 1960s manuscript, well after the war.)[28]

Even for those who criticized Hitler, writes historian David Clay Large,
the complaints "did not extend to the German fans in general, whose
treatment of black athletes was seen to be respectful and friendly."[29]

But that leaves the question of how a Native American would be
treated. Of Tarzan Brown, Bill's friend Jock Semple wrote later:

Just about all the Americans thought the Indian would make hash of the Japanese and the rest in the big Marathon race. Tarzan had a fondness for German beer, however, and on top of that he got into trouble. He picked on a couple of Nazi Blackshirts and rapped together a couple of their heads. . . . Tarzan only made the Olympic race after the Americans sprung him from jail following his fight with the Nazis. Asked why he got into a fight with them, he told me one time, "I didn't like them."[30]

At the time, Bill denied reports of intoxicated Americans on the streets of Berlin. "I know it's not so," he said. "I never saw an American under the weather."[31] Of course, just because he didn't witness such behavior doesn't mean it didn't happen. (Plus, Bill's definition of "under the weather" might exceed conventional norms.)

In any case, the old-timer had high hopes for Brown, Kelley, and McMahon in what he considered the Games' premier event: "The climax of every Olympiad is the Marathon, and fittingly so, for no other event furnishes such dramatic finishes, a grueling test of man's speed, grit, and endurance."[32]

But there was no drama for the Yanks. Not in the race, anyway. Brown had developed a hernia, and his late-night roistering likely didn't help his condition. After struggling for sixteen miles of the course through the Grunewald forest, the Narragansett dropped out. For unexplained reasons, McMahon quit too. Kelley finished eighteenth.[33] "Here again the American runners fell by the wayside," wrote a disappointed Bill. It was the third straight Olympiad without an American medal in the long grind. In fairness, Bill noted, "The winner had been living [in Berlin] for three months and was well acclimated and in rare form."[34]

That winner, in the Olympic record-setting time of 2:29:19, was Sohn Kee-chung of Korea, then occupied by Japan. Less noticed in the West, Sohn's victory was a moment of defiance and enduring inspiration for the Korean peninsula. When photographed receiving his gold medal, Sohn deliberately carried a small potted oak tree to cover up the Japanese flag on his jersey.[35]

Despite that, and despite Germany's impressive haul of medals, "almost everybody present awarded the trophy—in their minds, at least—to Jesse Owens," writes historian Duff Hart-Davis. "In a single week he had revolutionized the speed events and opened up a new vista of sporting possibilities for the human race. Everyone recognized that he was a supreme athletic genius, the God of the Games."[36]

After the Games, the city of Hamburg, whence the American and other teams would depart the country, hosted various sporting exhibitions and sendoff parties for the athletes. For some reason, Bill decided to walk there. The distance from Berlin is about 175 miles, and "the only German I could speak was 'prost' [cheers!]." Yet even decades later, Bill had warm memories of the hospitality of ordinary German people that summer, two years before Kristallnacht, three years before the invasion of Poland, five years before Pearl Harbor.

> Starting at the Brandenburg Tor at the Unter den Linden, at noon I walked forty miles before dark, which at that season of the year over there was about ten o'clock. I slept in a hay stack and was up and on the road at four o'clock in the morning, walking twenty miles before I stopped in a small hamlet for breakfast at 8 a.m. Continuing on till noon where I sat and soaked my feet in a small stream at the side of the road. Here I slept for a couple of hours. Resuming my walk, I covered sixty miles before crawling into another haystack for the night. I was about eighty miles from my destination, having covered about one hundred miles in two days.
>
> The third day I reached [Perleberg] at about two P.M. having covered about forty miles. As this was an historical town, having been the scene of a battle in the Germanic wars. Also of interest to me here was located one of the Youth Hotels. Before leaving Berlin I had paid five marks to join the Jungendherberge, an organization similar to the Y.M.C.A. These places for young men and women traveling by bicycle or walking through Germany and many other countries in Europe as well as in Ireland. A member could put up for the night for ten pfennig and have coffee and rolls in the morning for five pfennig. So I decided to lay over and see what they were

like. Here I met many young boys all riding bicycles and touring their country on a vacation.

On registering here the caretaker called up the mayor and informed him he had an American there, whereupon the mayor sent a young man down to escort me up to meet the mayor. This young man could speak English, as could most of the young students whom I met at the hotel that night. I was shown all the historical spots in the city and given a picture and historical book of the city, which I still have. That night at the Inn all the boys wanted to hear all about America and many of them had relatives who had emigrated to the States. All of the boys gave me their names and addresses to send them cards of America. Told me not to walk but to hitch hike as you do in America.

Next morning I was on the road at daylight, with many handshakes and *"Auf Wiedersehen,"* I continued on my way to Hamburg. This was my worst day, as it started to rain, and I had to foolishly refuse the offer of many rides from passing truck drivers, but I wanted to finish the walk on foot. I reached the edge of town just before dark and stayed in a small inn for the night, about an hour from my destination. 180 miles in four days.

This trip taught me how true are the many truths one's mother teaches us in childhood. Be humble, kind, and courteous. I could speak no German, but I did know how to be courteous and the German saying was "Mitt hat in hand all doors open." Ain't it the truth.[37]

After the farewell celebrations, the team boarded the S.S. *President Lincoln* and embarked on the journey homeward, first stopping again at Le Havre, France, where they witnessed a scene out of a Disney movie:

We had hardly tied up when we noticed a cat wildly running along the pier, meowing at the top of his voice. On board ship sailors were excitedly shouting to it. As soon as the gang plank touched the dock, the cat madly dashed up the run to be gathered into the arms of a sailor. The cat had been ashore courting a French pussy cat and the ship had left without him. The cat had been meeting every ship that touched port, looking for the Lincoln.[38]

From there, Bill once again stopped in his ancestral homeland, where the ship picked up a passenger who, perhaps like Bill's mother and his paternal grandparents, had a foot in two worlds but no regrets about emigration:

> On leaving Cobh, an old Irish musician plays "Come Back to Ireland" on his cornet, and needless to say it sounds beautiful. On the trip home, a middle-aged Irishman shared the cabin with me. He had been saving his money for twenty years, he told me, to take a trip back to his old home. Every morning at daylight he was up looking out the port hole, and his morning prayer was "Thank God I am a day nearer America. America is Heaven."[39]

Back in Port Chester, in the weeks leading up to the Columbus Day marathon, the local Rotary and Knights of Columbus clubs invited Bill to speak about his experiences in Berlin. In addition to retelling tales of the Games, Bill unfortunately (in hindsight) defended the controversial AOC president: "Brundage, the most criticized official at the Games, was a real, true sportsman and a real gentleman." Bill never forgot Brundage's gesture, the loan of his own gold-embossed pass that allowed the bricklayer access to the stadium. Even thirty years later, Bill insisted in his unpublished manuscript that Brundage "took all the censure for the suspension of Eleanor Holmes [sic], when as a matter of truth he didn't vote on the question, the floor voting unanimously for the suspension."[40]

Had Bill known of Brundage's anti-Semitic leanings, he might have felt differently. Ahead of his time in some ways, L. J. Kennedy had drilled into his children the principle of equality over prejudice. Bill was ever quick to tell listeners of the gameness of Jewish runner Levi Levinson, and always grateful to Chicago's Hebrew Institute for helping him back on his feet after his bout with typhoid fever.

But on the basis of what he'd seen of Brundage in the context of athletics officialdom, Bill admired the more successful contractor as a "booster for amateurism, [who] always paid his own way. I recollect some years ago at one of the A.A.U. conventions he tried to enact a law that no man could be on the governing board who in any way made money from amateur athletics, save the secretary and his assistants. Needless to say it was defeated."[41]

⌣⌢⌣

Despite his hernia, Tarzan Brown won the 1936 Port Chester Marathon, on October 11, giving a "sterling exhibition of stamina and courage" to defeat Pat Dengis "after a thrilling duel."[42]

As for "Old Bill Kennedy of East Port Chester, who won't call his marathoning off until they shove him into a box," he lagged in thirty-fifth place early in the race, then steadily climbed ahead. "When the daddy of them all crossed the finish line in eighteenth, he was greeted with an ovation that outranked that given the winner." His time was 3:19:19.[43]

That was the last Port Chester Marathon that Bill ran. (He would continue his involvement as an official.) The memory of the crowd shouting "Here comes Bill" endured into the twenty-first century with Eileen Lawlor Kennedy, who recounted the story of watching the race from her family's front porch on Pearl Street near the Boston Post Road. Years before marrying Bill's nephew Paul J. Kennedy Jr., a young Eileen had joined in the applause for the local hero.

But the day's victor, Brown, had his own heroics in store. The very next day, Brown ran, and won, a marathon from Boscawen to Manchester, New Hampshire. Two marathon victories in two days—and four for the year (Boston and Bridgeport being the others).[44] If only Brown could have managed Berlin instead of Bridgeport.

⌣⌢⌣

It was time to retire. Bill announced that the 1937 BAA grind, his one hundredth marathon, would also be his last. Jerry Nason greeted this news in the *Globe* with wistfulness:

> Twenty-five years of ankling down the pike from the bucolic surroundings up Ashland and Hopkinton way have witnessed Bill's stubborn

thatch of wiry brown slowly but surely become a silver plume; a majestic banner ruffled by the breeze of many a cool April day.

Ninety-nine Marathons has old Bill raced since 1912, and only twice has he failed to finish the 26 miles-and-plus. That's an aggregate distance of 2575 ½ miles, figuring the yardage beyond the miles. This will be his 100th Marathon and, he feels, his last. Considerably more than 10,000,000 people have, at one time or another, paused by the roadside between the rural communities and downtown Boston to throw a cheery word as Bill plodded by.

And he hasn't forgotten those cheery words. "I shall never forget," he writes George V. Brown, "the kind treatment I have received from the finest sportsmen in all the world—the people of Boston and vicinity."

So closely has Kennedy grafted himself to the Patriots' Day race that virtually everyone who sees him pass, young and old, knows him on sight. There never has been a quick glance at a program number to identify old Bill. The glint of the dim April sun on that silver mane bobbing around the turn ahead is enough.[45]

Bill's daughter Juanita, now Mrs. George Bishop, came from Port Chester with his five-month-old grandson and namesake to watch what was supposed to be Kennedy's farewell to marathoning. There were no surprises for the fifty-three-year-old's last big race—well, except for an experimental mustache, which Bill Rae of the *Herald* said made him look "more like a lawyer than a bricklayer." Bill finished twenty-seventh—but that was enough to top the defending champ: twenty-two-year-old Tarzan Brown.[46]

Is that why Bill changed his mind about retirement? Or was it the example of "Old Peter Foley," who ran the marathon again that day, unofficially, at age eighty-three? Either way, Bill admitted right after the race, "I suppose I'll be fool enough to run again next year."[47]

The winner that afternoon was Walter Young, a "gangly 24-year-old Canadian [who] survived a stirring battle to the finish with the heavily favored Johnny Kelley of Arlington and left the stricken Irishman reeling at Coolidge Corner to win," in 2:33:20.[48]

Young had reason to hope for more than a pat on the back for his triumph. After Brown won the previous year, the trustees of Wilcox

Park in Westerly, Rhode Island, gave him a job as groundskeeper. Unemployment persisted in 1937 as the economy headed into a second dip after a modest surge in the mid-thirties. If an athlete could benefit indirectly from his accomplishments, that could mean food on the otherwise empty table. Young was so low on cash that he had to pawn the Waltham watch he had won in a twenty-mile race in North Medford, Massachusetts, a few weeks before the Boston Marathon. The youthful carpenter's apprentice and his wife had been on relief almost since their wedding day, and now the couple had a three-year-old son.[49] The Youngs' hometown of Verdun, Quebec, had taken up a public subscription to send the runner to Boston.

When reporters told Mrs. Young of her husband's victory, the economic benefit was uppermost in her mind: "Now maybe he'll get that job. [Verdun town officials] told him he'd have a good chance of getting it if he won. Now he's done it. Gee, that's swell." Though the news of the victory was the greatest thrill of her life, Mrs. Young said, she didn't plan to celebrate: "A party? I'll say there won't be any party. Have a heart, mister. It's hard enough to get enough food to live on without throwing any party. You know, this racing game isn't so much fun for me or Walter. All he's got out of it so far is a lot of cups and that sort of thing."[50]

But soon there was good news for the Youngs: Walter indeed got that job, with Verdun's public safety department, looking after the city's playgrounds, plus promoting Verdun by entering more races.[51]

‿◞◟‿

George V. Brown died on October 17, 1937. Hundreds traveled to tiny Hopkinton for his funeral service at the Church of St. John the Evangelist. Manager and starter of the marathon since the dawn of the century, Brown "bespoke Boston of the day when the B.A.A.'s blue postern light gleamed on Exeter Street," wrote Austen Lake in Boston's Brahmin paper, the *Evening Record.* "The tarnished trophies and frayed banners in the hallway, the upstairs odor of rubbing lineaments [*sic*] and locker room, the clatter of the squash courts—all that were part of the defunct B.A.A. were also part of George V. Brown and his character."[52]

The BAA wasn't, in fact, altogether defunct, thanks to Brown's efforts since the 1935 bankruptcy and clubhouse closure. The Hopkinton herd owner had kept a bare-bones organization going, with the winter track meet and the spring marathon still extant on the calendar. But what would happen now, without Brown around?

Fortunately, Brown's son Walter picked up the baton (and the starter's pistol). As vice president of the Garden-Arena Corporation, he would shoulder the responsibility for the BAA Games (the indoor track meet), allowing the club to collect the revenue to stay afloat and perpetuate the April marathon, as his father had done.

"Without Walter Brown, the Boston Athletic Association would most certainly not exist today," writes the club's official chronicler, John Hanc. "In fact, if not for his ministrations, it would have likely been a dimming memory by the end of World War II."[53]

As he had hinted, Bill returned to run Boston in 1938 and 1940. In between, he acted as referee at the '39 Port Chester plod, won by Pat Dengis. (Sadly, Dengis would die in a plane crash by the end of that year.) At the post-race banquet, Bill got "the biggest and most sincere ovation of the entire day," and in his remarks he was still the old union man, even if he no longer served as president of the marathoners' association. "Bill assailed the Amateur Athletic Union for neglecting marathon runners on the United States Olympic teams," reported the *Item*. "The old-time favorite of long-distance fans pointed out that the vast majority of Olympic coaches are 220-yard men, milers and other short distance performers. He urged the runners to stick together and demand first class representation on 1940 and other Olympic teams."[54]

The 1940 Olympics, slated for Tokyo, didn't happen. By then, Europe and Asia were engulfed in war. And even before the Japanese bombed Pearl Harbor, President Roosevelt, in September 1940, signed the Selective Service and Training Act, guessing the time was nigh when a new generation of doughboys (or, this time, "GIs") would have to go "Over There."

~~~

On Patriots' Day 1941, Bricklayer Bill Kennedy ran his twenty-fifth and—for real this time—final Boston Marathon. Out of a field of 154, fifty-seven-year-old Bill "amazed all and sundry by finishing 24th," with a time of 3:11:29, behind his old competitor Clarence DeMar, who was twentieth, in 3:05:37. Of course, both came in behind Les Pawson, the winner, and Johnny Kelley in second.[55]

After Semple crossed the finish line in eighth, "the [crowd] interest went up and down like an elevator. It perked up for DeMar [then] boomed for old Bill Kennedy." To the last, the fans gave the bricklayer a bigger hand than they did the printer with seven times the former's victories. Then again, Bill never slugged a fan who got too close—as DeMar did that very day, twice (one at Woodland Park, the other at Cleveland Circle). One wag suggested Mr. DeMarathon should be rechristened "Mr. Socko."[56]

A *Herald* reporter interviewed Bill, along with the other athletes, "in the barren basement of Boston University's Soden Building, hard by the finish line" (that is, the BAA's former clubhouse, which BU let the association use once a year). "'Sometimes they ask me why I don't give up marathoning,' [Bill] cracked. 'I always tell 'em I'd rather give up brick-laying. Honest, I get more tired laying bricks than I do running these things.' He skipped off smartly toward the shower room."[57]

With that, an era came to a close. Fittingly, rumors flew that war would end the Boston Marathon itself (as it did the Port Chester run). But the response from Walter Brown, "the youngish big shot of the BAA," was:

> "Nuts! Why should we give up the marathon race? We've been going along with it for almost 50 years and we'll keep on for another 50, I hope. A few years ago my father (George V.) had the answer to a similar rumor. He said that if there ever was a move to abandon the

Marathon he would conduct the race himself. And I feel the same way about it!"[58]

As things turned out, with America entering World War II by the end of that year, Walter Brown would indeed have to hold the Boston Marathon together almost single-handedly, at least in financial terms.[59] And perhaps at times he looked to Bricklayer Bill Kennedy as an inspiration for never giving up.

But though Bill was out of the race now, he wasn't done influencing the course of the event. A chance meeting during the war would change the face of the Boston Marathon for decades.

10

GO WEST, OLD MAN

Bill began the Second World War much as he had the first, on a construction site, building a military training camp. But this time around, that was as far as he'd go in the war effort; he was much too old to consider enlisting. Shortly after the Japanese attack on Pearl Harbor, Bill and his brother Joe worked together on Camp Kilmer in New Jersey. By summer 1942, Bill was in Geneva, New York, helping to build Sampson Naval Training Base, on the shores of Seneca Lake.[1]

At Sampson, Bill bumped into Jock Semple, who was stationed there as a drill instructor. Jock told Bill how he'd hoped his experience as a DI would help him become a coach after the war, but he figured he couldn't be a track coach because he hadn't gone to college. Bill had another idea. As Semple recalled, "He suggested I should use that experience to become a physical therapist." The Scotsman thought about this and filed the idea away for later consideration.[2]

Throughout the war Bill was on the move again, traveling for work. In 1943 he was driving through Alton, Illinois, and stopped at a tavern. "Noting the proprietor was a Greek," Bill recalled, "I spoke of the Olympic Games." Over his refreshments, Bill talked about the

1906 Games at Athens, when the marathon was won by William J. Sherring of the St. Patrick's A.C. in Toronto.

The proprietor smiled.

He told me he saw the race as a boy and of a Greek admirer who presented the winner with a young nanny goat, and of the embarrassed Sherring asking him [the boy, now the tavern owner] to carry it for him. Who as soon as Sherring turned his back ran off with the goat, much to the winner's relief. This man was Nick Bavas (now deceased). He told me he had looked up Sherring since coming to America and they had a good laugh over it.[3]

Bill ran his last recorded race the following January 8, 1944. He was in New Orleans, working at the Delta Shipyards, where he patched ships' plumbing with asbestos. Now sixty, "Old Bill . . . could have been mistaken for the year 1943 making a belated exit," wrote a local AP correspondent. Bill finished the six-mile Jackson Day race with a time of 48:55, fifteenth out of a field of twenty-two.[4]

"If the Lord had built me with a speedometer, I'd show about 100,000 miles of marathon running," Bill claimed. "That's counting training, too. I've run 112 full-distance marathons of better'n 26 miles. And so many of these runt races I can't remember."

As Bill recalled it, when "this newspaper chap" asked "whether I smoked or took a drink, I answered in the affirmative."[5] The writer then took a little license in the story: "[Bill] attributes his incredible energy to 'good, bonded whiskey, and carefully-aged tobacco,'" as well as "a spartan abstinence from hot dogs."

~⌒~

After the war, Bill and Jessie (see fig. 10) boxed up his trophies and scrapbooks and their other belongings and moved permanently back to St. Louis. It's unclear when exactly, but by June 1952, a character in *Mickey Finn*, the nationally syndicated comic strip by Bill's friend Lank Leonard, mentioned how "that bricklayer, Bill Kennedy . . . has moved out of town." (The strip was set in Port Chester.) Perhaps he

FIGURE 10. Bill and Jessie in later years.

felt the move was fair to Jessie, after all their time in "Old Saw Pits."
But he'd write to a niece, "I long for the East."[6]

Bill continued work as a brickie, and in 1953 he served as a del-
egate at an American Federation of Labor convention in St. Louis.
The "spry 70-year-old [was] seen bounding through the convention
headquarters hotel lobby, chatting with members," reported his union

newsletter. "Even a quick look at his graceful, quick movements [is] enough to label him an athlete."[7]

Still laying brick and still advocating for labor a few years later, he wrote a letter to Governor Fred Hall of Kansas, commending him for vetoing anti-union legislation: "You must be a goodly man dear Gov. Hall, a fair and honest man, to understand and refuse to sign the 'Right to work bill' known in your state as House bill No. 30." Echoing his father in his ability to work across the aisle on occasion, Bill continued: "I am a Democrat, but if I can ever vote for you, I would be proud and boastful to do so. The laboring classes in the State of Kansas, both union and non union, as well as all fair minded people, must be proud of such a man as Governor Hall. I salute you."

He signed the letter, " 'Bricklayer Bill' Kennedy."[8]

Both of Bill and Jessie's daughters had moved with their husbands from New York to southern California—Louise to Compton, Juanita to Long Beach. But Jessie's sisters were still in St. Louis, and their grandchildren remember "Uncle Bill" in this era, often showing up unannounced on a Sunday, having walked two to four miles from his house. Holding court in the living room with a cigar in one hand and a mug of beer in the other, Bill regaled the kids with tales of the Boston Marathon. They also remember "wacky" Jessie's fits of fury. In one recollection, she was "screaming" at her visiting daughter Louise "while throwing a bunch of Uncle Bill's trophies down the long flight of stairs" in their home.[9]

Bill kept working as a bricklayer until at least age seventy-nine. And while he stopped running, he still walked four to six miles a day, often around Forest Park—site of the 1904 Olympics, by this time part of Washington University of St. Louis. "Crowned with bushy white hair, he stands erect," reported the *Post-Dispatch* in April 1962, "a proud, wiry little man who speaks of bygone years with a laugh and an Irish brogue."[10]

Bill kept in touch with his fellow old-timers and always got a kick out of the fact that so many of them were still around, in the 1960s, despite the ominous warnings of self-styled experts in the early days of marathoning.

"Bob Edgren once wrote, 'It's a killer sport,'" Bill recalled, paraphrasing columnist Edgren's pronouncement in 1917 that "the Marathon was founded on a run that killed the runner. . . . Marathon runners last only a short time."[11] Not so, Bill reported with glee in 1963:

> Sid Hatch ran over fifty marathons with two one-hundred-mile races and at 80 years is hale and hearty in a suburb of Chicago. Monteverde ran one hundred marathons as well as his walk across the continent and at 93 still walks every day out in Los Angeles. Joe Forshaw at 83 still attends to his business at St. Louis. Johnny Hayes is around N.Y. in his seventies as is Harry Parkinson, Zuna is out in Reno, Nev.[12]

One glaring exception was Mr. DeMarathon himself. Clarence DeMar, who ran his final Boston Marathon in 1954, died in 1958 at age seventy. Significantly, however, DeMar died of cancer—*not* of "athletic heart." Dr. Paul Dudley White, who became famous as President Dwight Eisenhower's physician, had examined DeMar at different points in the 1950s and declared, "Not only was DeMar's heart normal in size, but the arteries were softer than could be expected. The aorta was still elastic, so it hadn't hurt him to run over 200 marathons, and it will not hurt anyone who keeps in good condition."[13]

White's colleague Dr. James Currens told the *Globe* how DeMar had shown up for one test wearing old, mismatched sneakers. The doctors rewarded him with a brand-new pair, and he ran on a treadmill for the test. "When it was over," Currens said, "Clarence trotted out of the office, down the street and back to work."[14]

White and Currens did much to publicize the benefits of regular exercise—needed more than ever as desk-bound middle-management jobs became more prevalent in these years. "To the old-fashioned doctor's idea that heavy work or exercise damages the heart," Bill wrote, "Dr. Currens retorts 'It's probably the lack of exercise that does it.' That's what we marathoners have been preaching for over sixty years."[15]

As well as the study of DeMar's heart, something of a posthumous examination of DeMar's personality took place as local athletes shared their memories of a man known for not sharing much. "DeMar wasn't a mixer," noted the *Globe,* "and few of the marathoning or road racing group ever got to know him very well." But apparently South Boston boxer Mike Conroy was one of those few:

> "I met him years ago and we used to talk," Mike said. "We were friendly and one day I asked him to come over to South Boston to race in one of our first 10 mile races. He accepted right away. He was the biggest name in road racing and his presence made our race.
>
> "Afterward I told him I wanted to pay all his expenses. He said to me: 'Buy me an ice cream soda and we'll call it square.' There never will be another like him."[16]

In part to preserve his own memories and the legacy of not just De-Mar but all the workingmen marathoners he'd met and all that they'd experienced, Bill decided in his old age to write it all down, hoping to publish a book. "I bought me a typewriter and am trying to teach myself to write on it," he told a friend, "as my hand writing is not too hot."[17]

Bill managed to learn, and he typed up some of his favorite "tales of the road, which gave me a laugh and partly answers [the question] 'what do you think about [while running]?' "

> Joie Ray in his younger days was a printer and lithographer, and [had] hundreds of his pictures made up. It was Joe's custom to autograph them and pass them out to anyone within reach. Coming home on the ship from the Amsterdam Olympics, one of the girl swimmers was trying to coax a trinket from another girl. On being refused, she says "I will trade you one of Joie Ray's pictures for it."

Several of us American runners were up in Toronto to run in a race. We were invited over to Percy Wyer's house for a light lunch before the race. Percy was the Canadian champion at the time and weighed about one hundred pounds. He was cooking some soft boiled eggs. His mother, who weighed over two hundred, sat in a chair rocking. The eggs were taken off the stove. Percy was hunting through closets and drawers. Patiently we waited, colder the eggs became, his mother kept on rocking. Finally one of us says "Percy, what are you looking for? Those eggs are getting cold." "Well, I was looking for those little egg cups to serve them in." And his mother kept on rocking. . . .

Bewhiskered "Pop" Weeks of Yonkers and his wife were seated in the N.Y. subway, a few days before the running of the Evening Mail Race. The paper was full of pictures of runners, among them Mr. Weeks, who always finished among the medal winners.

Two young ladies seated across the aisle were looking at the pictures on the sport page, and seeing the whiskered man in a track suit, one spoke, "Look at this old man with whiskers running in this race. If I was his wife, I would sure stop that."

Leaning across the aisle with a stern look, Mrs. Weeks says, "Young lady, I am Mrs. Weeks, and just how would you stop him? I have been trying to stop him for years."

One more on Weeks and I will sign off. Weeks and I were seated together coming down to N.Y. from a race at Amsterdam N.Y. Discussing running, I asked him, is your family interested in your running?

Looking at me with a whimsical smile, he replied, "If the greatest race in the world was finishing in front of my house and I was coming in the winner, none of my family would look out the window."

After running a ten mile race at Yonkers, Dan Ferris the then Secretary Treasurer of the Amateur Athletic Union, gave me a ride into N.Y. in his Ford with his wife and three children in the back seat. As we passed 145th Street on Jerome Ave., the light turned and Dan crossed on yellow. A big Irish cop halted us and pulled out his book. As he started to write out a ticket, he glanced into the back seat, where three pairs of big saucer-eyed and frightened eyes stared into his. Hesitating with his pencil, he turned to Dan and asked, "And who may these children belong to?"

"They're mine," answered Dan.

"Huh," says the big Turk, putting his book in his pocket. "Ye need the money more than the city of New York does, begone my lad." No wonder we love the Irish.[18]

___

Besides entertaining, Bill hoped to inspire. He expounded on what he called "gameness," persistence in the face of adversity or pain or just plain exhaustion. He emphasized that the notion went beyond sport:

> It is evident not only in athletics, but in business work, or our every day life. Gameness is will power, and it is in proportion to this, whether we continue to carry on despite discouragement or quit and let the other fellow do it.
>
> I saw Gene Tunney take an awful beating from Harry Greb in the old Madison Sq. garden, shortly after the first war. He was battered, butted and elbowed, yet he refused to go down. His head was "bloodied but unbowed," yet [he] carried on to become champion of them all.
>
> Eugene Criqui the French Poilu came over here and knocked out Kilbane for the world's title. A few months later he fought and took an awful beating from Johnny Dundee at the Polo Grounds. Fighting before a partisan crowd of Dundee rooters, with their unsportsman-like "Boos!" ringing in his ears, as he arose from repeated knock-downs, refusing to quit, until he was no longer able to get up from the floor. A real gamester.
>
> In my own sport I saw the bloodied foot prints of Joie Ray on the floor of the Boston A.A., after [his] finishing 3rd in the 26 mile run. . . .
>
> Any man can be game when he is winning but it takes guts to keep plugging when you know you are hopelessly beaten.
>
> For instance, in the Boston Race, there are over 200 starters, the first eight receive major trophies, the next 25 bronze medals, and the following men receive nothing. The leaders run through a lane of cheering thousands, yet for three hours, the forgotten men go struggling by. Few cheer them on as most, having seen the winners go by, have departed. Tired and footsore, the men are finishing something they have started, keeping faith with themselves, game-sters every one of them. . . .

You can see the same thing in everyday life, men and women overcoming handicaps in life, no plaudits for them, just the satisfaction of an obscure actor on the stage of life. Many of us become discouraged at times and give up too easily, not only in athletics but in our every day life. We all have our setbacks, dame fortune smiles on you at times, and then she turns on you and frowns. . . .

There it is, men, to the best of my ability. Go out and win, and if not this time, try again—from the losers come the winners and champions of the future.[19]

One who had taken Bill's advice of years before was Jock Semple. Returning to Boston after the war, Semple built on his firsthand knowledge of competitive sports and his drill instructor experience with a little bit of book learning and became a physical therapist. Walter Brown hired him as athletic trainer for the Celtics. Semple worked with Bob Cousy and the other Celtics greats of the 1950s and 1960s, taking them out for early morning runs and giving them rubdowns on his trainer's table after games in the Boston Garden.

Meanwhile, Walter Brown appointed Semple co-director of the Boston Marathon. The fiery Scotsman received runners' entry forms, distributed bib numbers, and managed many other practical aspects of the race. On top of that, Semple launched a personal mission to recruit a BAA team that would finally produce a winner for the hometown club. (The club, it should be noted, at this point pretty much existed solely in Semple's desk in the Garden.)

In this latter capacity, Semple discovered and mentored John J. Kelley—no relation to the great John A. Kelley. ("By a fillip of teasing fate, I bore the monarch's name," the poetically inclined John J. said.) "Kelley the Younger," as he would come to be known, attended Boston University on a track scholarship when he began training for the marathon—still an unconventional activity for a college student in the fifties. Like Semple and the other old-time plodders, Kelley knew something about hard work. He lugged boxes in a jewelry store basement and flipped burgers in a fast-paced cafeteria to help put himself through college. But he was still a college athlete, which for a runner of that era meant a sprinter. But despite his considerable prowess on the track, Kelley was drawn to the road—appropriate for a Kerouac fan. In particular, he felt the pull of the great road race that passed practically under the window of his dorm room by Kenmore Square. To the chagrin of Kelley's BU coaches, Semple persuaded him to join the BAA squad and helped him develop his talent for distance running.[20]

In 1957 Kelley beat the favored Finns and Koreans to win the Boston Marathon—the first American to do so since the war—while setting a new record for the course, 2:20:05. "More important," said Semple, "he made it respectable for college athletes to run on the roads, which some people—mostly college track coaches—formerly had thought were good enough only for us broken-down working guys."[21]

～⌒⌒/

Shocked and saddened by the death of President John F. Kennedy in November 1963, Bill donated to the Kennedy Library Fund. In August 1964 a letter arrived from the president's widow, Jacqueline. "I am most deeply grateful for the contribution," she wrote, "especially because you worked so hard to earn the money." Mrs. Kennedy added that her late husband would have appreciated "the touching response of you young people." Now eighty years young, the bricklayer treasured the letter despite the clerical error.[22]

Bill Kennedy suffered a stroke in 1965. He survived, bedridden at home for several months, with a nurse visiting to check on him every other day. "His heart was strong," recalled great-nephew John Mernah. "It wouldn't let go."[23]

With that strong heart, Bill managed to walk again, and to write again. There is no evidence that Bill had been particularly religious before, but the stroke made him think more seriously about God. He attended a Catholic retreat, which seemed to work wonders for him, as evidenced in letters he wrote to a nephew also named Bill—Bill Nolan, the son of Nellie, Bill Kennedy's first fiancée. We're told that

Nolan regularly bought tickets for Kennedy in the Irish Sweepstakes, the lottery set up to benefit hospitals in Ireland in the middle decades of the last century.[24]

Oct. 20th / 1966

Dear Bill:

Well the Irish S [Sweepstakes] is history for this year. And as the Irish-man told his pal after they begged a meal "Well Mike we won't thank God for this meal. We've had it. We will thank him for the next."
  Bill don't hold this check so long. Cash it. As a stroke effect your brain & your memory, I have no pains whatsoever but leg & foot are weak. Tho I walk 30–45 min. every day, exercise my leg 1000 times a day. Am confident I will conquer it; for I believe and say the Rosary twice a day.
  The Retreat was the best thing that ever happened to me. The lesson of silence and meditating. Nothing in life is chance. It is either a reward or a punishment and men who ran Marathons, with the hours & miles they have traveled on the roads in training & competi-tion alone with their thoughts & meditations do a lot of praying.
  I have been asked so many times if I pray for to win. No, I prayed for will power to keep going when tired & discouraged. I have run & walked over 50,000 miles in my career of over 100 full distance Mar-athons & nearly 200 lesser distances [and] I enjoyed every mile of it.
  So I accept this stroke as the will of God. We all have sinned & regretted for as the poet said "Of all sad words of tongue or pen the saddest are those it might have been."

April 10 / 67

Dear Bill:

Your kind letter with Sweepstake ticket received some time ago for which I thank you very sincerely. The winners really from what I have read are needy people, for which I thank God.

Alice at the time she visited our house had a very bad cough. I
hope she is cured of it as I was slightly alarmed.

As to myself, my leg is still weak. Tho I am confident it was an
act of God. That I no doubt deserved. And it can only be cured by
God's will and prayer, and I believe, having had several miracles. I
am praying for another.

Bill as one grows older he becomes smarter. I now realize men
are more sentimental than women. . . . Jessie tells me, "You are a
cripple for life."

I look at her & smile to myself. For I have knowledge. My fall of
70 ft 1909 at Des Moines my miraculous escape.

Fifty yrs ago the 19th of this month was a miracle. In the spring
of 1914, I was discharged from Hospital after 14 weeks with typhoid
fever. Chicago. Doctors and nurses all advised me never to run again
in competition as the fever takes something out of you. Yet after a
year of no competition I won the Boston Marathon 1917 leading
over 100 competitors from U.S. Can[ada] and Europe. It to me was
a miracle.

So long Old Pal. You will be like Jessie calling me wackey. Laugh
& the world laughs with you.

Bill[25]

‿◡‿

Bill outlived his three younger brothers. (Recall that Owen had died
as a child back in the nineteenth century.) In August 1967, a few
months after Bill wrote the second of these letters to Bill Nolan, Paul
(grandfather and great-grandfather of the authors) died. Though
they were both bricklayers, Paul was ten years younger than Bill, and
that chasm was only compounded by their geographical separation
since the war. This lack of closeness bothered Bill. He contrasted his
family with their Camelot namesakes, writing: "Had we been as the
Kennedys from Mass. what a difference it would have meant in our
lives. But we drifted apart and lost track of one another."[26]

Bill didn't make it to Paul's funeral. But six months later, in February 1968, their brother Joe died. It was with Joe that Bill had first embarked on that great westward adventure when they were teenagers. Now, at age eighty-four, the last of L. J. Kennedy's sons made his final trip east. He must have been in reasonably good shape at the time, as Joe's granddaughter Jo-Ellen Pearson remembers Uncle Bill doing calisthenics in her Bronx living room the morning of the funeral.

Two months later, in April 1968, Bill's thoughts almost certainly turned, as always, to Boston and the Patriots' Day marathon. It had been more than a decade since the triumph of Johnny Kelley the Younger. No American had won since then, a fact that increasingly bothered Bill. "In late years the men of the Old World seem to have more of it than the American youth," he wrote, rankled that runners from Finland and Belgium had a lock on the event once seen as "symbolic of the American Champion."[27] Bill had to wonder if he'd live to see an American win the race again.

On April 19, college student Amby Burfoot toed the line in Hopkinton. Back in high school in Groton, Connecticut, Burfoot's cross-country coach had been none other than Johnny Kelley the Younger. Kelley encouraged Burfoot to pursue long-distance running, even though Burfoot (echoing Kelley's own story) got a scholarship to run short distances, on the track. Burfoot had pushed himself, and in 1967 he'd run his first Boston Marathon—the last to include both Kelleys (Older and Younger) in the field, and the first to include a woman (Kathrine Switzer) running with an official bib number, despite the efforts of a crazed Jock Semple to physically tear the bib off of her mid-run. Though Burfoot stopped twice to relieve his bowels, he finished seventeenth, in 2:28:05.

Now here he was, on Patriots' Day 1968. Burfoot ran with the lead pack through Wellesley. After that, the race became a duel between Burfoot and Bill Clark. As they scaled the dread Newton hills, the sun at their backs, Burfoot glanced down nervously at Clark's steadily plodding shadow. But Clark cramped up slightly on the hill. From the press bus, Semple in his burr roared at Burfoot, "Give it hell on the downhill, Amby!" Burfoot obliged, and he held on for the win, in 2:22:17.[28]

An American had won the Boston Marathon. The news found its way back to St. Louis. Five days later, Bill passed away.[29]

Perhaps the timing is a coincidence, but we can't help but think that Uncle Bill had been holding on during those final years, waiting for that news. And now, Bill Kennedy went home supremely happy.

EPILOGUE

Nellie got the trophy. The silver cup that Bricklayer Bill won at Boston in 1917, likely his most prized possession. Jessie had no interest in it, and it ended up with Nellie, Bill's original love among the Herbert girls. She displayed it proudly in her front room for the rest of her life. Though she'd broken off their engagement long ago, perhaps in a way Nellie still carried a torch for Bill. The sad twist in their failed romance is that the man she married instead, John Nolan, died young, leaving Nellie to raise their five children alone. Like her mother, she took in boarders. She did laundry. Eventually she bought a bakery, naming it Nellie's Bake Shoppe. And she did it all with a positive attitude. "She had an awesome sense of humor," remembers one of her granddaughters.[1]

The Boston Marathon, too, adapted to changing realities. By cleverly filling out her entry form as "K. Switzer," Kathrine Switzer had become the first woman to run the race wearing an official bib (the cause of rules-stickler Semple's rage) in 1967. She was not the first woman to run the marathon, however. Roberta Gibb did that, unofficially (by simply jumping in), in 1966. But neither would be the last. Thanks to their example, more and more women advocated to enter, and in 1972 the race officially opened up to the other half of the population. Nina Kuscsik was the first winner in the female division, in 3:10:26.[2]

That same year, Frank Shorter won the Olympic marathon, the first American to do so since Johnny Hayes in 1908. Tragically, in those same Games at Munich, Palestinian terrorists killed eleven Israeli Olympians. USOC president Avery Brundage was slated to retire from his post anyway and soon stepped down, but the Munich tragedy made a sad bookend to his long and controversial career. He died three years later.[3]

Shorter had never run Boston, and he horrified the Globe's Jerry Nason when he informed the sportswriter that under new regulations, the Hopkinton–to–Back Bay route was "illegal." He meant it was no longer considered an Olympic qualifying course. Not only is it too steep downward overall, but also it's a point-to-point race rather than a loop, so theoretically a tailwind could benefit runners the entire way.[4]

Still, thanks in part to Shorter, big changes were afoot in people's perceptions of road running as well. Bostonians liked their Johnny Kelleys and cheered on the runners along Comm. Ave. every Patriots' Day. The rest of the year, not so much. In '72, when a scruffy, long-haired Bill Rodgers ran around Jamaica Pond, passing motorists threw beer cans at him and shouted, "Get a job!" (Why they had beer cans in their cars if they were such upstanding types themselves is another question.) But in 1975, when Rodgers—a protégé of Amby Burfoot—ran the Boston Marathon wearing a handmade "BOSTON" T-shirt, he won over the straight crowd. Spectators chanted "Boston, Boston," as he bested Canadian Jerome Drayton in a duel for the lead at the early mark of mile eleven and held on for the win.[5]

Rodgers went on to triumph three more times, and to win the new New York City Marathon (founded in 1970) four times. He inspired thousands to take up road running, for competition or just for their health. Thanks in part to Rodgers, running would become the mainstream activity it is today, and the line of apprenticeship that produced him can be traced back—via Burfoot via Kelley via Semple—to Bricklayer Bill Kennedy.

The old-time plodders all would have recognized the conditions that Rodgers and his own pioneering peers labored under even in the 1970s. Remember how Kennedy had split his YMCA bed with Mellor? And how he and five other runners had crammed into a car, with four hidden under the rumble seat to evade the ferry fare? Now read Tom Derderian's account of how, decades later, Rodgers "traveled to races in old cars filled with his fellow runners."

> When they went to Philadelphia two runners rented a hotel room with two double beds. Six other runners came up the back stairs. They took the mattresses off the box springs and put them on the floor so that the room accommodated all eight runners—two on each mattress and two on each box spring. When Rodgers and his friends returned to Boston, no one had a single dime left; they had to return via back roads because they could not afford the turnpike tolls.[6]

Times did change, though, even in Boston. The BAA marathon went professional in 1986 with the sponsorship of the John Hancock insurance company. In a new era of pro elite runners sponsored by shoe companies, cash prizes were needed to attract top talent and keep the historic race relevant. This was Nason's worst fear realized. He decried the event's going "commercial."[7]

But in a way, the prize money won by a few elites is beside the point. Nowadays, nearly thirty thousand people run the marathon every Patriots' Day. The overwhelming majority run for the love of the sport, for their health, and for the camaraderie.

And increasingly, they run for a good cause. A half century after Bill Kennedy sent his manuscript to a niece who worked at Harvard University Press, his great-grandnephew met with a Harvard paleo-anthropologist. Daniel Lieberman's research suggests that endurance running is what made us human. In packs, our ancestors ran down game; that unique ability allowed the meat diet that grew our brains.

Lieberman argued that the purpose of distance running has evolved along with us.

"Why are people running 26.2 miles for charity?" Lieberman asked rhetorically. "The Boston Marathon raises more than twenty million dollars a year for charities. And I think that's because we've always run to help each other. Back in the old days, people ran to hunt, for security." In Native American and other traditions, foot races were part of ceremonies to ensure the rains, and fleet-footed messengers kept communities connected. "Running has always been a communal event that was part of helping each other, and I don't think that today's marathon movement is any different."[8]

In that way, the mutual-aid spirit of the old workingmen marathoners lives on, whether runners are sharing a ride, a meal, a crash pad, a length of tape, or a training tip. Whether their friends chip in toward their charities, or their spouses take on extra chores and child care duties to make possible those long weekend runs. Running might seem like a solitary sport, but it turns out to be a collective endeavor.

As we opened this book with Bill's words, so it seems fitting to close in the same manner:

> Why is the winner's time in the Boston Marathon always much faster than the same men run elsewhere? This has always been a debatable question among distance runners, officials, and followers of this sport. . . .
>
> But oh that Boston Race. Every man in it is an experienced runner, with few exceptions. They have known for years it would be held on this day, and have been pointing for it and are well trained to run this distance. Once that gun goes off you are on your own, no one can help you here, you can't see the men behind. Get out in front if you can, and run to stay there. You can't lap him with early speed and take his pace, you ponder where each is placed, is he gaining, where is DeMar? Stop to tie a shoelace, to take a sip of water, even

to look behind you and a runner goes by. No let up until you hit that tape on Exeter St.

There is no monotony on the road. New faces, jokes, cheers, each turn of the road, so much nearer your goal, each hill climbed is behind you. . . .

The wonderful crowd along the course spurs you on, with words of encouragement. You can't quit here. Sure, you are tired, your feet blistered, you feel sick to your stomach, you feel like quitting. But where on each side of you are cheering sympathetic people cheering you on, can you let them see you quit? Hardly. "Carry on" as the Tommies used to say. Finally that turn to the right at Exeter and you are home.

The well-policed course, the sportsmanship of the spectators, and the class of the competition all tend to make fast running at this race. . . .

That's my theory of the fast time. But who cares? It's a great race to win.[9]

NOTES

ABBREVIATIONS

AWC	Army War College
BA	*Boston American*
BDA	*Boston Daily Advertiser*
BDE	*Brooklyn Daily Eagle*
BER	*Boston Evening Record*
BET	*Boston Evening Transcript*
BG	*Boston Globe*
BH	*Boston Herald*
BJ	*Boston Journal*
BMP	*The Bricklayer, Mason and Plasterer,* union newsletter
BP	*Boston Post*
CDT	*Chicago Daily Tribune*
KPEU	William J. Kennedy, "Keep Pickin Em Up," unpublished manuscript, ca. 1963
NYT	*New York Times*
NYTrib	*New York Tribune*
PCDI	*Port Chester Daily Item*
S&S	*Stars and Stripes*
SLPD	*St. Louis Post-Dispatch*
WSU	Washington State University

PROLOGUE

1. "When Life Flashes before Your Eyes," *Popular Science*, Apr. 12, 2010, popsci.com.
2. State of New York, *Thirtieth Annual Report of the State Department of Health*, Feb. 15, 1910; Pamela Cooper, *The American Marathon* (Syracuse: Syracuse University Press, 1998), 67.
3. KPEU, 38.
4. "Port Chester" (list of short items), *NYTrib*, Sept. 13, 1896.
5. Cooper, *American Marathon*, 8–9, 17; "The Marathon Race," *New York Evening Post*, Sept. 18, 1896; "World's Records Smashed," *BDE*, Sept. 20, 1896.
6. "World's Records Smashed," *BDE*, Sept. 20, 1896.
7. Quote: "M'Dermott Won It," *New York Herald*, Sept. 20, 1896; telegraph poles: "Miscellaneous Notes," *New York Evening Post*, Aug. 31, 1896; condition of roads: Eric Jaffe, *The King's Best Highway: The Lost History of the Boston Post Road, the Route That Made America* (New York: Scribner, 2010), 189–90.
8. "World's Records Smashed," *BDE*, Sept. 20, 1896.
9. KPEU, 22.
10. KPEU, 2–3.

1. BRICKIE, BOXER, KNICKERBOCKER

1. Pamela Cooper, *The American Marathon* (Syracuse: Syracuse University Press, 1998), 9–10.
2. Charlotte Porter and Helen Clarke, eds., *The Poems of Robert Browning* (New York: Crowell, 1896), 428.
3. Richard D. Mandell, *The First Modern Olympics* (Berkeley: University of California Press, 1976), ix–x, 72.
4. Cooper, *American Marathon*, 10–20; David Davis, *Showdown at Shepherd's Bush: The 1908 Olympic Marathon and the Three Runners Who Launched a Sporting Craze* (New York: Thomas Dunne, 2012), 27; John Cumming, *Runners & Walkers: A Nineteenth Century Sports Chronicle* (Chicago: Regnery Gateway, 1981), 8–9.
5. "Honors for Americans Sustain Their Reputations at Olympic Games," *NYT*, Apr. 11, 1896; Cooper, *American Marathon*, 10–20; John Hanc, *The B.A.A. at 125: The Official History of the Boston Athletic Association, 1887–1912* (New York: Sport Publishing, 2012), 48–51.
6. Cooper, *American Marathon*, 18.
7. For this and all other quotations from the *Eagle* article on this race, see "World's Records Smashed," *BDE*, Sept. 20, 1896.
8. Eric Jaffe, *The King's Best Highway: The Lost History of the Boston Post Road, the Route That Made America* (New York: Scribner, 2010), 173–85, 189–90.
9. "Great Athletic Records," *NYT*, Sept. 20, 1896.
10. Hanc, *B.A.A.*, 53. This passage originally appeared in Patrick Kennedy, "In the Running: 1897 to 2014," *BU Today*, Apr. 18, 2014.
11. "Record Time," *BG*, Apr. 20, 1897.

12. "Harvard Sports," *BG*, Apr. 26, 1897; Tom Derderian, *The Boston Marathon: The First Century of the World's Premier Running Event,* Centennial Race ed. (Champaign, IL: Human Kinetics Publishers, 1996), 3-6.

13. "Record Time," *BG*, Apr. 20, 1897.

14. Cooper, *American Marathon,* 4.

15. KPEU, 4.

16. Kennedy family oral history; Bill Kennedy to Ann Louise McLaughlin, Mar. 13, 1963.

17. Kennedy to McLaughlin, Mar. 13, 1963.

18. Kevin J. McCarthy, *Gold, Silver and Green: The Irish Olympic Journey, 1896–1924* (Cork: Cork University Press, 2010), 7.

19. Kennedy family Bible, in authors' possession; "L. J. Kennedy Dies, Veteran Builder Here," *PCDI,* Dec. 26, 1931; Kennedy family history, compiled by Ann Louise McLaughlin (undated, unpaginated), in authors' possession; "L.J. Kennedy Dies," *PCDI,* Dec. 26, 1931; U.S. Census, 1880, accessed via Ancestry.com.

20. U.S. Census, 1870 and 1880; authors' interviews with Ann Louise McLaughlin; Wendy Gamber, *The Boardinghouse in Nineteenth-Century America* (Baltimore: Johns Hopkins University Press, 2007), 34–76; Kennedy Bible and family history; *U.S. Veterans Gravesites, ca. 1775–2006,* accessed via Ancestry.com; "'17 Marathon Winner Slows Down at 78—to Four Miles," *SLPD,* Apr. 22, 1962.

21. Jonathan Gill, *Harlem: The Four Hundred Year History from Dutch Village to Capital of Black America* (New York: Grove Press, 2011), 117–18 and 141; Edwin G. Burrows and Mike Wallace, *Gotham: A History of New York City to 1898* (New York: Oxford University Press, 1999), 1123–24; Bill Kennedy to Arthur Veasey, Dec. 13, 1959.

22. Municipal records, Port Chester, NY; Kennedy family history; U.S. Census, 1900; KPEU, 51; Bill Kennedy to Governor Fred Hall, Jan. 21, 1956 (Kansas Historical Society), and Arthur Veasey, Dec. 13, 1959.

23. Owen Bernard Maginnis, *Bricklaying* (New York: O. B. Maginnis, 1901), 7–22. Some of Patrick Kennedy's passages about Bill Kennedy learning bricklaying and taking up boxing were originally published in "Bricklayer Bill's Ultra-Marathon of a Life," *Narratively,* Oct. 1, 2014, http://narrative.ly.

24. McLaughlin interviews.

25. "Kennedy Captures 9-Mile Road Run: Veteran Successfully Celebrates 24th Anniversary as Athlete," *NYT,* Sept. 25, 1922; Bill Kennedy to Arthur Veasey, Dec. 13, 1959.

26. "Gouging match": Foster Rhea Dulles, *A History of Recreation: America Learns to Play,* 2nd ed. (New York: Appleton-Century-Crofts, 1965), 144–45; "metronomic": Michael Isenberg, *John L. Sullivan and His America* (Urbana: University of Illinois Press, 1988), 45.

27. Arne K. Lang, *Prizefighting: An American History* (Jefferson, NC: McFarland, 2008), 49; *NYT,* Jan. 25, 1900.

28. "Goddard Whips Maher," *National Police Gazette,* Dec. 24, 1892.

29. Lang, *Prizefighting,* 49; Isenberg, *John L. Sullivan,* 33; McCarthy, *Gold, Silver and Green,* 47–48.

30. KPEU, 36.

31. "'17 Marathon Winner Slows Down," *SLPD*, Apr. 22, 1962; Hanc, *B.A.A.*, 18; Elliott J. Gorn, *The Manly Art: Bare-Knuckle Prizefighting in America* (Ithaca: Cornell University Press, 1986), 201.
32. Municipal records, Port Chester, NY.
33. McLaughlin interviews.
34. U.S. Census, 1900.
35. "L. J. Kennedy Dies," *PCDI*, Dec. 26, 1931; Kennedy family oral history.
36. Authors' interview with Joan Kennedy Harvey, Dec. 31, 2015.
37. L. J. Kennedy's daybook, Jan.–Dec. 1893, in authors' possession; Bureau of Labor Statistics, Consumer Price Index inflation calculator, bls.gov; S. Morgan Friedman's inflation calculator, westegg.com/inflation; McLaughlin interview, Apr. 2, 2011.
38. U.S. Census, 1910.
39. L. J. Kennedy's daybook, Dec. 29, 1880.
40. "L. J. Kennedy Dies," *PCDI*, Dec 26, 1931.
41. This anecdote and the ones that follow are from McLaughlin interviews.
42. McLaughlin interviews plus author conversation with Jo-Ellen Pearson (Joe Kennedy's granddaughter), Apr. 2013, and Bill Kennedy to Arthur Veasey, Dec. 13, 1959.

2. ON THE ROAD (AND RAILS)

1. Clark Spence, "Knights of the Fast Freight," *American Heritage Magazine,* Aug. 1976, americanheritage.com; Jack London, *The Road* (1907; New Brunswick: Rutgers University Press, 2006), chap. 2; John Lennon, "Riding the Rails: The Place of the Passenger and the Space of the Hobo," *Americana: The Journal of American Popular Culture* 3, no. 2 (Fall 2004). Patrick Kennedy's passage about Bill Kennedy riding the rails was originally published in "Bricklayer Bill's Ultra-Marathon of a Life," *Narratively,* Oct. 1, 2014, http://narrative.ly.
2. "'17 Marathon Winner Slows Down at 78—to Four Miles," *SLPD,* Apr. 22, 1962.
3. Edward Achorn, *The Summer of Beer and Whiskey* (New York: PublicAffairs, 2013); Eoghan Miller, "St. Louis's German Brewing Industry: Its Rise and Fall" (M.A. thesis, University of Missouri–Columbia, 2008).
4. St. Louis City Plan Commission, *Physical Growth of the City of Saint Louis* (St. Louis: City of St. Louis, 1969); *Ground Plan of the Louisiana Purchase Exposition* (St. Louis: Buxton & Skinner, 1904).
5. "Valuable Prizes for Olympic Games," *NYT,* Oct. 4, 1903.
6. Sources for 1904 Olympics include "American Runner Wins," *NYT,* Aug. 31, 1904; and Karen Abbott, "The 1904 Olympics May Have Been the Strangest Ever," *Smithsonian,* Aug. 2012, smithsonianmag.com.
7. KPEU, 26.
8. KPEU, 26–27.
9. "10 Unbelievable Performance-Enhancing Substances," *Mental Floss,* Oct. 11, 2010, mentalfloss.com.
10. KPEU, 27.

11. Pamela Cooper, *The American Marathon* (Syracuse: Syracuse University Press, 1998), 22–23.

12. Tom Derderian, *The Boston Marathon: The First Century of the World's Premier Running Event*, Centennial Race ed. (Champaign, IL: Human Kinetics Publishers, 1996), 28–35.

13. John Rickard Betts, *America's Sporting Heritage: 1850–1950* (Reading, MA: Addison-Wesley, 1974), 98–101; Cooper, *American Marathon*, 12.

14. "From Present Entry List Prospects for Local Marathon Race Are Bright," *St. Louis Republic*, Feb. 12, 1905.

15. Christine Forshaw O'Shaughnessy, "Joseph Forshaw, Marathon Runner," *Journal of Olympic History*, May 2004, 15.

16. Ibid.

17. "St. Louis Boy Wins 25-Mile, Heart-Breaking Race, Finishing in Burst of Speed," *SLPD*, May 7, 1905.

18. "Marathon Runners Get on Their Marks," *SLPD*, May 5, 1906.

19. "Hatch, of Chicago, Wins," *SLPD*, May 6, 1906.

20. "History's Most Remarkable Run," *SLPD*, June 3, 1907.

21. "Bill Kennedy Here for the Marathon," *BG*, Apr. 17, 1915; KPEU, 64.

22. "John J. Hayes Wins Marathon Run," *NYT*, Nov. 29, 1907.

23. "Why He Lost the Race," *NYT*, Oct. 20, 1907.

24. For the 1908 Olympic marathon, see David Davis, *Showdown at Shepherd's Bush: The 1908 Olympic Marathon and the Three Runners Who Launched a Sporting Craze* (New York: Thomas Dunne, 2012), 64, 68, 97–102, 131, 155–69, 186; Derderian, *Boston Marathon*, 43–47.

25. KPEU, 28; Benjamin Cheever, *Strides: Running through History with an Unlikely Athlete* (New York: Rodale, 2007), 202.

26. "Women Get Marathon Craze," *University Missourian*, Feb. 12, 1909.

27. KPEU, 45; "Live Tips and Topics," *BG*, Apr. 12, 1913.

28. Bill Kennedy to Arthur Veasey, Dec. 13, 1959.

29. Joe Forshaw, "Marathon Running," in *Spalding's Athletic Library*, group 12, no. 317 (New York: American Sports Publishing, 1909), 71.

30. This discussion is drawn from e-mail interviews with Matt Migonis, Dennis Doherty, and Christopher Straub, another marathon runner and a Harvard neurobiologist, Oct. 2015.

31. KPEU, 9.

32. "Erxleben Beats London Marathon Record 6 Minutes," *SLPD*, May 1, 1909.

33. Ibid.

34. "Hatch, Chicago Paper Carrier, Wins Marathon," *SLPD*, May 3, 1908.

35. "St. Louis Boy Wins," *SLPD*, May 7, 1905.

36. "Erxleben Beats London Marathon Record," *SLPD*, May 1, 1909.

37. "Hatch, Chicago Paper Carrier," *SLPD*, May 3, 1908.

38. "Erxleben Beats London Marathon Record," *SLPD*, May 1, 1909.

39. "No Winner of Past B.A.A. Marathon Runs in Monday's Event," *BG*, Apr. 7, 1915.

40. KPEU, 62.

41. Cheever, *Strides*, 12–15; "Swift Pony Paced Jackie Miles," *BG*, Apr. 25, 1926.

42. KPEU, 36–37.

43. This discussion is drawn from U.S. Census, 1910; interviews with Ann Louise McLaughlin and John Mernah.

44. Records of weather observations for October 21, 1909, held by the office of the state climatologist of Iowa, show that the wind picked up between 11 a.m. and noon, reaching speeds of twenty-nine miles per hour. The passage on the Des Moines incident is from Kennedy, "Bricklayer Bill's Ultra-Marathon."

45. "Workman Falls," *Des Moines News*, Oct. 21, 1909.

46. "Falls 50 Feet and Alights on Man's Head," *Rock Island Argus*, Oct. 21, 1909; KPEU, 64.

47. *Holmquist v. C.L. Gray Const. Co.*, 151 N.W. 828 (1915).

48. KPEU, 64.

49. Ibid.

50. Ibid.

51. Missouri marriage records; interviews, phone calls, and e-mails with Ann Louise McLaughlin, Joan Kennedy Harvey, Rita Bishop, Tracey Bishop Holton, John Mernah, Tim Nolan, Patricia Nolan Schmidt, and Mary Nell Nicoletti, 2010–2014.

52. KPEU, 36.

53. KPEU, 5.

54. "Careful Planning Helps Pillivant Win Classic," *SLPD*, May 15, 1910.

55. KPEU, 53; "Dust-Choked Horde Plods Home behind Hatch, in Marathon," *SLPD*, May 14, 1911.

56. "Dust-Choked Horde," *SLPD*, May 14, 1911.

57. U.S. Census, 1920; *California, Death Index, 1940–1997*, accessed via Ancestry.com.

58. "Taft Meets John Hayes," *NYT*, Feb. 5, 1911.

59. "Muss in City Hall after Marathon" *NYT*, Feb. 7, 1911.

60. KPEU, 4, 6.

61. "Yonkers Marathon," *NYT*, Nov. 26, 1911.

62. "Sidney H. Hatch Wins Marathon," *NYT*, Dec. 1, 1911; "A Traditional Run That Refuses to Die," *Wall Street Journal*, Sept. 17, 2010.

63. "Sidney H. Hatch Wins," *NYT*, Dec. 1, 1911; KPEU, 22, 48.

64. "Sidney H. Hatch Wins," *NYT*, Dec. 1, 1911.

3. STRIDES, SETBACKS & LAURELS

1. "BAA Marathon Race Tomorrow," *BG*, Apr. 18, 1920.

2. "Roosevelt May See Race Here," *BG*, Apr. 11, 1912; "Forshaw Here for Marathon," *BH*, Apr. 17, 1912.

3. "Beautiful Trophies for Prize Winners," *BG*, Apr. 15, 1912; "Entry List for the Marathon," *BG*, Apr. 18, 1912.

4. "Roosevelt May See Race Here," *BG*, Apr. 11, 1912; "Beautiful Trophies for Prize Winners," *BG*, Apr. 15, 1912; "Marathon Group Looks Good," *BG*, Apr. 19, 1912; "Belief That Seasoned Athlete Will Win," *BH*, Apr. 15, 1912.

5. David Blaikie, *Boston: The Canadian Story* (Ottawa: Seneca House, 1984), 67.

6. KPEU, 57.

7. "Ryan Sets Record Winning Marathon," *BH*, Apr. 20, 1912.

8. "Finds Course in Good Shape," *BG*, Apr. 16, 1912; Ryan First in Marathon," *BG*, Apr. 20, 1912.

9. "Record May Fall in Marathon Race," *BG*, Apr. 16, 1911; "Ryan First," *BG*, Apr. 20, 1912; Patrick Kennedy interviews with Dale Lolar and Chris Sockalexis, for "Running as Tradition," *Harvard Gazette*, Apr. 14, 2016.

10. "Ryan First," *BG*, Apr. 20, 1912.

11. KPEU, 18, 57; "Mike Ryan's Marathon," *NYT*, Apr. 20, 1912; "Ryan Sets Record Winning Marathon," *BH*, Apr. 20, 1912; "Hatch Chosen as Olympic Runner," *CDT*, Apr. 20, 1912.

12. KPEU, 55.

13. Unless otherwise noted, all quotes about this race are from "Spurting at the Finish, Joe Erxleben, St. Louis, Wins Marathon," *SLPD*, May 5, 1912.

14. KPEU, 55.

15. "How He Won the Great Race," *SLPD*, May 5, 1912.

16. "H. Ratican Is Star of Hibernian Meet," *SLPD*, June 24, 1912; "Kennedy Is First in Annual M.A.C. Eleven-Mile Run," *SLPD*, July 21, 1912.

17. KPEU, 39–40.

18. "Chicago Stars Here to Run in M.A.C. Marathon," *SLPD*, Apr. 18, 1913.

19. All quotes about the 1913 St. Louis Marathon are from "Kennedy, I.A.C., Loses 12 Pounds Winning Slowest M.A.C. Marathon," *SLPD*, Apr. 20, 1913.

20. KPEU, 32.

21. "Winner of the M.A.C.'s Modified Modified Marathon and Runner-Up Interfered With by Congested Traffic," *SLPD*, May 18, 1913.

22. "Kennedy Wins Nine Mile Run," *CDT*, June 1, 1913.

23. U.S. Census, 1920; *California, Death Index, 1940–1997*; "Long Run to Fritz Carlson," *CDT*, June 22, 1913.

24. Race preview coverage in this paragraph and the next: "Grant Park Stage Set for Greatest Athletic Display," *CDT*, June 28, 1913.

25. The account of this race is drawn from "W. J. Kennedy First in Grind Opening Grant Park Meet," *CDT*, June 29, 1913, except where otherwise noted.

26. "Heat Doesn't Annoy Bricklayer," *New York Sun*, June 29, 1913.

27. KPEU, 6.

28. "Bricklayer Athlete Wins Grueling Race," *Tacoma Times*, July 4, 1913.

29. Untitled sports item, *Chicago Day Book*, June 30, 1913.

30. KPEU, 35–37.

31. KPEU, 21. The quotation is from *Richard II*.

32. KPEU, 32.

33. KPEU, 20.

34. "Kennedy Has Typhoid Fever," *CDT*, Nov. 21, 1913; *Typhoid Fever*, Centers for Disease Control and Prevention, cdc.gov; Chicago School of Sanitary Instruction, *Chicago's Health* (Chicago, 1914).

35. "Kennedy Still in Serious Condition," *CDT*, Dec. 2, 1913.

36. KPEU, 64.

37. Joseph Ferrie and Werner Troesken, "Water and Chicago's Mortality Transition, 1850–1925," *Explorations in Economic History*, Apr. 2006, 15; "IAC Team Needs Star Sprinters," *CDT*, Dec. 24, 1913.

38. KPEU, 64.

39. KPEU, 47.

40. KPEU, 46.

41. Timothy Chandler and Tara Magdalinski, *With God on Their Side: Sport in the Service of Religion* (New York: Routledge, 2002), 76; Hal Higdon, *Leopold and Loeb: The Crime of the Century* (New York: Putnam, 1975), 123.

42. KPEU, 39.

43. "Hatch Takes Run," *CDT*, Sept. 21, 1914.

44. KPEU, 11.

45. "Kennedy Colorful," *Schenectady Gazette*, Nov. 8, 1927; "A Man of Iron," *Schenectady Gazette*, Oct. 19, 1934.

46. Jock Semple with John J. Kelley and Tom Murphy, *Just Call Me Jock: The Story of Jock Semple, Boston's Mr. Marathon* (Waterford, CT: Waterford Publishing Company, 1981), 57.

47. KPEU, 12.

48. "Bill Kennedy, 1917 Marathon Winner, Tells What Lures Runners Back Year After Year," *BG*, Apr. 18, 1923.

49. KPEU, 12; "Bill Kennedy Here for the Marathon," *BG*, Apr. 17, 1915. On this meeting, all Kennedy and Sweeney quotes, respectively, are from these two sources.

50. Blaikie, *Boston*, 83–95.

51. "Here Is One Marathon Runner Who Will Be Surprised If He Wins," *BG*, Apr. 13, 1915.

52. For quotations from Sullivan's article, see "Time 2:31:41 1/5," *BG*, Apr. 19, 1915.

53. KPEU, 12.

54. "Fabre Wins Marathon on His Fifth Attempt," *BG*, Apr. 20, 1915; Tom Derderian, *Boston Marathon: The First Century of the World's Premier Running Event*, Centennial Race ed. (Champaign, IL: Human Kinetics Publishers, 1996), 70–71.

55. "Women Would Run in Big Race," *BG*, Mar. 31, 1915.

56. "Live Tips and Topics," *BG*, Apr. 21, 1915.

57. KPEU, 11.

58. "Live Tips and Topics," *BG*, Apr. 21, 1915.

59. Blaikie, *Boston*, 71–82; KPEU, 18.

60. In race previews, Bill Kennedy is listed as "unattached" in "Hatch to Defend Title Tomorrow," *CDT*, July 30, 1915, and as "formerly with the Illinois A.C." in "Name Twenty Stars for Long Road Race," *CDT*, Sept. 23, 1915. Bill's quote comes from "Mrs. W. J. Kennedy Gets a Wire," *BJ*, Apr. 20, 1917.

61. "Soccor [*sic*] Club House of the Big Chicago Union," *BMP*, Dec. 1915, 19.

62. "Two Arthur Roths in the B.A.A. Run, with Either Likely to Win," *BG*, Apr. 17, 1916.

63. "Cream of World's Long Distance," *Boston American*, Apr. 16, 1916.

64. "Roth of Dorchester Wins the Marathon," *Boston Globe*, Apr. 20, 1916.

65. KPEU, 58.

66. Ibid.

67. "Resumes Bricklaying," *BG*, Apr. 21, 1916.

68. Ibid.

69. "Sidney Hatch Wins Marathon," *CDT*, May 7, 1916; "Hatch Wins Marathon, Kennedy Places Second," *CDT*, July 30, 1916.

70. KPEU, 47.

71. "Westerners Shine at Travers Island," *NYT*, Sept. 24, 1916.

72. KPEU, 16.

73. "Governor a Guest at the Brockton Fair," *BG*, Oct. 7, 1916.

74. "Rutgers in Bad Shape, News of Athletics, *NYT*, Oct. 31, 1916.

75. "Dunbar's," *BJ*, Apr. 14 and 17, 1917; "When the Irish Ruled New York Sports," *Wall Street Journal*, June 14, 2010; Ian McGowan, "A Brief History of Celtic Park," Winged Fist Organization, wingedfist.org. Also see Joseph Edward Cuddy, *Irish-America and National Isolationism, 1914–1920* (New York: Arno Press, 1966).

76. E-mail from Timothy Nolan, Oct. 17, 2014.

77. "Kyronen Takes Zero Marathon," *CDT*, Dec. 24, 1916.

78. " '17 Marathon Winner Slows Down at 78—to Four Miles," *SLPD*, Apr. 22, 1962.

79. "Kyronen Takes Zero Marathon," *CDT*, Dec. 24, 1916.

80. " '17 Marathon Winner," *SLPD*, Apr. 22, 1962.

4. "WE MUST REPEL THE FINNS"

1. Weather reports in *NYT*, Jan. 12, Feb. 6 and 14, and Mar. 1, 1917.

2. "Artisan First in Marathon," *BH*, Apr. 20, 1917.

3. KPEU, 8.

4. "Kennedy Wins the Marathon," *BP*, Apr. 20, 1917.

5. David Kennedy, *Over Here: The First World War and American Society* (New York: Oxford University Press, 1980), 5; Robert H. Zieger, *America's Great War: World War I and the American Experience* (Lanham, MD: Rowman & Littlefield, 2000), 50–51.

6. Shipping news, *NYT*, Feb. 10 and 21, 1917.

7. "Kennedy Leads Field Home," *NYTrib*, Feb. 12, 1917.

8. "Dorchester Club Boys May Meet N.Y. Runners," *Boston Evening Record*, Mar. 10, 1917.

9. "Schuster Is First in Marathon Race," *NYT*, Feb. 23, 1917.

10. "Schuster Sets New Mark in Marathon Race," *New York Sun*, Feb. 23, 1917.

11. "Curley's Hat and Spring Arrive," *BA*, Mar. 1, 1917.

12. Kennedy, *Over Here*, 10; Zieger, *America's Great War*, 51.

13. "Plans Announced for B.A.A. Marathon Run," *BH*, Mar. 13, 1917.

14. "Arthur Duffey's Comment on Sports," *BP*, Mar. 27, 1917.

15. Tom Derderian, *Boston Marathon: The First Century of the World's Premier Running Event*, Centennial Race ed. (Champaign, IL: Human Kinetics, 1996), 71–75; "Leading Amateur Runners in Country in B.A.A. Marathon," *BER*, Apr. 5, 1917; "Only a Fortnight Before the Annual Marathon Run," *BA*, Apr. 5, 1917.

16. "Duffey's Comment," *BP*, Mar. 28 and Apr. 15, 1917.

17. "Duffey's Comment," *BP*, Mar. 29, 1917.

18. "Celts Protest Entry of U.S into the War" and "Urges Loyalty by Catholics to America," *BJ*, Apr. 2, 1917; "President Declares Germany Is Now at War with America," *BP*, Apr. 3, 1917.

19. "Lodge on Top in Fist Fight," *BG*, Apr. 3, 1917.

20. "Only a Fortnight," *BA*, Apr. 5, 1917.

21. "Leading Amateur Runners," *BER*, Apr. 5, 1917.

22. "Duffey's Comment," *BP*, Apr. 5, 1917.

23. Workers of the Writers' Program of the Work Projects Administration (WPA) in the State of Massachusetts, *Boston Looks Seaward: The Story of the Port, 1630–1940* (1941; Boston: Northeastern University Press, 1985), 204.

24. "U.S. Warship Hunts Raider," *BA*, Apr. 8, 1917; WPA, *Boston Looks Seaward*, 205. Patrick Kennedy originally wrote much of this passage on Boston and the war for "A Race against Fear," *BG*, Mar. 23, 2014.

25. Kennedy, *Over Here*, 5; WPA, *Boston Looks Seaward*, 204, 208.

26. WPA, *Boston Looks Seaward*, 207; "German Submarine Sinks Three Barges," *BG*, July 22, 1918; and see the retrospective feature "Surprise Attack," *Cape Cod Times*, Apr. 18, 2013.

27. Editorial, "Embarkation in Great War Spells Doom of Strong Drink in U.S.," *BA*, Apr. 6, 1917.

28. "Duffey's Comment," *BP*, Apr. 8, 1917.

29. For Sweeney's article, see "Already There Are 25 Entries for B.A.A. Marathon Which There Is Talk of Calling Off," *BG*, Apr. 11, 1917.

30. "The 2017 Boston Marathon by the Numbers," *BG*, Apr. 18, 2017; "2017 Boston Marathon Registration Dates Announced," *Runner's World*, July 7, 2016, runnersworld.com.

31. "Marathon Run Will Be Held" *BH*, Apr. 12, 1917.

32. "Duffey's Comment," *BP*, Apr. 15, 1917.

33. "Bob Dunbar's Sporting Comment," *BJ*, Apr. 16, 1917.

34. For Rogers's article, see "Crisis of a Two Year Feud Reached When Kolehmainen Meets Kyronen in Marathon," *BER*, Apr. 7, 1917.

35. "Marathon Runners Are Expected Here Today," *BT*, Apr. 16, 1917.

36. KPEU, 9.

37. "Duffey's Comment," *BP*, Apr. 11, 1917.

38. "Bill Kennedy Coming Today," *BG*, Apr. 20, 1917.

39. KPEU, 68.

40. "Opera Singer to Plug Along Marathon," *BER*, Apr. 11, 1917; "Decides to Run Marathon," *BG*, Apr. 12, 1917.

41. "62 Now Entered in Big Marathon," *BA*, Apr. 17, 1917.

42. "Montreal Star in B.A.A. Classic," *BJ*, Apr. 11, 1917; Derderian, *Boston Marathon*, 154; "Marathon Run," *BH*, Apr. 12, 1917.

43. "Opera Singer," *BER*, Apr. 11, 1917.

44. *Boston Traveler*, Apr. 13, 1917.

45. "Official Guide of the Railways, 1910," Central Pacific Railroad Photographic History Museum, cprr.org; Matthew Boylan, "Cross Country Travel in 1912," Mar. 15, 2013, New York Public Library, nypl.org/blogs; "Coast Runner Coming," *BET*, Apr. 16, 1917.

46. "Two Prominent Entrants for B.A.A. Marathon Run Tomorrow," *BG,* Apr. 18, 1917.

47. "Promising Field," *BP,* Apr. 8, 1917.

48. *BER,* Apr. 11, 1917.

49. For the Sweeney article, see "Bill Kennedy," *BG,* Apr. 14, 1917.

50. "Artisan First," *BH,* Apr. 21, 1917.

51. KPEU, 11; "Bill Kennedy," *BG,* Apr. 14, 1917.

52. KPEU, 11.

53. "'Bill' Kennedy, 1917 Marathon Winner, Tells What Lures Runners Back Year After Year," *BG,* Apr. 18, 1923; "Hatch and Roth Are Among the Missing, but Not for Long" *BA,* Apr. 13, 1917. We trace the conflation to "Bricklayer Bill Kennedy in BAA Marathon," *BH,* Apr. 14, 1929, and 'Bill Kennedy Promises to Be in Prize Winners,'" *BG,* Apr. 18, 1932, continuing in "Bill Kennedy, 1917 Victor, Enters Boston Marathon," Apr. 11, 1934, and beyond.

54. Boston College *The Stylus,* Feb. 1, 1906.

55. All Cathedral race coverage is from the following newspaper articles of Apr. 15, 1917: "Kennedy Wins Road Race," *BG;* "Bill Kennedy Wins Cathedral Annual Ten-Mile Run in Field of 22 Starters," *BP;* "Kennedy Wins Big Cathedral 10-Mile Race," *BA;* and "Kenneday [*sic*] Home First in Race," *BH.*

56. "U.S. Raid in Melrose; Guns and Powder Seized," *BA,* Apr. 14, 1917. In his book *Dark Invasion, 1915: Germany's Secret War and the Hunt for the First Terrorist Cell in America* (New York: HarperCollins, 2014), Howard Blum chronicles imperial Germany's very real sabotage campaign in America.

57. Derderian, *Boston Marathon,* 74, 367; "'Bill' Kennedy," *BG,* Apr. 18, 1923.

58. "Promise a Clear Marathon Course," *BG,* Apr. 17, 1917.

59. "62 Now Entered," *BA,* Apr. 17, 1917; "Expect Governor at Marathon," *BG,* Apr. 18, 1917.

60. "Start Search of White Mts.," *BER,* Apr. 17, 1917; WPA, *Boston Looks Seaward,* 205; U.S. National Park Service, Division of Publications, *Charlestown Navy Yard,* handbook (1995), 47; "U-Boat Fires Torpedo at American Destroyer," *BA,* Apr. 17, 1917.

61. "At Least 125,000 Likely to See B.A.A. Marathon," *BG,* Apr. 17, 1917.

62. Ibid.

63. "Report Naval Battle in Massachusetts Bay," *BA,* Apr. 18, 1917.

64. "Marathoners Await Start of Big Race," *BA,* Apr. 18, 1917.

65. Event listings and coverage in *BG,* Apr. 18 and 20, 1917, and *BJ,* Apr. 20, 1917.

66. "Live Tips and Topics," *BG,* Apr. 20, 1917. From this point through the race's aftermath, unless otherwise noted, quotations are drawn from "Kennedy Wins," *BP;* "Kennedy Wins," *BG;* "Artisan First," *BH;* and "Runners Past 30 Marathon Stars," *BJ,* all dated Apr. 20, 1917.

67. Cartoon in *BP,* Apr. 19, 1917.

68. KPEU, 4.

69. KPEU, 14; "Winner of B.A.A. Marathon Went Back to His Bricklaying Job," *BT,* Apr. 20, 1917.

70. Weather report, *BG,* Apr. 20, 1917; Clarence DeMar, *Marathon: The Clarence DeMar Story* (1937; Tallahassee: Cedarwinds Publishing Company, 1992), 40; KPEU, 6; "Live Tips," *BG,* Apr. 19, 1917.

71. Derderian, *Boston Marathon,* 41.

72. "Kennedy Confident," *BP,* Apr. 20, 1917.

73. "In Close to Record Time," *BG*, Apr. 21, 1908; "DeMar Wins the Marathon and Smashes the Record," Apr. 20, 1911.

74. "'Bill' Kennedy," *BG*, Apr. 18, 1923.

75. "Bill Kennedy Promises to Be in Prize Winners," *BG*, Apr. 18, 1932.

76. "'Bill' Kennedy," *BG*, Apr. 18, 1923.

77. Ibid.

78. "A. V. Roth Wins Marathon," *BG*, Apr. 19, 1916.

79. Amby Burfoot, "Running Scared," *Runner's World*, May 2008, runnersworld.com; Derderian, *Boston Marathon*, 154–55.

80. Derderian, *Boston Marathon*, 2; Caleb Daniloff, "Marathon Motivation: Be the Brickie," *BU Today*, Apr. 17, 2009; Jock Semple with John J. Kelley and Tom Murphy, *Just Call Me Jock: The Story of Jock Semple, Boston's Mr. Marathon* (Waterford, CT: Waterford Publishing Company, 1981), 55–56.

81. KPEU, 8.

82. KPEU, 64.

83. Bill Kennedy to Arthur Veasey, Dec. 13, 1959.

84. DeMar, *Marathon*, 30–36; "Drew Shows Speed," *BG*, May 31, 1913. Some portions of the passage about DeMar, written by Patrick Kennedy, were originally published in "In the Running: 1897 to 2014," *BU Today*, Apr. 18, 2014.

85. "It Will Be Boston vs. New York in Tomorrow's Race," *BG*, Apr. 18, 1917; U.S. Census, 1910; Steve Flynn, Ashland Redevelopment Authority plaque series *Marathon Park: It All Started Here*, Marathon Park, Ashland, Massachusetts.

86. "De Mar Wins," *BG*, Apr. 20, 1911.

87. "The Scout Honor Roll," *Boys' Life*, July 1917.

88. William Marchione, Brighton-Allston Historical Society, "Annexation Spurned: Brookline's 1873 Rejection of Boston," bahistory.org; U.S. Census, 1920; KPEU, 58.

89. "Winner of B.A.A. Run an Interesting Fellow," *BT*, Apr. 21, 1917.

90. "'Bill' Kennedy," *BG*, Apr. 18, 1923.

91. "Investigate Charges against Merchant in Marathon Run," *BA*, Apr. 20, 1917; Alex Hutchinson, "Hot Drinks v. Cold Drinks for Cooling," *Runner's World*, May 27, 2014, runnersworld.com.

92. *Twelfth Annual Report of the Police Commissioner for the City of Boston* for the year ending Nov. 30, 1917.

93. "Kennedy Back at Work," *BET*, Apr. 20, 1917.

94. The news made the front pages of, e.g., the *Topeka State Journal*, *Evening Herald* (Albuquerque, NM), and *Evening Times-Republican* (Marshalltown, IA), all Apr. 19, 1917; "Germany's Line Still Crumbling," *BP*, Apr. 20, 1917.

95. KPEU, 44.

96. KPEU, 64.

97. "Winner of B.A.A. Marathon Returned to Work Today," *BT*, Apr. 21, 1917.

98. John Hanc, *The B.A.A. at 125: The Official History of the Boston Athletic Association, 1887–1912* (New York: Sports Publishing, 2012), 28–29; "B.A.A. Pledges Its Support to Wilson," *BG*, Apr. 24, 1917; for the speeches, see "Kennedy Not Only Ran Great Race, but Accepted Prize in Fine Speech," *BG*, Apr. 20, 1917; "Kennedy Confident," *BP*, Apr. 20, 1917; "Artisan First," *BH*, Apr. 20, 1917; "Kennedy Wins," *BG*, Apr. 20, 1917.

99. "Kennedy Wins," *BG*, Apr. 20, 1917.

100. "Runners Past 30," *BJ*, Apr. 20, 1917; "Widespread Interest in the B.A.A. Marathon," *BJ*, Apr. 18, 1917.

101. "Kennedy Wins," *BG*, Apr. 20, 1917; Joe Falls, *The Boston Marathon: The Incredible, Zany Story of America's Greatest Foot Race and the Men and Women Who Have Run in It* (New York: Macmillan, 1977).

102. Derderian, *Boston Marathon*, 76; "Artisan First," *BH*, Apr. 20, 1917; "Kennedy Wins," *BG*, Apr. 20, 1917; DeMar quoted in KPEU, 65.

103. "Kennedy Wins," *BP*, Apr. 20, 1917.

104. "Bill Kennedy, Marathon Victor, Right Back on His Job as Bricklayer," *BA*, Apr. 20, 1917.

105. "Winner of B.A.A. Marathon," *BT*, Apr. 21, 1917.

106. "Investigate Charges," *BA*, Apr. 20, 1917.

107. "Bill Kennedy, Marathon Victor," *BA*, Apr. 20, 1917.

108. "Investigate Charges," *BA*, Apr. 20, 1917.

109. Hanc, *B.A.A.*, 9–13.

110. "Kennedy Back at Work," *BET*, Apr. 20, 1917.

111. For quotes from Spargo's column, see "Speaking of Sport," *BT*, Apr. 21, 1917.

112. "Merchant Is Disqualified," *BG*, Apr. 21, 1917.

113. For the quotes from this column, see "Duffey's Comment," *BP*, Apr. 22, 1917.

114. Derderian, *Boston Marathon*, 74–77.

115. *Rand McNally Boston Guide to the City and Environs* (New York: Rand McNally & Co., 1916); "Pie Alley Café Closes Doors," *BG*, Jan. 10, 1915. Reasonable people disagree on the spelling and meaning of this quirky byway, officially named Williams Court. Some say it is properly Pi Alley, after the "pi," or discarded letter type, that compositors would track in from the print shop floor. (Why they called this type "pi" is another story.) Others like the "Pie" spelling, supposedly a tribute to the meat pies that workers lunched on. The latter seems to have edged out the former during this time period.

116. "Bill Kennedy Promises to Be in Prize Winners," *BG*, Apr. 18, 1932.

117. KPEU, 41.

118. *Commercial and Financial New England Illustrated* (Boston: Boston Herald, 1906); U.S. Census, 1910, 1920; Boston City Directories, 1892, 1893, 1916.

119. KPEU, 42.

120. "Bill Kennedy Promises to Be in Prize Winners," *BG*, Apr. 18, 1932; U.S. Bureau of Labor Statistics, *Union Scale of Wages and Hours of Labor, May 15, 1917* (Washington, DC: U.S. Government Printing Office, 1919).

121. KPEU, 43; emphasis added.

122. "Elks Honor Grand Exalted Ruler," *BG*, Feb. 17, 1911.

123. KPEU, 43.

124. Derderian, *Boston Marathon*, 99–100.

125. KPEU, 48.

126. KPEU, 16; "Bill Kennedy Promises to Be in Prize Winners," Apr. 18, 1932.

127. "Live Tips," *BG*, Apr. 23, 1917.

5. OVER THERE

1. David Kennedy, *Over Here: The First World War and American Society* (New York: Oxford University Press, 1980), 149.

2. Ibid., 154; Congressional Research Service, "American War and Military Operations Casualties, Lists and Statistics," Jan. 2, 2015.

3. "Hennigan First in Marathon," *NYT*, July 5, 1917.

4. Robert H. Zieger, *America's Great War: World War I and the American Experience* (Lanham, MD: Rowman & Littlefield, 2000), 86, 37.

5. "Hingham Naval Camp Is Opened," *BG*, Aug. 14, 1917.

6. "Bill Kennedy Was Bound to Get into the Army," *BMP*, Dec. 1917, 12; Leslie Jones photography collection, Boston Public Library. Jones's word choice is unfortunate in retrospect: a munitions ship would in fact blow up and devastate Halifax, Nova Scotia, later that year.

7. "Steel Work on Fore River Plant at Squantum Going Up Tomorrow," *BG*, Oct. 23, 1917.

8. "City for 10,000 Springs Up in a Month on Squantum Marsh," *BG*, Nov. 11, 1917.

9. New York Adjutant General's Office, Abstracts of World War I Military Service, 1917–1919, series B0808, New York State Archives, Albany; *Service Records, Connecticut, Men and Women in the Armed Forces of the United States during World War, 1917–1920* (Hartford: Office of the Adjutant General, 1941), 791. Veterans' records accessed via Ancestry.com unless otherwise noted.

10. "Brockton Fair Booms Salute," *BG*, Oct. 6, 1917.

11. Ibid.; "New Record Set in Brockton Marathon," *BG*, Oct. 6, 1917.

12. "Live Tips and Topics," *BG*, Oct. 6, 1917.

13. Clarence DeMar, *Marathon: The Clarence DeMar Story* (1937; Tallahassee: Cedarwinds Publishing Company, 1992), 38; *World War I Selective Service System Draft Registration Cards, 1917–1918*, Washington, DC: National Archives and Records Administration; "Bill Kennedy, 1917 Marathon Winner," *BG*, Apr. 18, 1923; Clarence DeMar, "They Mean Well, But . . . ," *American Legion Monthly*, Apr. 1936, 14–15, 43–44; *Illinois in the World War: An Illustrated History of the Thirty-Third Division*, vol. 1 (Chicago: States Publications Society, 1921); "Kolehmainen Home First," *NYT*, Nov. 30, 1917; *Applications for Headstones for U.S. Military Veterans, 1925–1941*, Washington, DC: National Archives.

14. "Quincy Strike Halts Two Launchings," *BG*, Nov. 3, 1917.

15. Kennedy, *Over Here*, 262; Zieger, *America's Great War*, 117.

16. "Bound to Get into the Army," *BMP*, Dec. 1917, 12; National Cemetery Administration, U.S. Veterans Gravesites, ca.1775–2006; Biography and Service Record of William J. Kennedy, State of Missouri Adjutant General's Office (record mailed to authors by the Missouri Historical Society); New York Adjutant General's Office, Abstracts of World War I Military Service, 1917–1919, series B0808, New York State Archives, Albany; "Live Tips and Topics," *BG*, Dec. 3, 1917.

17. "Live Tips," *BG*, Dec. 3, 1917.

18. "Georgio Captures Yonkers Marathon," *NYT*, Nov. 30, 1917.

19. Pamela Cooper, *The American Marathon* (Syracuse: Syracuse University Press, 1998), 57, 87.

20. Army War College (AWC), *Historical-Technical Report of the Twenty-Third Regiment of Engineers, U.S. Army* (Carlisle, PA, 1922), pt. 1, chaps. 1–4, paginated inconsistently.

21. Kennedy, *Over Here*, 185; Zieger, *America's Great War*, 89.

22. John R. Betts, *America's Sporting Heritage: 1850–1950* (Reading, MA: Addison-Wesley, 1974), 136; Clarence DeMar, "They Mean Well, but—," *American Legion Monthly* 20 (Apr. 1936): 14–15, 43–44.

23. "Track Stars Are Rated," *NYT*, Dec. 31, 1917.

24. Tom Derderian, *Boston Marathon: The First Century of the World's Premier Running Event*, Centennial Race ed. (Champaign, IL: Human Kinetics Publishers, 1996), 77; "Camp Devens Division Team Wins Marathon," *BG*, Apr. 20, 1918.

25. Derderian, *Boston Marathon*, 79; "Camp Devens Division Team Wins Marathon," *BG*, Apr. 20, 1918.

26. AWC, *Historical-Technical Report*; "Engineering Work in Base Section No. 1," *Cornell Civil Engineer*, Dec. 1919, 110. Some of the passages on Bill and Company I were originally published in "Bricklayer Bill's Ultra-Marathon of a Life," *Narratively*, Oct. 1, 2014, http://narrative.ly.

27. "Live Tips and Topics," *BG*, Aug. 24, 1918.

28. Washington State University (WSU) Libraries, Digital Collections, image 1007, undated newspaper clipping.

29. AWC, *Historical-Technical Report*.

30. "The Battle of Dreadful Roads," *S&S*, Sept. 20, 1918.

31. AWC, *Historical-Technical Report*; Zieger, *America's Great War*, 94–101; KPEU, 38.

32. Derderian, *Boston Marathon*, 76; *Illinois in the World War*, 335, 350, 359; Edward G. Lengel, *To Conquer Hell: The Meuse-Argonne, 1918* (New York: Henry Holt and Co., 2008), 275, 301.

33. U.S. Army War College, *Camouflage for Troops of the Line* (Washington, DC: GPO, 1920), 12–16; photograph by Margaret Hall, January 1919, Massachusetts Historical Society.

34. Kennedy, *Over Here*, 356–58.

35. *The Highwayman* (U.S. Army, 23rd Engineers), Nov. 22, 1918.

36. AWC report; WSU clipping.

37. Zieger, *America's Great War*, 108.

38. *The Highwayman*, Nov. 22, 1918.

39. Wait C. Johnson, ed., *Official Athletic Almanac of the American Expeditionary Forces* (New York: American Sports Publishing Co., 1919), 65. In addition to these most competitive events, any and all servicemen could enter countless one-off contests at their local bases in a variety of sports, including (but not limited to) pig-a-back relay, Indian wrestling, hop-step-jump, indoor baseball, rooster fight, dog fight, tug-of-war, potato race relay, hopping relay, wand wrestling, and medicine ball throw.

40. "Inter-Allied Games Will Mark Victory Jubilee," *S&S*, May 23, 1919.

41. Johnson, *Official Athletic Almanac*, 65; Betts, *America's Sporting Heritage*, 137–38; *S&S*, Dec. 27, 1918; Matthew P. Llewellyn, *Rule Britannia: Nationalism, Identity and the Modern Olympic Games* (New York: Routledge, 2014), 129.

42. "Overconfidence May Beat U.S. in the Allied Games," *S&S*, May 9, 1919; *PCDI*, undated clipping in authors' family collection.

43. *PCDI*, undated clipping; New York State veterans' records; Bill Kennedy to Ann Louise McLaughlin, Mar. 13, 1963; "Crack Athletes of S.O.S. Go to Colombes to Train," *S&S*, Mar. 21, 1919.

44. DeMar, *Marathon*, 41–42.

45. "Passing the Buck," *S&S*, May 16, 1919.

46. KPEU, 30.

47. "Boston Roads in Fine Shape," *BG*, Apr. 17, 1971.

48. For this account, see KPEU, 31; "S.O.S. Meet Goes to Intermediate Section Team," *S&S*, May 9, 1919.

49. "Great A.E.F. Marathon," *Daily Times* (Geneva, NY), May 15, 1919; "Seventy Kilometer Relay Race," *S&S*, May 16, 1919.

50. "Seventy Kilometer Relay Race," *S&S*, May 16, 1919.

51. William C. King, *King's Complete History of the War* (Springfield, MA: History Associates, 1922), 749; Llewellyn, *Rule Britannia*, 129.

52. KPEU, 31; untitled item, *S&S*, May 23, 1919.

53. All quotes in the passage on the Memorial Day race come from "Private Tells President of Chateau-Thierry Race," *S&S*, June 6, 1919. Other sources include *S&S*, May 16 and 23, 1919; *NYT*, Aug. 29, 1919; undated clipping, *PCDI*; Thomas F. Meehan, *History of the Seventy-Eighth Division in the World War, 1917-18-19* (Wilmington, DE: U.S. Army, 1921); DeMar, *Marathon*, 41; Johnson, *Official Athletic Almanac*, 175.

54. Johnson, *Official Athletic Almanac*, 65, 69; "A.E.F. Athletes Are Announced," *South Bend News-Times*, June 22, 1919; "America's Main Dependencies at Inter-Allied Athletic Meet," *NYTrib*, June 22, 1919.

55. KPEU, 65.

56. DeMar, *Marathon*, 41.

57. Undated clipping, *PCDI*; "Inter-Allied Games Will Mark Victory Jubilee," *S&S*, May 23, 1919; DeMar, *Marathon*, 41.

58. KPEU, 51.

59. DeMar, *Marathon*, 42.

60. Kennedy, *Over Here*, 358–59.

61. "Americans Win Relay," *NYT*, July 4, 1919.

62. Undated clippings, *PCDI*; Adjutant General's Office, Abstracts of World War I Military Service, 1917–1919.

6. PARIS OR BUST

1. "Blue Denim Suits for All Homegoers," *S&S*, Apr. 11, 1919.

2. "Bill Kennedy Returns," *PCDI*, undated clipping.

3. "Bricklayer-Runner Arrives for Classic," *BG*, Apr. 17, 1920.

4. "De Mar and Stenroos in Marathon Battle Today," *BG*, Apr. 19, 1926.

5. John R. Betts, *America's Sporting Heritage, 1850–1950* (Reading, MA: Addison-Wesley, 1974), 138.

6. "Kennedy Recalls Marathon Win 50 Years Ago," *SLPD*, Apr. 19, 1967.

7. "Marathon Mark Broken by Zuna," *BG*, Apr. 20, 1921.

8. Ibid.

9. Frederick Lewis and Dick Johnson, *Young at Heart: The Story of Johnny Kelley, Boston's Marathon Man* (Waco, TX: WRS Publishing, 1992), 14.

10. "Veterans Class in Hub Marathon," *New York Evening Telegram*, Apr. 20, 1922.

11. "As 11 Years Ago, DeMar Wins, *BG*, Apr. 20, 1922.

12. "Kennedy Captures 9-Mile Road Run," *NYT*, Sept. 25, 1922.

13. "Titterton First in 10 ½ Mile Greek-American Club Road Run," *NYTrib*, Oct. 2, 1922.

14. Ibid.

15. "Kennedy Wins Six-Mile Road Run in 36:45," *NYTrib*, Oct. 9, 1922.

16. "Ritola Leads Pack in Long Road Race," *NYT*, Oct. 13, 1922; KPEU, 45.

17. "Colorful Picture by NY Bricklayer," *BG*, Apr. 18, 1923.

18. "Heart Bad, Runs 25 Miles for a 'Little Exercise,'" *NYT*, Apr. 20, 1923; "Old Favorites to Fore in 1923 Marathon," *BG*, Apr. 20, 1923.

19. KPEU, 62–63.

20. "Marathon Course Slightly Changed," *BG*, Apr. 17, 1923; Tom Derderian, *Boston Marathon: The First Century of the World's Premier Running Event*, Centennial Race ed. (Champaign, IL: Human Kinetics Publishers, 1996), 41.

21. "Live Tips and Topics," *BG*, Apr. 16, 1923; "Ruth's Homer Beats Sox before 74,200," *BG*, Apr. 19, 1923.

22. KPEU, 22; "Michelson [*sic*] Breaks 3 Marathon Marks," *NYT*, May 21, 1923. All *Times* quotes on this race come from this article.

23. KPEU, 23, 41.

24. Ibid., 23.

25. Ibid., 33.

26. "Michelson [*sic*] Victor in Marathon Run," *BG*, June 17, 1923; "Live Tips and Topics" *BG*, June 22, 1923; KPEU, 41.

27. "Jack Lamb of Biddeford Wins Marathon," *Portsmouth Herald*, Aug. 22, 1923; "That Marathon Race and Thanks," *Portsmouth Herald*, Aug. 29, 1923.

28. "Live Tips and Topics," *BG*, May 22, 1923.

29. "Baltimore Granted Olympic Race Trial," *Washington Evening Star*, Nov. 22, 1923.

30. *Washington Evening Star*, Mar. 8, 1924.

31. "Zuna, Millrose A.C. Star, Wins Pontiac-to-Detroit Marathon," *NYT*, Mar. 30, 1924; David E. Martin and Roger H. W. Gynn, *Olympic Marathon: The History and Challenge of Sport's Most Challenging Event* (Champaign, IL: Human Kinetics, 2000), 117–19.

32. "Runners in BAA Classic Distance April 19, Must Cover More Than Mile More Than in Previous Years," *BG*, Apr. 1, 1924.

33. "Marathon in Boston to Be Olympic Test," *Schenectady Gazette*, Apr. 15, 1924. See also "Six of 144 in Marathon to Uphold US Prestige at Olympic Games," *BG*, Apr. 18, 1924.

34. "Swoop": "Marathon in Boston," *Schenectady Gazette,* Apr. 15, 1924; Newspaper Row visit: "Live Tips and Topics," *BG,* Apr. 19, 1924. See also "Pick Zuna and DeMar to Lead Marathoners," *BG,* Apr. 19, 1924.

35. "Marathon Run Olympic Test," *BH,* Apr. 19, 1924.

36. "There's Much More to Hopkinton Than Starting Point for Marathon," *BG,* Apr. 17, 1932.

37. "Marathon Entry of 144 Only Has Been Exceeded in Three Other Grinds," *BH,* Apr. 18, 1924.

38. "Frank Zuna Vindicated after Special Test with Williams in Paris," *BDE,* June 30, 1924.

39. "Wonder Man DeMar Wins Marathon in Record Time," *BG,* Apr. 20, 1924. Unless otherwise indicated, all details on this race come from this source and Derderian, *Boston Marathon,* 97–101.

40. "Wonder Man," *BG,* Apr. 20, 1924.

41. "Marathon Runners Dress in Odd Fellows Hall" and cartoon, *BH,* Apr. 20, 1924.

42. "Frank Zuna Vindicated," *BDE,* June 30, 1924.

43. Emphasis added. McCabe at the *Herald* accepted Geiger's pronouncement but blamed the BAA's checkers. "Because [Williams] was missed by most of the checking parties all the way along the route from South Framingham until Cleveland Circle at the head of Beacon Street, there was a question raised on his ability to get home as fresh as he did.... [T]here was a feeling for a while but things were not just right. That is all due to the officials not checking on enough of the contestants." Note that McCabe, too, acknowledges Williams's "fresh" appearance.

44. For quotes from this article, see "Protest Hurja A.C. Runner," *BG,* May 2, 1924.

45. KPEU, 48; "Frank Zuna," *BDE,* June 30, 1924.

46. KPEU, 48.

47. "America's Olympic Candidates Getting Ready for Tryouts," *BDE,* Apr. 20, 1924.

48. "2 Olympic Records Beaten in Tryouts," *NYT,* June 8, 1924.

49. KPEU, 48.

50. Authors' conversations with Eileen Lawlor Kennedy, Ann Louise McLaughlin, Joan Kennedy Harvey, Larry Coffin, and Roger Kennedy; "America's Olympic Candidates," *BDE,* Apr. 20, 1924.

51. KPEU, 6.

52. KPEU, 48.

53. "Clean Bill for Williams in Marathon Mixup," *BG,* May 6, 1924.

54. Martin and Gynn, *Olympic Marathon,* 117–19.

55. "Zuna Vindicated," *BDE,* June 30, 1924.

56. Clarence DeMar, *Marathon: The Clarence DeMar Story* (1937; Tallahassee: Cedarwinds Publishing Company, 1992), 53.

57. Ibid.

58. "Stenroos, Finn, Wins Olympic Marathon; DeMar, U.S., Is Third; 40-Year-Old Woodcutter, Running First Race in 15 Years, Captures Historic Event," *NYT,* July 14, 1924; " 'Bill' Parry Fires Heavy Broadside at Promoters Who Capitalize Athletics," *BDE,* Aug. 10, 1924.

59. Martin and Gynn, *Olympic Marathon,* 122, 119.

60. Derderian, *Boston Marathon*, 102–4; "Frank Zuna Vindicated," *BDE*, June 30, 1924.

61. KPEU, 48.

62. "Cooling Shower Coming Tonight to Cool Us Off," *Long Island Daily Press and Long Island Daily Farmer*, Sept. 2, 1924.

63. KPEU, 22.

64. KPEU, 14.

7. GOOD TIMES

1. "Miles, Nova Scotia Boy Wins in Record Time," *NYT*, Apr. 13, 1928.

2. "Linder Enters Boston Run," *BG*, Apr. 20, 1926.

3. "De Mar Arrested at Dawn," *NYT*, Apr. 3, 1926.

4. "Men of All Classes," *BG*, Apr. 13, 1925; "All Ready for Starter's Gun," *BG*, Apr. 17, 1927.

5. KPEU, 35.

6. "Pick DeMar to Win Marathon," *BH*, Apr. 19, 1926.

7. KPEU, 32.

8. "Clarence DeMar, Winner Four Times," *BH*, Apr. 19, 1925.

9. "Field of 121 Entered," *BG*, Apr. 20, 1925.

10. "Can DeMar Win His Fifth Marathon?" *BG*, Apr. 19, 1925; "Field of 121 Entered," *BG*, Apr. 20, 1925.

11. KPEU, 58.

12. "Clarence DeMar, Winner Four Times," *BH*, Apr. 19, 1925; "Despite Bad Heart, DeMar Is Favorite," *BH*, Apr. 20, 1925.

13. KPEU, 33–34.

14. Jerry Nason, "Joy! We Win!" *Boston Magazine*, Apr. 1965, 41; "Mellor Captures Boston Marathon," *NYT*, Apr. 21, 1925; "Mellor Wins Marathon Duel," *BH*, Apr. 21, 1925.

15. Tom Derderian, *Boston Marathon: The First Century of the World's Premier Running Event*, Centennial Race ed. (Champaign, IL: Human Kinetics Publishers, 1996), 103; "Mellor Wins," *BH*, Apr. 21, 1925.

16. KPEU, 34.

17. "Mellor Wins," *BH*, Apr. 21, 1925.

18. "Mellor First in Marathon," *BG*, Apr. 21, 1925.

19. "Mellor Starts with Chew of Tobacco," *BH*, Apr. 21, 1925.

20. "Field of 121 Entered in Today's Marathon," *BG*, Apr. 20, 1925.

21. "Mellor Starts," *BH*, Apr. 21, 1925.

22. "Mellor Chicago Wins Marathon Duel with DeMar," *BG*, Apr. 21, 1925.

23. KPEU, 32–33.

24. "Mellor Starts," *BH*, Apr. 21, 1925; "Mellor First," *BG*, Apr. 21, 1925.

25. "Live Tips and Topics," *BG*, Sept. 21 and 22, 1925.

26. KPEU, 66.

27. Pamela Cooper, *The American Marathon* (Syracuse: Syracuse University Press, 1998), 67–68.

28. "Many Famous Harriers to Run," *PCDI*, Oct. 9, 1925.

29. "Field of 92 Races in Marathon Today," *NYT*, Oct. 12, 1925; "Michelson [*sic*] Victor, 250,000 See Race," *NYT*, Oct. 13, 1925.

30. "Cygnet's Club Star Took the Lead in Rye," *PCDI*, Oct. 12, 1925; "Michelson [*sic*] and Kennedy Receive Great Ovations," *PCDI*, Oct. 13, 1925.

31. "Michelson [*sic*] and Kennedy Receive Great Ovations," *PCDI*, Oct. 13, 1925. Also see "Cygnet's Club Star Took the Lead in Rye," *PCDI*, Oct. 12, 1925.

32. "Athletes Are the Guests at Local Banquet" and "Runners Form Association Here," *PCDI*, Oct. 13, 1925.

33. "Marathon Runners Form Association," *NYT*, Oct. 15, 1925.

34. "Athletes Are the Guests" and "Runners Form Association Here," *PCDI*, Oct. 13, 1925.

35. "Famous Brooklyn Marathon to Be Revived in February" *NYT*, Nov. 12, 1925; "Marathon Route Chosen," *NYT*, Nov. 28, 1925.

36. "DeMar and Stenroos in Marathon Battle Today," *BG*, Apr. 19, 1926.

37. "Boston Trail Short, Declares Stenroos," *NYT*, Apr. 19, 1926; Hal Higdon, *Boston: A Century of Running* (Emmaus, PA: Rodale Press, 1995), 59.

38. "Grocer's Boy from Sydney Mines," *BH*, Apr. 20, 1926.

39. "Miles Felt Certain He Could Show Way," *BG*, Apr. 20, 1926; "Swift Pony Paced Jackie Miles," *BG*, Apr. 25, 1926.

40. Miles, Nova Scotia Boy, Wins in Record Time," *BG*, Apr. 20, 1926.

41. "Miles Sure Prayers Won Marathon Run," *BG*, Apr. 21, 1926.

42. "Swift Pony," *BG*, Apr. 25, 1926.

43. "Marathon Hero Has a Busy Day," *BG*, Apr. 22, 1926.

44. "Big Farewell to John C. Miles," *BG*, Apr. 26, 1926.

45. Jock Semple with John J. Kelley and Tom Murphy, *Just Call Me Jock: The Story of Jock Semple, Boston's Mr. Marathon* (Waterford, CT: Waterford Publishing Company, 1981), 24–31, is the source of all quotes in this passage unless otherwise indicated.

46. Erastus Long Austin, ed., *The Sesqui-Centennial International Exposition* (1929; New York: Arno Press, 1976); "The Sesquicentennial Exposition of 1926," City of Philadelphia, phillyhistory.org/blog; "DeMar Captures Another Marathon," *NYT*, June 3, 1926.

47. "DeMar Is Winner in Marathon Race," *NYT*, Oct. 13, 1926; "DeMar Is Supreme," *PCDI*, Oct. 13, 1926.

48. "Our Interest Is Growing," *PCDI*, Oct. 13, 1926.

49. "Rejection Likely of Non-Citizen Ban," *NYT*, Nov. 15, 1926.

50. Ibid.; "Non-Citizen Ban Proposed by A.A.U.," *NYT*, Oct. 31, 1926; "Paddock's Record Accepted by A.A.U.," *NYT*, Nov. 16, 1926.

51. KPEU, 46–47.

52. "Linder, Winner in 1919, Enters April 19 Marathon," *BG*, Apr. 14, 1927.

53. "Find Marathon Course Is Short," *BG*, Apr. 13, 1927; "500,000 to Watch Annual BAA Marathon Run," *BH*, Apr. 19, 1927.

54. "1926 Victory of Miles," *BH*, Apr. 18, 1927.

55. "DeMar Wins Marathon," *BH*, Apr. 20, 1927.

56. "DeMar Victor in Marathon," *BG*, Apr. 20, 1927.

57. "DeMar Wins," *BH*, Apr. 20, 1927; "All Ready for Starter's Gun," *BG*, Apr. 17, 1927.

58. Clarence DeMar, *Marathon: The Clarence DeMar Story* (1937; Tallahassee: Cedar-winds Publishing Company, 1992), 59.

59. Derderian, *Boston Marathon*, 112–13.

60. "DeMar Victor in Marathon," *BG*, Apr. 20, 1927.

61. DeMar, *Marathon*, 59.

62. "DeMar Takes Race under Broiling Sun," *NYT*, Apr. 20, 1927; "DeMar Victor," *BG*, Apr. 20, 1927.

63. "DeMar Takes Race," *NYT*, Apr. 20, 1927; "DeMar Wins Marathon," *BH*, Apr. 20, 1927.

64. "DeMar Victor," *BG*, Apr. 20, 1927.

65. Derderian, *Boston Marathon*, 114.

66. "Melrose Veteran Sets Record," *BH*, Apr. 20, 1927.

67. "What of the Laggard?" *BG*, Apr. 24, 1927.

68. "DeMar Kept Busy after Big Victory," *BG*, Apr. 20, 1927.

69. "Marathon Champion," *BH*, Apr. 21, 1927.

70. "Fear DeMar's Last Race Has Been Run," *BG*, Apr. 23, 1927.

71. "A Man of Iron," *Schenectady Gazette*, Oct. 9, 1934; "DeMar Is Favored to Win Marathon," *BG*, Apr. 19, 1928.

72. "Bill Kennedy in BAA Run," *BH*, Apr. 15, 1928; "This Race Today Was Not So Tough," *BH*, Apr. 20, 1928.

73. "Boston A.A. Run on Thursday to Be First of Series of Olympic Marathon Tests," *NYT*, Apr. 15, 1928, emphasis added. Also see "De Mar Favorite in Record Field of 285," *NYT*, Apr. 19, 1928.

74. "Marathon Association Annual Meeting Tonight," *BG*, Apr. 19, 1928.

75. DeMar, *Marathon*, 60.

76. "Cites Marathon to Stress Plea for Harriers," *PCDI*, Oct. 11, 1929; Cooper, *American Marathon*, 71.

77. "Gavrin Enters 1929 Marathon," *PCDI*, Oct. 4, 1929; "Finance Problem Threatens Future Marathon Here," *PCDI*, Oct. 9, 1929.

78. "For Town Pride's Sake," *PCDI*, Oct. 10, 1929; "Budget Complete, Ready for Race," *PCDI*, Oct. 11, 1929.

79. "Michelsen Wins Port Chester Run," *NYT*, Oct. 13, 1929.

80. "Michelson [*sic*] and DeMar," *PCDI*, Oct. 14, 1929.

8. HARD TIMES

1. KPEU, 49.

2. "Six Lotteries Raise $500,000 for Marathon," *BH*, Apr. 17, 1930; "Grand Jury to Probe Marathon Lottery," *BG*, Apr. 24, 1930.

3. "De Mar Wins His Seventh Marathon," *BH*, Apr. 20, 1930; "Finishing Abreast," *BP*, Apr. 20, 1930; Tom Derderian, *Boston Marathon: The First Century of the World's Premier Running Event*, Centennial Race ed. (Champaign, IL: Human Kinetics Publishers, 1996), 129.

4. "1929 Victors to Run Again in P.C. Race," *PCDI*, Sept. 30, 1930.

5. "Canada Knows Port Chester Better Than Big U.S. Cities," *PCDI*, Oct. 14, 1930.

6. "Komonen Is First in Marathon Race," *NYT*, Oct. 13, 1931.

7. KPEU, 48.

8. "Marathon Sidelights," *PCDI*, Oct. 13, 1931.

9. "Hundreds Pay Final Tribute to L. J. Kennedy," *PCDI*, Dec. 30, 1931.

10. "Lawrence J. Kennedy," *PCDI*, Dec. 28, 1931.

11. "Bill Kennedy Promises to Be in Prize Winners," *BG*, Apr. 18, 1932.

12. "Bill Kennedy Pays Wellesley Man for Soda Water He Drank in Last Year's Race," *BG*, Apr. 18, 1932.

13. "Marathoning Hobby, Sociable, Ageless, Poor Man's Recreation, Says Kelly," *BH*, Apr. 8, 1934.

14. "Marathoners Elect McVicar President," *BG*, Apr. 20, 1932.

15. "Harriers Pledge Support to Kennedy Plan for 1932 Marathon," *PCDI*, Sept. 27, 1932.

16. "Between You and Me and the Lamp-Post," *PCDI*, Oct. 1, 1932.

17. "Harriers Pledge Support to Kennedy Plan," *PCDI*, Sept. 27, 1932.

18. "Between You and Me and the Lamp-Post," *PCDI*, Oct. 1, 1932.

19. "Kennedy Girl Injured When Cars Collide," *PCDI*, Oct. 10, 1932.

20. "Johnny Semple Wins K. of C. Race," *BG*, Oct. 13, 1932.

21. Jock Semple with John J. Kelley and Tom Murphy, *Just Call Me Jock: The Story of Jock Semple, Boston's Mr. Marathon* (Waterford, CT: Waterford Publishing Company, 1981), 62.

22. "Frank Lalla, Rye Boy, Wins Marathon," *PCDI*, Oct 17, 1932.

23. "Kennedy Slated for New Term as V.F.W. Head," *PCDI*, Oct. 11, 1932; "Frank Lalla, Rye Boy, Wins Marathon," *PCDI*, Oct. 17, 1932.

24. "'Bill' Kennedy's Race," *PCDI*, Oct. 17, 1932.

25. John Hanc, *The B.A.A. at 125: The Official History of the Boston Athletic Association, 1887–1912* (New York: Sport Publishing, 2012), 72.

26. "Marathoners Urge B.A.A. Run Continue," *BG*, Apr. 20, 1933.

27. "Pawson Puts Work, Education Higher Than Marathon Honors, but Hopes to Run in the Olympics," *BH*, Apr. 21, 1933; Derderian, *Boston Marathon*, 124–25.

28. "Pawson Puts Work, Education Higher," *BH*, Apr. 21, 1933.

29. "Marathon Hit by Depression," *BH*, Apr. 18, 1935.

30. "Kelley Wins Marathon; Near Record," *BH*, Apr. 20, 1935; "Kelley Finishes Alone but Entire Clan Shares Victory in BAA Clubhouse," *BH*, Apr. 20, 1935.

31. Hanc, *B.A.A.*, 72.

32. Ibid., 72–74; "Doomed B.A.A. Clubhouse," *BG*, Oct. 9, 1935.

33. "Touching Scenes at Old B.A.A. Clubhouse as Members Collect Their Belongings and Say Farewell," *BG*, Aug. 4, 1935.

34. "Mayor Banister to Award Prizes in 10th Marathon," *PCDI*, Oct. 11, 1934; "Dengis Wins 1934 Marathon in 2:31:30," *PCDI*, Oct. 12, 1934; "Port Chester Run Taken by Dengis," *NYT*, Oct. 13, 1934.

35. "Mayor Banister, at Banquet for Runners in 10th Annual Race," *PCDI*, Oct. 13, 1934.

36. "62 Answer Starter's Gun in Marathon," *PCDI*, Oct. 12, 1935.

37. "Pawson Edges Dengis in Port Chester Grind," *BG*, Oct. 13, 1935; "Pawson Conquers Dengis by 10 Yards in Marathon," *PCDI*, Oct. 14, 1935.

38. "Pawson Conquers," *PCDI*, Oct. 14, 1935; Pamela Cooper, *The American Marathon* (Syracuse: Syracuse University Press, 1998), 81.

9. THE ROAD TO BERLIN

1. Benjamin G. Rader, *American Sports: From the Age of Folk Games to the Age of Televised Sports* (Englewood Cliffs, NJ: Prentice-Hall, 1990), 205; Steven A. Riess, *Sports and the American Jew* (Syracuse: Syracuse University Press, 1998), 31; Daniel Brown, *The Boys in the Boat: Nine Americans and Their Epic Quest for Gold at the 1936 Berlin Olympics* (New York: Viking, 2013), 216.
2. "Kennedy Scores Long Run Victory," *CDT*, July 5, 1913 (Kennedy won a fifteen-mile race, the feature event of the Portage Park Citizens' Celebration Association, while Brundage, a member of the sponsoring organization, took first place in the high jump, second in the broad jump and discus throw, and third in the shot put); "Met. Officers Head A.A.U. Committees," *NYT*, Dec. 26, 1926.
3. Brown, *Boys in the Boat*, 225–26.
4. "Kelley and Pawson Rated as Co-Favorites," *NYT*, Apr. 20, 1936.
5. "Scotty Rankin to Compete," *BG*, Apr. 6, 1936.
6. "Jewish Champion Enters B.A.A. Run," *BG*, Apr. 10, 1936.
7. "Marathon Runner Gets Divorce," *BG*, Apr. 17, 1936.
8. Clarence DeMar, *Marathon: The Clarence DeMar Story* (1937; Tallahassee: Cedarwinds Publishing Company, 1992), 19.
9. "Memory of Dead Mother Spurs Brown to Victory as Legs Begin to Fail," *BG*, Apr. 21, 1936.
10. Jock Semple with John J. Kelley and Tom Murphy, *Just Call Me Jock: The Story of Jock Semple, Boston's Mr. Marathon* (Waterford, CT: Waterford Publishing Company, 1981), 48, 55–56; Tom Derderian, *Boston Marathon: The First Century of the World's Premier Running Event*, Centennial Race ed. (Champaign, IL: Human Kinetics Publishers, 1996), 151–53.
11. "Memory of Dead Mother Spurs Brown to Victory," *BG*, Apr. 21, 1936. Portions of this passage were originally written by Patrick L. Kennedy in "Running as Tradition," *Harvard Gazette*, Apr. 14, 2016.
12. "Brown Marathon Victor," *BH*, Apr. 21, 1936; "Tarzan Brown Not Certain of Post on Olympic Team," *BG*, Apr. 22, 1936.
13. "Essence of Sport, *BG*, Apr. 21, 1936.
14. Brown, *Boys in the Boat*, 290–95; Frederick Lewis and Dick Johnson, *Young at Heart: The Story of Johnny Kelley, Boston's Marathon Man* (Waco, TX: WRS Publishing, 1992), 74; Laura Hillenbrand, *Unbroken: A World War II Story of Survival, Resilience, and Redemption* (New York: Random House, 2010), 28–30.
15. "Kennedy Lauds Conduct of Brundage at Olympics," *PCDI*, Oct. 2, 1936; "Olympic Rules Too Strict, Bill Kennedy Tells Rotary," *PCDI*, Oct. 7, 1936.
16. David Wallechinsky, *The Complete Book of the Summer Olympics* (Woodstock, NY: Overlook Press, 2000), 143; David Moraniss, *Rome 1960: The Olympics That Changed the World* (New York: Simon & Schuster, 2008), 415; "Olympic Rules," *PCDI*, Oct. 7, 1936.

17. "Olympic Rules," *PCDI*, Oct. 7, 1936.

18. "Kennedy Lauds Conduct," *PCDI*, Oct. 2, 1936.

19. KPEU, 66.

20. Brown, *Boys in the Boat*, 305–8.

21. Ibid., 297, 299, 332.

22. KPEU, 49. James Leo "One-Eyed" Connelly was a former boxer and champion gate-crasher who used ruses—posing as a sheriff's deputy, a painter, a press assistant, and so on—to gain free entry into more than a hundred pro boxing matches.

23. Ibid.

24. Rader, *American Sports*, 203–4; "The Olympic Torch's Shadowy Past," BBC News, Apr. 5, 2008, news.bbc.co.uk.

25. "Olympic Rules," *PCDI*, Oct. 7, 1936.

26. Rader, *American Sports*, 205.

27. David Clay Large, *Nazi Games: The Olympics of 1936* (New York: Norton, 2007), 233; Jeremy Schaap, *Triumph: The Untold Story of Jesse Owens and Hitler's Olympics* (Boston: Houghton Mifflin, 2007), 193; "Owens Back, Gets Hearty Reception," *NYT*, Aug. 25, 1936.

28. "Olympic Rules," *PCDI*, Oct. 7, 1936.

29. Large, *Nazi Games*, 234.

30. Semple, *Just Call Me Jock*, 51.

31. "Kennedy Lauds Conduct," *PCDI*, Oct. 2, 1936.

32. KPEU, 26.

33. Semple, *Just Call Me Jock*, 48–51; Pamela Cooper, *The American Marathon* (Syracuse: Syracuse University Press, 1998), 84.

34. KPEU, 29.

35. "The Forgotten Story of Sohn Kee-Chung, Korea's Olympic Hero," *The Guardian*, Aug. 27, 2011.

36. Duff Hart-Davis, *Hitler's Games: The 1936 Olympics* (New York: Harper and Row, 1986), 226.

37. KPEU, 67–68.

38. KPEU, 64.

39. KPEU, 66.

40. "Kennedy Lauds," *PCDI*, Oct. 2, 1936; KPEU, 49.

41. KPEU, 49.

42. "Brown Easily Conquers Dengis," *NYT*, Oct. 12, 1936.

43. "Indian Beats Pat Denghis [*sic*] by Minute," *PCDI*, Oct. 12, 1936.

44. "Brown Wins Marathon Second Time in 2 Days," *NYT*, Oct. 13, 1936.

45. "Kennedy, 25 Years a Runner, Quitting after BAA Event," *BG*, Apr. 8, 1937.

46. "Young 'Welter' Boxer at Hopkins," *BH*, Apr. 20, 1937.

47. Ibid.

48. "Young Wins," *BG*, Apr. 20, 1937.

49. "Brown Regrets Mother Can't Share Triumph," *BG*, Apr. 22, 1936; David Blaikie, *Boston: The Canadian Story* (Ottawa: Seneca House Books, 1984), 125–26.

50. "No Party for Race Victor, Says Wife," *BH*, Apr. 20, 1937.

51. "Young Appointed Policeman," *BG*, Apr. 30, 1937.

52. Cited in John Hanc, *The B.A.A. at 125: The Official History of the Boston Athletic Association, 1887–1912* (New York: Sport Publishing, 2012), 75.

53. Ibid., 78–80.

54. "Kennedy Gets Big Ovation at Marathon Race Banquet," *PCDI*, Oct. 9, 1939.

55. "Pawson Outlasts Kelly to Win Third Marathon" and "Order of Finish in Marathon," *BG*, Apr. 20, 1941.

56. "Pawson Wins 3d BAA Marathon," *BH*, Apr. 20, 1941; "DeMar Socks Pair of Hecklers," *BG*, Apr. 20, 1941.

57. "Pawson Finds Haven after 26-Mile Grind," *BH*, Apr. 20, 1941.

58. "Abandon Marathon? Nuts!" *BG*, Apr. 26, 1941.

59. Hanc, *B.A.A.*, 79–80.

10. GO WEST, OLD MAN

1. U.S. World War II Draft Registration Cards, 1942, Ancestry.com.

2. Jock Semple with John J. Kelley and Tom Murphy, *Just Call Me Jock: The Story of Jock Semple, Boston's Mr. Marathon* (Waterford, CT: Waterford Publishing Company, 1981), 73.

3. KPEU, 27.

4. Unless otherwise indicated, information about this race comes from "Bill Kennedy 15th in Annual Marathon Race," *Sarasota Herald-Tribune*, Jan. 9, 1944.

5. KPEU, 52.

6. "Mickey Finn," *Idaho Falls Post-Register*, June 22, 1952; Bill Kennedy to Ann Louise McLaughlin, Mar. 13, 1963, and Mar. 4, 1964.

7. "Bricklayer Bill Kennedy," *BMP* 57, no. 12 (1953): 242.

8. Bill Kennedy to Governor Fred Hall, Jan. 21, 1956, Kansas Historical Society.

9. Phone interview with John Mernah and e-mails from Patricia Mernah and Maureen Mernah Wheeler, Apr. 2014.

10. KPEU, 5; e-mail from Patricia Nolan Schmidt, Oct. 29, 2014; "'17 Marathon Winner Slows Down at 78—to Four Miles," *SLPD*, Apr. 22, 1962.

11. "Danger Lurks in 'Over Doing' in Athletics," *BG*, Apr. 22, 1917.

12. KPEU, 5.

13. "Athletic Heart Theory False, Dr. White Says," *BG*, June 25, 1958.

14. "DeMar Ran His Heart into Perfect Condition," *BG*, Nov. 16, 1961.

15. KPEU, 62.

16. "Marathoners of Past Call DeMar Greatest," *BG*, June 12, 1958.

17. Bill Kennedy to Arthur Veasey, Dec. 13, 1959.

18. KPEU, 64–67.

19. KPEU, 56, 9.

20. This passage by Patrick Kennedy was originally published in "In the Running: 1897 to 2014," *BU Today*, Apr. 18, 2014.

21. Tom Derderian, *Boston Marathon: The First Century of the World's Premier Running Event*, Centennial Race ed. (Champaign, IL: Human Kinetics Publishers, 1996), 326, 248–52; Semple, *Just Call Me Jock*, 21.

22. Mrs. John F. Kennedy to Bill Kennedy, Aug. 24, 1964.

23. Phone interview with John Mernah, Apr. 2014.

24. E-mails from Mary Nell Nicoletti, Oct. 2014.

25. Bill Kennedy to Bill Nolan, Oct. 20, 1966, and Apr. 10, 1967.

26. Bill Kennedy to Ann Louise McLaughlin, Mar. 13, 1963.

27. KPEU, 5, 17.

28. Derderian, *Boston Marathon*, 306–12.

29. *U.S. Veterans Gravesites, ca. 1775–2006*, National Cemetery Administration, Washington, DC; *SLPD*, Apr. 26, 1968.

EPILOGUE

1. E-mails from Mary Nell Nicoletti, Oct. 2014.

2. Tom Derderian, *Boston Marathon: The First Century of the World's Premier Running Event*, Centennial Race ed. (Champaign, IL: Human Kinetics Publishers, 1996), 329–48.

3. On Brundage, see Allen Guttmann, *The Games Must Go On: Avery Brundage and the Olympic Movement* (New York: Columbia University Press, 1984).

4. "A Heavy Price," *BG*, Apr. 17, 1982.

5. Bill Rodgers, *Marathon Man: My 26.2-Mile Journey from Unknown Grad Student to the Top of the Running World* (New York: Thomas Dunne, 2013); Derderian, *Boston Marathon*, 366–73. This passage by Patrick Kennedy was originally published in "A Race against Fear," *BG*, Mar. 23, 2014.

6. Derderian, *Boston Marathon*, 367.

7. "A Heavy Price," *BG*, Apr. 17, 1982; Derderian, *Boston Marathon*, 483–93.

8. Patrick Kennedy's interview with Daniel Lieberman was originally published in "Running as Tradition," *Harvard Gazette*, Apr. 14, 2016.

9. KPEU, 53.

INDEX

Ade, George, 219–20

Amateur Athletic Union (AAU), 29, 35, 90, 203–5, 209–10, 215, 221, 223, 229–30, 254–55, 270–71

American Expeditionary Forces (AEF) races, 169–83

American Legion, 260

American Olympic Committee (AOC), 24, 34, 56, 191, 197, 202–3, 205–8, 212, 223–34, 235–36, 255, 258, 266

Ashland, Massachusetts, (Stevens Corner), 12, 56–57, 83, 116, 135, 194–95, 200

Babb, Edward E., 136, 139

Bishop, George, 247, 268

Blake, Arthur, 9

Boston Athletic Association (BAA), 4, 9, 11, 29, 59, 83, 140, 231, 239, 249–52, 269–72, 281

Boston College, 98, 122, 125–26, 201

Boston Marathon: bicycle attendants, 27, 57–58, 87, 120, 215–16; course route in 1917 (cartoon drawing of), 116; gambling scandal, 239; physical exams, 57, 212, 217–18, 233–35; pre-World War I, 4, 11–12, 56–59, 82–83, 86–87, 96–97, 116–33; thirties and forties, 239–40, 245, 255–57, 267–70; twenties, 186, 188–90, 194–95, 197–205, 215–19, 224–26, 231–33; women in, 83–84, 285–88; World War I relay race, 162–63

Boston Post Road, 10, 205, 208

Boston University, 251, 271, 281–82

boxing, 16–18, 76–77, 280
bricklayers' union, 16, 22, 73, 87, 186,
    229, 275–76
Brown, Daniel James, 255, 260
Brown, Ellison "Tarzan," 256–57, 262–
    63, 267–69
Brown, George V., 83, 99, 104, 106, 113,
    116, 120–22, 200, 251, 256, 268–72
Brown, Walter, 270–73, 281
Brundage, Avery, 255, 258–61, 266–67,
    285–86, 288–89
Burfoot, Amby, 122, 285, 288–89
Burke, Tom, 9, 12
Busch, August Anheuser, Sr., 72–73
Byram, Connecticut, 229. See also East
    Port Chester, Connecticut

Carlson, Fritz, 67–69
Carr, Ray, 233–34
Cheever, Benjamin, 35
Chicago Hebrew Institute, 69, 76–77,
    266
Christensen, Chris, 62–63, 68
Columbia Athletic Club (St. Louis),
    73–74
Comiskey, Charles, 86
Connors, Johnny "Cigars," 71
Conroy, Mike, 278
Coolidge, Calvin, 89–90, 226
Cooper, Manuel, 69, 71, 76
Cooper, Pamela, 236
Cunningham, Bill, 233
Curley, James Michael, 96, 98, 115, 211
Currens, James, 277–78
Cygnet Athletic Club, 78, 189, 192,
    195–96, 198–99, 202–5, 223, 228,
    240–41, 246

Davis, David, 34
de Bruyn, Paul, 245–46
de Coubertin, Pierre, 9
DeMar, Clarence, 4, 6, 59, 105–6,
    126–34, 137–39, 145, 148, 156–57, 159,
    161, 172, 177, 180, 182, 190, 194, 198,
    200–203, 207, 212–13, 215, 218–20,

222–23, 226–28, 232–37, 239–41, 256,
    271, 277–78, 290
Dengis, Pat, 251–53, 267, 270
Dineen, Joseph F., 234
Derderian, Tom, 138, 148, 208, 218, 233,
    250, 289
Doherty, Dennis, 36
Don Bosco Catholic Club, 240–41
Dorchester Athletic Club, 81, 86
Drayton, Jerome, 288
Duffey Arthur, 97, 101, 144–45
Duffy, Jimmy, 84–85
Dunbar, Bob, 101

East Port Chester, Connecticut, 78,
    189, 229, 246, 247
Edgren, Bob, 277
Erxleben, Joe, 38–39, 47, 60–61, 64–66,
    82

Fabre, Édouard, 56, 82–83, 104, 138
Faller, Fred, 153, 174, 176, 181–82, 184
Fenway Park, 56, 59, 86
Ferris, Dan, 279
Fitzgerald, John F., 59, 211
Foley, Peter, 139, 150, 268
Forshaw, Joe, 31–32, 34, 36, 48, 51, 55,
    59–61, 64–66, 82, 277
Fowler, Bob, 31–32

Garcelon, Billy, 250, 252
Geary, Edward, 146–49
Gianakopoulos, Nick, 184
Gibb, Roberta, 287
Gordon, Burgess, 217–18
Graham, John, 9
Grant, Dick, 12
Greenwich, Connecticut, 3, 71, 89, 247

Hallahan, John, 131, 138, 186, 190–92,
    202, 218, 242
Hanc, John, 251, 270
Hart-Davis, Duff, 264
Harvard University, 12, 100, 119, 127,
    203, 214, 234

Hatch, Sid, 32, 37, 48–49, 51–53, 58–60,
    64, 69, 78, 82, 84, 87–91, 106, 113, 116,
    118–19, 121–23, 128–35, 137–39, 145,
    150, 157, 159, 166–67, 171, 220, 277
Hayes, Johnny, 14, 34–35, 49, 90, 159,
    252, 277, 288
"Heartbreak Hill" (Newton hills), 12,
    87, 105, 122–23, 125, 135, 142, 201,
    232, 257, 285
Henigan, Jimmy, 80–81, 109–12, 153,
    157, 235, 241
Herbert family, 43, 46–47, 62, 188, 276,
    282–84, 287
Hicks, Thomas J., 28–31, 34
Hitler, Adolf, 254, 260–62
Holmquist, John, 45–46
Hopkinton, Massachusetts, 198–200,
    212, 231, 235, 250, 256, 267, 269–70,
    285, 288

Illinois Athletic Club (IAC), 6, 63, 74,
    77, 85
Inter-Allied Games, 169–83
International Marathon Runners'
    Association (IMRA), 6, 223–24,
    229, 234–36, 245, 250
International Olympic Committee
    (IOC), 254, 260
Isenberg, Michael, 17

Jarrett, Eleanor Holm, 258–59, 266
Johnson, Augustus, 205–6
Johnson, Cornelius, 262
Johnson, Frank, 38, 48, 64–65
Johnson, Wait, 169

Kelley, John A. (the elder), 189–90, 245,
    250–51, 257–58, 263, 268, 271, 281
Kelley, John J. (the younger), 190, 281–
    82, 285, 289
Kenmore Square, 12, 59
Kennedy, William J. "Bricklayer
    Bill": AEF races and Inter-Allied
    Games, 160–161, 169–83; AOH
    race, 153, 157, 174; Berlin Olympics,
257–67, 264–65; Boston Marathon,
    55–59, 80–84, 86–88; Boston Mara-
    thon and 1917 victory, 116–39, 189,
    190, 194, 271; boxing and running,
    16–17, 23, 33–36; Bricklayers'
    Athletic Club in Chicago, 86;
    Cathedral race (1917 victory), 103,
    108–12; Chicago 15-mile race (1913
    victory), 72; Chicago marathon
    (1913 victory), 67–70; Des Moines
    injury, 1, 44–46; Depression era,
    238–39; early life, 15–25; heart mur-
    mur, 194; Inter-State Sports Club,
    co-founder of, 246; letters to the
    Globe, 192–94, 242–45; local New
    York races, 191–92; Long Beach
    Marathon (1924 victory), 209;
    Morningside Athletic Club, 95,
    98, 107, 113, 148, 150, 186; Olympic
    hopes (1924), 203–5; *Port Chester
    Daily Item*, editorial, 249; Port
    Chester Marathon, role in, 221–22,
    246–47; Portsmouth, New Hamp-
    shire, 13-mile race, 197; St. Louis
    All-Western Marathon, 47–49;
    St. Louis All-Western Marathon
    and 1913 victory, 59–61, 63–66,
    88; stroke and death of, 282, 286;
    typhoid fever, 74, 284; World War
    I, service in U.S. Army (23rd Engi-
    neers), 137, 151–53, 157–59, 160–68;
    World War II, 273; work sites, 16,
    20, 44–45, 88–89, 113, 141–43, 153–
    55, 164–67, 186, 239, 273–74;
    Yankee Stadium marathons,
    195–96
Kennedy family, 13–16, 19–23, 52, 155,
    205, 267, 284–85; Jessie Herbert
    (wife), 62–63, 69, 91, 140, 158–59,
    186, 188, 274–76; Juanita Bishop
    (daughter), 67, 158, 188, 247, 276;
    Lawrence Joseph (father), 14–16,
    20–23, 89, 188, 241–42; Louisa
    O'Brien (mother), 15–16, 19–20;
    Louise (daughter), 49, 62, 80, 158,

Kennedy family (*continued*)
186–87, 268, 276. *See also* Herbert family

Knights of Columbus, 175–76, 223

Kolehmainen, Hannes, 97–99, 101–3, 105, 107–8, 112, 118–21, 124–26, 128–30, 132, 134, 137, 145

Komonen, Dave, 241

Koski, Karl, 232–33

Kuscsik, Nina, 288

Kyronen, Villar "Willie," 89, 91, 97–98, 102–5, 107, 116, 119, 121, 125, 128–29, 135, 156

Lake, Austen, 269

Lalla, Frank, 72, 78, 221, 248

Large, David Clay, 262

Leonard, Lank, 79, 274

Levinson, Levi, 60–62, 266

Levy, Mrs. Jack, 6, 71

Lieberman, Daniel, 289–90

Liebgold, Louis, 3, 11, 205

Linder, Carl, 104, 134, 145, 153, 156, 201, 207

Loeb, Jacob, 76

Longboat, Tom, 33, 128

Lorz, Fred, 27

Louis, Spiridon, 9

Lynch, Matthew, 178–80

Lynch, Mike, 51, 82, 246

Maloney, Harry, 173

Mandell, Richard, 9

marathon races: Baltimore (1923), 196–98; Bridgeport (1936), 267; Brockton Fair (1916), 89–90, 103; Brockton Fair (1917), 155–57, 159; Bunker Hill, 78; Chicago (1913), 67–70; Johnstown, New York (1916), 88; Manchester, New Hampshire, 247, 267; Pawtucket-to-Woonsocket, 241; Rockingham, New Hampshire (1932), 247; Sesquicentennial, Philadelphia (1926), 227–28; St. Louis All-Western,
30–32, 37–40, 47, 59–61, 63–66, 88, 159. *See also races under specific cities*

marathon running: alcohol, drugs, and tobacco, 16, 21, 28, 33, 34, 63, 71, 83, 85, 87–88, 189, 214, 217–20, 225–26, 244, 274; amateur status and prizes, 91–92, 147–49, 206, 209–11; conditioning and training, 19, 36, 81, 94; food and diet, 28, 31, 63, 66, 71, 73, 217–18; shoes, 31, 103, 123, 232–33, 239, 257

Marshall, Leslie, 248

Martin, Frank, 199

McCabe, Tom, 214–15, 218, 233

McCall, Samuel, 89–90, 117, 155

McCarthy, Kevin J., 14, 18

McDermott, John, 3, 11–12, 32, 205

McMahon, Bill, 257, 263

McNamara, Tommy, 221–22

Mellor, Chuck, 107–9, 118, 134, 145–46, 150, 157, 200–203, 217–22

Merchant, Albert Frederick, 106, 118–21, 124, 128–30, 132–34, 143–45

Michelsen, Albert "Whitey," 189, 195–97, 198–203, 208, 218, 221–22, 228, 236–37, 246

Migonis, Matt, 36

Miles, Johnny, 41, 225–26, 231–33, 239–40

Missouri Athletic Club (MAC), 30–32, 49, 55, 63–67

Monteverde, A. L., 51, 71–72, 250, 277

Nason, Jerry, 267–68, 288–89

New York: Athletic Club, 6, 30, 89; Bronx County Marathon (1917), 95; Brooklyn-Seagate Marathon, 224; German-American Athletic Club, 253, 256; Irish-American Athletic Club (IAAC), 28, 30, 34, 90; Knickerbocker marathon (1896), 2–3, 6, 10–11; Long Beach Marathon (1924), 5, 209; Millrose Athletic Association, 256; New

York City Marathon (founded 1970), 288; New York City modified marathon (1911), 49–50; Polo Grounds marathon (1909), 35; Yankee Stadium marathons, 195–96; Yonkers marathons, 33–34, 52–54, 91–92, 159

Nolan, Bill, 282–84

O'Reilly, John Boyle, 18–19, 140, 205
Olympic Games: 1896 (Athens), 2, 9, 11, 274; 1904 (St. Louis), 26–29, 276; 1908 (London), 14, 34–35; 1924 (Paris), 207, 208, 261; 1928 (Amsterdam), 236, 261; 1932 (Los Angeles), 261; 1936 (Berlin), 254–55, 260–64
Owens, Jesse, 262, 264

Pawson, Les, 253, 271
Pershing, John, 164, 183
Pheidippides, 8, 13
Pietri, Dorando, 34, 35
Port Chester ("Saw Pits"), New York, 1–3, 15–16, 19–23, 71, 89, 150, 185, 188–89, 205–6, 213, 222, 229, 238, 241, 249, 252, 258, 266–68, 274
Port Chester Marathon, 72, 221–23, 228–29, 236–37, 240–41, 246, 248–49, 252–53, 267, 270
Prohibition, 185, 251
Prout, William, 203–5, 221

Rader, Benjamin, 261–62
Rae, Bill, 268
Ray, Joie, 62–63, 67–68, 278, 280
Ritola, Willie, 229
Rodgers, Bill, 288–89
Rosi, John, 192, 197, 221, 223, 228
Roth, Arthur V., 86–87, 98, 105, 134, 145
Rozette, Billy, 47, 53
Ryan, Mike, 59, 207
Rye, New York, 3, 10–11, 16, 72, 223, 241, 246, 248

Schuster, Hans Christian, 95, 97, 113, 118–24, 128–30, 134, 143–45, 156
Semple, John "Jock," 80, 123, 226–28, 239, 247–48, 256, 262–63, 271, 273, 281–82, 285, 289
Sherring, William J., 33, 274
Shrubb, Alfie, 40
Shorter, Frank, 288
Silver, Max, 253, 256
Sockalexis, Andrew, 56, 58–59
S.S. *Manhattan*, 258–59
S.S. *President Lincoln*, 265–66
Stamford, Connecticut, 2–3, 10, 15
Steiner, Bill, 248, 256
Stenroos, Albin, 207, 225–26
St. Louis, 25–32, 35, 38–48, 51–53, 60, 63, 67–68, 73, 78, 86, 88, 152, 186, 188, 274–77, 286
Sullivan, Ed, 221, 252
Sullivan, James E., 29, 33, 34
Sweeney, Lawrence J., 80–82, 84–85, 101, 103, 106–7, 112, 114–15, 117–18, 122, 124–25, 127–28, 132–37, 139, 150, 159, 162–63, 192
Switzer, Kathrine, 285, 287

Taft, William Howard, 49, 86, 115
Tebeau's Farm, 199, 212, 217, 231, 250–51
Tewanima, Louis, 49, 56

USS *George Washington*, 162–63, 167–68
USS *Great Northern*, 185

Veterans of Foreign Wars (VFW), Port Chester Post, 249

Weeks, "Pop," 51, 279
Wellesley College, 58, 119, 201, 231
Wendling, Frank, 199, 201, 228
White, Arthur, 190–91
White, Paul Dudley, 277
Williams, Ralph, 201–8

Wilson, Woodrow, 68, 94, 98, 155, 157,
175–76, 180
Woollcott, Alexander, 165
World War I, 94, 99–100, 113–15, 151–
52, 157, 163–66, 183
World War II, 270–73
Wyer, Percy, 279

YMCA (Young Men's Christian
Association), 86, 103, 108, 113,
139, 148, 161, 164, 169–70, 172, 175,
289
Young, Walter, 268–69

Zamperini, Louis, 258
Zuna, Frank, 5, 51, 71, 174, 176, 189, 191–
93, 196, 198, 200–203, 206–9, 218,
222, 228, 277